Lewis in th

THE SCOTTISH WORKING PEOPLE'S HISTORY TRUST

Since its formation in 1992, the Trust has been committed to gathering the oral recollections of working men and women in Scotland about their working lives and about their educational, housing, recreational and other experiences. Four volumes of recollections have so far been published, edited by Ian Mac-Dougall: *Oh! Ye had to be careful* (Tuckwell Press, 2000), the recollections of eleven workers who had been employed at the former Roslin gunpowder mill between the 1930s and 1950s; *Bondagers* (Tuckwell Press, 2001), memories of eight women farm workers from south-east Scotland; *Voices of Leith Dockers* (Mercat Press, 2001), the personal recollections of seven Leith dock workers; and *Onion Johnnies* (Tuckwell Press, 2002), interviews with nine French onion sellers who worked in Scotland. In association with the Scottish History Society, the Minutes of the Mid and East Lothian Miners' Association 1894–1918 were published in 2004.

A substantial archive of other recollections has been built up, including those of miners, journalists, librarians, paperworkers, farmworkers, seamen, textile and building trade workers among others. Thanks to assistance from the Heritage Lottery Fund, many of these have been transcribed and transferred to CD to make them available to a wider public. The archive has been deposited with the School of Scottish Studies of Edinburgh University. The Trust believes that to gather and publish in edited form such oral recollections by working men and women is both important and urgent if hitherto often unexplored aspects of the history of Scotland within living memory are to become generally available and accessible.

IAN D. MCGOWAN
Chair, Scottish Working People's History Trust
May 2007

Lewis in the Passing

Edited by

Calum Ferguson

BIRLINN

in association with
The Scottish Working People's History Trust

First published in 2007 by
Birlinn Limited
West Newington House
10 Newington Road
Edinburgh
EH9 1QS

www.birlinn.co.uk

ISBN 13: 978 1 84158 547 5
ISBN 10: 1 84158 547 5

British Library Cataloguing-in-Publication Data
A catalogue record for this book is available from the British Library

The Publisher acknowledges subsidy from the
Scotland Inheritance Fund towards the publication of this book

Typeset by Iolaire Typesetting, Newtonmore
Printed and bound by Antony Rowe Ltd, Chippenham

Contents

Acknowledgements

Thanks to my friend Nancy Mitchell for introducing me to the work of the Trust and to Ian MacDougall, secretary of the Trust, who, with courtesy, provided me with support, encouragement and a sense of direction throughout the project's long gestation period. Thanks also to the agencies which gave me permission to use their photographs: Stornoway Gazette, Leabharlann Steòrnabhaigh and Sea Breezes.

I'm grateful to Ian MacDonald and Dr Joan MacDonald who proof-read the Gaelic texts and to Susan Reid, Tony Dilworth and Iona MacRitchie who transcribed my audio-taped interviews.

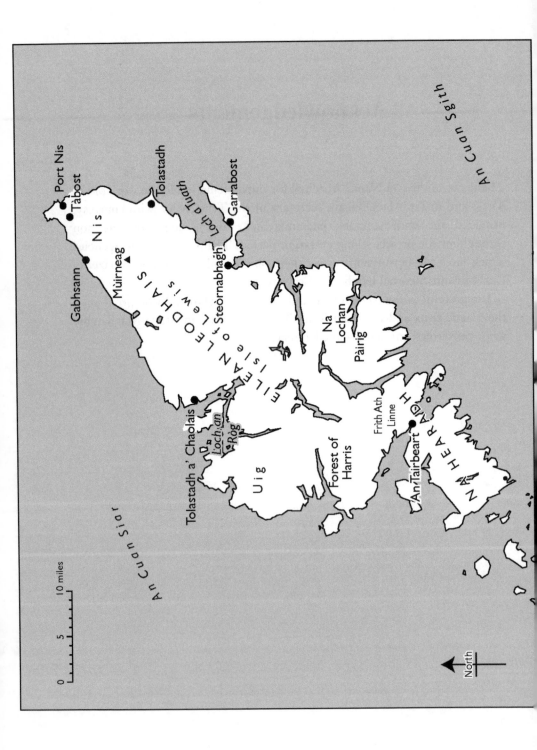

Introduction

The short autobiographies contained in this book are based on interviews which, over the past two decades, I conducted with twenty-one of my fellow islanders. Of my interviewees, sixteen were born in crofting villages on Lewis and were native Gaelic speakers, three were born in the town of Stornoway, one on the Scottish mainland and one in Canada. Most of those from the crofting villages were the offspring of croft tenants and had been born in black-houses, substantial thatched dwellings which, under the one roof, housed the family and their cattle and poultry. One was from a cottar family whose home was an earth-house built outside the wall that separated the arable ground of the crofts from the community's rough grazing. In crofting communities there were many such families who were landless and were regarded by the estate owner as, in every sense, beyond the pale. At that time, over-population was at the root of poverty.

The walls of an earth-house were made entirely of turf and the roof of driftwood which was thatched with heather or straw. As in a black-house, meals were cooked on an open peat fire in the middle of the living-room. Living in such dismal conditions forced many young couples to emigrate or to seek employment in factories or shipyards in the south of Scotland.

Most made a living from a combination of fishing and farming their few acres. Frequently, the loss of fishing-boats led to destitution among the dependants of crews lost. Periodic crop failures resulted in famine. But in the 1890s hundreds of island families benefited when Stornoway was developed as a major centre for the herring industry. In the summer season of 1898, about 700 fishing boats were based there. Thousands of barrels of salted herring and boxes of kippers were exported by steamers (known as 'Klondykers') to England, Germany and the Baltic states. Many of the boats fishing out of Stornoway were from mainland ports such as Peterhead, Fraserburgh and Buckie. Conversely, as the herring shoals migrated along the coast, Lewis boats followed and could be found fishing out of distant ports such as Stronsay in Orkney, Portrush in Northern Ireland or Yarmouth and Lowestoft in East Anglia. During the season, hundreds of girls from the Western Isles were employed, working in 'crews' of three as gutters and packers. The fishing bonanza lasted for only a few decades. As the twentieth century progressed, the herring and white fish industries declined, chiefly due to illegal trawling by fishermen from mainland ports such as Aberdeen and Fleetwood.

The autobiographies provide an insight into the lifestyle of islanders in the first half of the twentieth century and illustrate how deeply the island was affected by the tumult of historic events: the two world wars and the Great Depression.

During the First World War of 1914–18 every family lost kinsmen. As if the carnage of battles such as the Somme and Gallipoli were not enough, Fate had one final blow in store for the tortured families of Lewis and Harris. On New Year's morning 1919, as it was bringing seamen home from their war service, the naval yacht *Iolaire* foundered at the entrance to Stornoway harbour. In the disaster, 205 men perished – eleven from the village of Tolastadh bho Thuath alone and ten from the village of Seisiadar. In his Preface to the Island's Roll of Honour (1914–18), the editor gives vent to his utter despair at having to record the 'recital of losses in the finest of its manhood'; in no phase of the war was the cry of lamentation nor the agony of anxious hearts absent in any village in the land . . . Out of a population of less than 30,000 over 1,150 gave up their lives, not to reckon the distressingly large proportion of wounded and permanently disabled who have straggled back to their mourning homes. In his tribute to the 'proud record of Lewis in the Great War', Lord Leverhulme (the industrialist who owned the island) wrote, 'anxious mothers, their loving wives or sweethearts, their bonnie children . . . have not been demoralised. They have been ennobled by their sacrifice.' The tribute did little to relieve the grief of those who had lost their loved ones.

I was born ten years after the *Iolaire* Disaster. From a very early age, I was conscious of my having entered a world grief-stricken and still reeling from the war's seemingly never-ending punishment. Bereaved older women were attired from head to foot in unrelieved black, permanently committed to mourning their loss of husbands, brothers, sons or other kinsmen. Many sought comfort in religion and the Saviour's promise that, in the Hereafter, their fortitude and suffering would be rewarded. Morning and evening, long beseeching prayers were addressed to the 'God of Mercy'. In those dismal times, people found comfort in the togetherness of the community. Men and women gathered together to talk about their day-to-day challenges and their hopes for the future. To lighten the gloom and assuage the torment of their losses, stories were told of the Olden Days when the *sìthichean* (Little Folk) performed wonderful feats at harvest-time; of local women who had the gift of the second sight; of scary water-horses roaming the open moors or of the prodigal sons of Lewis who came home from the Cold Earth (Canada) accompanied by native women whom they had married 'in the wilderness'. Would that I had had the foresight and the equipment necessary to audio-record interviews with those neighbours who entertained the company when I was a boy – stalwarts of our community who carried the oral history of their ancestors and had survived the deprivation and conflicts of the half century between 1888 and 1938:

- John MacLeod ('Ain Uilleim), cousin of my mother and hero of the so-called Land Struggle, who spent nine months in Calton Jail in Edinburgh for his part in the Aiginis Riot of 1888

- Iain Tharmoid ('Torachan'), our next-door neighbour, gassed on the Somme and awarded a military medal for gallantry; and his brother Calum, who had spent several years in the Falklands working sheep

- Calum Uilleim MacKenzie, who knew stories about the ancient *Fèinne* and had won a major dancing competition in Peterhead still dressed in his fisherman's attire; and his son Iain, admired for his melodeon-playing and *seann-nòs* singing

- Murchadh Aonghais Campbell, the road-mender, who was wounded at Gallipoli; and his son Murdo, who spent four years in a German POW camp in the First World War and five years in the Second

- The crofting matriarchs who spun and wove the wool shorn from their blackface sheep and personally supervised all the preparations essential to their industry, including storing in a huge iron pot all the urine produced by their households

- Iain MacKenzie, who told us the Ulster story of Deirdre and Clann Uisne but was better known as one of the seamen who had managed to escape from the sinking *Iolaire* moments before her boiler exploded and she slid astern into deep water

The crofter-fishermen of those days were close to nature and depended largely on their harvests from the soil and the sea for their livelihood. My interviews with them would have recorded their knowledge of herbal medicines and natural dyes, their work songs, love songs, satirical poems and 'mouth-music', their mischief-making at the Old New Year, their courtship customs, their Christian faith, their superstitions and their age-old crofting and fishing skills.

In 1919, servicemen returning from the war discovered that a year earlier their island of Lewis and Harris had been purchased by the Lancashire industrialist Lord Leverhulme, a man whose declared aim was to uproot the islanders' identity as independent crofter/fishermen and turn them into tenured wage-earners. Lord Leverhulme's ambitious plans included the building of factories, piers, roads and railways, exploiting the rich fisheries in the island's coastal waters and annexing croft lands to create dairy farms. At first, resistance was muted and hundreds of the island men and women grasped the opportunity of working on the landowner's ambitious schemes which were costing him in excess of £200,000 per annum. However, the opposition of a minority, mainly ex-servicemen, resulted in confrontation and riot. In the end, Lord Leverhulme decided to abandon the work. Without alternative opportunities for employment, a large proportion of the island's workforce emigrated to the United States and Canada in 1923 and '24.

The emigrants had scarcely had time to settle in their adoptive countries before their lives were overturned by a major new upheaval. Triggered by the collapse of stock prices in the United States, the Great Depression was a worldwide economic downturn which started in 1929. The most industrialized nations, including the USA, Britain, France and Germany, were deeply affected. Figures for unemployment and homelessness soared. In the world's great cities, factories closed and construction virtually halted. Farming communities suffered as prices for crops fell by a half. Many of the islanders who had emigrated to North America returned no better off than they were before they left home. Indeed, many of my own contemporaries now resident in Lewis, including my wife and two of my cousins, were born in the USA or in Canada and were brought back as toddlers in the early 1930s.

When the effects of the Great Depression began to ease, shipping between the world's trading nations gradually resumed. For the breadwinners of the Western Isles, the Merchant Navy became their final safety-net. Able-bodied men joined the Royal Naval Reserve in droves and applied for work with shipping lines. By the beginning of the 1930s, the bitter memories of the Great War had begun to recede. The vitality of the adolescents and children roused the community to optimism and a sense of purpose. In summer, melodeon dance music brought the young together at crossroads and, even in the most downcast homes, set feet a-tapping. On winter evenings, organised ceilidhs and dances in village halls gave singers and musicians an opportunity of performing as semi-professional entertainers. In the 1930s, with the inception of gramophones, families were given ready access to performances by the singing stars of the Gaelic world, most of whom were resident in the cities of the Lowlands: Neil MacLean, Archie Grant, Allan MacLean, Jenny Currie, Margaret Duncan and Kitty MacLeod. At the same time, the 'wireless' began to familiarise Gaelic audiences with English voices and accents and music from distant lands. Islanders began to introduce English words and phrases in their everyday conversations, initiating into their language a dilution that, since then, has gathered pace as our world becomes ever more dominated by English-language television and the other media.

Less than twenty years after the signing of the Armistice of 1918, which signalled the end of the 'War To End All Wars', international tensions again grew in Europe as Nazi Germany began to re-arm. In September 1939, Germany invaded Poland and sparked off the most destructive war in history, involving the fighting forces of more than seventy nations and resulting in the deaths of some 60 million people worldwide.

At the beginning of the Second World War, of the 6,486 seamen in the Royal Naval Reserve (of whom many were employed on British merchant ships), 1,634 were provided by the townships of the Western Isles. As a consequence, when Germany's packs of U-boats began to sink hundreds of thousands of tons of British shipping during the first two years of the Battle of the Atlantic, there was severe loss of life among Western Isles seamen. In May 1945 the unconditional surrender of Germany restored peace in Europe and the people of Britain began the work of repairing the damage inflicted on the country's cities and towns during Hitler's aerial bombardments. The war in the Far East ended with the capitulation of Japan in September 1945.

In the half century since the post-war period of austerity ended, the living standards of the population improved with each successive decade. Much of the progress made stemmed from the work of the Labour government which came to power shortly after the Second World War. In 1942, a report by the eminent economist William Beveridge identified the 'five giant evils' of British society as squalor, ignorance, want, idleness and disease. The report proposed that all workers pay National Insurance contributions; in return, those in need would be entitled to receive benefits, e.g. sickness, unemployment and retirement. In 1945, the newly elected Labour government began the process of implementing the Beveridge committee's proposals with particular emphasis in the fields of education, health and unemployment, thus creating the Welfare State designed to care for the people of Britain 'from the cradle to the grave'.

In the mid 1950s, the government sanctioned huge civil engineering projects designed to improve road and rail links throughout the Highlands and Islands and to provide hydro-electricity, running water and sewerage even to remote villages and, coincidentally, provided employment for many thousands of ex-servicemen and women. Double-glazing, loft insulation and the acquisition of 'modern conveniences' brought the living conditions of the islanders into line with those enjoyed elsewhere in Britain. Those advances simultaneously coincided with the gradual demise of the crofting way of life but also, regrettably, the slow decline of Gaelic as the language spoken among the young of our crofting townships. However, in the past three decades, the BBC and several agencies funded from central government or the European Union have worked tirelessly and with considerable success to promote our ancient language.

Having finished my forty years of employment in the Lowlands in 1989, I retired to my native Lewis, since time immemorial recognised as an island of *seanchaidhean* – men and women gifted with an ability to captivate the listener with their powers of description and recall. When I accepted an invitation from the Scottish Working People's History Trust (Urras Eachdraidh Luchd-Obrach na h-Alba) to participate in their enterprise, I could not have imagined the amount of work the project entailed nor, indeed, the amount of pleasure I would derive from interviewing a score of my fellow islanders. I soon discovered a field no less fertile in narrative than that which had been so influential in establishing my identity when I was young. The majority of those whom I interviewed were aged between seventy and ninety and had begun their lives against the backcloth of the historic events which I have described. A few had childhood memories of the ever-mounting losses of the First World War and of *Oidhche na Truaighe*, the night of the *Iolaire* Disaster which traumatised the island in the early hours of 1919. They themselves were plunged into the second war against Germany and, in a number of cases, saw action against the enemy. I am grateful to the Trust for ensuring that several of the autobiographical sketches included in the book are given in Gaelic as well as in English.

For my interviewees whose youth was rooted in the ways and traditions of the old crofting-fishing economy, the enhanced standard of living has been nothing short of revolutionary. The land struggles of the late 1800s, the experience of the two world wars and the Great Depression were a backdrop to their lives and, in their old age, shaped their outlook on politics, their sense of social justice and the value they placed on education and personal fulfillment. I found among them a deep sense of spirituality. Most were Church members deeply committed to their Christian faith. They had lived through the catastrophes of the twentieth century and were without cynicism or rancour. My thanks to them and their families for allowing me to audio-record the interviews and to include in this book not only their autobiographical sketches but also photographs from their personal archives. I am privileged to have spent many hours in their company. *Ceud mìle taing airson an iomadh cèilidh!*

Kenneth MacLeod ('Curro')

1907–2002

I will be ninety-one years of age on the 3rd of September. I was born in 1907. Kenneth MacLeod is my name in English but Coinneach Iain 'Ain Mhòir is the Gaelic name by which I wish to be remembered for it recalls the names of my father and grandfather. However, it may surprise you that in my native village of Pabail Iarach I'm not known by any of these names! Here they have a nickname for me: 'Curro'. It's a nickname I have had since I was a small child.

I live alone but I am very fortunate, for I have good neighbours. So far as my health is concerned, I'm OK apart from my legs and feet. I've got a cataract on my left eye. I was wanting to get rid of the cataract, but the optician gave me a pair of glasses instead. He said the glasses would be better for me, so I had to pay a hundred pound for that. Apart from those wee problems, I'm fine and my memory is still sharp.

I was brought up on my father's croft but the house we used to live in was very different from this one. Och well, the old house was very nice but it was one of the old thatched houses – a *taigh-dubh* [black-house]. At that time, many people in the village were living in thatched houses. Some of those had the fire for cooking and warmth on the hearth in the middle of the floor. Other thatched houses had chimneys. Some houses were more modern with slate roofs and with proper chimneys. They were proper 'white-houses'. Some people think that living in a black-house was awful. Well, I just want to say I think it was all right. I was very healthy while I was living there. In fact, everybody here was very healthy until Lewis was hit by tuberculosis. That was in the 1920s and '30s. Yes, at that time, there was a lot of TB going around here. Those were hard times for the families that had consumption. A sanatorium was built in Stornoway to take care of many of the TB invalids in the island. Every week, you'd hear of somebody dying – somebody that you knew. It was usually young folk who were dying of consumption – *A' Chaitheamh* [the Wasting].

While I was at school, I think I enjoyed it – but only sometimes! Some of our teachers were very hard on us. Oh yes, the hardest in the world! I left before James Thomson became the headmaster. Thomson was quite a well-known Gaelic poet and he came the year after I left, I think, 1922. But the bloke before him as headmaster, he had three daughters and a son as teachers in our school. Yes, the three daughters and the son and the father were all teaching in the Bayble School. A sort of family affair! There was about eight teachers altogether and four of them would be from the one family, plus the father. His name was Donald MacIver – the famous MacIver who composed 'An Ataireachd Ard' – one of the greatest songs in our language. Wonderful bard but, as a teacher, he was awfully hard. Oh, he was bad but no worse than all the other teachers of that generation. They were all the same. The two infant teachers in the school were two from Garrabost. They never spoke any English to us – none at all. I still remember how they taught us one of the letters: '*S man Slabhraidh*' [S like a pot hook]. Now, I have to admit that these two were good teachers and fair. It was after the infant classes when the teaching was in English that the teachers turned up the heat on us. I remember one day I was singled out by Annie MacIver. Somebody in the class was doing something he shouldn't. She blamed me for it and brought out the tawse.

She said, 'Put your hand out, boy!'

I wouldn't put my hand out to receive a stroke or two of the tawse. I said, 'It wasn't me, ma'am. I am not to blame and I'm not putting my hand out to get somebody else's punishment!'

And she started crying. I don't know who was more shocked by that – her or me. As children, we thought that every one of those teachers were bad-tempered and cruel. Yes, every one of them. Well, the MacIver son died about two or three years after he started teaching in the school. He was in the army in the First World War and he died with pneumonia.

There was the teacher, Norman MacIver, and when he called you out to be punished, you couldn't refuse or you'd really be in dead trouble. You had to put out both hands one on top of the other, like that. And the teacher holding the tawse would come down with it from the shoulder, right down your hands and then back up the back of your hand. That's the way he used to do it. I remember three of us and, oh, we got it. I don't know what we'd done. We'd done something anyway. Calum was one, and Tarmod from Garrabost and myself. When they got a couple of strokes of the tawse they started crying. As soon as they started crying, he stopped. 'Well,' I said to myself, 'you won't make me cry if you're there all day!'

Now, there were two classes in the one room. A woman teacher had the other class. Well, she couldn't stand seeing all the harsh punishment that this fellow was doling out. She came and spoke to our fellow who was hammering away at us and said, 'It's time you stopped that nonsense with the tawse.' He wasn't so bad after that. But he didn't live long enough, anyway, after that. He died before I left school.

As schoolboys, we had quite a lot of fun and games. We used to make up games and play round the houses. We played shinty; that was one of the games. We never had football – not while I was at school. In fact, I had left school before I saw a football. Shinty was the game we had most at school.

There were fistfights every day. Just the fists and never the boots or head-butting as the young fellows have today. All Queensbury Rules! When we fought as schoolboys, there'd be big blokes round you there all the time to see that you fought fair. There was a bad habit in those days, where the big boys arranged fights between the little boys.

When I left school, I started helping on the croft. Well, I had to do that long before I left school. All the children helped. But it was good when you felt you were becoming an adult. I began then to look at girls. But I was shy, like. First of all I remember the open-air dances we had. We used to congregate at a bridge, a wooden bridge between Upper and Lower Bayble. Well that's where we used to dance in those days. Aye, that was the way in my time. The music would be provided by a melodeon or sometimes an accordion. That gave us a good opportunity for meeting girls. Oh, yes, girls – everybody was there, girls and all. I started courting when I was aged about sixteen. When a young couple were courting, the bloke would be going into the house in the dead of night. They were all black-houses in those days and it was easy to enter them without too much stir! When I was courting, I used to go to the girl's house two nights a week. Of course, I was visiting just the one girl – not different ones. Yes, the same girl. I was going with her for two years. She was my first girl. I cannot rightly remember why we stopped seeing each other. After that, perhaps there was a different girl, but I was mostly after the one girl. She'd be expecting me, of course. Oh, you'd just tap on the window and she'd come to the door. In fact, the first time I went to the window there was me and another bloke. There were two sisters there. And I think we got in. I'm not sure now how we got into the house. Well, of course, their brother might have been out and all and the door would be open. They were sleeping in the box-bed by the fire. The box-bed by the fire, yes. Sometimes you would go to bed with the girls if there was plenty of room. If there was four, one had to get up and spend all night by the fire. The boy would never manage to get under the blankets. Oh, no, no. There was nothing like that. No hanky-panky, and of that you can be sure. It was just the thought of getting under the blanket that counted! We were young and innocent. That's how it was.

As I remember it, I was very happy growing up. That is, before I left home, which was before I was seventeen. In the summer, there was plenty of food. Plenty fish of every kind in the bay there. And potatoes. We would be eating potatoes and herring and meat in the winter. Oh, we had plenty to eat – the same as we have now. The big difference was that almost all the fish and most of the meat was salted. They say that salt is not very good for you. Well, I don't know about that. All I can say is that it didn't do me any harm anyway! Salt herring and salt meat and potatoes was the staple diet but there was also all sorts of things: eggs, plenty of milk, butter and cream and bannocks made with flour. In the winter we ate salted butter – butter salted in the previous summer or autumn. Oh, I ate that, yes. Some people used to say that salt butter was too strong to taste. But really it wasn't too bad. I didn't think nothing of eating it when I was young.

I was aged ten when my father was lost in 1917 in the First World War. Apparently he was in a small ship, some small minesweeper or some small vessel like that. They sailed from Aberdeen and straight into a minefield. The ship was blown up. He left four sons and one sister. After that my mother was getting a little pension and that helped her, I'm sure. I don't know exactly how much it was but I think she got about thirty shillings a week.

We used to eat oatmeal and barley-meal. Of course, we grew lots of both barley and oats on the croft. I remember very clearly going to the Garrabost mill with the grain. My auntie had a horse and cart and I was allowed to drive the horse and cart, even though I was still going to school. I would have been a big boy at the time. I thought it was very interesting to see how they converted the grain to oatmeal and barley-meal. They used to heat it up first, warm it up and then put it in the kiln. When the grain had become roasted, they then put it to the mill and turned it into meal. The mill is just along the road there, a mile or so away at Garrabost. In those days, the crofters came to the Garrabost mill from miles away. We were lucky to be so close to it. Oatmeal and barley-meal were very important to us at that time. You would eat that in the form of porridge and of bread – bread was made on a griddle. The final stages of the baking was done by standing the bread against peats beside the fire.

My favourite meal would be fresh fish – any kind of fish. My father was in a boat before the war. At that time, there was twelve boats here in Pabail – ten or twelve anyway. They used to work great-lines right out in the Minch there. Instead of going to Stornoway with it and sell it fresh, they most often used to salt it and dry it up in the wind and sun. And I remember when they were drying it up, there were two people working for the double sheds down there – the salting houses. They used to dry the fish on the rocks and that. And when they had enough they would then take it to Stornoway with the boat and sell it. There was mostly cod and ling and that was the fish they were curing. The fishermen used to take home the other fish that they couldn't take to market – skate and eels and coalfish and so on. That kind of fish was for the house. I was once in a boat where we used to get *falmair* [hake] in the nets. Small ones, about so big, about seven inches up to fifteen inches. We used to catch them in the nets, actually. That's all the *falmair* that I ever saw being caught in these waters. I never saw one on a hook.

At that time, the boats used to catch halibut. They were going out specially for halibut. And I remember my uncles. My father was lost in 1917, in the war, when I was aged ten. We were all heartbroken. It was a terrible time for my mother especially. And my uncles had a boat here after the war – that's the First World War – and they had a halibut and they took it to Stornoway. It weighed a hundredweight! It took four of the crew to pull the creature into the boat and they got £7 for the one fish. There was an old man just along the road there and he said it was a better sale than the price you'd get for selling a cow! You wouldn't get so much for a cow in those days!

You could get really big halibut around our coasts. I was working myself for two or three months on the great-lines after the Second World War. I came home in I think it was March. I got demobbed on 10 March 1946 and we started, five or six of us on a boat we had. Well, we caught the occasional halibut on the great-lines, which, as you know, had large hooks. We used herring for bait usually but when they went fishing for halibut they used to split conger eels – split them and dried them and that was some of the bait they used to use because that would last on the hooks. The herring, well, that would sometimes get pulled off. But dried conger was the best bait they were using for halibut. Of course, normally when they baited a great-line hook to catch the cod, they put a half-herring on. Well, they used to go out drift-netting to catch herring. In those days, herring round the coast here was more or less all the year round.

Of course, working the seas around our islands can be a very dangerous occupation. There was four boats lost down there in one day, I think. The crews had gone down to the shore as usual ready to put to sea, but a *bodach* [old man] here advised them not to go out. He forecast that it was going to blow a gale. At that time it was a fine morning, nothing moving. And then they went out and the weather turned foul. The wind came up and the sea grew wild. Four of the boats were lost. I have heard that there was a drowning every two years between 1801 and 1901. And it didn't stop this century. The drownings continued. Quite a few drownings out of Bayble here but only one drowning at sea in a boat in my time, but my grandmother lost three brothers fishing out there.

As I have already told you, I left home when I was sixteen and a half years old, joined the RNR [Royal Naval Reserve], and after that I went to the fishing for three years, 1926, '27 and '28. I was doing very well, too, at the fishing. I was on a lucky boat. That's what we called a boat that made good catches and earned a bit of money. We called her a 'lucky boat' because of that. But I became restless and wanted to see more of the world. I went off to London and joined the Merchant Navy. Yes, I went to sea when I was very young and I wouldn't be as fluent in English as I am now. No, I wasn't so fluent, but I could understand everything, and speak – a little anyway. The blokes I was going fishing with couldn't speak the King's English either! Not at all. They spoke a kind of English the East Coasters speak!

Well anyway, aged sixteen and a half, I joined the RNR. That was in 1924 when I joined. I gave my wrong age, said that I was eighteen. I got away with it, but the next crowd that tried it got caught and they were fined two pounds each. Yes, four young lads from here. One of them was my first cousin. In the RNR, we did six weeks' training, and after that you went for training every two years. You were supposed to go, but more often you went every third year. But when I worked in the Merchant Navy, sailing, I just couldn't get away. So, for me and other boys working deep-sea, it became every third year.

I was on a ship on the New Zealand coast when the Second World War started on 3 September 1939. There was a group of ten or twelve of the crew who were Royal Naval Reservists . . . We were there in Auckland and we sailed from there to Halifax in Nova Scotia, in Canada, and from there across to London. We were all called up then and we went head–first into the war. Hardly a boy was left in the whole village of Bayble when the call-up came. Just one or two perhaps; everybody else was in the Merchant Navy. My eldest brother had emigrated to Canada in 1924 when he was aged eighteen. Well, he ended up in the American army but he never came across here at all during the war, but, some years after the war, he came back. That was in 1951, and he was home for about four or five months. I'm sorry to say that I lost touch with his family.

Now the biggest disaster to hit the island was what happened at the end of the First World War, with the sinking of the yacht, the *Iolaire*. Yes, that was the biggest disaster ever. Over two hundred men drowned on 1 January 1919, coming home from the war. Och, I remember the morning after the disaster as good as anything! I was eleven year old then. I remember it all. There was a next-door neighbour of ours lost on her. A first cousin of my mother was lost. Two cousins of my mother lost there. There was one or two from Pabail Uarach lost on her. I remember those boys very well, yes, very well. But there was a few men from here were saved. There were at least three who managed to make it to the shore. A bloke from Ness swam ashore with a rope. Almost all who survived got ashore on that rope.

Four years after the *Iolaire* Disaster, emigrant ships took away almost all the young men who had survived the war. The first emigrant ship that came was in 1923. She was called the *Metagama*. Well, there were only two men, two boys and two girls emigrated from here. But when the next emigrant ship came – the *Marloch* – that's when my brother went. There was a crowd of them went – nearly one from every house. And there was a few of them on the third emigrant ship taking the young people to Canada. I was in the RNR at that time and I wasn't at home in 1924, so I missed all that.

The loss of so many was a devastating blow to the families, when all the young people left the community. Of course it was, yes. Well, there wasn't many left. Well, there were only a few left. There had been lots of people here before the war – big families. There was one family with eleven children, I think! There were families, two or three houses away from here, with ten in each. Lots of other families with seven, eight or nine. So you can imagine what our villages were like before 1918, before the war started – full of young people, and then after 1924, when the emigrant ships sailed away with the young people who had survived the war. The place was almost empty. It was a sad and lonely place for the few young people who were left.

The crofter's year was governed by sun, the seasons and by the tides. I remember the routine of the year very well. After the harvest was taken in off the fields, there was no rest for the family. The grain of the barley and oats had to be prepared for the mill. That would be in November, I would say, before the New Year. The process of separating the barley grain from the straw was called *suathadh*. That was done with bare legs. Oh, they were just working around it with their bare feet. It was funny the way they did it. Not a drop left. Just the bare straw left? Hard work, though! The ears of barley were full of these nasty bristles that could sometimes get into your nostrils or ears. Very uncomfortable! They were used to the work, of course. They didn't think much about it. It would be done in November and was all complete by New Year. Everything.

In December they would be winding down. A ceilidh at night – visiting the neighbours for a blether. That was very important in the communities at that time – visiting each other and renewing friendships. That really was what the ceilidh was all about – friendship and laughter. But then in January or February, the end of January anyway, they would start fishing with the great-lines. With the short days of the middle of winter they would put to sea and lay their great-lines down on the seabed, between half a mile and a mile off the coast. They were big sturdy boats with six or seven in the crew. The men also were sturdy – good strong fishermen, often at sea in wind and sleet. Dangerous work at times.

There was no Santa Claus in my day – or if there was he kept most of his presents to himself! You'd be lucky to get a few sweets. Christmas and the New Year were just like any other day. At *Oidhche Challainn* – the Old New Year, around 12 January – we boys used to go out and play about. On New Year's Day some of the men would be in the pubs, drinking in Stornoway. They would walk to the town and back again just to get a few drams. Yes, they would, just for a few drams! It wasn't common for people to have a bottle of whisky in the house. Not then.

Now, in February, the meal-chests are all stocked up. Some people used to complain of *ganntar an earraich* – 'the shortages of the spring', when some of the supplies were running short. They used to say that but, thinking back, I don't think they were any worse off in the spring than at any other time of the year. On the other hand, maybe my family was one of the lucky ones, for we never felt that starvation was round the corner.

Now, when the winter was finished, they would get cut the peats and then the fishing would start on the 10th of May. They would be all away by then to the fishing on the east coast [of Scotland] and wouldn't come home until September. That is when they had to do the harvesting. After the harvesting was done and all the oats and barley were safely stowed away and the potatoes safely stored, they would go off to the herring fishing in Yarmouth. They would be there till the end of November. Sometimes some of them would be away at the fishing till Christmas time.

Most of the teenage girls here were employed at the fishing – gutting the herring. There were two or three girls who went to work in factories in

Dundee. There were two sisters – one married in Peterhead and the other in Glasgow. Well, they used to go to the fishing, but then they used to go as servants in hotels or in the big houses in places such as Glasgow or Inverness. Yes, they went on service to the big houses. They had to be big, you see, to have domestic servants like that.

My mother and her friends were going to the fishing. She used to say that when her generation were going to school, they used to carry a peat with them every day – a peat to keep the fire in the classroom going during the day. Now, by the time I was going to school, the school authorities were cutting peats and supplying them to the school. The work of cutting and drying the peats and supplying it wasn't done by the teachers but by workmen employed for that purpose.

When I was in the Merchant Navy I never saw fights between the deckhands but I heard a lot about fights among the firemen. There would be about thirty firemen on a ship. They sometimes fought among themselves. That's how they got their bad name. But very, very seldom would you see people like me, the seamen, fighting among themselves. They used to go ashore and get drunk and things like that, but we never used to fight. Don't get me wrong. The Highland boys would fight if they had to fight, oh, yes. But I was in some ships where most of the crew were from Stornoway and that was a lovely ship to be on. She was called the *Port Sidney*. All our boys were good seamen. But two or three of them were pretty old at that time. Well, I thought they would be very old. I was very young myself then. I was the bloke who'd do the jobs aloft – up the mast and the funnel and things like that. If you were painting them, well, I would have to go and make everything ready for stock painting. And the mast, you would have three men on the mast. I was bo'sun in the last ship I was on. Well, I was bo'sun before that. I was three years bo'sun's mate in the ship called *Rangitane*. And she was lost in 1941. She was shrouded out by two German surface raiders. They fired one salvo and there was only one casualty – a girl from Invergordon, a stewardess. She was killed. I wasn't on her then. Before sinking the *Rangitane*, the Germans split up the crew. They took half of them to Germany as prisoners of war, and the other half, they put them ashore on an island in the Pacific – the island of Nauru. And a bloke from Aird was there too, a brother of 'Broman' [Angus MacKay]. The lad taken prisoner was known as 'Uircean'. At the end of the war, he was released from Nauru and settled in Australia.

In my young days, almost all the single men were daft for booze. They spent every penny they earned. Well, I was young and I got mixed up in a crowd like that. And I went to sea with some of them too. There were members of the crew who used to get drunk. They'd come back on board drunk then. Whenever that happened, I would get out of their way. Well, they were just young fellows.

Silent pictures then. No talkies then. Cowboy pictures. I used to go, in New Zealand. I used to go to watch the wrestling. There used to be good wrestling. World champions, too. I seen a Canadian, Macready was his name. He was the world champion at that time. He was there every season. They had seasons of it, like. I used to go to the boxing too. But in the States we saw all the big-time boxing on television. Well, you got plenty of boxing on the radio, but that was different to the television. In the 1930s you'd sometimes be up half the night, listening to the Joe Louis fights on the radio. He was the world heavyweight champion, a great fighter. Now later on, when I was on ships on the coastal trade round the coasts of Britain, I wasn't drinking a lot. Just a 'nip and a pint' here and a 'nip and a pint' there. Whenever we berthed in a port and I knocked off duty, I used to go ashore to a restaurant or café to get something to eat and then go to a cinema. In the old days, I used to make for a pub and spend my time ashore socialising with drinks with whoever happened to be willing to chat with you. No, no, that was no use to me once I became a bit older.

I didn't get married. There was the girl I was going with when I was very young. She was a really nice girl. There were others but nothing serious. Anyway, I never got married. I went to London when I was twenty-one, you see. I was away for years and it was all those years before I came back. By then I had lost sight of the girl I told you about. My life was full of booze in them days. Typical sailor. Of course, she knew it would be hopeless marrying somebody so fond of the drink.

By the time I laid off the drink, I was too old to marry. Still an' all, I'm not complaining. I've been round the world many times and seen everywhere I ever wanted to see. I live here on my own in my native village surrounded by kind neighbours, and what more could an old sea dog like me want!

Mary Crane

1910–2002

I'm not going to say how old I am! But I'll tell you I am no spring chicken! I am well over eighty but I don't remember how many years. I was born in a thatched house that by today's standards was a very poor home. But, in those days, we didn't think it was poor. It was just the ordinary kind of home. Everybody had a house quite like it. But it wasn't a black-house with the fire in the middle of the floor. It had gables with a chimney which had a lum. But, as I said, it was a thatched house.

I remember the awful years of the First World War when news of my father's death came. I must have been four at the time and remember standing with other children at Innis Mòr's house. My mother was across the wee stream that was midway between our house and our neighbour's. I could see that she was crying and I wanted to run to her but for some reason I didn't. She was just standing there, looking at three men approaching. It was the minister and two elders who were coming and my mother knew that my father was dead. That was 1915, the second year of the war. Yes, and I remember that quite vividly. I think I was four or five.

My father was a gunnery officer on some kind of warship and he took ill with appendicitis and died in Mesopotamia. There was nobody to operate on him and he died of peritonitis. Months afterwards, sailors from the island who knew him came to see us because they had visited his grave. I don't know if they're still alive or no, but they went to see my father's grave. Sad days.

I was born in 1910 but hadn't gone to school at that time of my father's death. I hadn't, because I'll tell you how I know. Because I had lost my father, I went to school with a black ribbon on my hair and a black pleated dress that my mother had made. I was the first person in that school with a black dress. Unfortunately, as the war progressed, more and more black dresses and ribbons appeared.

Just after three years, my Auntie Marion lost her husband as well. That was in the *Iolaire* tragedy, on the first morning of January 1919, just a few weeks after the Armistice that ended the Great War. More than 200 men drowned coming home after the war – having survived the German shells in the trenches. They were coming home on New Year's Eve and were only half a mile from the safety of the Stornoway quay. It was just horrible – all those bodies coming ashore at Holm. So there were the two sisters, my mother and Marion, with nine children between them to support. Following the sinking of the *Iolaire* money poured in from all over the world. I become upset by the memory of it but it's good to keep your memory of these things.

The next of kin of the men lost on the *Iolaire* each got a gift of money. War widows, the likes of my mother, got only a small pension – more than five shillings a week, I think. There was so much money put out for each and every child, and there were six of us. Some of the families who had lost their breadwinners and their *bata làidir* [mainstay] were quite poorly off. I remember my mother sending basins full of meal this way and that, in the twilight, so that people wouldn't see that she was sending those gifts to the poor. I was usually the one carrying one basin and Ewen was carrying the other – oatmeal and flour. As a matter of fact I would go as far as saying that it wasn't only our own family that my mother's widow's pension brought up. In those days, most people in our community – but not all – behaved as though we were the one family. They were kind to one another.

My mother was a great Christian. In the end, she died in the cancer hospital in Glasgow, in the 1950s. She was able to speak Gaelic and English fluently. People were coming from all over to see her – a truly holy lady. She was exceptional. I was there all day, you know. Because I was in Glasgow and the rest of her children were in Lewis, I had to be at the hospital with her. She was an inspiration to all of us.

It was all crofting and fishing in Lewis when I was little. But I was only a child. I remember my brother Donald – the eldest in the family – working at the small-lines. That kind of work carried on all year. That didn't stop except on the Sabbath, the Lord's day of rest when no work was done either on the croft or in the house. But apart from the Sabbath, baiting hooks and placing them neatly in a *sgùil* [large wooden or wicker tray] was a daily chore. The *sgùil* was the name of the broad tray in which they had the baited lines and carried them like that to the boat.

They sometimes baited the small-lines with *maoraich* [limpets] but sometimes with *feusgain* [shelled mussels] or small morsels of herring.

We collected the limpets down on the foreshore. We chipped them off the rocks using a special kind of knife or chisel called an *òrd maoraich*. They caught a lot of haddock, whiting, plaice and gurnets.

During the war, all the young men were away at the fighting. So the fishermen were just the old men. It was the old men who did most of the work – pulling the boats and that. Before I left home to come to the Lowlands, I was forever down on the *cladach* helping to pull the boats, or, when they were launching the boats, by pushing along with the men until the boats floated in the sea. I thought it was all good fun!

Our little community at the end of the Point Peninsula were all living in thatched houses. As a matter of fact, my mother was the first crofter in our end to build a modern 'white-house'. The walls of the house were made of poured concrete. My sisters and I carried all the shingle that went into the walls, on our backs in creels. It all came from the *cladach* – the foreshore. I was strong physically in those days. Anything the boys did, I could do it! Yes, Margaret, Kate and myself carried all that shingle in creels on our backs. That was really hard work but we were young and fit and were delighted to see the house going up. And, oh, what a lovely house when it was all done; what a big change for the better! But at the same time, though we were quite poorly off, we were on a par with everybody else. All the families were struggling, and I would say this, that although the home of my early years in Lewis was poor, it was a happy home.

My two sisters, Margaret and Kate, were older than me. The three of us carried the shingle. My mother decided she was going to build a Board of Agriculture house, and it was the first one in Point. It was an enormous, two-storey house and still is enormous! It had four bedrooms. Since then, it's been added to.

Our mother could have had shingle delivered by lorry from another part of the island – from the Bràigh perhaps – ten miles away. But the shingle on the shore was less than 100 yards from the site and it was cheaper to put it in a creel and fetch it! Unfortunately, there's no shingle left there now, I don't think. Other house-builders continued what we started and, between us, we spoiled our lovely shingle beach. Even so, I'm not ashamed of all the work we did for my mother and for our family. No, I'm not! I'm very proud of my back! The hard labour didn't do me any harm, nor did it make me any slimmer! In those days I was as strong as any man. I was able to carry 140 lbs on my back and often did – more than 200 yards at times. There is nothing shameful in admitting that. I was wholeheartedly in it. I cannot say that, when they were in their teens,

the boys in the family, my brothers, were hard-working on the croft.
They were not!

Why the boys didn't carry the shingle is a good question. I just don't know
why. I'm not going to say anything against my brothers, no, nothing. It
wasn't our family alone that allocated all the carrying work to the women.
The women were doing all that hard work because the boys were allowed
to be lazy, that's why. Some people say that the women of Lewis used to
protect their menfolk because so many men were lost through wars and
through accidents at sea. For sure, in the past hundred years or so there
were countless accidents in which boats went down, each carrying six or
seven men. As a result, there were a lot of widows and orphans in our
villages when I was young. But I don't really offer the heavy loss of men at
sea and in wars as the reason why the boys just sat at home while the
women worked like slaves. I don't believe that at all, no. It was just the
custom.

Everything was accepted as the way things should be done – even the bad
habits. Everything was traditional: the way people dressed and behaved; the
number of years a widow had to wear black clothes; the way family worship
was conducted night and morning; the way we regarded strangers – and so
on. One did it, the next one did it, and the next one did it and, after that,
it just became the custom – a tradition!

While we were working with the creel, we knitted, especially when we
were carrying the peats. But I wouldn't say that we knitted while we were
carrying the shingle. Not at all. The shingle was really heavy and we
always had a struggle going up the *bruthach* [steep rise] above the Carragh
Bàn. That *bruthach* was only about 15 feet high but it was quite steep and
by the time you got on to the level with your load, your thighs were
aching.

Cutting the peats was almost always done by the man. He cut the raw
peat with a kind of spade called a *tairsgear* which had a sharp blade more
than a foot long. While the cutter of the peat was above on the bank,
somebody had to be below to throw the blocks of peat as they were coming
off the blade. Guess who was always the thrower – a woman! The men
smoking away on their pipes or cigarettes and, at a leisurely pace, cut the
riasg [raw peat] Meanwhile, the woman was bent double to receive each *fàd*
[block of peat] that came off the *tairsgear* and threw it up to 3 yards away
from the face of the peat-bank. Now, the picture I'm painting might suggest
that the woman was some kind of crofting slave. In fact, the peats were a
very *càilear* [pleasant] form of activity. Everybody of my generation enjoyed

it – the cutting, the *rùdhadh*,* the carting home and the *stèidheadh* [stacking]. It was a communal activity, you see. People came together and had a good laugh. Any woman feeling exhausted by the throwing changed over so that she stood above working the *tairsgear* and the man became the thrower. Women didn't like doing the cutting for they weren't very good at it. The raw peat as you find it on the moor is tough and fibrous. Sometimes, it was almost impossible for the average woman to drive the blade through it – unless, that is, she was as big-boned and strong as a man. Now I was big and strong and I liked the cutting and found it easier than the throwing.

My three uncles went off to Canada before the First World War and for a long time we kept writing to them and they to us. In fact, they were the first Europeans to work the land in places south of Saskatoon. I suppose you could say that they were pioneers in Saskatchewan. Hundreds of their offspring live in Saskatchewan, Alberta and British Columbia. I kept in touch with their children and grandchildren for many years but I'm too old and tired now to make the effort.

Three MacKenzie brothers from No. 5 married three MacDonald sisters from No. 6. One of those couples were my parents. My father was the eldest of the boys, so he got the croft. The others, like myself, had to leave home. A fourth brother, Andrew, married Mary MacKay, a lovely auburn-haired girl from the village of Garrabost. Andrew and Mary also emigrated to Saskatchewan. Each of those early settlers got 160 acres of prairie land for only $10. But they had to work very hard to clear the land and to bring it in for growing crops like wheat. That was one of the conditions of their getting the land. One or two of the emigrants were quite homesick in the early years. Kay Brown, my uncle Andrew's daughter, came over to Scotland two or three times. She and her husband, Fred, loved Lewis. I remember being with them down on the shore one day and Kay said to me, 'Mary, dear, can you tell me something: whatever possessed my family to leave the Isle of Lewis?' There was homesickness there – even in the second generation. That was on a summer's day of course. On a winter's day Lewis would not look quite as attractive. It would look dismal if you didn't have a proper income and if your prospects were bleak!

I think that all the hard work I did on the croft in my young days made me supple and strong. Up to now, I can still clean the house and look after

* Building the blocks into standing clusters, within a few days of cutting, so as to allow the wind and the sun to dry them.

myself. I'm here now, am I not! Today's croft women have become such fragile, delicate creatures that they could not, or would not, do the work that I and my co-ages were used to. I cannot understand them! I would love to do it again. But, you see, it's a new generation, and they have different attitudes. In any case, they just don't have to do it. They are all so much better off than we were. In my day, no Lewis woman would object to her traditional role in the family. Her chores were set out for her from the beginning. She knew exactly what she had to do. If you didn't do what the rest of your co-ages were doing, they would look down on you. They would be talking about you.

Mind you, a few women that I know of did rebel against the manual labour that they were expected to do. My impression is that my Granny Margaret was an exceptional lady – in more ways than one. It is said that, in her young days, she was a very beautiful woman. But also, they used to say of her that she never got off her bottom to do any work! There was nothing wrong with her except that she didn't care to work. Her behaviour made her different from all the rest of the women around her. Every other woman enjoyed hard work and I certainly enjoyed it. Of course, I am called after our other grandmother, Granny Màiri, who was a really hard worker. She was a widow before she was forty and brought up her own six children and two orphans, though they only had two acres of Croft No. 6. True grit!

You ask me why I turned my back on the croft and the kind of work it entails. There was a very good reason for my leaving Point and the Isle of Lewis, which I love. You see, as a girl, I wasn't entitled to inherit the croft at No 5. Only the eldest son was considered to be the rightful heir to the tenancy. That was the crofting law. So I had to leave the nest and go to the city to fend for myself. But during my days under my parents' roof, I learned how to do hard work and that stood me in good stead in the Lowlands.

I was a clever pupil at school and I had the chance of getting a place at the Nicolson Institute. And if I were a child today with my level of ability I would probably be given a proper education. I remember that when I was at the last class of the primary school I had to take a letter from the headmaster home to my mum asking her to go up to see him at the school. My mother went but she didn't tell me, for many years, why the headmaster had sent for her. The reason was that the headmaster told her that there was a place for me in the secondary school. The reason why my mother did not see the matter through was that she couldn't afford to support me in digs while I was attending the Nicolson Institute. So I lost out on that important opportunity.

*

The first penny I earned was at the far-lines at Stornoway gutting herring. In those days, the herring industry employed many thousands of young men and women. The men worked the boats while the women gutted the herring and salted them in barrels. The fishing-boats were known as 'drifters' and they followed the herring shoals as they moved along the coast from the Minch all the way to the East Coast ports and then south as far as East Anglia. The girls worked in teams of three – 'crews' we called them. I didn't much enjoy that kind of work as it was exhausting and poorly paid. On the other hand, I enjoyed the company of the girls in our crew and of the hundreds of island girls who lived in lofts and lodgings in places like Fraserburgh and Yarmouth. It's a long way from Lewis to Yarmouth. We took the train from Kyle of Lochalsh and we travelled all the way from there for hour after hour. Of course, in those days there wasn't a dining-car on the train, so we had to do the best we could with cups of tea brewed up on a meths stove. With the tea we ate stacks of oatcakes which we had brought with us from Stornoway.

After working at the fishing, I went down to work in Claverhouse, in Dundee. I was working in a place where they were bleaching the cotton. That kind of work didn't suit me all too well. Then I decided to come to Glasgow on service, or, as we say in Gaelic, *air mhuinntireas*. My mother had copperplate writing and her English was good. She must have written to Dòmhnall Aonghais Mhòir [Donald Campbell] in Glasgow. He was related to us – a policeman – and he arranged for a member of his family to meet me off the train at Queen Street. And the funny thing was that Charlie Crane – the man who, years later, became my husband – was lodging in their house. I got introduced to Charlie during my first few days in the city. I came to Glasgow when I was in my twenties and have been resident here for about sixty years.

From the time I got my first job in Glasgow until I got married, I had only one employer. I worked for Dr Adams, a Jewish doctor. When Charlie and I got married Dr Adams even went to church to give me away. They were lovely generous people. They even paid for my wedding. So they were my adoptive parents in a way. I was a Presbyterian from the north but we got on very well! We respected each other and our different ways and we were as the one family. Mrs Adams was English. Both she and her husband died and their son and daughter then emigrated down south. I miss them very much. We were so close to each other.

My mother was very fond of Charlie – as fond as she was of her own three sons. Charlie was of English stock. His father and mother came from

Chester, and they were well-to-do people, I believe. It seems that they had done something wrong and they fled to Glasgow. They never went back south, but what the problem was we never found out. Although I am more fluent in Gaelic than I am in English, Charlie never tried to learn Gaelic. He just wasn't interested. Because all our acquaintances in Lewis [and] in Glasgow could speak English, he felt that making the effort to learn a new language would be a waste of his time.

There was a lively Highland community in Glasgow when I came here. I used to go to lots of ceilidhs and dances. Had I stayed up north, I would have had a totally different lifestyle, but there was no place for me at home and I often regretted that. There was no place for Charlie and me to bring up a family. Looking back, I might not have been happy going back to Lewis, even if a place had become available.

I have followed the Christian religion as my parents did before me. Unfortunately, I am no longer able to go to church, which I miss very much. Still, I read my Bible and listen to the worship on the television. I have a son Charles and a daughter Janetta and they are both very good to me.

I am very keen on the football. I'm a football supporter – Rangers! When I see my grandchildren with their faces with 'Rangers' on them, you couldn't help but be one of them. Although I tell you that I support Rangers I have never been to a live game. I have a lot of Catholic friends and I'm ashamed that there's all that trouble between the supporters of the Glasgow rivals' teams – between the Catholics and Protestants in Glasgow. It really is a shame and I don't approve of it. As far as I'm concerned, I'm a Highlander and a Protestant who has a lot of Catholic and Jewish friends. I love them all.

I live in this lovely flat in Ashfield, in Bishopbriggs, with carpets on the floor and beautiful furniture, lovely wallpaper and expensive ornaments, most of which I am given as gifts from my son and daughter, and my friends. It's quite a change from the days of my childhood when we had to live in a house which had a clay floor, limed interior walls and a sooty ceiling. So that was our black-house. Of course, that was when I was very young, growing up. As I told you before, my home in Lewis in my growing up years was a happy home in the sense that it was a Christian home, and I learned there that true happiness doesn't come from the material things you have around you in your home.

Angus MacLeod ('Ease')

1916–2002

I was born on a croft in the village of Calbost in South Lochs in Lewis and am aged eighty-two. In my youth, I was very happy living in Calbost but, like everybody else, I was forced to leave because of lack of work. You see, there's a lot of concern just now about crofting, and rightly so. There's depopulation on the island of Lewis and I don't quite agree with the emphasis they're laying on the absentee crofter, absentee crofter, absentee crofter . . . There wouldn't be absentee crofters if there was work in the crofting townships. The agricultural side of crofting cannot sustain anybody. You need some other work to augment what little you take out of the soil. The work that augmented crofting, in Lochs particularly, was the herring fishing. And the herring fishing has now gone.

A crofting family needs to have a second kind of occupation in addition to producing food from their three or four acres. And I maintain that the authorities never understood that properly. Oh, you look at all the royal inquiries, the royal commissions and all that and you will find that they talk about agriculture. They talk about viable crofts. There isn't a viable croft in existence. No such a thing! There never will be. Even if you have a whole crowd of people doing crofting together as a co-operative, they will need some other work to give them a proper standard of living.

My native village of Calbost is no longer a community, for it is almost empty of people. Empty! Empty except one young, middle-aged lady, who came there when her father died. The last man of Calbost was aged ninety-four and he has now died. He was born in 1902, incidentally, and the village then was at its height as a crofting community, with a healthy population of about two hundred. That man who is now dead, he saw it out. He was the very last man. And that's the story of the twentieth century; the nineteenth century rising, the twentieth century declining.

In my view, crofting, if it is to be successful, has to be communal. It is based on villages, as a rule, although you might find a cultivated croft here and there. But generally speaking, villages, or 'townships' as they are called officially, were basically collections of interdependent families. And in the olden days, you see, the work on the land was done by groups of families working together. They worked on the sheep together. Then a crowd of them got together and went to cut the peats and dried them and transported them home together. They even stacked them together so that each family had fuel for the fire for a whole year. All that was available to them on the village common. Without peat, there wouldn't have been crofter villages, for there was no other fuel available to the crofters. That was the peats and, then, they went to cut the seaweed, to plant the potatoes – various things like that they did together, you see. They even built their houses together. Oh yes, very much so. That's an important matter that must be remembered – the islanders' communal effort throughout the generations.

When a fellow was going to build a house, well, all you were concerned about when you were building a house was the roof. You see, that is why the landlords allowed you to take the roof, but you couldn't take the stones. The stones were his. The roof was your own. So you could cart the roof away. And when you moved to another place – or were forced to move – well, all the neighbours gathered round and you had that wall up probably in a couple of days. You formed your walls of stones and turf and then you roofed it. The only other thing you needed was an outer door.

Ever since they started going to the Caithness fishing, the fishermen were taking wood home from the mainland. They were going across to the mainland, opposite us here, to the Gairloch area and to the forests over there and taking timber back. I don't mean that they were stealing timber. Oh, no. Lewis people don't steal anything! They would have bought it with money they earned at the fishing.

Now their diet. They ate a lot of salted, preserved food which doctors of today advise you against. Och, medical advice! Don't be listening too much to them, or you might go the wrong way with your diet. The people's lifestyle in the real crofting days was very different from what it is now. Hard manual labour burnt off whatever food they were eating. Today's crofters hardly turn a spade! We rely on tractors and gadgets to do all the really hard work.

It is said that in the sixteenth century Lewis was self-supporting. But you must remember that the population was low and it was only between 4,000 and 6,000. It was only 6,000 in the eighteenth century. In the nineteenth century, there was an explosion from 9,000 at the beginning of the century to 29,000 at the end of it, you see. Now that's fact number one. Fact number two is that ever since the potato came* they were all right.

* Thought to have been introduced to the Highlands and Islands some 250 years ago.

There was an abundance of fish at the foot of the croft. Boats were small, but if necessary you would get enough fish by fishing from the rocks. Plenty of fish. Down through the years, from the introduction of the potato to my time in Calbost, the staple diet of the islanders was fish and potatoes.

My father was a weaver in South Lochs, where I was brought up. The road linking our villages to Stornoway was only completed in 1928. Transport before that was by boat. I was twelve years old when the road was built. But that didn't mean that before the road was built we were not familiar with the town of Stornoway. We came to the town by boat, you see. After the road link was built, we continued with the boat, but then when small buses started to operate the road came into its own.

Whenever my father came into the town – which wasn't often – he did some serious shopping. And he always brought home, as necessary, a boll of oatmeal, 140 lbs, and a boll of flour, 140 lbs as well. A rack of sugar, 112 lbs, and a box of margarine, 56 lbs. Can you imagine a housewife buying that in these quantities now? Now the money was scarce, so I'm also mystified as to how they managed to buy in such large quantities. Well, now, you had a boll of flour, a boll of oatmeal, a bag of sugar and a box of margarine, a barrel of salt herring and a pile of potatoes. Oh, you were as well off as could be! Good food, good wholesome food.

Now, that was in the 1900s. Earlier generations would have grown their own oats and barley. But, at that time, all the people in the island – all the people in Lochs certainly – bought their meal in the same way. You see, I don't think the local merchants were selling any 2 lb, 3 lb, 4 lb or half-stone bags of meal. The price of a boll of oatmeal was 17s 6d. That was before the Second World War. You see, I was in school in the '20s and I left at fourteen, in 1930. So, I'm still talking about it in 1930.

There was a mill on the stream in our village and I've been thinking about it quite a bit lately, and nobody ever told me who built it originally. I'm now fairly convinced that it probably was the Norwegians. Calbost is a Norwegian name, you see. In any case, the tacksman [farm tenant] owned it and then my grandfather had it. My grandfather kept it until he moved to Stornoway in 1902. He was a progressive man.

If you're well versed in history, you will know the way the world continues to change and evolve all the time. By the turn of the nineteenth century, the people of Calbost had evolved out of planting barley and making their own meal. Except for the mill that is in Garrabost in Point and the mill in Ness, all the others had ceased to operate. That was because the way of life changed, you see. They were earning money and did not have to go through the hassle of manuring the ground, planting cereals, reaping, stacking, threshing, winnowing and carting to and from the mill.

Now, you might be wondering about the question how were they able to earn the money with which to buy oatmeal and so on. To be truthful, I myself am puzzled because there was often no money. They would go to the fishing and if they had a poor season by not catching good shots of herring, they came back without any money. And if they came back with £6 or came back with £10, or anything between £10 and £20, they were rich! The herring fishing was good up to the beginning of the First World War. The fisher-folk were pretty well off, as far as herring fishing was concerned. Now the First World War put the finish to that, you see. Our markets were the Baltic states, Prussia and Germany and, well, after the First World War, Germany couldn't afford to pay for our cured herring. They were bankrupt. They paid but, as often as not, their money was worthless. So you see, life was hard without a steady income to meet the needs of the people here.

Some might think that with a deer forest on their doorstep and salmon rivers in the estate, Calbost and the other villages in South Lochs would be full of poachers. But, strangely enough, they weren't aware that the salmon were wandering about the coast here. They weren't aware of it. It's only our generation that discovered that the shoals of salmon were only a couple of hundred yards from our doorstep. It was we who took advantage of the discovery that the salmon were there for the taking. Oh, yes, yes, yes! And I was one of those who took advantage of God's given bonanza.

I remember, you see, I sent for a net to the mainland because I had an idea that the salmon were following our coastline. Some fellows from Lewis and Harris were going to the salmon fishing down in the south of Scotland. Well it occurred to some local fellows here, myself included, that there must be salmon on our coast as well. However, leave the salmon history alone, in case you misuse this recording and get me into trouble!* Now, the deer was another thing. You see, that's a sore subject in Lochs. The people of Lochs were in dire straits towards the end of the nineteenth century. They had three, four, five, even six families living on crofts which extended to only a few acres. The biggest Clearance of people in Lewis took place in South Lochs. Landowners cleared the people off the land to make room for commercial sheep-farming. The creation of commercial sheep-farms was the root cause of most of the Clearances. The first commercial sheep-farm

---

* Shoals of salmon on the coast were bound for the rivers on sporting estates and anybody discovered catching them in the open sea were (and still are) regarded as poachers and severely punished by the courts.

was established in Southern Park in the South Lochs district about 1802. And the whole of the peninsula of South Lochs at that time was inhabited. So to establish the farm they had to clear a number of villages in the very south. And then that farm kept expanding until it took in two thirds of the entire district: 42,000 acres and thirty-six villages of the Park Peninsula.

Now as time went on in the nineteenth century people were getting a bit militant and, you know, by the 1870s the people of the whole Highlands were pulling their socks up. And certainly, by the beginning of the 1880s, oh, well, they were getting a bit fedup of the situation and they were agitating. And then we got the Crofters Act in 1886. And what happened in Park? But in 1887, the landowners changed that farm from sheep-rearing to deer. The commercial sheep-farm became a sporting estate. Well, that was a slap in the face for the local people, just a year after the Crofters Act was passed safeguarding the rights of the crofters.* You see, the people had put up with the sheep-farm for a whole century. You can imagine how angry the people were. The poor people! This croft beside me here had six big families, living on just a few acres between them. Some of the families consisted of a man, a wife and nine or ten children. How did they manage to feed all those children, you ask me? Now, there you are, you see! There was deer at hand because the landowners made the sheep-farm a sporting deer-park for their prosperous clients from the south. Well, that's what we got in the Highlands, as a spin-off from the affluent Victorian society!

In my view, the men and women who stood up to the authorities in those days are worthy of our admiration. At the moment, monuments are being erected in different parts of Lewis, commemorating the very thing we were talking about – that is, the crofters' agitation for land law reform. The agitation for living space. When you consider that there were thirty-six families, more than 200 people, living on the fourteen crofts in Calbost. There was only 76 acres of arable, you see, to support all these people. Oh, man alive! Can you just imagine the conditions of the people? Fortunately the community owned a few boats. Oh, they had to rely on the boats to catch fish for the pot and fish to sell, but that was often a dangerous occupation in treacherous seas in winter and spring. That was the trouble, you see. That's why the people were leaving crofting communities. Young people want a wage packet every weekend. And that is why Calbost is now a ghost village with only one house occupied.

---

* Based on the finding of the the Napier Commission of 1883, the Crofters Act was passed in 1886, guaranteeing crofters security of tenure and fair rents and, in effect, greatly diminishing the power of the landowners.

People should know their history. And the authorities would learn a lot if only they looked carefully at what has happened to us in the past. There was the Napier Report that resulted in the passing of the Crofters Act. More recently, there was the Taylor Report and all these other reports. They always concentrated on crofting as if it was farming. Crofting is not farming. Crofting is not an industry either. It's a way of life. Even if you took any of the biggest villages in the island, it still wouldn't make a decent agricultural unit. There's an element of agriculture in it, but the big factor in giving the crofter a proper living is the employment which provides him with a steady income throughout the year. Now, when they made their Crofters Commission by the 1955 Act, and then a few years later when they set up the Highlands and Islands Development Board, why didn't they consider that fact? The Crofters Commission in the 1955 Act was designed to be looking after the agriculture. No word about what you really need in the twentieth century – ancilliary employment.

In the Highlands, and in Lewis particularly, we delight in arguing with each other. Because of that, we don't get anywhere. Unfortunately, they went and allowed their interests, which were aligned with the aims of the Land League, to fall by the wayside. The moment they got the protection of the Crofters Act, they lost interest in the wider movement. You see, that's what happened. The moment somebody gets what he wants – cheerio, he's not bothered about the other fellow!

Some people ask me why I worked so hard to resuscitate the Crofters Union. Well, I'll try to explain. I think the Highlander likes to argue and fight. Unfortunately, we are like that throughout the Highlands. However, the point is that I and a lot of people felt that the crofters should get together. Unity is strength, you see. Trade unions were a good thing and the sad thing about the twentieth century is that trade-unionism has fallen out of favour. I sincerely hope that the trend won't affect the Crofters Union. It has done a lot of good work and continues to do so. We have a good man at the helm and representatives in all the crofting areas.

I hear people say, 'Oh, the crofts are done now! Crofting has gone forever.' I come back to tell you that crofting's a way of life. It's not farming. Now that's why I keep harping on. Of course, today we're well off. We're a high-class people, you see! You will understand, of course, that I don't mean that in any class-conscious sense. What I mean is that, in the islands, we have a very special way of life and, whatever our economic circumstances, we are blessed to live in those islands with the language and culture we have. It's precious, you see.

Well, you know I'm very interested in local history and in those artefacts that were used by our forebears. I was the youngest of the family of six boys. The rest of our family wandered off all over the world and left me standing here in ill health. I determined not to go under! I've got a croft, so I said to myself, 'This is the very thing I want to do – to start collecting everything that people were throwing out and all the things that I myself would have been throwing out if I had not cared for preserving evidence of our history.'

If I could, I would take you all to my Crofting Museum in Calbost in South Lochs. You couldn't go to a better place than Calbost anyhow! It's only an hour from Stornoway. If you were in London you'd spend two hours sitting in traffic going nowhere as beautiful as Calbost! In fact, I was talking to somebody from London recently and he was telling me that he spent twelve hours a day travelling. Twelve hours, if you don't mind!

Now, I suppose that you are just on the point of asking me why I'm living in the town of Stornoway and not in Calbost! Well, you see, I was in ill health after the [Second World] war. I was two years in hospital in Glasgow and I wasn't long home when my mother died. And I tell you that in those days, before the present national health and welfare systems came around, you were paying two stamps, one for employment and one for illness – 1s 6d each or something like that. And if you became ill, you got 15s. Dole money amounted to 15s, or 15s if you fell ill – per week.

Now, as it happened, I fell ill in Glasgow. I was getting my 15s in hospital. I was in hospital nearly two years. After the first six months, they cut the money by half. That was the rule: 7s 6d. And in six months again they cut that by half again – to 3s 9d. So I came home with 3s 9d per week to support me. Gosh, it was tough going! You see, I was suffering from TB and expecting to die any day. But I had such a good doctor! Oh, I'm all for the doctors. There I was over in Calbost living as an invalid with an income that was just a pittance. I couldn't very well work peats, because I hadn't fully recovered. But, strangely enough, I recovered very well since then and did a lot of work in my time. So I turned my attention to the only thing I knew. I didn't have much education either. Such education as I have, I acquired it in the school of life. And a good university it is, and it teaches you a lot about a lot of subjects – particularly budgeting!

I decided to go into business – the Harris tweed manufacturing business. I had £26 in the Post Office. I don't know why or how. Well, I think I'll tell you why. If you found yourself stranded on the mainland, couldn't get a job, you were on the beach as a wreck and there you would lie stranded unless you had enough money to buy your ticket home. No use sending home for money, for there was none there either! I bought my ticket home to Lewis and, over and above the cost of the ticket, I must have had a little over. I think that I must have been putting a little by, each week, for a security – a bit of a wee nest egg. Anyway, I lifted my £26 out of the Post Office and I went and bought wool. Though I wasn't feeling very strong, I went and scraped the *crotal** off the rock. I had to do that personally: nobody else to do it for me because my parents were dead by that time. I knew how to dye the wool, for I had often watched my parents doing it. I put fire down at the loch and I dyed the wool. That was the trick, you see. After that was done, I took the dyed wool over to Newalls Mill in Stornoway, and before you could blink, and I was a Harris tweed manufacturer! That was me, the recovering invalid, in business!

My next move was like this. I got whatever yarn I could get both in Lewis and on the mainland and even in from as far away as England. That made me then, a yarn-importer. A yarn-importer in a very small way, you see. I don't know how I got in touch with Marshall Ingram, a firm in Princes Street, London, and I became their buying agent for Harris Tweed. And that was money for old rope there. A commission it was called. Well, I had to use initiative like that to survive. It came out of dire necessity.

Lord Leverhulme was the proprietor of the island in the 1920s. Now, in his own way, he was a different kind of landlord from his predecessors. At heart he was a good man. But, unfortunately, clever though he was, he was stupid. He went and started an argument with the crofters. He wouldn't give them land and that's one of the rocks on which he foundered – but not the only rock. He meant well. That's our trouble, you see. It's a question of judgement. Now Lord Leverhulme's judgement was bad when it came to crofters and land. On his estate on this island of Lewis there were many people being born into barns and had to stay there in barns throughout their lives. Yes, it's a fact! Some people were born into a barn, lived there all their lives and died in the same barn. The proprietor refused to allocate them crofts in the deer-parks. And all those thousands of acres with deer on them were sacrosanct. Stupid! The thing was so wrong. No wonder the people were alienated! Lord Leverhulme should have done his homework.

In my view, the system of landownership we have in the Highlands and Islands of Scotland is out and out wrong! It's wrong morally, physically and everything else wrong. And the land, in my opinion, should belong to the people who live and work on it. Now I am a bit sceptical, supportive but

---

* A form of lichen that produces a deep brown colour of wool.

sceptical, of the Small Trusts. You see, before we got this single Crofters Union, as you know, there were small Crofters Unions but they weren't effective. As usual, the one argued with the other or put forward a policy that was directly opposite to what the other one was putting forward. Consequently, the authorities paid no attention to them. They just dismissed them.

The Stornoway Trust* has not been successful, you see, because it's too small. The Stornoway Trust determined not to raise the rent of the crofters. Now, although the trustees don't seem to recognise the fact, the Stornoway Trust is a business. You've got to run a business in a business-like way. And long since, the time came long since, when rents should have gone up. Stornoway Trust should raise their income and exploit all the avenues open to it, including by increasing the rents. Over the decades, the trustees are usually better-off people. They're the wrong people to be running the Trust, you see. The big people in Stornoway, the merchants, what did they know about crofting? They're good people but, all the same, they are the wrong people to be the trustees.

I wrote a paper advocating that instead of having different trusts or agencies representing the interests of small districts, we should have only one trust for the whole of the Highlands and Islands. And that trust could also be a development association. You imagine all the rents that's paid for quarries and all the things that raise rents in the Highlands and Islands. They would have a vast income. But, you see, the lobby of the landowners is too strong to allow for change.† Oh, yes, they have a strong lobby because they understand what's what and have the expertise. You really have to be strong to tackle them. You have to be united, of course. And that's the trouble. We're not united on anything. Well there's a Scottish parliament coming and folk in that parliament have been talking about land since I was a boy. They're not doing much about it just now. But we live in hope.

I have to say that I liked the way of life in the black-houses. I was in many black-houses, in and out of them. And they were nice and warm, homely, clean. Today, when you look at a ruin, you can hardly imagine that the people living in them were clean and house-proud – as clean as they could be, given the smoke and lack of sanitation. You know, in the morning, they made the hearth clean and bright with 'whitening' [a form of lime] round

* In 1927, Lord Leverhulme (a Lancashire soap-manufacturer) gifted his estate in Lewis to his former tenants. The Lews Estate is run by the Stornoway Trust, an elected body.

† Apart from those living on community-owned estates, croft tenants must follow rules laid down by their landlords including, for example, how the mineral potential of the land may be exploited.

the fire. It was a welcoming sight to go into a house like that with a bright fire blazing in the middle of the floor. Then, in the next room with the box-beds and all that. Much like you see in our old place in Calbost, you know.

Now, ignorant people say all sorts of things about the black-houses but, in fact, they don't know what they're talking about. For example, they talk about the floor of the black-house as if it were an earthen floor. It wasn't an earthen floor at all. Black-houses were done cleverly and with due care and attention to their construction. Take, for example, the construction of the foundation. After clearing away the topsoil right down to the bedrock, they put down stones, small stones. They put them down in such a way as to allow water to drain between then. That's the kind of best way of draining water away, putting a lot of small stones. On top of that, they put clay. That's beaten clay, clay that became as hard as cement on top of it. They compacted the clay in the most enjoyable way imaginable. They invited everybody into the house and had a dance – a barn dance most likely. That's right. They had a dance, you see, to pack the floor well down. They would have the clay floor as hard as cement by the time they moved in. The last dance in Calbost of that nature was in 1945, immediately after the war. My brother was building a white-house and he put the floor in. It was a wooden floor of course. Well, a dance was held there just in the way of the old tradition when neighbours used to come and help compact the clay floor. It was the last time that that old tradition was observed.

Now take for instance the walls of the black-house. The wall consists of a double wall of stones. There's an inner stone wall and there's an outer stone wall. The space between them was packed full of earth. It was the forerunner of the present cavity wall in modern houses. In Lewis, we put our rafters and the roof on to the inner wall. In most other places in the Hebrides, they put it on the outer wall. In our style, the rainwater flowed down on to the peat between the two stone walls. Of course, grass grew on the peat to form what was called the *tobhta*. The *tobhta* was useful, for you could walk on it when you were repairing the roof or thatching the house. You might ask me where all the water went that poured off the thatch and on to the *tobhta*. It must have percolated down between the double stone walls. Now, as far as I can make out, they wanted the dampness in that filling between the two walls, for it kept the cold out and it kept the warm in. And another thing, the stones on the inner side of the wall, if you go and examine them, you see, there was a slight drop out the way for the water to go, not to come into the house but flow out the way into the cavity.

The black-houses were low and streamlined and the wind whooshed past them. They also toned well into the land. So our recent ancestors knew what they were doing so far as the building of black-houses was concerned. There was a science to it and they were masters of that science. Now, I see there on the television folks with dogs and cats and, you name it, mice or rats, in their arms. Where's the hygiene in that? I think the hygiene of their homes is worse than that of any black-house! Yes, you might say that I'm up in arms about people who talk down the old black-houses and haven't got a good word to say about how our forefathers lived.

But before I leave the subject of the black-house, may I refer you to the living conditions in our cities of those days, with their open drains used as sewers. The working classes of the cities were far worse off that we were in Lewis – worse off by a hundred times! Of course, many of the people in the cities of Glasgow and Dundee were people who had gone there from the Highlands and Islands and Ireland to look for work in the factories and shipyards. In many cases, they would not have been worse off had they stayed where they were.

There was a fellow John MacLeod born in 1827 at Kershader, South Lochs, and he eventually became a minister of the famous Iron Church at Strontian in Argyll. A wonderful Gael and a wonderful minister at a time when the people of the Highlands were very oppressed. And how did he manage that, born into a poor community in 1827? How did he do it? My standard of education was so poor that I could hardly write home when I was in Glasgow. I was born in 1916, a hundred years after him.

In the past, we lived in a spiritual society. There was friendship and a reliance on your neighbour that was based on the spirit of Christianity. There was a strong communal spirit and, in those days, that was absolutely essential. Among the things that are devalued in our society of today is religion. In my view, that is very regrettable.

The Edinburgh Ladies Schools were established in 1811.* And my goodness, after that the Gaels were able to read in the Bible what they had been hearing from others. Now they were able to read it for themselves. The Bible was a textbook and you couldn't get a better textbook than the Bible, you see. And that fashioned their character and still fashions our character to this day. The schoolhouses in Lochs weren't built till 1880! Education gave the most able in our communities good prospects abroad. It gave them wings! That was inevitable. Education sucked the best people

* The Ladies Association of Edinburgh was established in 1850 to support the establishment of Free Church Schools in the Highlands and Islands. As well as supporting the economic, intellectual and spiritual needs of the people, the association aimed to enable more Gaelic-speaking young men to become students for the ministry.

away. It's sucking them away now. But, things are changing now. Our culture is taken care of, our language is taken care of; our culture is taken care of in a large way. We talk about a university of the Highlands.* Oh, if only all those things would have come fifteen, even fifty years ago, a hundred years ago! But it's coming now and let's welcome it and do what we can to help the young folk.

On the question of religion in our island, I would say that you find one or two people who have a very blinkered view of the world we live in. The world is made up of all kinds of people – black, brown, pale-skinned, yellow-skinned and so on – all of them God's people, and they have all been created by Him. Our island people are very receptive of every stranger who visits our shores or comes to live here. But so far as religion is concerned, just a few of us cannot accept that there are different interpretations of the Bible and of how we should worship the Almighty.

Now, so far as religion is concerned, you have as many religions as there are cultures. You have to contend with people in committees and you know they frustrate progress, very often. The world is made up of all kinds. Now there are certain people that get the Free Church a bad name. There's nothing wrong with the Free Church. It has a good constitution. It's based on the Bible and has its own interpretation of how the Good Book wants us to behave. It's one interpretation. But one thing is certain, the Bible doesn't advocate that you call each other names and behave aggressively to one another, just because they are different and have different views of things. You have to be big enough to dismiss these people who behave badly for what they are – even though some of them are very influential in our society. Some of them are very influential and outspoken. But if you are sensible, you will peg away in your own quiet way and overcome the influence of those people and their nonsense, you see. The Bible clearly says do not judge others. It is not for you or me to decide who are God's people or who's in the Elect. That's the province of God. Leave it to Him. The Bible says there is a Heaven and also a Hell and I believe the Bible. You'll get your reward when you get there. That is something the Bible makes very clear. So you had better be sure that you end up on the right side. Of course, I'm only a simple, straightforward crofter and that is my philosophy anyway!

Angus MacLeod passed away on 25 October 2002. His 'Calbost Collection' of crofting artefacts and other memorabilia are on display at Museum nan Eilean, Stornoway.

* Now in existence.

Seonaidh a' Mhuilleir

1917–

Rugadh m' athair ann an Tàbost ann an Nis agus bha e pòsta aig Seònaid, nighean Aonghais Ghrèim à Siadar. Bha Aonghas Greum ainmeil anns an là ud airson a neart. Mar tha fhios agad, tha tè dha na clachan a thog e air rathad Bharabhais air a comharrachadh bhos cionn an rothaid. Co-dhiù, thug iad Aonghas Greum Moireasdan air m' athair mar ainm, às dèidh a sheanar. 'S e duine làidir a bha nam athair cuideachd, ach cha robh a neart idir ionann ri neart a sheanar.

Chan eil mi dhan Eaglais Shaor no dhan Aonadh! Tha mi dha na 'Bràithrean' – na *Brethren*. 'S ann mar sin a tha mise agus a bha m' athair romham. Tha Bràithrean againn air feadh an t-saoghail. Tha aon rud mu ar timcheall: faodaidh sinn a dhol a dh'àite sam bith dhan t-saoghal agus gheibh sinn ann daoine dhar seòrs' fhìn. Chan eil gu diofar càite – Ruisia no Sìona, chan eil gu diofar. Thall air taobh sear Alba tha mòran dhiubh ris an iasgach. Tha tòrr aca anns a' Bhruaich agus bailtean eile air Cost a Sear na h-Alba. Bha eòlas agamsa air tòrr dhaoine bhon a' Bhruaich. Dh'aithnichinn iad nuair a bha mi na mo dhuin' òg, bhon a' Bhruaich agus à Ceann Phàdraig. Ged nach eil na Bràithrean uabhasach làidir ann an Leòdhas, tha eaglais againn ann an Steòrnabhagh – an Gospel Hall ann an Ceann a' Bhàigh. Tha sinn a' creidsinn ann am baisteadh – baisteadh inbheach – agus tha sinn a' cuimhneachadh bàs an Tighearna a h-uile seachdain, oir tha an Fhìrinn ag iarraidh ort sin a dhèanamh.

Nise, innsidh mi dhuibh beagan mu dheidhinn eachdraidh an teaghlaich againn agus mar a thàinig mi gu bhith nam mhuillear ann an Garrabost. Dh'fhàg m' athair Leòdhas agus chaidh e a dh'obair a Pheairt, ach ann an 1911 dh'fhalbh e a Chanada, agus nuair a ràinig e null, lean e air gus an do ràinig e Bhancùbhar. Aon fheasgar, is e air sgur a dh'obair, chuir e air deise agus chaidh e airson cuairt sìos am baile, agus choinnich e ri nighean agus i ri coiseachd le Bìoball aice na làimh. Dh'fhaighnich e a' cheist dhi: "Can you tell me where the Brethren have their prayer meeting here?"

"Yes," ars ise, "that's where I'm going. You come along with me."

Agus b' ann mar sin a choinnich m' athair ri mo mhàthair! Chaidh mo mhàthair a-mach a Chanada ann an 1913 agus phòs iad ann an sin fhèin, ann a Bhancùbhar. Aon fheasgar, bha iad nan dithis air streetcar a' dol sìos gu meadhan a' bhaile: 's ann a thàinig seann bhoireannach a-steach dhan chàr. Cò bha sin ach tè a bha air Càrlabhagh fhàgail na pàiste agus air siubhal a-null dhan Talamh Fhuar. Bhruidhinn m' athair rithe agus thuirt e rithe, "Is e seo a' bhean òg agam."

"O," ars ise, "a bheil a' Ghàidhlig aice?" Thuirt m' athair nach robh. Ars ise, "'S e mallachadh a th' ann an sin!"

Mar a tha an seanfhacal ag radh, "Coinnichidh na daoine far nach coinnich na cnuic."

Bha am boireannach sin ag innse dham athair gun do thachair am beatha riutha nuair a chaidh iad a-null an toiseach . . . gum biodh iad a' cur bhuntàta timcheall bunan nan craobhan. 'S iongantach mura robh iad a' dèanamh sin chionn 's gu robh a' choille cho dlùth a' fàs agus nach robh iad aig an ìre sin air na craobhan a ghearradh sìos. Tha e iongantach leam nach robh àite sam bith eile aca airson am buntàta a chur ach timcheall bunan nan craobhan. Co-dhiù, dh'innis i dham athair gu robh iad, air aona bhliadhna, cho bochd agus gum b' fheudar dhaibh am buntàta a bha iad air a chur a thogail airson ithe. Cha robh aca airson a chur ach rùsgan a' bhuntàta a bha iad air a thogail.

Rud iongantach a th' ann, mar a tha Freastal ag obair agus mar a tha ar beatha air a riaghladh. Thachair rud iongantach ann an Garrabost – ach cha b' ann an-dè a bh' ann! Bha boireannach ag innse dhòmhsa mar a thachair dha a dà bhràthair. Thàinig aon dhiubh, Uilleam, dhachaigh air lìobh aig àm a' Chogaidh mu dheireadh. Fhad 's a bha e aig an taigh, dh'fhalbh e chon a h-uile taigh a bh' ann an ceann shuas Gharraboist. 'S chaidh e steach gu Beileag Iain Ruairidh aig a' Phost Oifis 's thuirt e rithe, "Uill," ars esan, "cha thill mise an seo tuilleadh."

Thuirt i ris, "Carson a tha thu ag ràdh sin?"

"Cha thill mise gu bràth tuilleadh," ars esan.

'S thuirt e cuideachd ri a mhàthair, "Chan eil mise dol a thilleadh tuilleadh."

"O, na bi 'g ràdh sin!"

Co-dhiù, dh'fhalbh e, ma-thà, agus nuair a chaidh e air an t-soitheach, chaidh an t-soitheach a chur gu Nova Scotia. Chaidh an criutha air tìr ann an sin. Thurchair gu robh bràthair aige ann an Canada, ach cha robh fhios aige glè mhath càit an robh e. Ach bha fhios aige air a seo, gur e pìobaire a bh' ann. Nise, bha iad air tìr anns a' bhad sin – chan eil fhios agam an tuirt i an ann an Quebec a chaidh iad air tìr. Co-dhiù, chaidh Uilleam suas chon na h-oifis 's dh'fhaighnich e dhaibh an robh beachd aca air a leithid seo a dh'fhear. 'S chan innseadh iad càil dha. Ach 's ann a bha e a' dol air ais chon na soithich nuair a chual' e pipe-band a' cluich. Mach leis gus am faiceadh e na pìobairean, agus nuair a ràinig e far an robh iad b' ann a bha a shùil air an duine a bha air an ceann leis a' bhaton.

Thuirt e ris fhèin, "Cha chreid mise nach e mo bhràthair tha siud!'

Bha bliadhnachan mòra bho bha a bhràthair air falbh. Bha esan na bhalach beag nuair a dh'fhalbh e. Mar a thachair, bha pioctar a bhràthar aige ann a shin, na phòcaid. Choisich e suas ri taobh an fhir air an robh amharas aige. Thug e mach am pioctar agus sheall e dhan an duine e fhad 's a bha iad a' coiseachd taobh ri taobh. Dh'aithnich a bhràthair gur e fhèin a bh' anns an dealbh agus chuir sin e gu math troimh-a-chèile. Ach cha b' e sin uireas! Chuir e ceàrr na 'cir-di-rols' a bha e a' dèanamh air a' phìob. O, chuir e am pipe-band ceàrr cuideachd! Agus choisinn sin dha a bhràthair an uair sin gu robh e, mar gun canadh iad, 'on the carpet'!

Agus thuirt an fheadhainn a bha bhos cionn a' ghnothaich, "Gu dè a dh'èirich dhut 's gun deacha tu ceàrr?"

"O," ars esan, "chunnaic mi mo bhràthair gun dhùil ris."

"Cà bheil e?"

'Tha e muigh an siud a' feitheamh rium."

"Thoir thusa steach e."

'S thug iad a-steach e is rinn iad diathad dhaibh. Agus chaith iad am feasgar còmhla ri chèile.

Thill am fear a bha ri seòladh air ais chon na soithich. Dh'fhalbh an t-soitheach gu ruige New York, ach air an t-slighe chaidh an t-soitheach fodha agus challeadh na bh' innte. Gnothaich duilich. Ach nach b' iongantach mar a bha am fear ud leagte ris a' bhàs mus do dh'fhalbh e!

Chaill mise mi fhìn balach. Chaidh a mharbhadh le càr. Aois ceithir bliadhna fichead. Agus nuair a chaidh mise a chruinneachadh nan rudan a bha e air fhàgail, bha an nighean a bha e dol a phòsadh còmhla rium. Agus thuirt i rium, "Oh, there's a poem that Iain wanted to keep. You can have it," ars ise.

Tha na briathran sin a sgrìobh mo mhac agam fhathast aig an taigh. Mas e do thoil, leughaidh mi dhut e. 'S e poem iongantach a th' ann.

> Now a young boy of twenty-four,
> A wreath will hang upon the door tomorrow
> Of the little place that once we called our home,
> And friends will come and hang their heads in sorrow,
> To pay their last respects to one gone on.
> But you remember the joys we shared
> Together at the start,
> How you promised me
> It would be till death do us part.

Tha mise na mo bheatha cho tric air faicinn rudan uabhasach dhan t-seòrsa sin a' tachairt, agus saoilidh tu gu bheil an fheadhainn dha bheil e a' tachairt air rabhadh fhaighinn gu bheil an t-uabhas a' dol a thighinn nan rathad.

Cluinneam feadhainn a' faighneachd, "Are you a religious person?" Chan eil mise "religious", ach tha mi nam Chrìosdaidh. Dhòmhsa, chan eil ann an 'religion' ach rud a tha a' cuingealachadh do bheatha agus a tha a' toirt a-steach na Hindus agus nam Muslims agus nan creideamhan eile a tha gad dhèanamh mothachail air Dia a tha a' riaghladh. But the Bible defines religion as this: "Pure religion undefiled before God and the Father is to visit the widows and fatherless in their affliction, and to keep oneself unspotted from the world."

Bho chionn ceud bliadhna, bha fear a bhuineadh dhomh ann an Nis: Alasdair Nicolson a bh' air. 'S ann à Borgh a bha a dhaoine, 's bha e pòsta aig piuthar mo sheanar – tè Peigi Mhoireasdan. B' e sin an dàrna pòsadh aice. Bhon a' chiad phòsadh, bha balach aig Peigi air an robh Dòmhnall. Chaidh esan a Chanada agus fhuair e air adhart gu math. Bha e ann a Winnipeg, 's bha elevators aige. 'S bhiodh balaich à Leòdhas ag obair aige.

Leis an dàrna pòsadh, bha Peigi pòsta aig Alasdair Nicolson. Agus bha e fhèin agus a bhean a' fuireachd ann an àite ris an can iad Asmaigearraidh, faisg air Dail, an taobh sa de Dhail. Ma thèid thu sìos a Nis, chì thu fhathast an làrach gorm aig Asmaigearraidh far an robh an taigh aca. Chaidh Iain, am balach a bh' aca, a dh'Ameireagaidh agus phòs e tè ann an sin, tè Nora Cushing – bana-Ameireaganach. Agus ann an ceann sreath, thàinig iad dhachaigh at the turn of the century. Bha iadsan dha na Brethren, 's bhiodh iad a' cumail choinneamhan ann an Nis. Bha iad an toiseach a' cumail choinneamhan anns an taigh aca fhèin. Ach an uair sin thog iad hàlla. Bhiodh Sgoil Shàbaid aca anns a' hàlla sin 's bhiodh mu chuairt air ceud leanabh a' dol innte.

Rugadh mise ann an Garrabost ann an 1916. Ach 's iomadh turas a bha mi, 's mi na mo bhalach, a' dol a-null à sin a Nis. Glè thric bhiodh m' athair gam thoirt ann air Latha na Sàboind às dèidh tìde diathad. Bha bhan aig m' athair, 's dheigheadh sinn a-null leis a' bhan airson na coinneimh feadh na h-oidhche.

Air chùl sin, thog 'Ain Fiosaiche agus a bhean, thog iad Edgemoor Hall, taigh-còmhnaidh agus eaglais bheag, fada muigh anns a' mhòintich, mu chuairt air trì mìle air an t-slighe eadar Sgiogarstaigh agus Tolastadh bho Thuath. Chaidh sin a dhèanamh airson gum biodh àite aig luchd nan àirighean far am faodadh iad a dhol dhan an eaglais nuair a bhiodh iad fada bhom bailtean. Tha cuimhn' agamsa, 's mi nam bhalach, a bhith a-muigh air a' mhòintich ann an sin far an robh taigh 'Ain Fiosaich, air fìor oir na creige, 's mi bhith anns an eaglais a bha sin, 's i làn dhaoine. Cuimhnich a-nise gu robh 'Ain Fiosaich agus a bhean dha na Bràithrean, agus mar sin bha e air a cheann fhèin. Seadh, cha robh esan no ise pàighte no càil. Chan eil duine againn dha na Bràithrean pàight' airson ar n-obair mar bhuill.

Bha fear à Nis anns an àm ud ris an canadh iad Ruairidh Ròigean, 's bha bus aige. Agus bhiodh Ruairidh Ròigean a' dol a-mach feasgar leis a' bhus, 's e làn òigridh; a' dol a-mach chon na mòintich, 's dheigheadh e cho fad' 's a gheibheadh e air Rathad Leverhulme. Choisicheadh na bh' aige de dh'òigridh an còrr dhan an t-slighe. An dèidh na seirbheis, dhèanadh Nora, bean 'Ain Fiosaich, dhèanadh i teatha dhaibh mus deigheadh iad air ais a-rithist. Bhiodh Ruairidh Ròigean air a' mhòintich nan coinneamh airson an toirt dhachaigh.

Bha bràthair aig 'Ain Fiosaich air an robh 'Billy' [Alasdair], am fear a rinn an t-amhran 'Eilean Leòdhais, Tìr nan Gaisgeach'. B' e sin a bhràthair. Bha càr aig a' ghille sin 's bha sin annasach ann an Leòdhas; cha robh mòran chàraichean ann anns an latha sin. Thurchair dha a bhith shìos ann an Nis, agus bha fear eile an sin le càr, 's thuirt esan ri Billy, "Bidh mise ann an Steòrnabhagh romhad."

Ma thubhairt, dh'fhalbh an dithis a' còmhstri mar sin ri càch-a-chèile. Gu mì-shealbhach, chaidh Billy leis a' chàr bhàrr an rathaid, faisg air Loidse Ghabhsainn, agus chaidh a mharbhadh. Tha mi 'n dùil gun do thachair sin mu chuairt air 1910.

Bha fear eile ann an Nis aig an àm ud a bha gu math ainmeil na latha. B' e sin Aonghas Greum. Nuair a bhathas a' deanamh an rathaid – am Pentland Road – rinn e euchd a bha gu math iongantach. Bha a' chlach mhòr a bha sin na suidhe, na cnap-starra, agus cha robh dòigh air a gluasad no faighinn cuidhteas i. Bha i anns an rathad orra gus an tàinig Aonghas Greum, agus chuir esan a dhàrna taobh i. Bha e glè thric a' dèanamh euchdan dhan t-seòrsa sin; ach cha dèanadh e càil ach nuair a bhiodh e na aonar. O, bha e iongantach làidir, 'eil fhios agad. A rèir aithris, bha e ann an Steòrnabhagh aon turas agus bha soitheach-cogaidh a-staigh. 'S bha boxing champion oirre. Anns an là ud, bhiodh a h-uile duine a' dol dhan an Imperial – taigh-òsta air an robh an t-ainm sin. Bhiodh na balaich a' cruinneachadh ann an sin, agus b' ann a thòisich iad a' tarraing à Aonghas Greum. Thuirt iad ris, "An tèid thu a shabaid ris an duine sin?"

Cha deigheadh Aonghas Greum a shabaid ri duine. Ach chùm iad air agus, anns a' cheann thall, thuirt e riutha, "Uill," ars esan, "beiridh mi air làimh air, mus buail mi e."

'S rug e air làimh air an duine thapaidh ud agus bha an grèim a ghabh e air an làimh dheis aige cho teann 's gun do thòisich a chuid fala ri sruthadh às na h-òrdagan aige. O, aidh, duine cumhachdach. Bha deilbh againn dheth uair – dealbh Aonghais Ghrèim agus dealbh mo sheanar – air gach taobh dhan mhantlepiece againn. Ach bhàsaich m' athair agus chaill mi na deilbh. 'S mòr am beud, gu dearbh.

Bha e shìos anns a' Phort – Port Nis – aona latha agus e a' tighinn dhachaigh leis a' chairt agus i làn eisg. Ach seo, 's ann a chaidh cuibhle na cairt ann an toll a bh' anns an rathad, 's chan fhaigheadh an làir air a tarraing às. Dh'fhalbh Aonghas Greum 's rug e air a' chuibhle agus bhrùth e i gus na thog e i às an àite anns na ghreimich i. Thog Aonghas còir a cheann agus thuirt e ris an làir, "A bhrònag bhochd, chan eil thu cur càil a dh'iongnadh orm nach do tharraing thu às i. Cha mhòr nach do dh'fhaillich e orm fhìn."

Chuala mise m' athair ag ràdh: "Nuair a bha mise na mo bhalach," ars esan, "bha cailleach laghach dà dhoras no trì bhon taigh againne." Dh'ainmich e cò i – a' chailleach a bha seo à Tàbost. Chan eil cuimhn' agam an-diugh ciod an t-ainm a bh' oirre. Co-dhiù, thuirt i rim athair, "Na gabh thusa iongnadh, a bhalaich, gu robh do sheanair làidir." Ars ise, "Dheigheadh e a-mach ann an sin anns a' mhadainn gu Mùirneag agus thigeadh e dhachaigh le fiadh air a mhuin. 'S bha iad ag ithe sin cho tric 's gu robh na fèidh aca cho pailt 's a bha na fàdan mònach!" Siud a thubhairt i. "Bha iad ag ithe sitheann an fhèidh," ars ise, "cho tric 's a bha iad a' cur feum air na fàdan mònach!"

Fhios agad, anns an là ud, cha b' e an aon seòrsa beatha a bh' aig daoine 's a th' againn an-diugh. Bhiodh balaich à Nis a' dol chon an iasgaich, agus bha iad a' coiseachd à Nis a Tholastadh, 's à Tolastadh a Steòrnabhagh. Bhiodh iad a' caitheamh na h-oidhche air an àirigh. Bhiodh iad a-muigh aig na h-àirighean far an robh taigh 'Ain Fiosaich ann an sin. 'S ann an sin a tha Mùim, Gil, Allt an t-Sùlair, Abhainn Chuidhsiadar suas gu Loch Nèill. 'S ann an sin a bha àirighean Thàboist, air feadh na mòintich ann an sin gu lèir. Bhiodh iad a' caitheamh na h-oidhche an sin còmhla ri daoine a bhuineadh dhaibh no clann-nighean air an robh iad a' suirghe. Thogadh iad orra anns a' mhadainn, agus an uair sin bha iad a' coiseachd gu Tolastadh agus à sin gu ruige Steòrnabhagh.

Bha aona nighean ann an sin agus tha e coltach, a rèir aithris, gur e 'livewire' a bh' innte. Air an fheasgar, bhiodh a' chlann-nighean a' dol sìos air leòidean casa a bha tuiteam sìos chon nan creagan far an robh feur math gorm. Bhiodh iad a' gearradh an fheòir dhan chrodh leis a' chorran. Bha iad a' dol sìos gu oir na creige ach bha ròp aca airson an cumail sàbhailt. Uill, thuirt an nighean a bha siud gun deigheadh ise sìos an toiseachd ro chàch, agus dh'fhalbh i. Air an t-slighe sìos, 's ann a bhris an ròp. Siud i tarsainn air a' chreig 's chaidh a marbhadh.

Thuirt 'Ain Fiosaich riumsa, "Cha d' fhuaireadh an dust aice gu làrna-mhàireach 's bha taigh-fhaire aca ann an sin air mullach na creige." Bha e 'g ràdh, cho fad' 's a b' aithne dha, gum b' e siud an aon taigh-fhaire a chaidh riamh a chumail a-muigh – a-mach à taigh. Bha sin gu math brònach – gu math iomraiteach anns an là ud.

Choisich mi fhìn an t-slighe ud, bho Tholastadh gu Sgiogarstaigh. Tha e mu ochd mìle. Tha taigh 'Ain Fiosaiche, chanainn-sa, mu thrì mìle air taobh muigh Sgiogarstaigh. 'S bha an uair sin, O, uill, chanainn co-dhiù còig mile no sia bho Tholastadh.

Bha peathraichean-athar agam a bhiodh air a' mhòintich aig Loch Nèill. Bhiodh iad a' coiseachd air Latha na Sàboind dhan an eaglais ann an Tolastadh. Bhitheadh. Bha iad cho dìleas, a dhuine. Bha antaidh eile agam a bha fuireachd ann an Stèinis. Bha i pòsta aig fear ris an canadh iad Murchadh Thòmais. Nuair a bha i na nighinn, bha i 'g obair ann an Loidse Ghabhsainn, air mhuinntireas ann an sin. Ag èirigh anns a' mhadainn, bha i a' bleoghan a' chruidh; bha i dèanamh na bracaist dhan an teaghlach; 's bha i, às dèidh sin, a' cur oirre a h-aodach ceart. Bha i an uair sin a' coiseachd à Gabhsann sìos a Thàbost. Bha bean m' uncail a' dèanamh copan tì dhi mus gabhadh i an rathad a-rithist, sìos trì mìle eile gu ruige a' choinneamh shìos ann an Lìonal. Anns an là ud, bha iad a' coiseachd mhìltean mòra gun saoilsinn càil dheth. Ach chaill sinne a' choiseachd sin. Ach cuideachd, bha neart iongantach anns na daoine. Uill, 'eil fhios agad, tha tòrr anns a' chleachdadh. Bha mise ag obair sa mhuilinn an sin, mi fhìn nam dhuin' òg, agus bhithinn a' dèanamh bollaichean min-eòrna. 'S cha robh duine anns a' mhuilinn ach mi fhìn. Bha mi a' cumail sùil air a' ghràn shuas an staidhre agus a' coimhead gu robh na drabhailtean làn agus, an uair sin, ri dol sìos an staidhre chon na mine. Agus bha mi lìonadh a' phoc agus ga chur air a' mheidh – deich clachan: 140 pounds. Bha mi an uair sin a' fuaigheal a' phoca agus ga chur air an làr airson a stampadh. An ath rud, bha mi a' togail a' phoca – a' breith air – agus ga chur suas do dh'àite air leth.

Bha a' mhuilinn a' dol a latha 's a dh'oidhch'. Bha, bha! Cha robh mi saoilsinn càil dheth. Cha dèanainn siud air leth no tomhas dheth an-diugh! A rèir coltais, bha muilinn Lochlannach ann an Garrabost aig toiseach tòis-eachaidh. 'S cinnteach gur ann air sgàth sin a thug iad Allt na Muilne air far an robh a' mhuilinn sin – còrr air leth a' mhìle bho Muilinn Gharraboist. Ach càit an robh a' mhuilinn Lochlannach fhèin suidhichte chan eil mi cinnteach.

Nise, bha muilinn ann an Steòrnabhagh – a-muigh aig Willowglen. Chaidh a' mhuilinn a thogail ann an Steòrnabhagh – ach cuin a chaidh a togail chan urrainn dhomh a ràdh, oir chailleadh na reacordan nuair a chaidh an Town Hall na teine. Bha sin mu chuairt air 1816. Thàinig na Mathesons ann an 1844, 's an uair sin chaidh an Caisteal a thogail. B' e John Latta am muillear a bha bhos cionn na muilne sin agus bha e a' fuireachd ann am Peighinn na Dròbh. B' ann an sin a bha taigh na muilne – air tac Pheighinn na Dròbh. Nise, chaidh John Latta a bha sin a mharbhadh anns a' mhuilinn. Chaidh a mharbhadh innte. Chan eil cuimhn' a'm cuin – timcheall air 1834. Ach co-dhiù, b' i sin a' mhuilinn a bha dèanamh na h-obrach do thòrr. Bha a h-uile duine bha timcheall ann an seo (Garrabost) a' dol innte. Nise, chaidh a' mhuilinn sin, cho fad 's as aithne dhòmhsa – chaidh i na teine. Chan eil fhios cuin. Chaidh i na teine co-dhiù, agus b' ann às dèidh sin a chaidh muilinn Gharraboist a thogail. Ann an 1893, thug Lady Matheson seachad feu airson a' mhuilinn a thogail ann an seo. Bha clachan-brathainn cha mhòr air a h-uile lot. Bha sin air a bhith aca a' dol air ais fada, fada. Agus ron a sin, bha clach mhòr aca, clach le slag innte, mus d' fhuair iad na bràthan; clach le slag innte, agus bha clach mhòr a' roiligeadh innte.

Thàinig m' athair mar mhuillear a Gharrabost ann an 1914, aig toiseach a' Chiad Chogaidh. Ron a sin, bha muinntir innte air an robh Robastanach. Agus b' ann an uair ud a bha Balaich an t-Saighdeir ann am Pabail: 's ann acasan a bha a' mhuilinn an uair sin. Nuair a thàinig m' athair a Gharrabost, bha a' mhuilinn sa gu a h-amhaich ann am fiachan. Ach, gu sealbhach, bha fear Aeneas MacKenzie na 'dhuine mòr' anns a' bhaile – cha chreid mi nach e fear-lagha a bh'ann dheth – agus chaidh iad thuige airson gum faigheadh iad thairis air an staing anns an robh iad. Thuirt esan gum faigheadh iad airgead bhon a' Bhac Disaster Fund. Uill, fhuair iad sin. Fhuair iad airgead bhon a' Bhac Disaster Fund. Cha chreid mi nach e trì cheud not a fhuair iad. Agus chuir sin a' mhuilinn air a casan. Phàigh m' athair air ais a h-uile càil a bha sin agus dh'fhalbh Balaich an t-Saighdeir. Bhàsaich iad agus chaidh feadhainn ac' a mharbhadh anns a' Chogadh. Anns an là a bha siud, bha daoine ag obair cruaidh – a h-uile teaghlach aig an robh lot. Bha triùir nighean ann am Port Mholair a bha ainmeil, eadhon aig àm an Darna Cogaidh. Anns a' Ghearran, bhiodh an triùir aca air an lot a bhreacadh le clèibh feamad mus èireadh càch. Ghreasadh iad sìos dhan a' chladach cho luath 's a dh'fhidreadh iad gu robh feamainn ga cur air tìr leis an rotach. Bha iad a' dol dhan an leabaidh tràthail, 's bha iad ag èirigh tràthail. Bha, 's bha iad a' dol sìos mus èireadh duine a bha anns a' bhaile. Abair gun robh pòr aca, le eòrna is coirc is buntàta. Uill, tha cuimhn' agams' orra, nuair a bha na bha sin a dhaoine a' tighinn chon na muilne, agus 's urrainn dhomh seo a dh'ràdh mun deidhinn: bha iad tòrr mòr na bu shona na tha sinne an-diugh. Agus bha iad a' dol dhachaigh às a' mhuilinn le dhà no thrì mhullaichean de mhin-eòrna agus bha iad cho sona 's a ghabhadh. Fhios agad, bha pailteas sgadain aca 's bha am buntàt' aca, 's cha robh iad ag iarraidh a' chorra.

Nuair a bha iad a' spadadh às nan taighean-dubha, bha 'n talamh a bha iad a' toirt a-mach às na seann bhallaichean a bha sin math dha-rìribh airson curachd. Chan eil fhios a'm an ann air sgàth an t-sùith a bha anns na ballachan a bha sin mar sin – fhios agad, an t-sùith a bh' ann, leis an teine bhith ann an teis-meadhan an làir. Ach 's e riasg a' chuid bu mhotha a bh' anns na ballaichean.

Bha tòrr a bharrachd eòrn' a' dol tron mhuilinn na bha de choirc. An-dràsta, gheibheadh tu faisg air a dhà uiread de mhin bho tomhas de dh'eòrna 's a gheibheadh tu bho choirc. Cha robh an coirc idir ri toirt seachad uiread de mhin agus a bheireadh an t-eòrna. Tha barrachd slige air a' choirc gun teagamh. 'S cha robh uiread de bhiadh anns a' choirc. Cha robh. Chì thusa gràinne de shìol eòrna: tha e tòrr nas motha agus tha barrachd biadh ann na tha an gràinne de shìol coirc. Nuair a thigeadh teaghlach le eallach mhòr de shìol eòrna no de shìol coirc, bhiodh iad uaireannan a' fàgail bolla no dhà de mhin-eòrna agus a' toirt leotha bolla min-flùir na àite. Bhiodh sinne riaraichte gu leòr a' toirt na min-flùir dhaibh mu choinneamh na min-eòrna.

Ach, gu ìre, bha am beatha air a cuingealachadh leis an lot. 'S e obair làn-thìde a bh' anns an lot. Agus eadhon tron a' gheamhradh, bhiodh feadhainn aca a' dol air an oidhche dhan t-sabhal a dh'obair, nuair a bha càch nan cadal. Bhiodh iad a' suathadh air an oidhche no a' bualadh a' choirc. Bhiodh cuid de dhaoine ri suathadh an àite dhaibh a bhith a' bualadh an eòrna le sùist – obair nach robh càilear! Bha na boireannaich a' suathadh air an casan luirmeachd agus bha na calgan a' cosnadh dhaibh gàgan a thighinn air an calpannan. Obair chruaidh a bh' ann. Ach bha iad dìcheallach. Anns an là ud, bha daoine, saoilidh mi, tòrr na bu dòigheil' na tha iad an-diugh. Cha robh iomagain orra, cho fad 's a bha biadh aca a-staigh. B' e sin na bha iad ag iarraidh. Cha robh nithean an t-saoghail a' dèanamh na bha sin de dhragh dhaibh idir. Bha iad dìcheallach – tòrr mòr na bu dìcheallaich' na tha daoine an-diugh. Ach bha uaireannan anns an robh bochdainn anns an Rubha.

Tha cuimhn' agamsa air boireannach anns an Rubha a dh'aithnicheas mi. Nise, dh'fhaodainn innse dhut cò th' innt', ach chan innis. Bha i a' fuireachd ann an taigh beag shìos ann an siud. Agus bha nighean leatha a-staigh ri bàsachadh. Bha i a' bàsachadh leis a' chaitheamh. Agus dh'iarr an nighean oirre rudeigineach a dh'itheadh i. Thuirt i ris an nighinn, "Chan eil, a ghràidh, càil agamsa a bheir mi dhut."

'S cha robh sin aice. Bha am boireannach bochd sin aig an daras agus i a' coimhead a-mach. Agus nuair a bha i a' coimhead a-mach air an daras, chunnaic i fear a' tighinn suas an rathad agus thill am boireannach a-steach. Chaidh an duine seachad ach thill e air ais agus bhuail e an daras. Thuirt an duine ris a' bhean bhochd a bha sin, "Seo!" ars esan. "Seo dhut! Thuirt an Cruthaidhear rium siud a thoirt dhut." Is chuir e nota na làimh.

Nise, tha cuimhn' agam cuideachd a bhith a' cèilidh air bean chòir ann am Pabail, agus bha mi a' bruidhinn ris an nighinn aice. Agus thuirt an nighean rium, "Nach teirig thu steach," ars ise, "a choimhead air mo mhàthair." Chaidh mi null chon na leapa far an robh i na sìneadh, agus thuirt am boireannach rium, ars ise, "Cha dhìochuimhnich mise d' athair gu bràth! Tha cuimhn' agam an duin' agam a thighinn dhachaigh bhon an iasgach. Cha d' fhuair iad càil aig deireadh an t-seusain. Cha d' fhuair tastan! Agus chaidh e null chon na muilne agus dh'iarr e air d' athair am b' urrainn dha min a thoirt dha."

" 'Uill'," arsa d' athair, " 'tha e glè dhuilich dhòmhsa min a thoirt dhut an dèidh na th' agad ri thoirt dhomh mar-tha.' "

Co-dhiù, dh'fhalbh e 's chuir e a' chairt a-null a Phabail le dà bholla mine thuige. 'S thuirt a' bhantrach aige rium, "Cha dhìochuimhnich mise gu bràth a' chobhair a thug e dhuinn. Cha robh càil againn a-staigh . . . càil againn!"

Nise, bha bochdainn ann an sin. Cha robh 'Assistance' aca man a th' aca an-diugh, no càil dhan t-seòrs' sin. Agus nuair a sheallas tu air ais ri eachdraidh an eilein sa, nach iomadh buille mhòr a thàinig air an t-sluagh a bha seo. Smaoinichibh an-dràsta air an *Iolaire*, nuair a chaidh i fodha a' toirt nan seòid dhachagh. Bha sin ann an 1919. Cha robh mise ach trì bliadhna dh'aois aig an àm sin. Ach bho dh'fhàs mi suas, tha deagh chuimhn' agam air an èiginn a bh' anns an eilean anns na 1930s leis a' chaitheamh, an uair a bha còrr air fichead neach 's a deich de dhaoine òg anns an 'Sani'. Feadhainn dhan a' chloinn-nighean bu bhòidhche a chunna mi riamh, 's ann anns an 'Sani'. Shaoileadh tu gu robh deàrrsadh anns na h-aodainn aca. Bha iad ann an sin, à badan air feadh an eilein. Bha sin. Uill, bhiodh m' athair-sa ri dol dhan an 'Sani' fad nam bliadhnaichean mòra. 'S iomadh coinneamh bheannaichte a bh' againn ann; 's iomadh gu dearbha. 'S cha tàinig càil riamh nar lùib dhan a' chaitheamh. Cha robh càil dhan sin co-cheangailte rinne idir. Cha robh.

Bha iad air tòiseachadh air leigeil às a bhith ag earbsa ris na lotaichean

anns na Thirties fhèin. Chuir an Dàrna Cogadh crìoch air a h-uile càil a bha
sin.

Thòisich daoine a' faighinn airgid an uair sin agus sguir iad dha na
lotaichean. Sguir iad a chumail bheathaichean. 'S cha robh feum aca dhan a'
mhuilinn às deidh sin. B' fheudar dhòmhsa seòrs' eile dh'obair fhaighinn,
bhàrr air obair na muilne. Bha mise 'g obair aig an Esso Station. Bha mi an
sin airson faisg air fichead bliadhna. Ach a dh'aindeoin sin, chùm sinn a'
mhuilinn a' dol an dèidh sin, agus tha i fhathast a' dol. Seach nach eileas a'
cur no a' buain arbhair anns an eilean, tha sinn a' faighinn a' ghràin a-nall
bhon a' mhòr-thìr.

Bha tòrr mhuilnean anns na sgìrichean air feadh Eilean Leòdhais. Tha
muilinn ann an Garrabost; muilinn ann an Griais; 's bha muilinn ann an
Nis; 's bha muilinn ann an Calanais; agus bha muilnean beaga gu leòr thall
taobh Ùig. Ma thèid thu null chon a' Riof ann an Ùig, chì thu loch air
mullach a' chnuic ann an sin, 's tha sruthan a' tighinn a-nuas bhon an loch
sin sìos chon na mara. Uill, bha ceithir dha na muilnean Lochlannach air an
allt a bha sin. Chì thu iad ann fhathast. Tha iad mar gum biodh iad a'
dearbhadh an t-seòrsa beòshlaint agus an t-seòrsa beatha a bh' aig ar
sinnsirean anns na linntean bho chian.

John Morrison

1917–

My father was born at Habost, Ness, and he married Janet, daughter of
Angus Graham from Shader, Barvas. That Angus Graham was famous in
his own lifetime by virtue of his great strength. As you know, there is one of
the enormous stones he lifted beside the Barvas Road and has been painted
white. It is prominent on the north side of the road. Anyhow, my father was
given the name Angus Graham Morrison, by way of recognition that he was
the grandchild of the famous strongman.

I belong neither to the Free Church nor to the Church of Scotland. I am
of the 'Brethren'* just as my father was before me. There are Brethren all
over the world and you will meet them wherever in the world you go and
that includes Russia and China. Many of the East Coast fishermen are
Brethren, for example, in Fraserburgh. When I was a young man, I knew
Brethren from there and from Peterhead. Though we are not very strong as
an organisation in Lewis, we have a church in Bayhead, Stornoway, called
the Gospel Hall. We believe in baptism – the baptism of adults; and we
remember the death of our Lord every week for the Scripture asks us to do
so.

Now, I'll tell you something of the history of our family and how I
came to be a miller here in Garrabost. My father went to work down in
Perth but, in 1911, took off to work in Canada. Having arrived there, he
continued his journey until he reached Vancouver. One evening, after he
had finished work, he decided to go for a walk down in the city centre.
There he met a girl who was walking with a Bible in her hand. He asked her
the question, 'Can you tell me where the Brethren hold their prayer
meeting?'

'Yes,' she replied. 'That's where I'm going. You come along with me.'
And that was how my mother and father found each other.

---

* A denomination pervasive throughout Scottish society; see *Brethren in Scotland (1838–
2000)* by Neil T.B. Dickson.

My mother went out to Canada in 1913 and they married there in Vancouver. One evening, they were on a streetcar in the city and an old woman embarked – a woman from the village of Carloway who had emigrated as a young girl. My father spoke to her and introduced my mother, saying, 'This is my bride.'

'Does she speak Gaelic?' enquired the woman. My father said that she did not.

'What a downright shame!' replied the woman.

The woman told my father that after her people arrived in British Columbia, they used to plant potatoes at the base of the apple trees. I imagine that that was early on, before they had managed to clear the land of the forest. Perhaps there was little land for them to plant their potatoes except near the base of their apple trees. Apparently they were so hungry that they had to lift the potatoes they had planted. They had only the peels [containing the 'eyes'] to plant.

Strange how in faraway places we can meet people with whom we can make a connection! As the old Gaelic saying goes, *Coinnichidh na daoine far nach coinnich na cnuic!* [Men shall meet, where the hills cannot!] Strange how Destiny controls our lives. A remarkable event happened in Garrabost some time ago. A woman told me what happened to William, one of her two brothers. During the Second World War he arrived home on leave and during that time he visited all the houses in the village. He visited Beileag 'Ain Ruairidh at the post office and, as he was bidding her farewell, he said, 'I shall not be seeing you again.'

She replied, 'Why are you saying that, William?'

'Because I know that I shall never be back,' he said.

He told his mother the same and she said to him, 'Please don't say that, my son!'

Anyway, time went on and he left Britain on a ship bound for Nova Scotia. It so happened that his brother was resident in Canada but William was not at all sure where in that vast country he was living. All he knew was that his brother was a piper. In Nova Scotia, he went ashore in Halifax. I believe it was in Halifax! In any case, he went to the immigration office there to enquire whether they could tell if his brother had passed through there. He had his brother's photograph and showed it to the officials but, not surprisingly, they were unable to help him.

As he was returning to his ship, William heard the music of a pipe band. He then saw the pipe band marching and as it approached where he was standing, his eye dwelt on the fellow leading the pipers with his baton, and he said to himself, 'If I'm not mistaken, I have found my brother.' He took his brother's photo from his pocket and, keeping step with the band, walked abreast of the pipe major. When his brother caught sight of his own image in the photo held by the man who, to him, was a stranger, he lost his concentration and caused the band to become all mixed up. The result was that there was something of an upset and William's brother was hauled over the coals. Those who had arranged the march wanted to discover what had caused the band to become so muddled in public. The pipe major apologised and explained that he had been accosted by a brother whom he hadn't seen for a long time.

'Where is this brother who has caused the problem?' they demanded to know.

'My brother is outside waiting for me.'

Well, the upshot was that William was brought in and the two brothers were treated to a nice dinner and, afterwards, spent the entire evening together. William returned to the ship, which was due to sail to New York. Unfortunately, during her voyage, the ship was lost with all hands. It was a terrible tragedy, one of the many that occurred during the war. Strange that William had a premonition of his death before setting out for the New World for the very last time.

Now, I myself lost a son, aged twenty-four. He was killed by a car. When I went to collect his belongings, I was accompanied by his fiancée. She said to me, 'There's a poem here that Iain wanted me to keep but you can have it.' I still have it and I'll read it to you. I think it is a wonderful poem:

> Now a young boy of twenty-four,
> A wreath will hang upon the door tomorrow
> Of the little place that once we called our home,
> And friends will come and hang their heads in sorrow,
> To pay their last respects to one gone on.
> But you remember the joys we shared
> Together at the start,
> How you promised me
> It would be till death do us part.

In my lifetime, I have often been aware of terrible things like that happening and one can easily believe that some individuals are given premonition of what is about to happen to them.

I am sometimes asked the question, 'Are you a religious person?' To that I have to respond that I am not a religious person in the sense that they imply. On the other hand, I readily claim that I am a Christian. To me, 'religion' as such is something that restricts one's life and that includes Muslims and Hindus and all the other religions that, in their different ways, acknowledge the existence of God. But the Bible defines religion as this: 'Pure religion undefiled before God and the Father is to visit the widows and fatherless in their affliction, and to keep oneself unspotted from the world.'

A century ago, Alasdair Nicolson, one of my relations, lived in Ness. His people belonged to Borve and he was married to Peggy Nicolson, my great-aunt. That was Peggy's second marriage. They had a son whom they gave the name Donald. Now, when that boy grew to be a man, he emigrated to Canada and got on very well. He settled in Winnipeg and owned elevators for storing grain. He employed a number of men from this island. Yes, Donald Morrison was quite a well-known employer over there.

Another son of Alasdair and Peggy Nicolson, who was called John [Iain in Gaelic], went to America and married an American girl called Nora Cushing. They came back to live in Lewis at the turn o' the century, about 1900. Iain was known here as ''Ain Fiosaiche' [Iain, son of the Visionary/ Diviner]. He and his wife lived in a place called Asmaigearraidh, on the south side of Dell, in Ness. If you happen to travel down to Ness, you will be able to see the green sward at Asmaigearraidh where their house was situated. Iain and Nora Nicolson were of the Brethren and held services in Ness. Initially, the services were held in their home but, after a time, they built a hall. They not only held services in the hall but also conducted a sunday school for about a hundred children.

I was born in the mill house at Garrabost in 1916. From the time I was a lad, I've been back and fore from Ness many times. My father was a devout Christian and often took me there, after dinner, on the Sabbath Day. We used to go with the van to attend the evening services.

'Ain Fiosaich built Edgemoor Hall, a dwelling-house and a little church together, out on the moor, about three miles past Sgiogarstaigh on the way to Tolastadh bho Thuath. The two buildings are close to the edge of the cliff, in a lovely spot. The purpose of the church was to provide the people who were resident on the shieling* during the summer months with a place in which they might worship. I remember as a child being out there in 'Ain Fiosaich's house right on the cliff edge and, beside it, the church which was

---

* For countless generations, it was the custom for members of a crofting family to trek out on to the moor with their cattle to live simply in a small hut called a shieling. By so doing, the cattle were given access to the rich pastures of the moor and, at the same time, the grass of the croft could be cut for hay.

full of worshippers. 'Ain Fiosaich was of the Brethren and, as such, was independent of any organisation. Neither John Nicolson nor his wife Nora was paid for what they were doing. No member of the Brethren is paid for any duty he or she does in meeting our spiritual needs.

There was a man in Ness called Ruairidh Ròigein who owned a bus. He sometimes travelled out on the Leverhulme Road running along the coast from Sgiogarstaigh with a full complement of young people. When the bus arrived at a place where the road petered out, the young folk would come out and walk the rest of the way to Edgemoor Hall. After the service, Nora Morrison would make tea for all her guests. Then the company would traipse back across the moor and would find Ruairidh Ròigein waiting for them with the bus to take them home.

'Ain Fiosaich had a brother called Billy – the fellow who composed the well-known song 'Eilean Leòdhais, Tìr nan Gaisgeach' [Isle of Lewis, Land of Heroes]. Billy owned a car at a time when there were very few cars in Lewis. He happened to be visiting down in Ness and met another car owner who said to him, 'I'll be in Stornoway before you!' The two set off in competition with each other. Unfortunately, Billy's car left the road near Gabhsann Lodge and he was killed. So far as I can remember, that happened around 1910.

Now, about that time, there was another fellow in Ness who was quite famous. His name was Angus Graham, the fellow who performed the feat of strength at the time that they were building the Pentland Road. An enormous boulder was in the path of those who were making the road and the workers found it impossible to shift it. It so happened that Angus Graham was on his way to Stornoway and offered to solve the problem. He somehow removed the stone to the roadside, where it remains to this day. He frequently performed feats of strength but he preferred doing so when there weren't any onlookers. Oh, he was abnormally strong. According to what I have heard, he was in Stornoway on one occasion when a warship happened to be visiting. Onboard her was a boxing champion of some considerable renown.

Angus visited the Imperial Bar, which was a favourite drinking-hole for a lot of men in those days. Some of the men of his acquaintance began to tease Angus about his reputed strength. Pointing to a stranger, one of them asked if Angus thought he'd be able to get the better of him in a fight. The locals joined in with the question, 'Would you be prepared to fight him?' Of course, it was well known that Angus Graham never involved himself in fighting but they kept at him until, in the end, he said, 'OK, but before coming to blows I want to show that there is no animosity between us. We'll shake hands.' The boxer came forward and shook hands with him but Angus Graham's hand-grip was so strong that the fellow was in agony. In the end, the blood began to drip from his fingernails. Aye, his strength was phenomenal. At one time, we had a photograph of Angus and another of my grandfather, his brother. They used to sit opposite each other on the mantlepiece but when my grandfather died, the photographs went missing. It's a great shame. I have no idea how they were lost.

He [Angus] was down in the Port of Ness one day returning with his mare pulling a cartload of fish. But here, didn't the wheel get stuck in a deep pothole and the mare could not manage to pull the cart free. Angus took hold of the wheel and rotated it out of the place in which it was held fast. Angus raised his head and said to the mare, 'You poor critter, I'm not at all surprised that you were unable to shift it. It almost proved too much for me.'

I heard my father say that when he was a lad, there was an old woman staying two or three doors away in Habost, Ness. She said to my father, 'No wonder your grandfather was as strong as he was. He would go off on a morning to Mùirneag and when he'd return, he would be carrying a deer across his shoulders. Venison was as common in their house as was peats for their fire!'

In those days, people lived a different kind of life from what we live today. To go to the fishing in Stornoway, the boys used to walk to North Tolsta and from there to Stornoway. They used to spend a night out on the shielings near where the Edgemoor Hall is situated. They'd stay the night there either with folks related to them or else courting girls. In the morning, they would continue to North Tolsta and thence to Stornoway.

In the evenings, the young girls used to walk down the steep slopes where there was green lush grass growing on the cliffs above the sea. They used to cut the grass with sickles and bring it back to the shieling for the cattle to eat. They were supported in their climb by a rope tethered above them at the clifftop. One of the girls, said to be a livewire, volunteered to be the first to descend. As she ventured down, the rope to which she was clinging snapped and she tumbled over the cliff and was killed. Her remains were not recovered until the following day. 'Ain Fiosaich told me that they held a wake for the dead girl on the following day at the cliff-top. So far as he knew it as the only wake ever held out of doors. It was a very sad occasion.

I once walked the journey from Sgiogarstaigh to North Tolsta, a distance of about eight miles. It's not like walking along a tarmac road, for the moor along the coast is quite broken in places. 'Ain Fiosaich's house is about five miles from North Tolsta.

I had aunts, sisters of my father, who had a shieling out at Loch Nèill. They walked from there to church in Tolsta every Sunday. Another of my aunts was at Steinis and was married to a chap known as Murchadh Thòmais [Murdo, son of Thomas]. When she was a young lass, she worked as a servant in Gabhsann Lodge. After getting up in the morning, she would go out to milk the cows. Then she had to make the family's breakfast. Having done those chores, she would go to her room and don her 'good clothes'. After that, she would walk all the way to Habost where my other aunt would make her a cup of tea. Refreshment taken, she would then walk the three miles to the church service at Lionel. In those days, people walked long distances and didn't think anything of it. But we have lost the ability to do that. The people were amazingly strong. Of course, a lot of that can be explained by their lifestyle. You might consider, for example, the demands on myself when, as a young man, I was working in the mill making bolls of meal. I was made physically fit by the nature of the work I had to do. I had to be upstairs to make sure that the hoppers were full of grain and also oversee the production of the meal downstairs. I had to fill the bags and then lift them on to the scales to make sure that they contained ten stones – 140 lbs. After that, I had to sew the bags and lift them on to the floor to be stamped. Finally, I had to lift the bolls and carry them to a separate place where they were stored.

The mill was in production day and night. Indeed, it was! I thought nothing of the demands on my strength. Of course, I could not accomplish half that amount of work today. It would seem that there were two Norse mills in this township at one time. Surely that is why Allt na Muilne [Mill Burn] in Lower Garrabost was so named. However, in spite of the name, there is nothing to indicate where a Norse mill might have been situated on that stream.

There was a mill at Willow Glen in Stornoway but how old that was no one can tell. The official records were lost when the Town Hall was burnt down about 1816. That was a terrible loss to the island. What I can tell you is that it was the major mill for this part of the island. The people used to take their grain to it from all the villages around Stornoway, including from Garrabost. John Latta had been the miller at the Willow Glen mill and his house was at the farm of Peighinn na Dròbh, just a mile or so outside the burgh boundary. Around 1834, John Latta was killed in an accident at the mill and, so far as I could ascertain, the mill itself caught fire (though not necessarily in the John Latta accident) and was a total loss. Now, Sir James Matheson bought the Lews Estate in 1844 and the Lews Castle was built shortly after that. The loss of the mill caused a lot of hardship to a lot of people.* Families had to grind their corn using querns. There was a quern on pretty well every croft. Working those grinding stones was hard work and very time consuming. They had to spend several hours grinding with the quern every few days. At the mill, they could get a year's supply of meal by attending here for one day. So there was a desperate need for a proper mill. After the demise of Sir James, the Lews estate became the property of Lady Matheson. It was she who, in 1893, granted a feu at Garrabost for the building of our mill.

My father became the miller at Garrabost in 1914 at the beginning of the First World War. Before that, the mill was operated by a Robertson family. It was at that time that Balaich an t-Saighdeir [the Soldier's Sons] were living in Bayble and it was they, in fact, who owned the mill. When my father took it over, the mill was up to the eyes in debt. But, fortunately, Aeneas MacKenzie, a gentleman of importance in Stornoway – a lawyer, I believe – helped to alleviate the situation by suggesting that the business could borrow money from the Back Disaster Fund.† I believe that £300 was released and that helped to put the mill on a sound footing. My father paid back every penny of that sum and Balaich an t-Saighdeir disappeared. Some of them died of natural causes but others lost their lives in the war.

In those days everybody had to work hard to earn a living, not least if you were a crofter. There were three old maids living together in the village of Portvoller – two sisters and a niece – and they, for many years, were well known because of the way they managed their croft. Even as recently as the Second World War, they were working the land as had been done in the nineteenth century, manuring it well and extracting excellent crops from it. In the spring, they used to be down on the seashore collecting seaweed which they then distributed by the creel-load all over their arable land. They used to get up while it was still dark and transported the seaweed on their backs before others in the village had stirred. Of course, they went to bed early and got the advantage by being the first to issue forth in the early morning! But what a bumper crop of potatoes and oats they had every autumn! I knew them well when they came to the mill with their grain. They were humble crofters but they derived a great deal of satisfaction from the bounteous harvest that

* Under Matheson, the community of Lewis was in fear of Donald Munro, factor and chamberlain, described as 'the godfather of a little legal mafia of cousins, operating in the law courts of Lewis and Edinburgh'; see *A Shilling for Your Scowl* by James Shaw Grant.
† Fund set up in 1895 to help the families of nineteen fishermen who drowned in Broad Bay during a storm.

resulted from their labours. They were contented people, far happier than
we are today though we are fortunate in having all the advantages of 'mod
cons' in the home, improved communications worldwide, a wonderful
welfare state and all the other advantages of living in the twenty-first
century. It is no exaggeration for me to say that the people who used to
come to me with their harvest of grain were much happier than we are
today. When they left the mill with their three bolls of barley-meal and a
year's supply of oatmeal and flour, they were as happy as could be. To be
truthful, if they had a plentiful supply of salt herring, potatoes and meal,
they were utterly content. If they had those and were confident that they
and their families would not go hungry in the following winter and spring,
they were completely satisfied.

The oats were shelled in the same way as we shelled the barley-meal.
Children particularly loved the taste of shelled oats. Whenever they got the
chance, the lads who used to come to the mill to help out used to steal a
handful of the *gràn-sgilidh* – the shelled oats! It was the nearest thing to
confections that children of those days had access to.

Occasionally, when I had to suspend operations because there was
something needing urgent attention like, for example, mending some piece
of machinery, our customers had to go elsewhere with their grain. I can
remember, to get ours done, my father having to travel to the mill at Gress
on the other side of Broad Bay. We ourselves would malt it here, of course,
before transporting it to Gress. In those days, there was an excellent little
mill at that village. It's a pity that it was abandoned. I remember being told
that the Aird crofters travelled by boat to Gress with their grain when our
mill happened to be at a standstill. Yes, they had to cross Broad Bay in boats
to get their grain milled.

As you know, the walls of the old black-houses were very thick – six
or sometimes eight feet wide They consisted of two stone dykes, an
inner and an outer dyke, with peat filling the space between. When they
were demolishing the black-houses, the peat that was being salvaged from
the walls proved to be very good soil for growing crops. I'd like to know
the reason for that soil being so fertile. Was it, perhaps, because of the
gallons of soot-bearing water that passed through it during the generations?

In my young days, much more barley-meal was produced by the mill
than oatmeal. You could get twice as much meal from a bag of barley grain
as you could get from a bag of oats. There's no doubt that the oat seed
consists of a greater amount of husk than does the barley seed. Very often,
when a family brought a large quantity of barley, they would barter a boll of

barley-meal for a boll of flour.* It was a common practice which was of equal benefit to both parties.

To an extent, the crofters' lives were governed by the demands of their land. Croft work was a full-time activity. Even through the winter, when the weather dictated that the people spent little time outside their houses, there was enough work for the crofter to do in the barn to keep some of them going late into the night. Their oats had to be threshed to separate the seed from the straw. The barley also had to be similarly treated, though in that case the grain was separated from the sheaves by a method called *suathadh*. This required women to rub the ears of the barley between their bare calves so as to expel the grain. It was a demanding job and one that most women disliked very much. One of the reasons for that was that the barley plant, when it comes in from the field, has 'beards' which have sharp edges. Now, when they pulled the sheaf between the calves, it was liable to cause abrasions of the skin. Och, the women had a hard life in those days and nobody who knows anything about it could argue with that. In spite of that, people seemed to be more content with their lot than their descendants are today. There was great satisfaction in knowing that you had achieved your goal in storing away enough food and fuel to keep the wolf from the door for the year ahead. That gave them a sense of achievement, knowing that by their own labours they had secured the future of their families on those fronts at least. Quite an achievement! On the other hand, one has to remember that not everybody managed to achieve that goal. Some families were unable to attain those goals because of illness, old age or adverse weather conditions during the growing season or at harvest time. At times there was real poverty in this parish.

I remember a woman of my acquaintance in the Point district – I could name her, but for obvious reasons, I won't! She lived in a small thatched house not so very far from here. Her daughter was bedridden and dying of consumption. The daughter asked her if she could have something to eat but, unfortunately, there wasn't any food that the mother was able to bring her. The woman said, 'My darling girl, there is nothing inside this house that I can offer you to eat.' And she was telling the truth, for they were pretty well destitute. The poor woman was desperate and went to the door and was just standing there looking out. She probably stood there for some time. After a while, she saw a man walking up the street and, so that her sadness would not be seen by him, she returned indoors. The man passed

* Flour is produced from wheat, which cannot be grown in the Highlands and Islands.

the house but hadn't walked very far before he returned to the house and knocked on the door. The woman presently came to the door and the man said to her, 'I wish you to have this. The Lord directed me to give you this.' He handed the woman a pound note.

I remember paying a visit to a house in Bayble. I first spoke to the daughter, who said to me, 'We'd appreciate your going in to visit my mother.' Well, I did as the girl said and, when I entered the house, I saw her mother, a widow, lying on her bed. As I shook the widow's hand, she said, 'I will never forget your father's kindness to my family. My husband had arrived home after a disastrous season at the fishing. He didn't bring home as much as a shilling. We were in dire straits, so that he was forced to approach your father to see if he would consider giving us an advance of meal. Your father replied, "It is difficult for me to do so, considering the fact that you are already in the red at the mill." In spite of our debt, your father sent the cart across with two bolls of meal. It was such a relief to receive that food as I had nothing inside this house with which to feed my family.'

Now, that woman was describing real poverty. In those days, there was no government 'assistance' as we have today. Nothing of that kind. The people of Lewis suffered terribly over the centuries. We all know of the losses to our population in the First World War between 1914 and '18, followed immediately afterwards by the loss of the *Iolaire* which took the lives of more than 200 men returning from active service. Then in the 1930s we had the scourge of *A' Chaitheamh* – the Wasting – the epidemic of Consumption when there were more than thirty young persons in the 'Sani' [Stornoway Sanatorium] dying of the disease. Some of the most beautiful girls that I ever saw were invalids in the Sani. There was a certain kind of luminance in their countenances. They were in beds there from all over the island. My father visited the Sani for many years and held many blessed services there. Indeed he did. Fortunately, he was never infected with tuberculosis. We were fortunate that our family escaped.

The Second World War, which started in 1939, saw an end to the crofting way of life. The rural population began to earn a living without their having to be slaves to the land. Planting and sowing crops, and also the rearing of cattle and sheep, diminished bit by bit. Of course, the result was that the decline in their harvest of barley and oats had a knock-on effect at the Garrabost mill.

Because of the reduction in demand for milling, I was forced to find other work to supplement my income. Until I retired, I was a petrol-pump attendant at the [Stornoway] Esso station for twenty years. But, in spite of the ever-reducing demand for milling of grain grown locally, we continued to keep the mill in good running order. Indeed, the machinery is in fine fettle and, from time to time, we import grain from the mainland and produce meal.

At one time, there were many mills in the different parts of Lewis. Long ago there was another mill at Garrabost and others at Gress, Ness and Calanais. And there were lots of small mills over in Uig. If you should go to the Riof in Uig, you can find a loch high up on a hill. On the stream draining that loch to the sea, you can see the ruins of no fewer than four Norse mills. Those ruins give us a sense of the lifestyle of our ancestors of long ago.

Andrew Cabrelli

1930–

I was born here in Stornoway in 1930. You might well ask how somebody with an Italian name and fluent in Italian came to be living in the north-west corner of the British Isles. The reason is that, from the beginning of time, people have been migrating from one part of the world to another, seeking to better themselves. It seems to be in the nature of people to migrate and explore and, if they find an environment to their liking, they settle and put down roots. And that is what happened in the case of our family.

I suppose that the first migration from Italy to Britain was more than 2,000 years ago when Julius Caesar came here with an army of invaders. But, in recent centuries, the first emigration from Italy to Britain was in the 1870s and 1880s. That was the first lot that came. The second one was round about between 1900 and 1912. Then the third one was after the Second World War but that involved a very, very limited number of people. My people came over to this country, I think, in 1912. So, apart from the period of the 1914 to 1918 war, where you had to go back to Italy for war service, we'd been in this country. That's the way we came to be in Stornoway.

Maybe it is surprising that there should be an emigration from Italy, or an immigration to Britain, at a time when the British, particularly the Scots, were emigrating to America. The nature of the emigration from Italy was different from that from Scotland. When the people moved from Scotland to the USA or Canada they did so as entire families. They did so because they were deprived of the means of making a living. In Italy it was only individuals that came away – not the entire family. For us in Italy, moving to another country was just a venture, you know. Italians moved to this country when they found a niche into which they could fit. They had expertise which was needed here and which they could provide. The niche that we wanted to get into was the cafeteria business or setting up fish and chips shops or ice-cream parlours. They call it an ice-cream parlour today. It wasn't actually then, but anyhow, that was the beginning of it.

I don't think the early Italians were like the Indians and the Pakistanis who came here and to other countries to make money which they sent home to support families back home. The Italians who came to this country didn't send money home to Italy – not to that extent anyway. I think that what happened was that they came here to settle. They tried to save enough to enable them to buy a house. Well, first of all, to buy a shop.

Many of the young people who came here worked for, say, a businessman who had four or five or six shops at the time. Their first goal was to put enough money aside to buy off the property from their own boss. The other goal was to take across maybe the wife or the future wife – you know, the girlfriend. The usual pattern was: go across, marry, and then come back and start a family here. And that is what most of them did. There were no old people involved – no grandfathers or grandmothers. They usually started a family here. That's the reason that most of the children of Italian incomers were born in this country.

Both my father and mother came from Tuscany. I suppose that where they came from, their native environment was rather like in the rural districts here. I mean that in the sense that there was a lot of intermarriages. The marriage of couples closely related happened because you couldn't easily go out of your own small village. You weren't welcome perhaps in other districts, so you tended to marry somebody who lived near you.

Italians coming to this country, like Scots going abroad, very often clung on to their own culture and to their own ways. Their minds were often more or less tied up to the place from which they originally came. You found that those who went to the cities created more of an Italian community. In small towns like Stornoway where there were only two Italian families, you were less of an 'Italian presence'. In Wick, there was only one Italian family. The numbers dictated whether it was possible to maintain a continuous contact with your own co-nationals and to retain a national identity.

I was born here in Stornoway. I was brought up here and had my initial schooling here in primary school. Just before the war broke out, we went off to Italy during the summer holidays of, I think, 1939. And we were caught over there by the war. Dad tried to make it back with the family, you know, but we didn't make it. Paris was as far as we got. After that, the way was all blocked, so we returned to Italy and stayed there for the war years. That was really tough because our property was here. But we were lucky in a way because our grandparents were still alive and they took us in. I was nine when the war broke out in 1939.

Well, I'll tell you, life for people like us, myself and my cousins and those who have lived, shall we say, 'across the divide' on one side or the other, was what you would describe in Gaelic as a *bùrach* [shambles]. Yes, you take a long time to become reconciled to your fate. Some things you learn, in whichever environment you are in, will stay with you throughout your life. They will stick in your mind. Now I'll give you an example of what I mean. I've told you before that my first schooling was in primary school here in Stornoway. So today, whether I'm here in Stornoway or in Tuscany – no matter where I am – I still add, multiply and divide in English! Basic things like that, that you have learned as a young child, stay with you for all your life.

So far as the politics were concerned, I remember that, in a way, our situation was very, very trying for my parents. Across in Italy we were strictly forbidden by our parents to speak English because, I mean, if we had done so outside of the house, our parents would probably have been deported. Something awful like that could have happened to them. So there were restrictions on our behaviour. And again, there was a small bit of animosity, too, when we came back here to live in Stornoway. I can understand why a few people felt that way. But I can understand that somebody who was on a ship torpedoed by the Italians would feel animosity towards us. It would be natural a survivor who was in a lifeboat, say, in the Red Sea without water or shelter would be bound to feel animosity no matter how broad-minded and forgiving he was. But I mean, generally speaking, I think that we were part of the community before and, to the majority of people, it didn't make any difference when we came back. We were still part of that community, as we are today.

I speak our Italian language here in my home. I speak Italian fluently, of course, and so does my wife Gianfranca and also my family. Whether your native language survives in the home all depends on who you marry. For example, if an Italian who comes here able to speak only Italian marries a British girl, she will be unlikely to speak Italian. She'll usually have English only. Now, in their house it is almost certain that only English will be spoken. It is the incomer who will be most likely to learn the language of the community in which he chooses to live. Inevitably, he will be forced to learn the new language. Now, if it was the other way about, so that both the man and the woman had Italian, they would talk that language to each other in the home so that Italian would rub off on their children as well. I say that though it's a fact that it takes a long time and a lot of patience to be able to pass to your children a language which is different from the language of the rest of the community. It takes a lot of effort.

Lewis, before the war, was a different place from what it is today. Some of the changes you can call improvements. Other changes, in my view, were not. Anyway, the changes took longer to come to the island because we were furthest away from the points of development on the mainland. But I concede that there have certainly been big improvements in transport – not only on Lewis but also in our ability to travel to the mainland and beyond. Advances in communications of all kinds have brought about a revolution in our way of living. Big improvements also in housing here. The housing is better and so also is the islanders' standard of living. When I was young, there were thatched houses on the outskirts of town, where we could go for a walk. That was as far as we used to explore. We had no cars or anything. I vaguely remember one or two thatched houses on the outskirts of the town. I think the first time that I was out in the rural villages was in the 1950s, when I returned to Scotland after the war. I was then the proud owner of a motorbike. I was never actually inside a thatched house or in a black-house where the people had the fire in the middle of the living-room. The people dressed differently in those days. There was a great preference for black clothing. I suppose it was probably the type of clothing that lasted them a lifetime. It was only put on on occasions when they came to town.*

There were great similarities between the way of life in Lewis and the way of life of my grandparents in Italy. Communities tended to be located miles and miles away from each other. When a person travelled out of his or her native community, it was like going on a voyage of discovery. That was so if you lived in a rural community in Lewis. You dressed for the occasion. In that sense, the way of life was exactly the same. There were also similarities in the houses. The centre fire; the chain hanging down over the fire; just a tiny wee hole for sunlight to come in, the smoke lingering in the house and your eyes having to adjust to the smoke inside the room. Your vision was just like a hawk's because you had to see in the dark! And things like that.

When I was young, there was more Gaelic spoken in Stornoway than there is today – definitely. Nearly everybody spoke Gaelic, except a few folks in town. There was a division in attitude between that of the people of the town and that of the country people. Maybe I wasn't in a position to be able to judge but my impression is that the people of one parish felt slightly better than the people of another. But then again, I suppose that is true everywhere. I mean, I'm sure it was only on the surface. There was no harm

---

* Not necessarily true. As late as the 1950s women living in the rural villages dressed in black whenever a family member died. In cases where the husband died, the widow usually remained in black for the rest of her life.

or aggression behind it. But there was a riposte between, say, Point and some of the other parishes, you know. So, I mean there was bound to be even a bigger break between the town-folks and the country-folk. Although there was nothing bad meant by it. Each of us carried our own flag. We had what you might call *esprit de corps*.

I can remember the war years very clearly. I don't think civilians ever forget a war because they're hammered from both sides, usually. In our case, we were lucky, in a way, because we were far away from the front. The only time in which we did come in contact with the actual war itself was in the beginning of, say, 1944. And then it became really bad when our village was very near the Gothic Line.* We were just at the foot of the Gothic Line, and, of course, then it became a bit serious because of strafing and bombing and all that. Luckily for us, it didn't last very long and we were soon liberated by the Americans. That happened I think in April, the twenty-fifth of April. They arrived in the district where we were. So that was the end of the war for us. Prior to that, there was a lot of bombardment from the air. We didn't see any hand-to-hand fighting. The reason for the aerial attacks was that our area is very mountainous with a lot of viaducts. So they were trying to bomb these, you know, so they would destroy the roads and railways leading to and from the ports. Of course, the bombs weren't intelligent! They often missed their targets and caused lots of civilian casualties. Our family was lucky. We weren't down in the city. We were up in the hills, in the countryside. But we saw it happening. We lost a lot of friends, yes. Friends, yes. Did I feel anger against the Americans and the British at the time? Well, I don't know. It was a very ambiguous position. Because even if you felt anything against them, then it was compensated for by the fact that probably the next day it could be the Germans that would be strafing our area. So each compensated the other. In a war like that the civilians are the ones who suffer most. It is said that some of the people of occupied Europe were very fearful of the advancing French and American soldiers. They claim that they regarded the Americans as much more brutal in their attitude than the British. But I don't subscribe to that. No. No, I'll tell you why. I know that the French had a very bad reputation for rape, for example. But then, after the war, we found out that these were de Gaulle's soldiers, you know – the French troops. Not the French from France. In fact, they were soldiers from some of the French colonies. They

---

* The defensive positions set up by the Germans in the north of Italy after the fall of Rome in June 1944.

were the culprits. When the Americans arrived, we were given the first white bread that we saw in years. But they were very, very kind.

As you know, Italy has the Apennine mountains separating the plains west and east, right down the length of Italy. My wife happened to be on the other side of the Apeninnes from where we were. Again she was fortunate, for the advancing British soldiers were there. The British army didn't feel any aggression towards the Italian people. Their first target was to defeat the Germans. But they never interfered with anybody. They were very nice. After the disasters of the war, we came back to the land of my birth here in Lewis. I remember that quite well. I remember that when I applied for my British passport the British Consul got in touch with me, saying that I would be called up for national service. This was in Florence. Having lived in Italy during the five years of the war, I had virtually no English left in my head. That meant that I had to start learning English all over again. For that reason, my call-up for National Service in the British Army was postponed for two years, with the result that I went to the British Army aged twenty instead of the usual eighteen. That was a wee bit of a *bùrach* you might think! In fact, that whole experience was a series of *bùrach*s. I had to start all over again, but this time I was luckier because I was working in the shop. At that time, I was mostly in contact with the staff. The girl that we had working for us at that time was very nice and helpful. And of course, you know, I was taught a few bad words in Gaelic and English, which is only natural. It happens. But honestly, the people around me were a tremendous influence on my development and the picking up again of my English. As I became more confident, I began to meet the customers. Contact with the customers made it even more easy for me to find my feet. The only thing I couldn't acquire was Gaelic. Just a few bad words, nothing else. Italian is very much a part of my life as a Lewisman – the Italian language, culture and music.

As I said, I was eighteen when I came back to Stornoway and, of course, I wasn't married then. I had a few acquaintances here, very nice girls. But, I suppose it's like everything in life, it's fate that comes into it. Whatever is laid down by fate just happens to you. I decided to go back to Italy on holiday. I'd never seen Gianfranca before in my life. She didn't come from the same place as my parents did. She happened to be there on holiday when I was there on holiday. We just met and fell in love. That was it!

What kind of food does an Italian Lewisman like to eat? When we go to Italy, we eat Italian. But I'll tell you something that might surprise you. When we return to either Heathrow or Gatwick and we have enough time, the first thing I do is make a beeline for the first chip shop there is on the premises and have myself a huge fish supper! I do that, no matter what time of the day it is. So I like lots of things which are available to this country but also a lot of different dishes belonging to Italy.

I love music and I have many records, but then again I don't play them. I don't often find the time for that. I occasionally do, you know. Of course, with having a café we had a jukebox with all of the '50s music. I still have all of these old records. And funnily enough, of all the music, Italian or British, it is one of these jukebox records that I most want to listen to – if I ever find the time. I don't know why. I have a very, very great sympathy for them and I like them very much. Perhaps it's because they bring back happy memories of people that used to drop into the shop. A lot of very, very nice people that we met that way. Of course, we were all young, after the war. It was something new and exciting to relax and chat. The days of the old jukebox was very different from today when everybody has two or three radios and televisions in the house. Then people had to come inside the shop to hear a record. They had to pay for it, I had it for free!

I still have a lot of friends in Stornoway though many have passed away in the half century since I came back after the war. But you know, even when we go out for a run to the outlying villages, we meet people and they recognise us. You can see in their eyes when they speak to you that they remember us from way back. I'm a man that needs the human contact, you know. If you respect people, I think you are respected – simple as that.

We still visit the place where my parents came from. If we can, we go away every year. Because of that we have to forsake going to other places on the Continent. We always go to the same place. It's just home from home, especially for me, because I was there as a child. So I like to go back. The place has changed, of course. It has changed as much as Stornoway, maybe even more. And the people that I knew have nearly all gone but the place itself is as welcoming as ever.

I went down once to Monte Cassino by car to visit the monastery and the war cemeteries there. It was a very moving experience. We drove back during the night and all I saw of Rome was the orange glow of the city in the night. That's the nearest I have ever been to Rome or to the Vatican. Even so, my religion is Catholic. I was very lucky to have two tremendous parents and they taught us that we were Catholic. But then again, religion has much to do with the coincidence of geography. If the stork had come along and instead of dropping me off at No. 20 North Beach, it had gone to No. 19 or No. 21, I wouldn't have been a Catholic. I'd have just been a Protestant or something else. So, I mean, we just took it as the will of God. On that basis we respect all the other acts of God. We respect the religions of the other people that we meet and that are dear to us.

Choosing between Italy and this country would be as painful as having to choose between my father and my mother. That's how it is. That's how attached I am to both this country and to Italy.

Maryann Martin

1909–1999

I was born on the twenty-fifth day of November, 1910. I am the daughter of Dòmhnall nan Trì Dòmhnallan, or, in English, Donald of the Three Donalds. There has been a Donald Martin on this croft for three generations – since some time after the war with Napoleon.

I'm not sure where the Martins came from originally. The family name, Martin, doesn't sound like a Lewis name. Anyway, my folks have been in Lewis for many generations and Lewis is not the worse for that! We are honest, peaceable, intelligent people and I don't mind telling you that. A famous member of our clan was called Martin Martin, who was a well-known traveller and scholar. In his day, he was tutor to the family of the MacLeods of Skye. That was a long time ago but some of the books he wrote are read to this day.

When I was a wee girl, we lived in a thatched house, a black-house, and it was lovely. In the black-house, we had the *cagailt* [the hearth] in the middle of the floor and a hole in the roof above it to let out the smoke. We were used to the peat smoke and didn't mind it. The smoke didn't bother us, you see. Not at all! The house was lovely and warm and there was always a big fire in the middle of the floor and everybody sitting round it. They were good days – just different. Nowadays, people say that we must have been kippered in all that smoke. But they don't know what they are talking about. If we were kippered we didn't mind it. The important thing is that we were very happy.

Of course, at that time we did not have running water in the house. Instead of that, we had a good well and had to go to the well every time we needed to. But we did not have to go very far. We were fortunate that we had a croft with a well in the middle of it. So we hadn't far to go for water. In my young days 'running water' meant that somebody had to go running to the well every few hours! That was sometimes a problem, for many of the families in the village relied on our well for their cooking water. In summer, we sometimes sat in a queue waiting our turn to fill our pails. But that was not really a problem for us when we were young. We were patient and we just had to sit and chat while the clear cold water came up from the underground spring into the well. It was fun to sit and chat, though the adults at home often became impatient waiting to get water to cook the fish and potatoes for dinner.

In the 1930s, my parents built a white-house with the chimneys in the two gable ends. That was 'the latest' in those days! In my very early days there were only a few white-houses in the village. They built it with help from the Board of Agriculture – the 'Grant and Loan' scheme. At that time, there were as many black-houses as white-houses in all the crofting villages that I knew.

While we were in the black-house, we thought it was comfortable enough, though when my parents moved into our new white-house, we realised that the old black-house was poor accommodation by comparison. Having said that, I should tell you that, in my childhood, I was very happy in the black-house but the white-house with the fires set back in the gable-ends was nice and clean and, to this day, it is my home.

Nowadays, people rely on the big stores in Stornoway for all their groceries and things. It was very different in the old days. There was nothing like that but we had everything we needed – but few luxuries. We had sheep and we had cows and we had hens – so we had everything we really needed. All we had to buy was tea and sugar. We had salt meat and salt fish, more than we could eat. We were fortunate. We ate fresh meat on Sunday but we had fish all week. In actual fact, during half the year, from about May until the winter set in, we had fresh fish – herring, mackerel, haddock, lythe, flounders, *cnòdain* [gurnets], saithe, ling, eel – och, and lots more that I cannot remember. Then, in winter, we ate mostly salt herring with the potatoes.

Doctors say that salt food is supposed to kill you if you take too much of it. But we didn't think that in those days – there was nothing like that said against salt food. That's only a new thing, the 'salt food is dangerous' business! In the old days, we lived on salt herring and everybody in my generation lived till their nineties! So that surely proves that all that salt herring didn't kill me. It's preserved me! We ate the salt herring and drank lots of water afterwards. Pints of good well water out of a *mug a' cheàird* [a tin jug made by local tinkers].

Every few years, we used to kill a cow ourselves and made four halves of it and sold three halves and kept a half to ourselves. Well, I mean, not halves, but quarters! We get £3 for the quarters we sold – a pound a quarter. We sold the meat to our neighbours next door. I remember fine. It would be about the time of the First World War – 1912 or '14 maybe. In those days, families had to make do with that sort of barter. Most of our neighbours were related to us . . . mostly all related. And if we weren't related, they were next-door neighbours. Everybody was friendly in those days, whether you were related or not. It didn't make any difference. We had to be friends because we planted the potatoes and worked the peats together. We did everything together: cut the peats together and carted them home together. We were forever friends and in and out of each other's houses. No formality, and treating everybody in the neighbourhood as if they were family. If we were at dinner, which was usually eaten between midday and one o'clock, a neighbour might walk in. Well, the neighbour wouldn't leave at once. You would say to him, '*Nach cuir thu do làmh dhan t-seirbheis?*' [Will you not have some?]

Well, that was an invitation to lean forward and take something from the ashets in the middle of the table – usually a boiled potato or a morsel of fish. We considered that to be good manners. The neighbour would eat the potato or fish while standing and then quickly depart. In those days, we ate our potatoes and fish from our fingers and didn't use knife and fork.

The working day was divided into four quarters. They started the day with a very early breakfast at half past six. Another breakfast at nine and then coming home for potatoes and herring at one o'clock. Then, they finished off with tea at about five o'clock in the afternoon. Sometimes, they kept on working until late in the evening – especially in the summer if the weather was fine.

We used to get our seed potatoes in the town, in the shops in Stornoway. But we also used to keep some of our own from one year to another. At the end of the harvest, we stored our own potatoes in a big *sloc bhuntàta* [potato-pit] in the fields. It was like a wee fortress with a deep moat round about it so that the sheep or rabbits couldn't easily get at it. It was full of potatoes – our family's treasure! We sometimes had a big pit of potatoes out there on the moor. We used to have it out there, on the hill at Tom nan Eun.

In my father's day, people travelled back and fore from the town [Stornoway] by walking the eleven miles. And in fact, more than once I walked it myself in the one day, not once but twice to Stornoway and back. More than twenty miles. We thought nothing of it. Of course, some families which had a shop owned a gig. The gig was a small carriage drawn by a horse. There were two gigs within half a mile of our home, so we used to get up to town on that sometimes.

Drove Day was a big, big day when I was young. On that day, we used to go to the market day in Stornoway, and we all went together and we walked there and walked back. Drove Day was called *Latha na Dròbh* and was always on the first Tuesday of July and we used to go then. It wasn't just cattle that was for sale. Everything was in it. There was all sorts of things. There was *aran-cridhe* [gingerbread] and sweeties and 'lucky-bags' with all sorts of things in it. It wasn't only cattle. It was everything! What an exciting day in Stornoway was Drove Day, which, in other places I've lived in, was called 'Market Day'. The cattle buyers, the drovers, would come from the mainland. They were coming from Inverness and these places.

Though I was only a little girl, I can remember news coming home of the men who lost their lives fighting in the First World War. I can remember the *Iolaire* Disaster very clearly. It happened on New Year's morning, 1919, when 200 men perished coming home from fighting the Germans. I remember that day very well because my uncles were coming home along with the rest of the sailors. The *Sheila* was the regular mail boat that carried passengers and goods between Stornoway and Kyle of Lochalsh. My uncles were desperate to get on the *Iolaire*, which was a fast yacht sent to help the *Sheila* bring the men home for Hogmanay. My uncles were very disappointed that they were unable to get a passage on the fast yacht. Their train arrived too late, you see. So they all went to the *Sheila*, which was a slow boat. Fortunate it was for them. What a disaster! More than two hundred island men lost their lives at the mouth of Stornoway harbour. The yacht ran aground at Holm there. So many men that we knew well died that night. My mother didn't know whether her brothers were on one boat or the other. And of course there were no phones or things like that in those days. I can tell you that there was a lot of broken hearts in our island at that time – a lot of widows and orphans and bereaved parents – yes, and sweethearts who were hoping to get married. It was a terrible time. We thought the First World War was the war to end all wars. I lived long enough to see that that was just not the case.

When I was young, Innis Uilleim [Angus MacLeod] was the kingpin in this district. In fact, he was the kingpin here since long before I was born. He owned a big shop and salting-houses and fishing-boats and what not. He and his wife and family lived in Portvoller House, the Big House just a hundred yards down the road from where I am sitting now. While the rest of the village were living in thatched houses, Innis Uilleim and his family were living in the lap of luxury. They expected everybody to do everything for them for nothing. The fact that the merchant's wife was a sister of my grandfather didn't make much difference. We still had to help for nothing.

But there was tragedy in Innis Uilleim's family in his young days. He lost his wife and family to the *Caitheamh*, which is the Gaelic name for tuberculosis.

Innis Uilleim's meeting Anna, his second wife, was a stroke of good fortune for him. She was my grandfather's sister. Innis Uilleim saw her in Stornoway as she was coming off the mail boat, the *Sheila*. He was meeting somebody off the boat. It happened that, at the same time, my grandfather was meeting his sister Anna. Innis Uilleim asked my grandfather who the young lady was. My grandfather told him that Anna was his sister. I suppose that she looked very glamorous coming home from Glasgow. Anyhow, Innis Uilleim fell for her. He said, 'Well, I'll like to get in touch with Anna tomorrow so that we'll see how things go.'

And that was how his interest in Anna started. They married and had a big family and lived in Portvoller House. In fact, they had ten children and when they grew up they went all over the world. During the First World War, they were in different parts of the British Empire. I left school when I was fourteen years of age. Nobody questioned me why I was leaving or why I wasn't leaving. I just left. At that time there were not any exciting openings for a young girl. Either you went to the herring fishing or else you went into service. That's all. There was nothing else on offer. I chose to go to service. I went to the hotels. I started in the Coffee House in Stornoway, worked there for a little while, then went to Glasgow. What a wonderful city! I was ten years working as a nanny in Glasgow, looking after a wee child. At that time, Glasgow was a lovely place. It had a reputation as a place full of gangs. But, in all my time there, we did not see any gangs. We used to walk from the 'Lewis and Harris' ceilidh dances at three o'clock in the morning all the way to Pollokshields and think nothing of it. The place was full of Gaelic and shouting 'Hello' to everybody on the streets. Glasgow was full of Gaelic coppers. No, it was lovely – just a lovely, exciting place. On Thursdays and Saturdays, my pals and I used to go to the Highlanders' Umbrella, down by the Central Station. We went there to meet other friends. Everybody used to gather there and we used to meet people from home who had come to Glasgow after leaving home. Gaelic speakers from other islands were there – from Skye and Uist and Islay and places like that, but more so from our own island.

Though my own language was Gaelic, my English wasn't bad. I still speak Gaelic better than I do English. But the English I had when I left home was different from the English they had in Glasgow. We were speaking 'Hielan' and they weren't. We used to say that if we were

'Hielanders', they were 'City Hooligans'! Och, it was just a wee bit of banter. But the Glasgow folk didn't look down on us. They weren't bad really, no. They were nice people then in Glasgow. Nice people they were, just as nice and friendly as could be. I went regularly to the dances. Like a fool, I couldn't miss a dance. I was that fond of the dancing. And though I wasn't religious, I went to church every Sunday to the Church of Scotland, but, if I be honest, we were not so fond of going to church. We went now and again but not all the time. Of course, there were very religious Gaels in the city, but we weren't of that ilk.

When the Second World War came, I was called up and I came home from Glasgow. I joined the ATS [Auxilliary Territorial Service] and went to work in Stornoway in the NAAFI [Navy Army and Air Force Institutes] – the organisation that looked after the servicemen and -women while they were at base. I didn't like working there. In fact, I hated it. Some of the servicemen who came in were very lecherous and made comments that I found offensive. I complained about their suggestiveness but nobody did anything about it. It so happened that I met a friend down town and she offered me a job in one of the hotels in town. And I said, 'All right, I don't like the NAAFI anyway!'

So I took the job and I was in the Lewis Hotel, working, and one of the 'High Heid Yins' of the NAAFI came in one day and saw me. He seemed surprised to see me in the Lewis Hotel. Anyway, he spoke to me and asked me what I was doing there and I told him that I wasn't going back to the NAAFI for the reason that I didn't like it. The man couldn't believe his ears! He says, 'You can't do that – just walk away from doing your duty! You were called up,' he says, 'and you've got to come back to the NAAFI like a shot or I'll have you up on a charge!'

'Not me!' says I. 'I'm not going back if I can help it. I'll not go back there any more, I'll stay here!'

Oh the fellow, an officer, was very displeased. He wouldn't hear of my staying employed at the Lewis Hotel. He kept at me: 'Good God, girl, haven't you heard there's a war on? Are you happy to be called a deserter?'

So I had to go. I went back to the general NAAFI but, shortly after that, I was given a transfer to the section serving the Women's Auxilliary Airforce. So that wasn't quite so bad. It was wartime, of course. Anything could happen. And one day something did happen that brought about a big change in my life. The boss came round into the kitchen and asked me and another girl if we would like to go overseas. Well, we didn't take the fellow all that seriously, so I signed the papers that he had. We just thought it was all a bit of fun and never thought seriously of what the word 'overseas' meant. We thought we might be going to Kyle of Lochalsh or somewhere on the mainland. Well, we had a big surprise in store for us. Instead of going to Kyle of Lochalsh, I ended up in the Middle East!

After eighteen months in Egypt, another girl and I were transferred and did about six month over in Palestine. I was working in a 'married family shop', a giftshop. Mercifully, after that I got home. We came on the first passenger-ship for months and months that had been allowed through the Straits of Gibraltar. Just months after that the war ended. That was in 1945 and I remember clearly the joy of VE Day – Victory in Europe. As soon as we were demobbed, we made for home. It was wonderful to come back home in peacetime.

After a spell at home, my friend and I rejoined NAAFI. We went to Germany to work in the 'married family shop'. I liked the work there all right but I didn't like the place

After Germany, I worked in hotels on the mainland until I was old enough to get the Old Age Pension. You might think, because of my wandering from place to place during my lifetime, that I am not really a Lewis woman at all! But I am very much a Lewis woman – very much so! I've been all over right enough, but I prefer Lewis to any other place. More than twenty years ago, when I retired, I came home – in fact, to the croft of my ancestors, the croft of Donald of the Three Donalds.

Once I settled down here, Chrissie, my sister, and I carried on doing the croft work. We were working and doing all sorts of things. We were planting potatoes and planting vegetables. We had all kinds of vegetables in the garden, turnips, carrots, onions, everything. Cutting peats. We had to do everything. There was nobody else to do it. To an extent, we were self-supporting. We had nearly everything we needed.

Speaking of myself, I decided not to get married. I thought I was better off as I was. I had three sisters, you know. Chrissie, was not married either and I felt that I couldn't leave my sister on her own. I lived with her here on the croft until she passed on. We were two spinsters living together with our relations and friends becoming fewer every year.

Now I live alone and go through my memories as I sit by the fire. I have seen in the village lots of changes since I came home. Yes, lots of changes, There's hardly anybody in the street today that I know. It's all, mostly all, English and all sorts. They're from everywhere. Oh, they're neighbourly all right, but that's it. They never come by to see us or anything like that. They're a different kind of islander – ones who wish to live apart and on their own. At one time, there was a real sense of community here in Portvoller. If you were needing milk or anything, you could go next door and get milk or anything else you were wanting. In our community, everybody was just like one – one big happy family. Very different to what it is today. And of course there was always plenty vegetables and plenty potatoes and our own barley-meal and oatmeal. I can remember the *being* [long stool] in the old black-house and it was full of sacks of oatmeal and barley-meal. Yes, the *being* was a kind of bench and it was laden with sacks of oatmeal and barley-meal. That was our supply for the year.

Our way of living has changed. Even our diet has changed. There's no potatoes and salt herrings nowadays. You don't get that any more. It's a luxury, a salt herring today. But otherwise we have the same sort of food really, but we buy it all the time. We don't have any croft animals or poultry so we can't kill a cow and we can't kill a hen. We have to buy them if we want it. We get it in Safeway in Stornoway right enough but it has a different taste altogether. It's not the same taste – not the same as we used to have when it was produced by our own croft, when we used to have basins full of cream and making fresh butter and crowdie and all these nice things that you can't get today. Folks don't have to plant their potatoes or cut their peats as we had to. They're working in town, every one of them. They are in good positions and have got lovely houses and cars, every one of them.

The influence of the Church is much less now. It has gone down quite badly. There's mostly older people going to church now. The young ones don't go. And the Gaelic service is only once a week. It is English mostly. The Gaelic language is much less spoken than it was in my day. But the older people do still speak it. In my own home, we never spoke anything but Gaelic, unless we had visitors who spoke only English. Naturally, I'm happier speaking in Gaelic but we can't speak it when there's English people coming in. We have to turn round and talk English to them, funny enough.

I do not think that my parents and grandparents would be happier if they were living now rather than when they were living here on the croft and working the land. I think they were happier in their own day because they produced almost everything they needed. They got a lot of satisfaction from growing their own. They raised their own cows and sheep and hens, made their own dairy products – cheese, butter, milk, crowdie – all the food that they wanted, without having to go to a van like what I've got to go. There was also as much fish as they could eat. What a wonderful place this was when I was young! Of course, the scenery of Lewis is just the same as it was – beautiful. It will never change, whoever comes to live in our villages and whatever language they speak. Now I am beginning to feel a wee bit sad.

George Smith

1929–

I live at Kenneth Street in Stornoway and, except for when I did my national service and when I go on holiday, I have lived in the same street all my life. My father was born in the parish of Lochs, in the village of Marabhaig. He came to Stornoway with his parents when he was a baby.

When my grandfather brought his family to Stornoway, the rural communities spoke nothing but Gaelic, whereas English was the language of the town, with the result that my father grew up with very stilted Gaelic or, as we say, in the old tongue, *Gàidhlig lapach*. My father started the shoe-repairs, the cobbling, in 1920 and was known to everybody as 'Dòmhlan'. His brother, who had been a cowboy on a ranch in Alberta, some 120 miles west of Calgary, came home and served his apprenticeship with my father. He became known as 'Marabhaig'. There were a lot of cobblers in the town in my father's day. I can't remember whether the number was fourteen or sixteen, working in six shops. There was Marabhaig's, Eachainn's, Johnny MacGee's, Fahdie's on Keith Street, Wee Murdo on North Beach and Dòmhlan's – our own. But, in addition to those, every village on the island had one or two cobblers. Wooden lasts, up in the loft of our shop, belong to an age when people used to get their shoes made. The wooden lasts have the customers' names inscribed on them.

My mother was born at Col, in the parish of Bac. She worked in the town, in a shop on Church Street, called Finlay's. By then, Father would have been in town for perhaps twenty years. He had older brothers and sisters and they lived in Bayhead. My parents lived at first in Castle Street, then moved to Kenneth Street, where they lived until they died. Their home in Kenneth Street, built in 1767, still exists and, in fact, is the oldest house in town. We have always known the house by the name Ardanmhor. Jim Grant [editor of the *Stornoway Gazette*] looked it up in the Feu Charter and found that the name Ardanmhor was that of the land on which the house was built. The Gaelic word *àrd* means 'headland'; *àrdan* is the plural;

mòr means 'big'. So the place probably meant 'The Big Headlands'.*
Certainly, the land at the end of Kenneth Street is high and, before the
town was developed, probably stood out as a sort of promontory. Anyway,
the house has a preservation order on it. It's across the way from our house
here in Kenneth Street – next door to the Royal Hotel with a garden in
between it and the shoe shop in Kenneth Street. It lies at right angles to
Kenneth Street and looks out over the inner harbour. No one lives there
now. We use part of it as a store and, downstairs, part of it as a workshop.

When I was a wee fellow, I had to wear a kilt. For years I was forced to
wear it and that is why I refuse to wear one today. Mind you, I did wear
one when I was in the Scouts and again, for a while, when I was in the
army. But I wouldn't bother with it as my regular, day-to-day attire. On
the other hand, I do believe that the tartan is good for tourism and is
identified with Highland Scotland everywhere. And although the kilt
was never worn here as what you might call the 'national dress', it is
something that is distinctively Scottish and I certainly would not say a
word against it.

I was educated in the Nicolson Institute, here in Stornoway. In the early
days, I can remember the 'Tin School', as it was called, and Mr Pryde, who
was the headmaster of the primary or elementary school. I can't remember
which of these terms was used in those days – in the 1930s. In the infant
school, it was the custom for Mr Pryde to take us on a Friday – maybe one
period on a Friday, just to smarten us up, I suppose! He was the only male
teacher. That was in the mid 1930s. I can remember those times reasonably
well.

My father, whom we referred to as the *Bodach* [Old Man], used to sit on
a seat in the *gàradh* – the garden – and I can recall the old fishermen calling
up to him as he sat there. He often shouted down to his friends and
acquaintances whom he spied walking in Cromwell Street. You couldn't do
that now of course, because of the noise of the traffic. But in those days the
street was so quiet that you could hold a conversation with a person on
the other side of the street. The old retired fishermen and the like always
wore a knitted 'polo' and trousers made of *clò Bucach* – a sort of heavy,
brownish, felt cloth. Those trousers had sloped pockets up near the
waistband instead of along the sides of the trouser as we normally have
today. That generation of fishermen were very sociable and also very

---

* It is likely that, at one time, the headland was owned or associated with a man called Iain
Mòr (Big John); in which case, Ardanmhor (Àird Iain Mhòir) should be construed as 'Big
Iain's Headland'.

knowledgeable, as they spent their lives working the sea and meeting people
from all over Britain and beyond.

Any poor soul that was born anywhere between Arbroath and Inverness
and came to Stornoway was regarded as a *Bucach* [pron. 'book-ach'] which
was a term originally applied to 'a man from the east-coast port of Buckie'.
If you weren't from here you were a *Bucach*!

For about half a century before my time, fishing was the main occupation
of Stornoway but it was still important in the 1940s. In my young days,
Stornoway was a much, much busier town than it is today. Here, the
population used to double at the height of the herring season. Not only East
Coasters and Shetlanders came to work out of Stornoway. Fishing boats
from as far away as Yarmouth used to come up and even brought their
horses with them as well. The horses were used for carting the herring from
the boats to the 'farlins' – the big troughs that held the freshly caught
herring. Teams or 'crews' of women and girls were employed at the farlins,
three girls to each crew. Two girls stood at the farlin gutting while the third
girl was kept on the hop sprinkling rough salt liberally as she packed the
gutted herring in barrel after barrel.

The horses were also used to cart a proportion of the herring down to the
kipper yards at places like Newton. There were a good many kipper yards in
those days: Woodger's and Duncan MacIver's and Louis Bain's, to name
just a few. I understand that, at the end of the herring season, the English
fishermen used to leave their horses here to be sold on their behalf. I was
told that some crofters looked favourably on the end of the season, as it
offered them an opportunity of buying those English horses.

'SY' were the registration initials used to identify boats belonging to
Lewis and Harris – from the Butt of Lewis down to Tarbert. The 'SY' was
always followed by three numerals stylishly painted on the sides of each
boat – fore and aft: SY345 and so on. If the boat happened to belong to a
village such as Bayble or Port of Ness, it always had the name of that village
painted on the stern or quarter. The sight of the harbour almost packed full
of fishing boats was unforgettable. The fleet of steam drifters was berthed
there by the score and stretched in a line, I would say from the King's
Lamp, as we call it, each with its stem against the pier. Then there was
another tier outside that again, with stems lying neatly between the first
tier's sterns. Round the Stone Point, you would get all the bigger boats, the
Bucaich and the Stornoway drifters. The smaller 'Lochies' which had only
three or four of a crew – little ones like the *Lady Marjorie* – lay in Bayhead.

Apart from the fishing there were other types of employment. Charlie
Morrison's, for instance, were ships' chandlers. That shop on Bank Street

was always one of the busiest shops in town. It still exists as an iron-mongers,* but on a much smaller scale than it did in my young days.

Shopkeepers used to swap yarns about interesting or funny things that happened in the shops and there were many such incidents! Let me tell you something that happened in Charlie Morrison's. Rope was sold by the fathom and, as you probably know, a fathom is equal to two yards. For the sake of speed, fathoms were measured by a man continuously pulling from the coil, pulling the rope across his chest from one outstretched hand to the other. It was assuming that his outstretched arms – his 'wing-span', as it were – measured close on a fathom. As that was the case, it was the biggest fellow on board a boat who was always the one sent up to the chandler's to buy rope. Obviously, the so-called 'fathom' measured by a small man would be less that the 'fathom' measured by a big man. According to Robert Morrison, a big *Leòdhasach* [Lewisman], came into the shop one day, to buy rope. The fellow was as big as a gorilla! He was there pulling out 'fathoms' bigger than any fathoms ever before measured in the shop. 'We were quite pleased to see the fellow doing that – measuring off his huge bundle of rope,' says Robert, 'for we had a wee surprise in store for him. We cut off the rope according to the length the man wanted, then put the bundle on to the scales. That is when we explained that that particular rope was being sold according to its weight!'

There were also plenty of bakeries in town and lots of little shops such as Walker's and Dòmhnall Chisholm's on Church Street. I can recollect going down with my grandmother at nine o'clock on a Saturday night, and getting fresh bread coming out of the oven – yes, still warm, newly baked, delicious bread. Almost all the old bakeries have now gone. Stag Bakery is still there but the likes of the Plasterfield Bakery and J&E's, and Johnny Oak's and Forsyth's, are all gone.

What with all the men from different places mixing together in the town, there was a constant babble of accents: *Bucaich*, English, Gaelic speakers, Stornowegians and so on. All different. And there would be the occasional fistfight – never involving me, I'm happy to say, or any of my associates! But they did have their fights downtown.

In the 1940s, the wee *Bucach* cooks on the fishing boats always had a hard time. 'Dodie' Campbell from Findochty first visited here before the First World War. In his later years, he became the skipper of the *Springing Well* and often fished from here. He used to tell us that, as a young lad, he got a hammering downtown in Stornoway on a Saturday night, for no other

* Stopped trading in 2001.

reason than that he was a *Bucach*. Mind you, Dodie may have been trying to steal somebody's girl. Who knows! There was a lot of intermarriage between the islanders and the visitors. A lot of the *Bucaich* married Lewis girls.

All the Lewis girls were skilful knitters. Even while they were walking along the street, arm in arm, they continued to knit. I've often seen them walking, arm in arm, five or six of them, moving along in a wave. I don't know how they could walk like that, while chatting and knitting.

Before the war, Harris Tweed and Lewis blackface sheep and their fleece were very important to the island. At the beginning of the summer, the Point crofters' sheep used to be transported to the Lewis Moor lying north and west of the town. Many of those animals were unhappy feeding on the rough deer-grass and heather out on the hills and, increasingly, became an unholy pest as they took to invading the town in search of tastier fare. They destroyed gardens and caused chaos in the streets. There was no heavy traffic in those days, really, so they could mosey in without getting run over. After cattle grids were installed on the approach roads, the problem eased but some managed to run the blockade and cause debate and argument between the townsfolk and the crofters. Some sheep are surprisingly intelligent and clever at solving problems. They learned how to lift latches and to take gates off their hinges. They had somehow figured out that most of the gates were supported on two-pin hinges. They got their horns under the lock and lifted the gate clean off its hinges. As you lay in bed, perhaps on a peaceful Sunday morning, you could hear them knocking the bins over – clatter after clatter! They could tip a bin, no bother – not the kind of modern 'wheelie bins' but much smaller buckets that people had in those days. They would get the lid off and start to rummage through the contents.

All the villages employed shepherds who were supposed to keep the hundreds upon hundreds of those marauders out on the wide, open spaces of the Lewis Moor. But the animals wished to enjoy *la dolce vita* in Stornoway – the sweet lawn grass, cabbages and sweet peas growing in people's gardens! I remember seeing a picture about 1950, in one of the daily papers, with a caption 'A Wet Day In Stornoway'. The picture showed six sheep standing in Woolworth's door, sheltering!

There was a lot of music in my young days. My father, my uncle and my aunt could all play instruments, though I can't carry a note myself! They could play the pianochord, which was something like a harpsichord, only it's plucked with a plectrum. They played banjos, ukuleles, violin, accordion, melodeon and an organ. Yes, they could all play well, but they didn't pass on their talent! Still, my brother is a reasonably good musician. In my day, dances were regularly held in the Town Hall. I didn't go to any dances till about the tail end of the war. Anyway, I wasn't much of a dancer. I've two left legs, I'm afraid!

My father and his employees made leather footwear. He probably had six men at the cobbling – most of them were from the country. No doubt, customers coming in from the villages had more Gaelic than English and, because of that, Gaelic gradually became the language most often spoken in the shop. People like myself, 'a townie', learning the trade became quite fluent. Well you had to, to function. My two brothers and I inherited the cobbling business and my Gaelic was further strengthened through dealing with customers. Unlike the old days, the shoe shop doesn't make shoes or boots any more. Initially, we got all our leather supplied by a firm called Bayne & Duckett in Glasgow, Parker of Dundee, A&W Paterson and John Paterson. They were what we called grindery merchants, supplying everything that was required in the footwear trade. Those companies have now all disappeared. You had soling leather and you had upper leather of different types: fine calf, bucks calf and goatskins.

They sold us rivets for making or repairing heavy boots, and tingles for shoes. Tingles are a sort of rivet without ribs. You would press the tingle into the leather with your thumb, then hit it with the hammer. Now, when you positioned the rivet, you held it between your finger and thumb to support it and then you drove it in with the hammer. For coarser work, for working boots and the like, you would use rivets. We also used a linen thread to make what we called a *streangan*. Two pulls from the middle of your body with your left hand and that gave you the right length of linen thread. You then rubbed it off on your knee to give it the twist. You made a five-string *streangan* or an eight-string *streangan*, depending on what job you were doing. If you were sewing, say, a fisherman's boot and the strap had gone from the heel, halfway up the leg, you would have to make a five-string *streangan*. But if you were sewing a sole on (which is the way they were done in the old days), you would have, at least, an eight-string *streangan*.

Before you started sewing, you rubbed the *streangan* on your knee so as to give it a wispy end on it and then you waxed it. I've seen it so cold in the workshop in winter that the wax hardened so fast that you couldn't keep going with the sewing for any length of time. Nowadays, machines do all that work and we are rid of all that hassle. Before the Second War, we got

German machines and an American Wirer Auto-soler. Then we got a Power Stitcher after the war. That stitcher used to be on the airport in Stornoway when the air force had a big contingent there – around 2,000 personnel, I believe. During the Second World War, some of the Air Force cobblers used to 'job' at the shoe shop, to earn a buck when they were off duty.

Today's generation cannot imagine what the Isle of Lewis looked like, during the Second World War. There were thousands of Air Force personnel, soldiers and sailors – men and women of different nationalities – all in uniform, of course, and mostly billeted in Nissen huts. There were Nissen huts in practically all the villages throughout the island. Quite a lot were on South Beach Street, Stornoway. At one time, you could see Italian, black-shirted, prisoners of war wandering about the town and they were housed in Nissen-hut encampments in the castle grounds. All the encampments were protected by a perimeter barbed-wire fence. There were camouflaged vehicles of every description in the streets of the town. All the time, there were bombers in and out of the airport. Heavy guns and machinegun nests overlooked the entrance to the harbour, and the harbour itself was a base for MLs [motor launches] and minesweepers. Rationing of food and clothes was the order of the day and everybody listened to the wireless for news of how the war was progressing. I was in school until November 1943. I did my national service from 1945 to 1949, and after my demob, I joined my father's firm here in SY. The work practices hadn't changed much over many years. It was the same old heartbreaking system. You still had to make *streangans* or 'wax-ends' as we sometimes called them. You were given lowly jobs like that to do. I suppose it's the same in any trade, the 'young fellow' gets to do the rubbish!

The boom days of the herring trade were before my time, of course, but I heard all about it. The exporters traded with the Baltic states directly from here. We have an old photograph showing Stornoway as it was about the 1890s and which, at one time, was a decoration in a railway carriage and ran behind a seat just above head level. I think it was by the famous photographer George Washington Wilson. Anyway, it shows sailing ships being careened on the shore in front of Lews Castle. There are also ships in Bayhead with their actual bowsprits projecting onto Cromwell Street. Can you imagine what it was like in those days when the bowsprits of ocean-going ships were sticking out over Cromwell Street – the main street of the town. What a sight that must have been! There's no pier, only an undeveloped shore. Of course, Stornoway in the old days used to trade with countries overseas. The father or grandfather of Miss Morrison, whose house is next door to ours, used to trade directly between Stornoway and the Baltic.

I've been told by Bill Lawson* that, in the 1700s, someone on Taransay (the little island off the west coast of Harris) used to salt whitefish and transport it in his own ship all the way to the slave plantations in the West Indies.

There was also a good shipbuilding trade in Stornoway. That's how the Patent Slip Mill (which became Newall's Mill) got its name. It was on that slip that the ocean-going ship the *D.L. MacKenzie* was built. I believe that she was armed with seven guns and that she was the last one they built. Yes, she was launched from there. I suppose they had to have guns in those days. The *D.L. MacKenzie* wasn't a warship, although she was equipped with guns. She was a merchant ship but the fact that she was armed tells its own story.

In the nineteenth century, Newton was full of sea captains just like Barony Square is today. Though it is within the burgh and even though it is within 200 or 300 yards of the middle of the town, native Stornowegians regarded Newton as a separate entity. I suppose that goes back to a situation many centuries ago, when the two places were separate villages. I remember my father and old Kenny Froggan having an argument about that. I should mention that K.J. MacDonald, the chemist, was known by that name – Kenny Froggan. Anyway, the two of them were talking about some old friend of theirs and my father referred to him as a Stornoway lad.

'No, no, no!' says Froggan. 'He's a Newton boy.'

'No!' my father says, 'He's from Stornoway!'

'You're wrong!' says Froggan, 'He was born east of the Pipe!'

My father had to agree – if you were born east of the dye-works' pipe, you were a Newton boy, west of the pipe and you were a Stornowegian.

There were thatched houses in Stornoway right up to the time of the Second World War. I remember them. But I'm told too that a lot of the Bayhead houses out past New Street were also thatched. Some of the low-built houses that were there, just after the war, were originally thatched houses. They were thatched cottages rather than black-houses. All they did was to remove the thatch and renovate the wall and interiors.

There wasn't a lot of crime here in my young days. I suppose there were a lot of misdemeanours like pinching turnips from gardens, maybe, but that

* The genealogist, Seallam, Isle of Harris.

wouldn't constitute crime, I suppose. Of course, in the old days – say in 1900 – you would be birched for a misdemeanour such as stealing turnips. Indeed, you would. You would get a couple of strokes of the birch for that.

Stornoway English has a lot of words that are foreign to people who are not from the island. But most of them are either Gaelic or adapted from languages current in the streets of the town in centuries gone by. I still hear the word 'cove' [male person], and 'bloan' [female person]. I always thought these had somehow been 'born' on the island, but they weren't. I've come across them, from time to time, in English books. We also used the Gaelic word *bodach* in English conversation. Lots of Gaelic words had come into the Stornowegian dialect in those days – words like an *ulpag*, heavy rock; *dòrnag*, a fist-sized stone; *steall*, for 'splash'; *bochd*, for 'poor'; and so on.

When I was at school, we used to refer to small change in terms of 'wings' and 'meiks'. A wing was a penny and a meek a ha'penny in old money. But those were the names of earlier Scottish coins, I believe. 'Half a dollar' would be 2s 6d – in old money when a pound sterling represented 240 pennies and not 100 pence. In those days, one pound sterling was worth four American dollars – that was during the Second World War. The 'two-bob bit' was another name for a 'florin' or 2s [10p]. Only readers of my vintage will know what all that means!

People from the villages beyond the bounds of SY were called 'maws' or 'scorps'. In fact, anybody who was not from Stornoway was a scorp. On the day that the Western Isles Council was set up, Norman Maclean wrote an article for the *Stornoway Gazette*, in which his comment was, 'The Scorps Won!' But using those words did not amount to serious animosity. Most of the duxes of the Nicolson Institute were from the rural villages and, year after year, proved themselves at school. They were often the best and very proud of their origins.

As an island, we have a reputation for being a pretty intemperate lot! One visitor to Stornoway remarked on the number of pubs and churches in the town. But, to be fair, I believe that a lot of the island boys who survived the First World War came home with a lot of problems. They came back from the trenches or the POW camps shattered and many of them used to come into the town to drink. Today, when you see on television what the soldiers of the First World War went through in the trenches of France and at Gallipoli, you say to yourself, 'How on earth could anybody survive those conditions?'

In any case, I just think that uncontrolled drinking is a Nordic bad habit.

You don't get that degree of drunkenness in Latin countries. Perhaps the problem is that our people can't carry their liquor! Maybe we haven't been eating enough green veg or the winter nights are too long and we don't get enough sunlight.

In former years, there wasn't any law that barred women from pubs. Yet, for a woman to be drinking in a pub had a certain stigma attached to it. It was the introduction of cocktail bars that made it respectable for girls to sit sipping a drink. As I can remember, there weren't any cocktail bars in Stornoway when I was young. They came in after the Second World War and that broke the taboo.

But another characteristic of Lewis folk is that, for the most part, we are a decent, religious and law-abiding society. Our Free Church congregation is one of the biggest church congregations in Britain, I understand. The congregation in the Kenneth Street church is a youngish congregation. When you cast an eye round in a morning, you realise it's a young congregation compared to most of the churches you see out of here. We have good preachers who accept the Bible for what it is – the Word of God. The point I am trying to make is that if you were you brought up in the fundamentalist tradition, you don't question anything in the Bible.

I was first in Austria during my spell of National Service. I was in the Sappers at first; finished up in Austria and then down to Trieste and met some Stornoway boys there. Duncan MacLennan was one and he was in the Registry there.

My sons and I rent a fair-sized area of the Lewis Moor from the Stornoway Trust and, from time to time, one or other of us goes out there with a shotgun and a dog. We've been shooting it now for about twenty-five years. One day, our youngest son, Iain, came off the moor with thirty-five birds on his own. We've never come close to that total. He's a good shot in that he can hit what he shoots at pretty well all the time. For a good number of years, it was a consistently good shoot. We built it up by potting the preponderance of old cocks. Unfortunately, in the last three years the bird population had declined and there's virtually nothing left on it. The year before last, we decided on a policy to stop shooting as soon as we had counted a hundred birds. In fact, the year before last, we saw only thirty-four birds on the first day we were out. Then we called a halt. We didn't shoot it. And then last year we counted only twenty-four birds. There's 55,000 acres in it but they are very hungry acres. I reckon you walk about a mile for every bird you shoot.

I think the decline is caused by two animals introduced to the Western Isles. The mink are killing the hens and the hedgehogs are eating the eggs. You see, the hen would probably stay with the chicks or the eggs whatever danger comes her way. The cock makes off as soon as he feels there's going to be trouble. I've heard said that even when there's a moorland fire, the hen will sit on the eggs until she's burnt. That's what the firemen reported after they've been out to a moor fire. However, I reckon it's the mink that are devastating the moor. It is estimated that there are between 5,000 and 6,000 on the loose in Lewis.

Occasionally, deer come on to the ground as well. On one occasion, Iain, our youngest boy, got one. He's a good shot but it's difficult ground to stalk. Unfortunately, the deer have no chance if they are up against poachers using 'quads'. 'Quads' are four-wheel vehicles that will go anywhere on the moor. In one of those vehicles, you can motor right up to deer. They don't know what the contraption is, so they don't take fright. I'm told that in a 'quad' you can run up to them, downwind of course, and shoot them off. Poachers have pretty well killed off all the deer that were on our acreage and I am very vexed about that.

In the 1960s there was a sudden boom in trade at the Shoe Shop. When the prefabrication yard took off at Arnish, a lot of money came into the island and changed the way of life here. There were about 2,000 people employed at Arnish, making oil platforms or converting rigs. There were, I think, around 1,200 living on a big liner, anchored in Glumag, the deep pool in the south-west corner of the harbour. Stornoway became a small 'boom town'. Arnish became a hive of industry with welding tools, steel presses and heavy hammers thumping away, six days a week. The Arnish buildings are still there, of course, but the industrial plant is gone and so is the workforce.

In the old days, Stornoway was a far more go-ahead place than it is now. Today, the town is no more than a conglomeration of residential houses, with a superstore at one end of the town and a superstore at the other. And that's it!

All told, there are about twenty-odd thousand people in Lewis and Harris, two-thirds of them living out on the country. The problem is that you don't have folk coming into the town centre any more. Would-be shoppers from the villages come in with their cars, just do a loop round the traffic islands at opposite ends of town, and, once they've shopped at the superstores, they're off again.

To my mind, the economy is heading down the tube because all the money earned by island folk or drawn as benefit is handed over in the supermarkets and gets banked on the mainland. There's no contracted work. Even the local authority is not issuing any contracts. The fishing is pretty well finished. The Arnish Yard is moribund and the tweed industry is at a low ebb. I am old enough to have a good historic perspective of the way things have declined. Unless there is some initiative taken by the government or even by local government, we will see the return of the bad old days with mass unemployment and depopulation.

Iain an t-Saighdeir

1911–2002

Tha sinn ann am Port nan Giùran aig No. 4. Seo a' chroit agam, an tè a cheannaich m' athair bho fhear timcheall air 1860. Aig toiseach tòiseachaidh, bha m' athair 's mo mhàthair leis an teaghlach ann an taigh-talmhainn. Cha robh anns an taigh bho thùs ach ceàrnach de riasg. Bha an t-àite-còmhnaidh am broinn an taighe cumhang. Bha na ballaichean aige uabhasach leathainn – mu chuairt air seachd no ochd a throighean – agus bha bunan nan sparran a bha cumail a' mhullaich air, leis an tughadh, air an cur an sàs air an fheur a bha fàs air na tobhtaichean. Nise, bha an taigh sin ann nuair a bha mise nam bhalach beag, agus tha deagh chuimhne agam air cho seasgair comhartail 's a bha e na bhroinn. An-diugh, tha e duilich dhuinn a chreidsinn nach robh saimeant aig ar sinnsirean anns an linn anns an deach an taigh-talmhainn a thogail. Am broinn an taighe, bha clachaireachd timcheall an oisein far an robh na leapannan. B' e sin uireas. 'S mathaid gu saoil sinn gu robh ar cuideachd san latha sin caran deireannach 's nach robh iad a' clachaireachd le cloich agus saimeant. Ach cha robh iad idir math air an dòigh. Cha robh airgead aca agus bha iad a' dèanamh a' chùis leis na stuthan a bh' aca ri an làimh. Nise, tro thìde, bha ballaichean taigh-talmhainn a' dol cruaidh a-staigh agus a-muigh. Bha teine mòr mònach daonnan ann am meadhan an làir agus bha am balla-staigh a' dol cruaidh. Air taobh a-muigh an taighe bha a' ghrian agus a' ghaoth a' dèanamh an obair fhèin! An ceann beagan bhliadhnaichean, rinn m' athair taigh-dubh dhan an taigh-talmhainn. Thog e balla cloich a-staigh agus a-muigh. Rinn sin na ballaichean na bu tighe buileach! Ach b' ann mar siud a bha a h-uile taigh-dubh anns an là ud: balla a-muigh agus balla a-staigh agus riasg eatarra. Cha robh mòran anns na bailtean ach taighean-dubha.

Cha robh a h-uile rud a' còrdadh ris na teaghlaichean a bh' anns na dachaighean ud, biodh iad nan taighean-talmhainn no nan taighean-dubha. Bha an teine mònach a bha air a' chagailt ann am meadhan an làir a' dèanamh sùith a latha 's a dh'oidhche. A rèir cò an àirde bhon robh a' ghaoth ri sèideadh, dhòrtadh sùith sìos air do cheann. Nan tachradh sin 's

gun deigheadh an sùith nad fhalt, bha agad ri do cheann a nighe anns a'
bhad. Tro na linntean, bha na bodaich a' creidsinn gu robh luach mhòr anns
an t-sùith airson na h-imrichean a mhathachadh; gu robh e math airson a'
choirc agus cuideachd airson na biastagan a chumail air falbh bho bunan
barran a' bhuntàta. Bha aca ris an tughadh a thoirt bho mullach nan
taighean a h-uile bliadhna – glè thric air latha brèagha aig deireadh an
fhoghair, an dèidh dhaibh an t-arbhar a bhualadh agus an sìol a ghleidheadh
air falbh sàbhailt' ann an cisteachan.

Tha an lot sa gu math torrach agus bha sinn a' toirt mòran aiste. Bha sinn
a' cur eòrna, coirc agus buntàta a h-uile bliadhna – agus pailteas dhe gach
seòrsa! Bhiodh sinn, gu ìre, a' cosnadh an aon àireamh de mhin a h-uile
bliadhna anns a' mhuileann an Garrabost: seachd bollaichean min-eòrna.
Bhiodh m' athair a' ceannachd min-flùr bhon mhuillear – ach cha b' ann le
airgead! Mu choinneamh an dà bholla min-eòrna sin, gheibheadh sinn dà
bholla min-flùr. Mar tha fhios agaibh, bha a' mhin-flùr ga dèanamh de
ghràn na criothnachd, 's bha sin a' fàs thall thairis – ann an Canada agus
rìoghachdan eile. Thuilleadh air sin, bhiodh sinn a' dèanamh dà bholla
mine de mhin-choirc. Mar sin, bha sinn a' tilleadh às a' mhuileann le trì
seòrsaichean mine: eòrna, coirc agus flùr. Leis na bha sin de bhiadh air a
stòradh am broinn an taighe, cha robh eagal oirnn a' dol chon a' gheamhraidh leis an teaghlach. A thuilleadh air a' mhin, bhiodh pailteas againn
cuideachd de bhuntàta agus de dh'iasg 's de dh'fheòil air a shailleadh. Mar
sin, cha robh acras no ganntar oirnn ann am Port nan Giùran!

Ged nach robh ganntar bìdh oirnn, cha robh againn ach beagan de
dh'àirnean am broinn na dachaigh. Bha ceithir sèithrichean againn agus
leth-dusan stòl. Bha preas mòr ris a' bhalla a bha cuideigin air a dhèanamh
de chraoibh a bha air a thighinn air tìr air a' chladach. Nach iad a bha
dìcheallach! Bha iad air a' chraobh a shàbhaigeadh sìos na plancannan agus
bha na plancannan aca air an gearradh gu grinn. Rinn cuideigin a bha
ealanta air an obair an t-saorsainneachd airson a' phris. Abair thusa
saothair! Nise, cha b' e aona phreas a bh' againn. Bha preas ann a bha
air a dhèanamh de dh'fhiodh dearg. Nise, bha preas eile ann le dreasair air.
Nach e "Welsh Dresser" a chanas tu ri sin? Airson an fhir sin, bhiodh
clann-nighean an sgadain ri toirt dhachaigh soithichean fancy à Yarmouth
agus Lowestoft. Bhiodh a' chlann-nighean a' dol deas chon a' chutaidh anns
na badan sin as t-fhoghar, agus an uair sin gu tuath as t-samhradh gu Ceann
Phàdraig agus a' Bhruaich.

Bha na leapannan air an dùnadh suas mar gum b' e bucais a bh' annta. 'S
e 'leabaidh-àrd' a chanadh sinn ris an t-seòrsa sin – seach gu robh mullaich
orra. Bhiodh trì leapannan dhan t-seòrsa sin nan sreath ceann-ri-cinn anns

a' chùlaist. Mu choinneamh nan leapannan bhiodh na cisteachan-mine. Bha ciste mhòr mhòr againne – tè a ghabhadh dhà no trì bhollachan mine. Aig ceann na tè sin bhiodh na cisteachan a bh' aig a' chlann-nighean airson a bhith dol chon a' chutaidh. Glè thric, bhiodh leabaidh-àrd eile shìos aig an teine. B' ann an sin a bhiodh sinn cruinn mun teine far am biodh bean an taighe a' deasachadh a' bhìdh agus, cuideachd, far am biodh an teaghlach aig a' bhòrd ga ithe. Bha na cisteachan math airson a bhith suidhe orra nuair a bhiodh sinn shuas anns a' chùlaist.

Aig ceann shìos an taighe [air falbh bhon chùlaist], bha a' bhàthaich, àite-còmhnaidh na bà. Bhiodh cearcan shìos an sin cuideachd. Rud iongantach a th' ann, ach cho fad' 's as cuimhne leam, cha robh droch fhàileadh shìos an sin idir far an robh a' bhò agus na cearcan. Nach eil sin àraid a-nise? An rud bu dorra anns an là ud, b' e nach robh taighean-beaga [toilets] anns na dachaighean. Cho tric 's a dh'fheumadh tu a dhol 'aonranach'. Bha agad ri àite fhaighinn far an robh thu air falbh bho shùilean dhaoine.

Cha robh a leithid de rud ann ri bhith a' gabhail bath, airson cha robh bath no uisge nam pìob againn. Dh'aindeoin sin, bha againn ri bhith gar glanadh fhìn. Cha robh comas agad air thu fhèin a bhogadh ach ann an aimsir ghrianach an t-samhraidh nuair a dheigheadh sinn nar balaich a shnàmh ann an geodha. Bha leth-bhath sinc againn, agus nuair a bha an cothrom agad, dheigheadh tu leis a' leth-bhath dhan chùlaist agus chuireadh tu ann bùrn blàth – bùrn a bha thu air a thoirt dhachaigh às an tobair agus a theasachadh air an teine-mònach. Ghlasadh tu an daras. Cha b' e glas iarainn a bha air an daras mar a gheibh thu anns a' bhùthainn – cha robh air ach glas-fhiodha. Chuireadh tu dhìot do chuid aodaich, ach bha thu fhathast le fiamh agus feagal gum fosgladh an daras agus gun tigeadh cuideigin a-steach a chitheadh tu luirmeachd! Anns an là ud, bha sinn cho nàr! Ag èirigh suas nam bhalach, cha robh e idir ann an gnè nan teaghlaichean a bhith còmhstri ri cach-a-chèile. Bha a h-uile teaghlach a' dèanamh an dìcheall ri cumail acrais agus ganntair bhon fhàrdaich fhèin. Cha robh farmad no iadach a' ruith nan daoine ged, mar tha fhios againn, nach do mhair an suidheachadh sin chon an là an-diugh! Bha sinn bochd anns an là ud, agus mura biodh croitean air bith againn agus iasg an Loch a Tuath, cha bhiodh sinn air a bhith beò.

Iasg na mara agus torrachd na talmhainn – seadh, ach bha sinn sealbhach cuideachd gu robh pailteas de riasg air cùl a' bhaile airson mòine a chumail rinn. Gun mhòine, ciamar a bha sinn air na taighean a theasachadh no am biadh a dheasachadh? Cha robh gual ri ar làimh. Nam biodh sinn airson gual a cheannachd, bhiodh againn ri fhaighinn à Steòrnabhagh air làraidh agus bhiodh cosgais mhòr air a bhith an cois sin. Cha robh sinn a' ruighinn air, oir cha robh airgead againn. Tha deagh chuimhn' agam air fear a bhiodh a' tighinn dhachaigh bho sheòladh agus, gach uair a thigeadh e, bheireadh e dhomh bonn sia sgillinn. Bha sin tòrr ga thoirt do bhalach beag. Nuair a bhàsaich mo mhàthair, b' e mo sheanmhair agus Cairstìona, piuthar mo mhàthar, a dh'àraich an teaghlach againn. Cha do dhìochuimhnich mi sin a-riamh. Eadhon nuair a thòisich mi ri dèanamh beagan cosnaidh, bhithinn a' cur thuca sia sgillinn a-mach às mo thuarastal. Cha robh sin mòr, ach anns an là ud cheannaicheadh e lof dhaibh. Lof! Abair thusa gur e luxury a bh' ann an lof do dhaoine bochd.

Nuair a bha mi òg, b' e latha sònraichte a bh' ann an 'latha buain na mònach'. Air an latha mhòr a bha sin, bhiodh sinn ri buain connadh na bliadhna do dh'aona theaghlach. Bha sin ga dhèanamh le sgiobadh anns an robh dusan no aon neach deug: fir agus mnathan, cuid a' gearradh leis an tairsgear agus cuid a' sadadh na mònach. Bha aca ann an aon latha ri buain de mhòine na chumadh an teaghlach a' dol le teine fad na bliadhna. Bha an teine ga chumail a' losgadh air a' chagailt a latha agus, gu ìre, tron oidhche. Nuair a bhiodh an sgiobadh againn a-muigh anns a' bhlàr, bhiodh sinn nar balaich a' feuchainn ri cuideachadh mar a b' fheàrr a b' urrainn dhuinn. Bhiodh bean an taighe a' fuireachd air ais airson am biadh ullachadh. Nuair a bhiodh i deiseil, chuireadh i sinne a-mach le dà chloich an làimh an urra, gam bualadh ri chèile le 'Gleog, gleog, gleog!' Bha am fuaim a bha sin a' dèanamh na chomharr dhan sgiobadh is gam fiathachadh dhachaigh gu am biadh. Mar dhuais, bhiodh sinne a' faighinn pìos lof le silidh air – rud a bha gu math annasach dhuinn.

Nuair a thàinig mi fhìn gu latha 's a bhithinn a' dol a-mach leis an tairsgear ann an sgiobadh, bha agam ri èirigh aig sia uairean sa mhadainn agus bracaist ithe de dh'uighean, aran agus teatha mus deigheadh sinn a-mach. Bha agad ri bhith air druim a' phuill aig seachd uairean. Mar bu tric', bha fear agus tè mun a h-uile tairsgear. Dh'obraicheadh sinn an sin nar dithis, an dàrna cuid gu h-àrd a' gearradh agus a' chuid eile gu h-ìosal a' sadadh, greis mu seach. Ghabhadh sinn anail mu chuairt air deich uairean, agus fhad 's a bha sinn a' dèanamh sin, ghabhadh sinn tuilleadh bìdh: an dàrna bracaist. Bha lit is bainne againne airson na tè sin agus copan teatha agus aran-coirc no flùr no eòrna le ìm. Aig leth-uair às dèidh meadhan-latha, gheibheadh sinn comharr airson an diathad a ghabhail. Bhiodh tu gu math acrach mus fhaigheadh tu fios gu robh am buntàt' 's an sgadan deiseil. Abair gu robh càil agad, an uair sin, airson an t-annlan sin ithe!

Thilleadh tu an uair sin chon a' phuill agus dh'obraicheadh tu gus am biodh e còig uairean feasgar. Bha thu 'n uair sin deiseil airson do theatha. Bhiodh hama is ugh aig cuid, no brot is aran. Ach bha feadhainn nach deigheadh chon an taighe airson a' bhìdh sin idir. Bha sin a rèir dè na rudan a bha aca ri dhèanamh aig na dachaighean aca fhèin. Air an làimh eile, an fheadhainn anns an sgiobadh aig nach robh bean no teaghlach agus a bha saor agus gun uallaichean, dheigheadh iadsan chon an taighe airson an teatha agus dh'itheadh iad an leòr. Tha fhios gu robh iad airidh air! Obair chruaidh, shàraichte, acrach a bh' ann a bhith buain na mònach airson fad latha. Air an làimh eile, bha e tlachdmhor a bhith dèanamh na h-obrach ann an sgiobadh.

Bha co-chomann againn agus àbhachdas – gàireachdainn – agus cha bhiodh an tìde fada dol seachad nuair a bha sinn an cuideachd a chèile. Mar sin, bha an co-chomann a' dèanamh na h-obrach na b' aotruime.

Air an lot againne, cha do chuir sinn each is crann a-riamh air an talamh airson a threabhadh. Cha robh againn ach na spaidean. Nise, nam biodh duine anns a' bhaile air chùl chàich, dheigheadh cuideigin às a h-uile taigh ga chuideachadh. Cha bhiodh na teaghlaichean idir ri tighinn cruinn airson am buntàta a chur, mar a bhiodh sinn a' dèanamh airson buain na mònach. Ach nuair a thàinig na tractaran a-steach às dèidh a' Chogaidh, bhiodh sinn a' cur a' bhuntàta le tractar agus bhiodh duine às gach taigh againn mar sgiobadh, a' leantainn a' chroinn fhad 's a bha e a' treabhadh, 's a h-uile duine a bh' anns an sgiobadh dian a' cur a' bhuntàta anns an sgrìob. Dh'fheumadh tu cumail na curachd a' dol mar a bha an tractar a' treabhadh, oir bha an tractar agus am fear a bha leis air am pàigheadh anns an uair. Tha caochladh air a thighinn air a h-uile càil a bha sin. Chan eil teaghlach anns a' bhaile a' cur bhuntàta airson a bhith aca rè na bliadhna – dìreach sgeòid bheag de bhuntàta-luathaireach airson a bhith aca aig toiseach an t-samhraidh. Cha mhòr gu bheil duine a' gearradh na mònach, agus dh'fhalbh àbhachdas an sgiobaidh. Chuir sinn cùl ri sgìths latha buain na mònach, nuair a bhiodh tu ri buain no ri sadadh airson deich uairean a thìde san latha!

Anns na seann làithean, bhiodh na fir à Port nan Giùran agus à Port Mholair ag iasgach le eathraichean mòra anns am biodh seachdnar de chriutha. Cha robh e na annas dhaibh a bhith a' seòladh tarsainn a' Chuain Sgìth chon na mòr-thìr a thogail fheusgan anns na lochan-mara thall an sin. Bha sin mu chuairt air deich mìle fichead, a' mhòr-chuid dheth leis an t-seòl. Bha aca ris am feusgan fhaotainn airson na lìn-bhige a bhiathadh, oir b' e am feusgan am biathadh a b' fheàrr airson iasgach nan adag. Bhiodh iad uaireannan a' dol chon an Loch Mhòir [Loch Broom], an loch a tha dol a-steach a dh'ionnsaigh Ulapul. Bhiodh iad cuideachd a' dol chon an Loch

Bhig [Little Loch Broom]. 'S iomadh sgeulachd a chuala mi bhuapa air mar a bhiodh a' tachairt dhaibh. Uaireannan, chlòthadh a' ghaoth gu ìre nach biodh gluasad lùths anns an t-seòl agus bhiodh aca ris an t-eathar a chur fo ràmh. Cha robh rìan ac' air a' chòrr a dhèanamh. Tha astar mu chuairt deich mile fichead eadar Port nan Giùran agus beul an Loch Bhig. Tha àite a-staigh ann an uachdar an loch ris an can iad Leac Mailm, agus b' ann an sin a bhitheadh iad, mar bu tric', airson am feusgan a thrusadh. Aig amannan bhiodh muinntir Chataibh a' dèanamh a-mach nach robh còir aig na Leòdhasaich a bhith tighinn an siud idir. Bha iad a' cumail a-mach gu robh am feusgan leothasan. Cha b' ann aon uair a bha trod eatarra! Innsidh mi beagan dhuibh mu dheidhinn rud a thachair air Latha Sàboind agus eathar à Port nan Giùran air fuireachd thall airson an reothart a ghlacadh air Diluain. Chaidh balaich an eathair dhan eaglais mar bu nòs.

Chaidh faighneachd dha na balaich an robh duin' aca a bhiodh deònach air ùrnaigh a dhèanamh. Thuirt bràthair m' athar gu robh, gu robh aon fhear, Dòmhnall MacLeòid, a bha uabhasach math air ùrnaighean a dhèanamh.

Nise, am fear a bha bràthair m' athar air a chomharrachadh air an ainm ud, fear air an robh am far-ainm 'My', cha deach innse dhàsan idir gu robh bràthair m' athar air siud a dhèanamh. Cha robh fhios aig 'My' bochd dè dhèanadh e nuair a thòisich iad a' gairm ainm anns an eaglais. Chùm na h-èildearan orra ag eubhachd ainm: "A Dhòmhnaill MhicLeòid, nach èirich sibh airson facal a radh!"

'My' bochd, bha e le a cheann crom leis an nàire. Cha robh facal aige ach "O, mo chreach! Chan eil mise comasach air sin a dhèanamh ann am fianais dhaoine!"

Faodaidh sinn a bhith cinnteach nach robh duine a' fàgail na h-eaglais air an là ud aig nach robh truas ri 'My' bochd! Abair faochadh! Agus tha mi cinnteach gu robh pailteas aige ri radh ri bràthair m' athar cho luath 's a chuir iad cùl ris na coigrich a bha mun cuairt orra.

Uaireannan bha an turas chon na mòr-thìr a' toirt dhà no thrì lathaichean. Bha e a rèir dè an àirde bhon robh a' ghaoth. Le pailteas gaoithe, cha toireadh an turas a-null ach eadar sia no seachd a dh'uairean a thìde. Leis an t-seòl làn, shiùbhladh na h-eathraichean mòra ud gu math luath. Bho àm gu àm, bhiodh tubaistean uabhasach a' tachairt. Ann an linn m' athar, bha bàthaidhean ann a bha cur nan teaghlaichean a bhuineadh dha na fir a chailleadh chon na bochdainn. Chaidh eathar fodha am badeigin faisg air Ceann an t-Siùmpain, mu chuairt air mìle air falbh bho a ceann-uidhe ann am Port nan Giùran. Bha i a' tighinn à Steòrnabhagh gu ruige Port nan Giùran le luchd fiodha. Tha e iongantach mura deach i air a beul fòidhpe fhad 's a bha i a' tighinn timcheall air a' Ghrianan. Cha d' fhuaireadh corp duine a bh' innte.

Tha mi gu math sealbhach gu bheil mi beò anns an là an-diugh agus gu bheil mi comasach air a' phiseach a tha air a thighinn air na bailtean againn fhaicinn. Nuair a bhios mise ag innse do chlann na dòighean anns an robh sinn beò anns an t-seann aimsir, tha e duilich dhaibh a chreidsinn gu robh sinn cho deireannach agus cho bochd dheth. Ach feumaidh mi radh, dh'aindeoin 's cho bochd 's a bha daoine, bha iad sona agus coileanta ann an iomadach dòigh. Ged a bhiodh iad air a bhith fuireachd ann an caistealan mar a bha na h-uaislean, cha b' urrainn dhaibh a bhith na bu toilichte. Cha robh iadach no farmad nam beatha. Bha a h-uile teaghlach gun càil aca anns an robh luach. Air an làimh eile, bha rud aca nach ceannaicheadh òr no airgead. B' e sin an creideamh agus an earbsa agus an tac a bha iad a' dèanamh à facal an t-Soisgeil a thug Iosa Crìosda dhuinn uile.

Tha mi air a bhith nam bhall dhan eaglais airson trì fichead bliadhna 's a seachd – bho bha mi nam bhalach. Tha buaidh air a bhith aig an t-Soisgeul air an teaghlach againn airson iomadach linn.

An-diugh, tha iomadach meur dhan Eaglais Chrìosdaidh againn anns na h-Eileanan agus cuideachd eaglaisean a bhuineas do chreideamhan eile. Bidh foghlamaichean a' deasbad air iomadach cuspair a thaobh na beatha sa agus a thaobh na sìorraidheachd. A bheil Iutharn ann? Agus eadhon a bheil Nèamh ann? Cha do chuir ceistean dhan t-seòrsa sin dragh orm a-riamh. Cha do rinn smaoin air Iutharn mo chur mun cuairt. Chan eil càil cudromach nam bheatha-sa cho buadhmhor ri làthaireachd Dhè. Bho thàinig mi gu bhith gabhail ris an làthaireachd sin, cha robh teagamh no rud sam bith gam bhuaireadh thaobh na sìorraidheachd. Tha eòlas agam air buaidh Dhè tro rudan a tha air tachairt nam bheatha. Cha robh aig neach sam bith ri mo threòrachadh air an rathad sin. Fhuair mi lorg air an Tighearna air mo ghurt fhìn. Thachair sin dhomh air a' chiad latha a bha mi anns an eaglais ann an Garrabost. Cha robh fhios agam dè a bha air tachairt dhomh! Cha b' urrainn domh sgur a ghal. Thàinig e a-steach orm gum b' e peacach a bh' annam. Dh'innis mi do bhanacharaid dhomh – tè a bha na bu shine na mi fhìn – mar a bha mi air mo bhuaireadh.

Thuirt mi rithe, "Na innis do dhuine an staid anns an deacha mi agus mar a tha mo chogais air a buaireadh."

Fhreagair i, "Chan innis mise ort idir, ach chan fhada gus an innis thusa dhut fhèin dè bhios agad ri dhèanamh!"

'S bha i ceart anns a' chomhairle a thug i dhomh. Chaidh mi air ais còmhla rithe dhan eaglais ach bha mi uabhasach diùid, lìogach! Bha mo

bhràthair, Uilleam, air tòiseachadh a' leantainn sia mìosan roimhe sin, agus
anns a' cheann thall thàinig e mach gu bhith na mhinistear. Co-dhiù, thug
Uilleam dhan eaglais mi ann an Seisiadar, agus nuair a bha sinn a' dlùthadh
air an eaglais, thuirt e rium, "Nuair a ruigeas sinn, bidh iad air an t-seinn
agus bidh an daras fosgailte. Thèid sinne steach nar dithis agus cha
mhothaich duine dhuinn."

Chaidh sinn a-steach nar dithis, agus cho luath 's a shuidh sinn agus a
chrom mi mo cheann, thòisich mi ri gal. Nuair a sheas am ministear airson
searmonachadh, thuirt e, "Tha agam ri innse dhuibh gu bheil mi a' dol a
leigeil bhuam an t-searmoin a bha mi a' dol a dhèanamh. Ach bheir mi
dhuibh searmon a bhuineas do dh'fhear a tha na shuidhe còmhla rinn air an
fheasgar." Rinn am ministear an searmon air an earrainn sa anns a'
Bhìoball: an treas caibideil de dh'Eòin, an deicheamh earrainn fichead:
Feuch uisge. Ciod a ta bacadh mise bhith air mo bhaisteadh? Fhuair mi
comhartachd mhòr ag èisteachd a' mhinisteir agus dh'fhàg an t-eagal a bha
orm ro Iutharn agus Breith na Sìorraidheachd. Fhuair mi eòlas air gràs an
t-Slànaigheir agus dh'fhalbh m' eallach dhìom. Dh'aindeoin sin, bhithinn
uaireannan gu math ìosal nam spiorad agus uaireannan air mo thogail suas
le aoibhneas. Tha mi a' smaoineachadh gu robh Dia airson sealltainn
dhomh gu robh mi fhathast nam pheacach agus gu robh E airson mo
chronachadh airson m' aingidheachd agus gus leigeil ris dhomh nach robh
mi idir saor bhon pheacadh. Tha earrainn ann an Gnìomharan nan Abstol a
tha ag radh *Is èiginn dhàsan fàs ach dhòmhsa bhith air mo lughdachadh.* Anns
a' Bheurla tha e a' ciallachadh "It's important that He grow but, first, that I
have to be diminished."

Tha na dh'ionnsaich mi de theagaisg an t-Soisgeil air a bhith dhòmhsa na
iùil bho bha mi sia bliadhna deug. Chan eil cuimhn' agam gu robh mi riamh
a' guidheachdainn no ris a' mhisg, ach bha mi trom air an tombac. Leig mi
dhìom an tombac airson gu robh mi cus fo a bhuaidh. Bha mi a' coimhead
air a bhith fo bhuaidh an tombac mar pheacadh.

Tha mòran anns a' Bhìoball mu dheidhinn murt is marbhadh. Tha sin
lìonmhor anns an t-Seann Tiomnadh. Cha do rinn mise murt a-riamh ach
chan eil sin gam shaoradh bhon pheacadh, airson tha am peacadh ann an
nàdar mac-an-duine. Chan eil sinn cho rèidh ri càch-a-chèile 's bu chòir
dhuinn. Bidh buairidhean eadar teaghlaichean, agus uaireannan eadar buill
dhan aon theaghlach. Is e sin an t-adhbhar gu bheil cogaidh anns an
t-saoghal.

Ach bha mise ann an cogadh – an Dàrna Cogadh Mòr – agus cha robh sin
idir a' buaireadh mo chogais gu robh mi ann a' sabaid ris an nàmhaid, agus

man tha fhios agad fhèin b' e sin a' Ghearmailt fo riaghladh Hitler. A' chiad soitheach air an robh mi, 's ann a-mach à cost Shasainn a bha sin, sloop ris an canadh iad a' *Weston*. Bha sinn air tòir na U-boats. Anns a' chiad seachdain a bha mi air a' *Weston* fhuair sinn fios gu robh soitheach ann an gàbhadh agus ann an cunnart a dhol fodha. Ghluais sinn aig astar airson a cuideachadh. Bhuail sinn oirnn le ar sùil air a' chuan. Ann am beagan ùine, chunnacas an rud seo air uachdair na fairge romhainn agus tonnan na mara a' bristeadh air. Chaidh ar gairm gu Action Stations agus, ann an ùine ghoirid, bha na gunnachan againn dearg a' losgadh air an rud a bh' ann. Bha dùil againne gur e U-boat a bh' ann gu cinnteach, ach cha robh ann ach druim soithich a bha air a dhol fairis agus a bha air a beul fòidhpe air uachdair na mara. Leis an eireapais a bh' oirnn, cha robh mise air faighinn a dh'iarraidh nam putanan a bh' againn airson an cur nar cluasan. Rinn tartar nan iorchaillean uiread de mhilleadh air mo chlaisneachd agus gum b' fheudar dhaibh mo chur dhan ospadal.

Thug mi naodh seachdainean anns an ospadal 's bha sin glè mhath, oir fhuair mi cuideachd naodh seachdainean de lìobh seach gun robh mi air a bhith san ospadal. Ach cha do chuir sinn crìoch air a' Chogadh dhomh! Nuair a thill mi gu Portsmouth, chaidh sealtainn dhomh am mine-sweeper air an robh mi gu bhith, agus trì latha às dèidh sin dh'fhalbh sinn air turas a thug mi iomadach mìle mìle bho chladaichean Bhreatainn. Chaidh sinn cho fada ri Cape Town mus d' fhuair sinn beagan ùine air tìr. Bha an t-soitheach ga h-ullachadh airson ionnsaigh a thoirt air eilean mòr a bha na Gearmailtich air a chur fòidhpa fhèin. B' e sin Madagascar, air taobh sear Afraga a Deas. Bha ceudan de shoithichean-cogaidh againn dha gach seòrsa: crùsairean mòra cumhachdach, diostròidhearan agus bàirdsichean làn shaighdearan. Chuireadh sinne air falbh ro chàch, airson rathaidean a sguabadh mus tigeadh na soithichean-cogaidh leis an armachd. Bha sinn a' sguabadh a-steach fad an t-siubhail, a' glanadh air falbh nam mèinn-ichean a bh' anns an rathad air na invasion barges a bha a' tighinn às ar dèidh. Ged a dheigheadh sinne ar marbhadh, cha robh e gu diofar! Fhuair sinn air adhart gu math. Bha sinn a' dèanamh chon na tìr, a-steach gus na ràinig sinn faisg chon na creige. Bha sinn gu bhith ris a' chreig mus deacha gin dha na bàirdsichean romhainn airson a dhol gu tìr. Uill, bha sinn air ruighinn cho faisg air an fhearann 's nach robh na Gearmailtich air bodraigeadh mèinnichean a chur cho faisg air a' chladach.

Bha sinn fortanach, oir cha robh an luchd-faire aca air ar fidreachadh a' dlùthadh orra. Le sin, bha sinn air am muin mus do mhothaich iad, agus chaidh iad às an toinisg! Bha sinn cho faisg air a' chladach 's gur ann sìos oirnn a b' fheudar dha na gunnaichean aca a bhith losgadh oirnn. Nuair a chaidh na bàirdsichean air tìr 's a thòisich am blàr, chaidh an t-adhar na smàl dearg leis a h-uile gunna mòr is beag a' tàirneanaich agus a' tartair. Bha mi miannachadh gum biodh duine ann a dh'aithnichinn, no duine ann air an robh beagan eòlais agam. Ach b' ann fada air chùl sin a fhuair mi mach gu robh sin ann! Bha fear às na Hearadh ann – Uilleam MacGhillFhinnein. Willie MacLennan. Fada, fada an dèidh a' Chogaidh, bha e ann an Inbhir Nis na mhinistear. Tha e air obair a leigeil dheth bho chionn ùine. Chaidh a leòn gu dona ann am Madagascar agus chaidh clàr airgid a chàradh anns a' chlaigeann aige. Chaidh. Uill, bha sinn ag obair ann an sin nuair a fhuair sinn air na rathaidean-mara a dhèanamh air dhòigh 's gu robh e sàbhailt' gu leòr. Nuair a bha sin againn air a dhèanamh, chaidh sinn air acair. Bha cabhlach mòr shoithichean ann. Ach bha an nàmhaid fhathast a' toirt dùbhlan dhuinn. Bha dà bhatraidh air mullach beinne, agus 's e 'Edinburgh Castle' an t-ainm a bh' aca air a' bheinn sin. Bha an dà bhatraidh sin a' losgadh sìos air na soithichean – a' losgadh oirnn agus a' losgadh. B' fheudar dhuinn gluasad air falbh bhon acarsaid a bh' againn agus acrachadh an àite eile. Ach seo, 's ann a thàinig dà chrùsair agus ghluais iad a-steach chon na creige. Loisg iad sin agus cha b' fhada gus an robh a h-uile càil a bh' air a' bheinn na thàmh. Chuir an dà chrùsair smùid à 'Caisteal Dhùn Èideann' agus a h-uile gunna a bh' oirre!

Bha mi ann an cunnart mo bheatha iomadach uair, mar a bha a h-uile duine a bha air tìr, anns an adhar agus aig muir. Fad còig bliadhna a' Chogaidh, no glè fhaisg air, bha mi air mine-sweepers. Bha againn ris na mèinnichean a bha an Gearmailteach air a chur anns an rathad air na soithichean againn a sguabadh air falbh. Bha mòran dhan obair sin againn ga dhèanamh a-staigh ris na cladaichean – glè thric, mìle no dhà air falbh bho far an robh an nàmhaid. Chaidh losgadh oirnn uair is uair, agus air na soithichean eile a bha ris an aon obair.

Sheòl sinn tron a' Mhuir Ruadh suas tron Suez Canal agus bha sinn a' sguabadh mhèinnichean fad an t-siubhail a-null fearann na h-Èipheit fhad 's a bha an t-Arm againne a' sabaid ris an Arm Ghearmailteach le Rommel air an ceann. 'S iomadh balach tapaidh air gach taobh a chaill a bheatha anns an fhàsach eadar an Èipheit agus Libia. Iomadach fear cuideachd air na soithichean a bha a' leantainn nan Arm leis a h-uile seòrsa rud air an robh feum aca, eadar ammunition, biadh, gunnaichean, connadh, tancaichean agus saighdearan. Bha an cunnart ann air a h-uile ceum. Bha sia no seachd dha na mine-sweepers againn ag obair a-staigh ris na cladaichean a' dèanamh na slighe glan. Glè thric chaidh losgadh oirnn, agus 's e gleidheadh Dhè a bh' air an t-soitheach againn nach deach a bualadh, ged a bha na seilichean aig a' Ghearmailteach a' tighinn gu math faisg oirnn. Sguab sinn na mèinnichean mus deach an t-Arm air tìr ann an Siosailidh agus a-rithist fad an t-siubhail suas ri cost na h-Eadailt. Anns a' cheann thall dh'iarradh oirnn a dhol ris an aon obair ri cladaichean na Frainge, mus deach an armachd air tìr aig D-Day.

Saoilidh mi gur e an rud bu mhiosa a chunna mise fad a' Chogaidh, gur e rud a thurchair dhomh fhaicinn ann am Portsmouth. Thachair e tràth anns a' Chogadh, goirid an dèidh dhomh fhìn faighinn a-mach às an ospadal. Bha mi air tilleadh às an ospadal chon nam barags. Thòisich na Gearmailtich a' slacadaich air a' bhaile tron latha. Mar a thuigeas tu, bha tòrr millidh ann. Chaidh na poilis agus an luchd-smàlaidh a ghairm a-mach agus, anns a' cheann thall, dh'iarradh oirnne – na seòldairean – a dhol a-mach airson na fir sin a chuideachadh. Cha tèid dìochuimhn' agam gu bràth air an t-sealladh a chunna mi, agus b' e sin clann nan sìneadh marbh far na thuit iad. Bha an sgoil san robh iad air a bualadh le bom. A' faicinn chloinne nan laighe gun lùths agus gun ghluasad am measg na bha briste mun cuairt orra, bha e na chràdh do chridhe a h-uile neach a bha 'n làthair. Bha sinn a' slaodadh air falbh nan cabraichean agus gach trulais a bha air am muin agus a' giùlain chorp air falbh bhon an sgoil. Bhriseadh e do chridhe a' faicinn na cloinne: na cuirp bheag neoichiontach ud le am beatha air a toirt bhuaipe. Chan eil fhios agam cia mheud a chaidh a mharbhadh, ach chaidh tòrr. Bhathar ag radh nach do theàrn leanabh idir às le a bheatha. Rud maslach.

Tha cogadh na uabhas. Mar a thubhairt mi, tha e soilleir nach do dh'èist mac-an-duine fhathast ris na facail aig Iosa Crìosda.

John MacDonald

1911–2002

I was born in 1911 at 4 Port nan Giùran, which is a village overlooking the Loch a Tuath [Broad Bay, Lewis]. Before World War Two, I was employed on fishing-boats and at deep-sea sailing.

I came back to the island of Lewis when peace returned in 1945. Yes, and I started at the herring fishing at once. I've got a croft here at No. 4, Port nan Giùran. I believe my grandfather bought this croft from another man around the 1860s. I don't know who the man was. And do you know how the croft house was built? It was a *taigh-talmhainn* – an earth-house. That means that it was of a square entirely of turf. Whereas the living space was somewhat limited, I would guess that the walls were about seven or eight feet thick. I remember, as a little boy, sleeping in that house and I can tell you that it was cosy enough for me to feel perfectly safe in it and comfortable and, so far as I can remember, perfectly weather-tight. Today, it is strange for us to think that there weren't any stones or cement used in the construction of a *taigh-talmhainn*, that is, except for a small section round where the beds were.

The turf used in the construction was cut just out at the back of the house here, which was very handy. The roof was laid over the turf square and was thatched. The rafters were put straight on to the grass that was covering the turf. There was a certain skill to making those turf houses. When the turf dried, the walls became quite solid. The reason for that was that there was a roaring peat fire in the middle of the house all day, so that there was a lot of warmth inside the building, you see. Oh, yes, yes! Through time, the walls became very hard. But in my parents' day, my father decided to convert the turf-house so as to become a *taigh-dubh* – a black-house. He did that by building stone walls both outside and inside the turf walls. Yes, stone walls that provided a kind of cladding for the turf. That was the way the black-houses were when I was young – stone walls outside as well as within. Och, there were plenty of those black-houses everywhere in the island.

Of course, there were advantages and disadvantages to living in a house like that. You know, how will I put it now, with certain kinds of wind, it brought soot down on to our hair and you had to wash it out! But that was because the fire was on an open hearth in the middle of the floor and the smoke was constantly making soot on the thatched ceiling. Of course, the smoke was all through the house. Generations of crofters living in the black-house thought of the soot as a precious commodity. They used the soot-covered thatch as compost for their fields. Apart from its value as manure, the crofters believed that the soot helped to keep away harmful bugs. They stripped the thatch off the houses every year. That job was usually done on a good day in the autumn after the threshing was over and all the grain had been stored away safely in chests.

Our croft here at No. 4 produced a lot of crops. We were sowing barley, oats and potatoes every year. It was all for use by our own household. Sometimes we would get about six and seven bolls of barley-meal. And we would get about two of oats. And my father used to change two bolls of the barley-meal at the mill in Garrabost, you know, and get two bolls of flour in exchange. The flour was from wheat, which we don't grow in the Western Isles. So you would have the three types of flour then. You would have the wheat flour, the oatmeal and the barley. It was very nice to get the flour into the house along with the barley and the oats. You could face the winter with those supplies secure in the meal-chests inside the house. Then, on top of all that, you had your salt meat and fish and potatoes. So long as we had those stored away by the end of the autumn, there was no likelihood of our experiencing starvation at Port nan Giùran! When I was young, there was no such thing as keeping up with the Joneses. The reason for that was that everyone was too busy keeping the wolf from the door! There was no jealousy or envy. The people were very poor then. If it wasn't for the crofts and the Broad Bay fish there, we could not have survived. You could say that everybody survived by the sweat of their brows. The men and women had to work hard both on the crofts and at the fishing.

Now, I'm going to tell you a bit about the furniture we had in the early days. There was just four chairs in the house but we had at least half a dozen stools. And there was a big cupboard which we called a 'press' and they were telling us it was made out of a log that had come ashore and it was cut up in slices. Planks you would call them. We had one of those of redwood. And we had another press with a dresser on it. It was like a Welsh-dresser, yes. And the girls coming back after the herring season used to bring home all sorts of fancy dishes from Yarmouth and Lowestoft. The girls used to go south to the gutting at Yarmouth and Lowestoft in the autumn, then north in the summertime to Peterhead and Fraserburgh.

The beds we had were closed-in beds which, in English, are called box-beds. In our bedroom, there were three beds, one after the other in a row. There was also one down by the fire in the living-room, which was also the kitchen. Now, on the other side of the room – opposite the beds – there were the chests of meal. We had a big, big one. It would take a few bolls of flour and oatmeal too. Following that big one came the chests that girls had at the fishing. Very often there would be a box-bed down by the living-room fire. That's where the family sat as the housewife cooked the meal and also where the family sat at the table at meal-time. Whenever we sat up in the bedroom, we used the chests as seats.

At the opposite end of the house away from bedroom, there was the *bàthaich* – the byre. That's where the cow was housed. Yes, and the chickens, too. And strangely, you were not conscious of any smell down in the byre. Now, in the old days, we were very handicapped. There was no bathrooms or toilets, you know. You had to use your own discretion. Certain areas of the shore were often visited for moments of contemplation!

Getting a bath was also awkward. There was a big portable zinc bath and you'd take it up into the *cùlaist* [bedroom]. None of the interior doors had locks but the front door had a wooden lock which was not at all like the metal ones you'd buy in a shop. So you took your bath, preferably when there wasn't anybody in the house but yourself. You'd half-fill the bath with water drawn from the well. Of course, you had first of all heated it in a *prais* [iron pot], over the fire in the living-room. Sometimes it was rainwater. But before you stripped ready to wash yourself, you would lock the front door.

The thing that made life possible in rural Lewis was the fact that we could cut peat which provided us with heating for the home. There was no coal. We could have bought coal from Stornoway, but we couldn't afford to do that. I remember a man that used to be in the Merchant Navy when I was a little boy. Every time he would come home, he would give me sixpence. That was a lot to give to a little boy. When my mother died, it was my aunt that brought us up, you know. I never forgot that, so when I started earning, though I was not getting much of a wage, I would write a letter to my aunt and enclose a sixpence. She would get a loaf for that. At that time, a loaf was a luxury.

When I was a boy, *latha buain na mònach* [peat-cutting day] was a very special day. That was peat-cutting day when all the fuel required by the family was cut by a team. Twelve or fourteen men and women would work together and spend one whole day cutting enough peat to provide fuel to keep the home fire burning day (and, to an extent, at night) for a whole year. When the *sgiobadh* [team] was out in the moor to cut the peats, young lads like myself were on hand to make ourselves useful. When the housewife was ready, the boys were sent out on to the moor, each carrying two pebbles. As we went, we'd be clacking the pebbles together to make a noise. That was the signal for the *sgiobadh* to come home for their meals. As a reward, each of us would get a slice of bread and jam.

Now, when I grew up, I myself used to be in a *sgiobadh*. I would get up about six o'clock and then had breakfast. On that important day, we cut enough peat to keep the family fire going for a whole year. You'd have to be in the peat-bank about seven o'clock – blow high or low! There used to be six or seven men each, with a *tairsgear* [cutting-iron]. For each iron, there would be two persons working – one person up top cutting and the other down below, throwing spell about.

Now, we'd have a second breakfast later on. Eggs for first breakfast. Then, three hours later, a breakfast of porridge. That would be at nine o'clock or so. And then boiled potatoes and herring around half past twelve or one o'clock. And then we had tea about five o'clock. Now that was finishing time. Some people who had pressing domestic business to attend to, would refuse to come after five for another meal. They would go back home to their own houses. But those peat-cutters who were young and carefree would usually accept the invitation and come for a meal at the house for whom the peats were cut that day. They would be hungry, you see – hungry all the time. Yes, a day in the *sgiobadh* was a long weary day and probably more days to come after that until all the neighbours had their supply of peats ensured. Much of the croft work was a communal effort. Everyone mucked in together. Oh, they were all coming together, you know. If anybody in the village was behind the rest in planting or lifting the potatoes, somebody from each of the other families would go and help. They were that friendly, they were all coming together and there was a lot of laughter.

We never used a horse and plough on the croft, just spades. In my early days, families planted their own potatoes with the spade. Each family planted their own. Then when tractors came in and did away with a lot of the spadework, you needed a *sgiobadh* to keep up with the tractor because the driver with his tractor was paid by the hour. Of course, all that is gone now. Nobody plants a year's supply of potatoes – just a wee patch to get a few meals of 'earlies' at the beginning of the summer. Hardly anybody cuts peats, so we don't have the laughter of the *sgiobadh*. No, nor do we have the tiredness of ten-hour days!

When I was a lad, the men of Port nan Giùran and Port Mholair worked in fishing-boats – big boats which had seven-man crews. They used to cross the Minch up to thirty sea miles to get to sea lochs of the mainland. They did that because they needed mussels to bait their small-lines. Oh, yes, they sailed their boats all the way to Loch Broom – the Loch Mòr, as it was called. That's the loch that goes in to Ullapool. Yes, sometimes I heard them tell of their experiences there. I heard them saying that, when there was no wind, no sailing could be done. No sail, so it had to be oars only. The men had to row all the way from Port nan Giùran over to the other side. Thirty miles and that took a lot of rowing!

And there's a place up in the far end of Loch Broom called Leckmelm. That's where they were getting the mussels. Now, sometimes the fishermen who lived on the other side, over by Loch Broom, weren't very happy with the men of Lewis coming over there and taking the mussels which, they claimed, were theirs by right. That was just some of them who felt like that. On one occasion, my uncle was a crewman in one of the Port nan Giùran boats that went to Leckmelm for mussels. They would probably have arrived over there on a Friday or Saturday and decided to stay there till Monday to catch the spring tide. Well, they went to church on the Sabbath Day. When they went to the church in the morning, the local elders asked the visitors, 'Is there any member of your crew who be willing to pray during our service?'

My uncle replied, 'Indeed, there is. Donald MacLeod from Port nan Giùran does a fine prayer.'

Now Donald MacLeod, whom we called by the nickname 'My' knew nothing of this and, when his name was called in church to get up and pray, he was shocked. All eyes were on him and the elders kept on calling his name in church to get him to stand up to pray.

Poor My had his head bowed. He was so embarrassed and kept saying, 'Oh, no, but no, no! I can't!'

No doubt, poor My was delighted when the service was over. And when they were out of earshot of the elders, he probably gave my uncle a good talking-to. Sometimes the round trip over to the mainland took a few days. Of course, the wind, if it was favourable, would help a lot with the voyage. With plenty wind, they wouldn't take long coming across – perhaps six or seven hours. With a full sail, those big boats could travel very fast. From time to time, there were terrible accidents when a boat would founder with six or seven men in her crew. That all happened before my time. Yes, before the First World War. Right enough, but in my father's day there were some terrible drownings. There was one boat that sank with all hands, somewhere off Tiumpanhead within a mile from Port nan Giùran.

They were coming from Stornoway with a load of timber. It is thought that the boat capsized and she went down with all hands. They didn't get any of the bodies. The families of those lost suffered terribly. Those were hard times. Oh, they were working hard those people, yes.

I am very fortunate to have lived to modern times – to be living to see the modern times with all these improvements in people's living conditions and homes. When you start telling people about the deprivation of my young days, they laugh. They do, because they find what I say difficult to believe! But my impression is that the people of those olden times were happy. They were happier than people are today. Perhaps they were happy because there was no envy between them and there was a lot of friendship. Nobody had anything of any value to speak about. But they had one thing that was valuable – precious beyond words. They had faith in the Gospel of the Lord Jesus Christ.

I have been a member of the Church now for sixty-seven years – since I was a boy, really. Well I was converted, you see, when I was very young. The influence of the Gospel has always been strong in our family. When I was young, there were three [Protestant] churches – the Free Church and also the United Free Church. Over and above that, there was the Church of Scotland. And before my time, my granny used to tell us that some members of the three congregations weren't very friendly to each other. Before the United Free Church got a church [building] of their own, the congregation used to pray in the rocks down there on the shore and, if the weather was bad, they all came into Donald MacAulay's house.

Today, Lewis has many religious denominations – even in the Christian Church. Some theologians argue about this and that. Is there a Hell? Is there a Heaven, even? Well, I never considered whether or not there is Hell. To me, my awareness is of the existence of God. Since I was converted, I have known with absolute certainty that there is God. I know that for certain because of things that have happened in my own life. It wasn't anybody else who told me about God's influence on our lives. I have discovered God for myself. On the very first day I ever went to church at Garrabost, it happened. Well, I didn't know what was wrong with me. I couldn't stop crying. And then I came aware that I was a sinner and I told a friend, a lady who was much older than me, that my conscience was troubled.

'Oh, please,' I says, 'don't tell anybody about it. I'm not saved.'

She said, 'No, John, I won't tell anybody but you'll soon tell yourself what you must do.'

And she was right. I agreed to go with her to church but I was so shy! My brother William had been converted six months before that. Of course, he became a minister of the Gospel. Anyway, he took me to church with him in Sheshader and he said, 'When we arrive at the church in Sheshader, they'll be singing and the door will be open. We'll go in and nobody will take notice of us.'

The two of us entered the church together and, as soon as I sat down, I bowed my head and started to cry. When the minister stood up to preach, he said, 'I must tell you that I have abandoned the sermon I was going to give you tonight. But I've been given another service which has something to do with somebody who sits before me.' The verse in the Bible he took for his sermon was 'See, here is water; what doth hinder me to be baptized?' [Acts: 36]. And that sermon comforted me and my fear of Hell vanished. I knew that there is a Saviour and we do not have to fear anything if we recognise that fact that Jesus is our Saviour. But during the past sixty-seven years, it has not been plain sailing for me. Sometimes, I would be feeling very high up and sometimes very low in my spirits. I think God was letting me know that I continue to be a sinner. He wasn't punishing me for these sins and was keeping me from becoming complacent. There's a verse in the Acts of the Apostles, *Is èiginn dhàsan fàs ach dhomhsa bhi air mo lughda-chadh.* In English, that means, 'It's important that He grow but, first, that I have to be diminished.'

The teachings of the Gospel have been my guide ever since I was sixteen. I don't remember ever swearing or being drunken; but I was a heavy smoker and I stopped because I took smoking to be a sin, for it was a form of self-indulgence.

There's a lot in the Bible about murder and all this. You get a lot of them in the Old Testament. I've never committed any of these terrible things. But still I'm a sinner, for I am, human being, by nature frail and full of myself! Because we are not following the ways taught us by Jesus, all sorts of terrible things happen in our lives. We do not behave to each other as Jesus wanted us to. It is because of that that there are quarrels between families. It is also the reason that there are wars.

I fought in the Second World War and I have to tell you that I was not conscience-stricken for fighting against Hitler's Germany. At the beginning of the Second World War, I found myself in Portsmouth on board the sloop *Weston*, on which I was quartermaster. Word came through that Britain had declared war on Germany. I was told by the petty officer of the watch to go round the ship blowing a whistle and shouting, 'Hear there! Hear there! Britain has declared war on Germany!'

Oh, what a lot of noise among the boys that day, for none of them was looking forward to going to war! The *Weston* had just come into port to go through a refit but the navy decided that she should be readied immediately to put to sea. In my first week on the *Weston*, we received word that there was a ship in distress some distance from us. We made all speed towards the given position with everybody on the bridge scanning the horizon. After a time, we saw a dark hull with the sea breaking over it. 'Action Stations' was called and, soon, our guns were blazing at the shape that looked ominously like a U-boat. It transpired that the object was a ship which had capsized. In our haste to open fire, I had forgotten to insert my ear-plugs, with the result that my hearing was so badly affected by the thunder of the guns that I had to be sent to hospital. My fate could have been worse, for, after recovering, I was given nine months ashore, doing shore duty. There were about a dozen of us doing odd jobs in a naval dockyard, but when our recuperation was over, everybody was given a draft to go here, there and everywhere.

I was assigned to a modern minesweeper. We sailed from Portsmouth and travelled as far as Cape Town before we were allowed time ashore. The ship was being prepared for an assault on Madagascar, a large island which the Germans had managed to subjugate. Madagascar lies to the east of South Africa. The fleet being prepared for the assault included big powerful cruisers, destroyers and barges packed with troops. We were the first to be dispatched and our remit was to clear a channel for the fleet to sail through with its armour. We swept all the way in with the invasion barges in our wake. If we were to perish, that was not to be of great concern to the powers that be, but we succeeded in our task. We swept all the way until we were close to the shore. In fact we were very close in before we were overtaken by the barges. By that time we had reached shallow water where the Germans hadn't bothered to sow mines. That was just as well, for the enemy lookouts had not sighted us as we approached. We got right in on top of them and took them completely by surprise. So close in were we that, to fire their guns, they had to fire downwards – to get our range. When the barges landed and our troops went ashore, the battle flared so that the sky became red as every gun, big and small, thundered and roared. I remember that in those circumstances, I wished that I were in the company of someone I knew; but there didn't seem to be any such person. Yet, it wasn't long after that adventure that I got to know a Harris man – Willie MacLennan. He had been badly wounded during the Madagascar campaign and had to have a silver plate inserted in his cranium. Some time after the war, he served for a time as minister to a congregation in Inverness.

When we had cleared the mines, we found a place at which to anchor. By that time there was a large fleet of ships lying offshore. The enemy was still roaring at us with their guns. Two of their gun batteries were on the crest of a hill that became known to us as 'Edinburgh Castle'. Two of our cruisers appeared one day and came in so that those batteries were within range of their big guns. A few salvoes from them was followed by silence from Edinburgh Castle!

I was for a long time at the wheel, you know, as we were sweeping. The captain told the first lieutenant, 'Send down for one of the hands and tell Mac he has to stand there all day.' The captain seemed to have a lot of faith in my ability to steer the ship while we were sweeping. After a long time, they stopped sweeping. They had decided to take in the sweeps so that they were fully trimmed. It was then I was allowed to go down for a rest. As I was on my way down the companionway, I met the stoker coming up from the engine room. He was just beginning to talk to me when, all of a sudden, a mine burst in the sweep. You can't imagine the destruction it caused. I saw that the stoker who had been talking to me was knocked to the floor. He had been hit by shrapnel and there was an awful split in the chest. Though I was standing beside him, I escaped without a scratch. We lost seventeen of the crew to that one explosion. Our first lieutenant, Jim MacLachlan from Glasgow, was one of them – a real gentleman. His arms were crossed like this and they were broken; also a big wound in his back. The male nurse on board was known as Sick Bay Terry. He gave us rolls of cottons and ice, you know, to help us look after the wounded until they got to the hospital ship. Jim MacLachlan didn't become unconscious. Every time I came back to him, I saw that he was still with us. As I said, he was a gentleman, very appreciative and brave. He was bleeding terribly. Each time I put a new roll of cotton on his back, he would say, 'Oh, thank you, Mac, thank you Mac.' He was taken on board the hospital ship still conscious, but we knew that he couldn't survive. He was dead by nightfall. It brings the tears. After Madagascar, we were directed to sail north along the coast of Africa, then through the Suez Canal and into the Mediterranean. There were, of course, other minesweepers doing the same work, sweeping along the coast of North Africa clearing mines as the Eighth Army advanced against Rommel. Many a fine lad on both sides lost his life in the deserts of Egypt and Libya. Many also on the ships which were in support of the army carrying all sorts of supplies such as ammunition, artillery, food, fuel, tanks and troops. Danger was present at all times. Six or seven of our minesweepers were constantly there clearing the way for other vessels. We were often under fire and only by the will of God were we spared as some of the German shells exploded very close to us. When Montgomery's armies defeated the Germans in Egypt and then in Libya, we were sent to sweep mines along the south coast of Sicily. Then, on D-Day, we got our final shelling from the Germans when we were in against the coast of Normandy. Again, our ship escaped unscathed.

But of all the awful things I witnessed during the awful years of the war, the one that haunts me belongs to an experience I had while I was ashore at Portsmouth. It was early in the war and I had been ill in hospital. After I was released from hospital, I was stationed in barracks to await my being given a berth on a ship. The Germans started bombing the port during the day and we were all called out of the barracks to help the police and firemen. During one of the raids, a school received a direct hit. I'll never forget the sight of dead children. We were helping with the task of taking the children out of the demolished building – all of them limp and lifeless. You know, it would break your heart. I don't know how many were killed. A lot. I don't think any of the children survived the bomb. I don't think so. That was the thing that most touched me. War is awful. As I said, mankind hasn't yet heard the gentle civilising words of Jesus our Saviour.

Iain Crichton

In 1934, I was born in Pabail Iarach [Lower Bayble], a village on a peninsula called the Rubha, on the east coast of Lewis. Before the Second World War, Pabail Iarach was a crofting village but now the crofting lifestyle is pretty well disappeared from the island. Anyway, Pabail Iarach is where my folks came from, but I didn't really get to know the place very well because I had a long period in hospital as a youngster. When I was three or four years of age, my parents decided to move to Marybank on the outskirts of Stornoway. That was in November 1938, just a year before the outbreak of the Second World War.

As I said, when I was a very young lad I became seriously ill. The doctors and the surgeon in the hospital told my parents that I had inflammation of the spinal cord – something like that. It may have been caused by an injury that I got when I was a toddler and fell on a stone floor. In those days, at the time of the Second World War, food was rationed and all my relations brought food to the hospital to keep me in good trim. Of course, on the crofts we were better off than the folk in the cities. There were sheep and hens and as much fish as could be landed by the old men – the only men who weren't fighting the war. Anyway, I was encased in plaster from my neck down to my toes. At that time, the number of medical staff in the Lewis Hospital was quite limited – again, because of the war. My treatment, perhaps, was not up to the standard that an invalid child would receive today. But, to cut a long story short, so far as my health was concerned, I didn't start getting myself properly sorted out until I got out of hospital in 1945 or '46. The hospital staff did their best for me but it was when I got out into the world outside that I began to make real progress.

As you know, I am passionately fond of Scottish dance music, which I first heard on radio, through headphones in the hospital. I just took a great, great liking to it. I thought to myself that if I ever got well I would learn how to make music like that. After that, my interest in accordion music developed at a gallop! I was fortunate in becoming friendly with a very talented gentleman – a fellow by the name of Alex Elliot, an Englishman who, at that time, was in charge of the local ENSA [Entertainment National Service Association]. During the Second World War, ENSA was an official organisation that entertained the men and women serving in the forces. At the time, there were many hundreds, perhaps thousands, of Royal Air Force, Army and Navy men and women stationed here on the island. Any road, Alex Elliot used to take time off from his official duties to come up to the hospital and go round the wards with his piano-accordion. And what a great way that was to cheer up the patients. Until then, I had only seen melodeons and other wee boxes like that. When I saw the instrument that Alex was playing, it looked to me like a piano standing on end! It was so big! Of course, I was in plaster from my neck down to my toes. But whenever Alex Elliot came by the bed and played, my toes began to twitch! I loved to hear the music of the accordion and I suppose my enjoyment of it showed in my face. Alex used to say, 'Well, lad, I can see that you're very interested in music.'

This day, he came in and said, 'I've got an old piano-accordion which is needing one or two things done to it. Perhaps you would have a go at learning to play it when I get it mended.'

Well now, although he said he was going to let me have a go with it, I knew that playing the instrument was going to be a bit of a problem because of the way my body was encased in plaster. Mind you, I already had an inkling of how the notes were set out on the keyboard, for I'd seen a piano being played. But I immediately set about sorting out a keyboard on paper trying to visualise how the notes would be arranged when I got my 'shot' of Alex Elliot's accordion. About a fortnight later, Alex brought his old accordion in for me. It was a wonderful thing to do and it did me the world of good. Alex said, 'There you are now! If you can learn to play a tune on that in a fortnight, you can keep it.'

It was just what I wanted to hear! Within a very short time, I learned how to play every tune I knew. And the way I managed to play was this. I used to throw a towel to the boy in the next bed so that the two of us pulled the beds together. The two of us would then stand the box up on my plaster, which, of course, was rock-hard. I then got the other boy to work the bellows and, as he did so, I would run my fingers up and down the keyboard. There was a piano on the ward at one time and the accordion had the same keyboard, two blacks, then three blacks, two blacks, three blacks and so on. I'd worked that out myself. But I just knew, instinctively, you know, the tunes I knew. Well, the next note that follows goes up a couple of notes or one note, or it goes down two notes, you know. The keys were on the right hand side. Moving the fingers up and down along the keys was something that seemed to have already been built into me. It was part of my genes, you might say!

When I started getting better, there wasn't even a physiotherapist in the hospital. There was a nice woman called Miss Lochhead, who was a gym teacher at the school, and she used to turn up to give me exercises. Encouraged by her, I began to make a few steps. When I got up, I'd have a go at walking, taking just a few steps. It seems that I began to get up and take a few on my own when Miss Lockhart wasn't there! The nurses knew fine that I used to sneak out of bed and go from patient to patient hanging on to the beds. I remember one day the surgeon was late in coming round the wards. He used to come round in the mornings. Oh, I wouldn't dare get up if I knew the surgeon was on the ward. Anyway, I thought that day that he wasn't coming at all, so at about three o'clock I was standing at the end of my bed, playing the mouth organ that had been sent to me as a present from Canada. The door suddenly burst open and there was the surgeon! He didn't look at anyone else in the ward but just came straight up to where I was. Och, as best I could, I got into bed like a shot! I can tell you that the man was not pleased! He sent for my mother. Of course, though he wasn't showing it, he was delighted by my progress. On the other hand, you know, he was annoyed that I was messing around. He wanted to give me the impression that he was wild.

He had a chat with my mother. 'I was delighted,' he says, 'when I saw Iain standing up today. But I want you to tell him that he's not to get up again until he's got permission. I don't want all the good that's been done to be undone.'

Well, I got better and I got out of hospital in 1946, and when I got home it was an uphill struggle to get fit. I could only hirple around with support. Hour after hour I persevered and, in the end, I became very fit. In the end, I could play football and play with the other boys for three hours non-stop. I could even outrun some of my co-ages in the village.

After the war, my father came home and we moved out here to Marybank. We then owned this croft which had about two and a quarter acres. My father bought a cow and after that we had plenty of milk and all the by-products of the milk – butter, crowdie and cream. When we started cultivating the croft, I thoroughly enjoyed planting oats and potatoes and cutting the grass and making haystacks and cornstacks. My mind was focussed on keeping fit. I even sent for a 'Charles Atlas' course and followed the instructions – for a wee while, anyway! I was absolutely determined that I was going to be able to do what all my mates were able to do.

It's hard for me to believe today, but I didn't start school until I went to the Laxdale Junior Secondary School when I was thirteen years old. No wonder my [formal] education is so limited!

In those days, I went on holiday to my native village, Pabail Iarach, a number of times and I joined in with whatever activity was going on down there in the community. I loved going out on the boat with my uncle and cousins. I enjoyed being with all the people who were related to me or were our close neighbours at one time. At that time, housing in Pabail was not of a high standard. There were many black-houses. I had an aunt and an uncle living in a black-house in Pabail Uarach [Upper Bayble] and I remember spending a week or two with them – most enjoyable and most comfortable. The walls of the black-house were built of stone and, of course, the roof was thatched. They kept cattle in one end of the house and lived in the other end. However, their home wasn't quite like the traditional black-house. The reason for that was that it didn't have the fire in the middle of the living-room with the smoke billowing all over the house. In fact, the house had a gable so that the smoke escaped up the chimney. Since the Second World War, crofters have been helped by grants and loans given by the Board of Agriculture or by the local council, so they are able to afford to build much better homes. Nowadays, there isn't one black-house left in the whole peninsula of Point. Some of the houses in Pabail are very posh!

In October 1951, I started working in the office of a local contractor, an electrical contractor. I ended up in charge of the office, doing all the taxes and different things that are involved in office work. I was employed with the same gentleman for about thirty years. My being able to converse in Gaelic was very much to my advantage during the years I worked in an office. When people from the country came in, wanting a job done, they preferred me to discuss with them in Gaelic what was involved. Unfortunately, that period in my life came to an end quite unexpectedly. The contractor I was with ceased trading and I was made redundant. Anyway, by that time, my sight began to deteriorate.

Of course, I am now sixty-four years old and I have been a musician for a lot of years. While I was busy doing office work during the day, I was also having a very hectic life in the evening. In fact, I was making more money playing my accordion than ever I was with my day work. An example then – in 1951, electricians were pretty well paid, getting £6 10s a week. As a clerk, I was getting only £2 or slightly more than that. But early on, when I was about nineteen, I was invited to join the Stornoway Dance Band and I was delighted to jump at the chance! We used to play not less than three nights a week – sometimes even five nights a week. At the time, the Stornoway Dance Band was the only dance band in town, so we played at every function that was being held in the town and elsewhere! My mother was fed up washing and ironing white shirts to keep me going! But, och no, it was a great experience and through playing I met lots of people. We played at the YMCA every Wednesday night. The recognised fee for that was 18s a night for each member of the band. We played either at the Town Hall or at the Drill Hall every Friday and at the Town Hall every Saturday. And you'd get not less than a pound there, maybe £1 10s. In addition to that, you'd be playing at the odd wedding. In those days, the Crown Inn was the place for the weddings. It was a wonderful time in my life. Over the years, I became associated with Scottish dance music and pipe music and with the musical tradition of the Highlands and Islands. I liked to compose tunes even in the old days when I was with the Stornoway Dance Band. I'd teach my latest new tune to the boys in the band and we'd play it, say, for a Canadian barn dance or a reel or a two-three dance. At that time, I neither read nor wrote music. In fact, I still don't bother much with 'the dots'! The result was that once the Stornoway Dance Band played one of my tunes, it just disappeared into thin air and was lost for all time. That was because I hadn't bothered to get somebody to write it down for me. Of course, in later years, all that changed!

One of the first tunes that I can remember being written down was a four-part, two-four march called the 'Queen's Welcome to Tarbert'. You might ask me why I would give a good Gaelic tune a title like that! Well, the reason was this. The queen was visiting here in the Western Isles at the time and the folk around Stornoway became very excited because the royal yacht was anchored out in the bay there. However, it didn't hang around SY* for very long. It went round in the evening to Tarbert, Harris, and anchored there. Whether by accident or design, our band had been invited to go that very night to play at a dance in the Tarbert Hotel. In those days, we didn't often play outside of the town of Stornoway. Anyway, Mr Cameron who owned the Tarbert Hotel was really pleased that we had accepted his invitation and he treated us very well. And so he should! The road to Tarbert over the Clisham† was a pretty treacherous one and we were dog-tired by the time we got home in the wee small hours! Anyway, the function turned out to be a bit of a damp squib – for the band, at least.

---

* Referring to registration initials painted on boats based at Stornoway.
† Situated close to the border between Lewis and Harris, the Clisham is the highest hill in the Outer Hebrides.

We played and played but none of the royal party appeared at the dance, after all. They might have paid a visit to the hotel but they certainly didn't come to listen or to dance to the music of the Stornoway Dance Band!

While I was with that band, we only had the one microphone between five of us! When it came the time to be playing for a Gay Gordons or a Strip the Willow, the microphone was usually pushed up to me so that my playing would be dominant. The leader of the band was the pianist – a fellow called George MacAulay. 'Well,' George would say, 'the next dance is going to be a Gay Gordons. What are you going to give us tonight, Iain?'

I remember one night that I'd just been learning a pipe tune called 'Pipe Major Willie Gray's Farewell to the City of Glasgow's Police Pipe Band'. When I told George the name of the tune I was going to play, he scratched his head and said, 'Look here, son, it's a tune we're wanting, not a bulletin!'

In those days, the dances we played were not all traditional. No, they were not! Some were very modern – the very latest danced in the smart places in the cities of the south. The dances in the town were practically all modern – quicksteps, slow foxtrots, modern waltzes, tangos, sambas, all that sort of thing. Today, you might call those traditional dances, but when I was a young man, they were regarded as the dances of the young generation.

A few years after I joined the Stornoway Dance Band, I formed my own – the Lewis Ceilidh Band. I did that mainly because I wanted to play pipe music: I wanted to play Gaelic songs and stuff like that, that we weren't doing in the Stornoway Dance Band.

We seldom played out in the country villages. Some of the dances out there were pretty rowdy. I know, for example, that some dances in Aird* were pretty rough. Aye. The country dances outside the town were a wee bit rowdy at times. A bit too much drink, you know!

Now, I'll tell you how I met Ishbel, the young lady who became my wife. And who is sixteen years younger than I am. I admire her so much and love her. I do, but she doesn't like my saying so, I think. Let me tell you that the interview I did last Saturday on radio was in Gaelic. After the broadcast, somebody phoned me up to say, 'Most of that programme was taken up with you praising Ishbel.'

Now, I knew her father many years before I met Ishbel. Some time after

* At the extremity of the Rubha.

I got out of hospital, I was told that there was a gentleman in the village called Torquil MacKenzie and that he was very knowledgeable about pipe tunes and Scottish traditional music. I wanted to meet him and used to spend a lot of time watching out for him as he passed along the road leading to Peighinn na Dròbh where he lived. Our house was quite near the corner that he had to pass on his way home. I used to watch from the window to see him coming up along the road and often made a point of being there at the corner, just to meet him.

When he got to know me, he was quite happy to spend time with me. We would spend maybe an hour sitting at the corner and him going through pipe tunes while I tried to learn them. We just sat there together whistling, while I tried to pick up the pattern of the tune. He was a very patient man. Very enthusiastic, though. I learned the tunes that way, much more accurately than the people who are playing them today. They learn them off sheet music but they put their own twists and turns into them. In my day, we kept strictly to what was in the pipe notation. So it was quite wonderful. Unfortunately, Torquil MacKenzie was not a well man and died one Sunday night after an attack of asthma. What a loss! He was only forty-four years old: a tragedy for his wife and family. News of his passing made me very sad indeed.

Torquil's daughters, Ishbel and her twin sister, Kathleen, were born at Peighinn na Dròbh. It was years and years later, after her father died, that I got to know Ishbel. She was then about, I don't know, twelve or thirteen. In those days, I used to help out a friend of mine who had a taxi. Well, I sometimes drove the taxi for him and, occasionally, did runs up to the MacKenzies' house. That's really how I first met Ishbel. I remember seeing her when she was only in her gym frock! Even then, she loved Scottish dance music, and once or twice I took 'the box' up to the MacKenzies' house and I played a few tunes to get the toes tapping. We seemed to get on all right then but, of course, it was a number of years before we really got together. We got married in 1971. And we're still together coming up to twenty-seven years later. I must have been doing something right!

Ishbel and I work well together on my music. Not very long ago, our sixth book of original tunes was nearly ready to go in to the printers when I had a bit of a mishap. I had promised that the music would go in to the printers on such-and-such a day but, instead, ended up getting a wee heart attack. So I said to Ishbel, 'What's going to happen to the book we were going to deliver to the printers?'

No problem! While I was in hospital, Ishbel spent her time sitting at the bedside – but she wasn't there just to chat! No, she spent hours with me working on my music. For a number of years now, she has been writing out all the music! You might well ask where, without attending any college, did Ishbel learn to do the notation? The answer is that she is completely self-taught.

I published Books 1 and 2 in the 'Puirt à Eilean Leòdhais' [*Tunes from the Isle of Lewis*] series, in which all tunes were written out by somebody else. And then I published a book called *Tunes for the Piper*, which consists of forty-seven original tunes. One night, shortly after that book was published, Ishbel told me while we were having our tea that she had redone all the handwritten manuscripts in the book, because some of them were atrocious scrawls. I was flabbergasted! She had written them all out in her own inimitable hand. Then, she announced, 'I would like now to write out all your tunes from scratch.'

You'd be right in thinking that Ishbel is very clever but also very industrious. She is as passionate about music as I am. Ever since she started the work, she's written out hundreds of my tunes. She's got an amazing grasp of them all now. When I compose a tune, I play it with the box and record it on audiotape. Ishbel then listens to the recording, learns to play it on her own wee keyboard and, from there, writes it on to the manuscript. When she's finished a batch, she sends photocopies of her manuscripts to John Renton, a band leader in Inveraray, for checking. We call him 'Our Vet from Inveraray'! The musicians on the mainland are absolutely amazed that Ishbel is able to do what she's doing. They much prefer her handwritten manuscripts to the stuff that's done on computer. And that is a very big compliment. She is a very special person – very gifted.

That book I mentioned, *Tunes for the Piper*, was probably the one that went to most places worldwide. It went out to shops in Canada, America, Australia, New Zealand and even to South Africa. It has become so well received that I've had correspondence from all over the world.

Obviously, we don't know all the places where my compositions are being played. But I hear Robbie Shepherd regularly playing my tunes on the BBC radio. My last book has just come out. It was reviewed in the *Stornoway Gazette* last Thursday and I just got copies of it on Friday. You know, a funny thing happened that day: I was signing a couple of copies of the book and listening to a BBC programme called *Mr Anderson's Fine Tunes*. As I was listening to a particular tune played by a folk group, I found myself singing along with it. What a lovely little melody, I thought to myself! After a wee while, I realised it's one of my own tunes. They mentioned the name of the tune but didn't mention the name of the composer! I was a wee bit annoyed at the time.

Of course, once your material goes out into the public domain, anyone can use it. I'm very happy to hear that my music is being played in different places. I'm a member of the Performing Rights Society and a member of the Mechanical Copyright Protection Society, so I get the royalties for my music through them.

Somebody was saying to me recently that there must be only a limited number of tunes left in my head. Well, all I can tell you is that, so far, the well has not run dry! But, it's a fact that when I was unwell recently I didn't do any composing, but, och, when I feel well, I could see me composing a tune every day, depending on how the spirit moves me. According to the people who are playing my tunes, I never repeat myself, and that is something I'm very thankful for.

I find the morning is the best part of my day. Quite often, I work steadily from five till about half-past seven in the morning, before the Gaelic programmes start on the radio or the phone starts ringing! I like the peace and quiet of the very early morning.

My impression is that the youth of the island have less interest in traditional music. Their interest is going down very rapidly. But on the other hand, there are one or two really good musicians – youngsters who are pipers. One or two are under the age of eighteen. There's a young fiddler – I'm looking at his photograph over there – he's fourteen, Alastair White, and he's absolutely brilliant. Now individuals like him have been getting tuition from an early age. Alastair actually started getting tuition on the fiddle when he was only six and a half. He and the other youngsters can read the dots on the paper and interpret the music no bother – just as easily as if they were reading the newspaper! Alistair has been tending, maybe, to go towards the folk scene with the fiddle music, but he'll be brought back on to an even keel very shortly because he's going to Pipe Major Ian Murdo Morrison for tuition on the chanter. He will eventually go on to the pipes as well. So that'll keep him right. I myself don't do any tuition. I can't because I haven't got enough knowledge of the written music. However, I am very happy to listen to the youngsters playing and advise them on their phrasing and tempos and so forth.

Healthwise I'm not very fit. In fact, I'm not fit at all! I was thinking, the other day, about the changes that have taken place in our island during my lifetime – how the way of life and the attitudes of the young have changed. Sunday, for example, is becoming just like any other day of the week! Some restaurants are open; the pubs are open. Well, I was most thankful when I was in the Stornoway Dance Band and the Lewis Ceilidh Band that there was Sunday – a day of rest. Because, although I'm not a religiously inclined person or anything like that, Sunday was a day when the people never went into the pubs and the shops were all shut. No ferries or planes. Now there's talk of all that changing. And it probably will change because that's the way the up-and-coming generations want it to be. They want every facility on a Sunday that they have during the week. Well, I hope it doesn't come to that in my time!

In my youth, Gaelic was the native language of most of the people of Lewis. Even though I was in hospital for over five years I didn't lose it. During those long years in hospital Mother spoke nothing to me but Gaelic during the visiting hours. And my uncles and aunties who came in, they spoke nothing to me but Gaelic, with the result that I retained the language. After I got out of hospital, I was brought up among the kids out here on the outskirts of town where they talked nothing but English. But somehow I still kept my mother tongue.

As people began to turn their back on the old crofting way of life, they began to lose interest in their own language and traditions. But today, people's attitudes are changing again. A lot of Lewis folk who have only English wish to learn Gaelic, you know. They realise that they missed out on a lot in not having the language of their forebears. My music has definitely come out of the Gaelic tradition. In fact, I was phoning a friend of mine on the mainland the other day, a piping adjudicator, Finlay Macrae, who lives in Dingwall. Finlay is now over seventy and, when he was aged ten, he started learning the bagpipes by practising on the chanter. He's got a great liking for my tunes. When he hears one of my new tunes, he phones up to say, 'That tune is full of the Lewis peat, Iain!'

Early on, I decided that if I ever did publish my tunes, I'd dedicate each one to one of my friends. And so my tunes are almost all for people I know. I mean, I don't believe in composing pieces inspired by themes from nature – for moving clouds, for wild seas or trees or hills or whatever! I decided also that, in my books, I would have a little story along with every tune – a wee biographical note about the person to whom I have dedicated the work. I feel that it adds something to the work I am doing. And that has taken a big trick with the folk who play my tunes.

Actually the one that I composed last week is an exception. It's going to be called 'The North Tolsta Memorial Cairn', which commemorates the war dead of the village of North Tolsta up to the end of the Second World War. Not a great deal has been said about this yet. I think they're playing it very low-key, but I've seen illustrations of the cairn. The land round about it has been landscaped, and close by there's a place, a car park, for about a dozen cars. It will be officially unveiled either the end of this month or in July. I'm delighted that I have been asked to make that little contribution to the occasion.

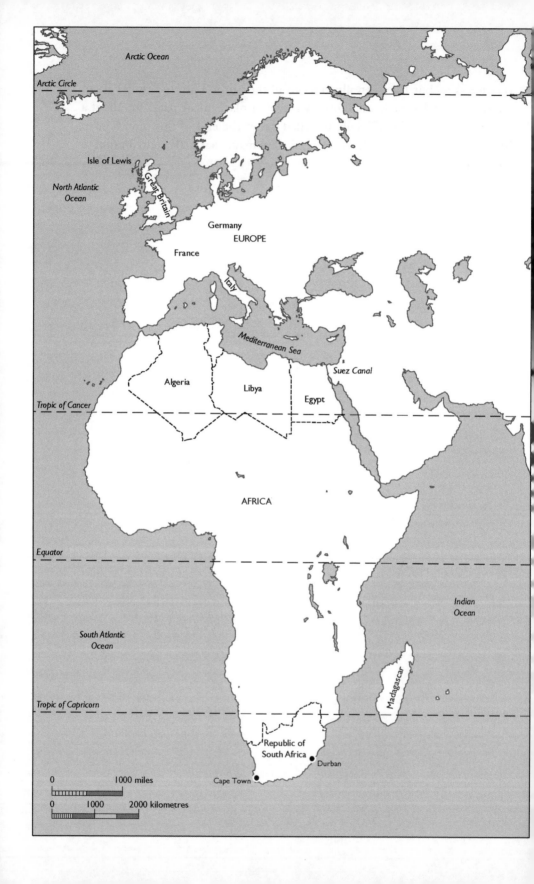

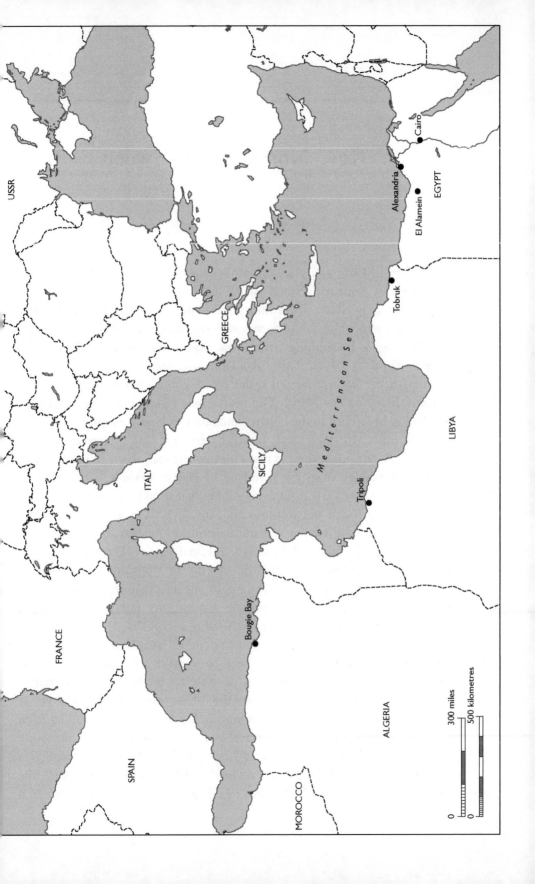

Rev. Norman MacSween

1920–

I was born in 1920, at a place called the Lagan Domhainn [Deep Dell] on the island of Scalpay, a small island lying off the east coast of Harris. Scalpay is only about three miles long and half that in width. The community into which I was born was lively and comparatively prosperous and, in spite of its seeming remoteness, was seasonally in touch with the outside world by virtue of the island's fishing industry.

At birth, my feet were seriously deformed. Unfortunately, we didn't have a doctor living on our island. The nearest was resident at Tarbert, Harris, and had to be fetched to the Lagan Domhainn by boat, a round trip of more than six miles. In those days, travelling by boat was preferred to going overland. At one point, there is just a narrow channel, about 200 yards wide, separating Scalpay from the mainland of Harris. Once you crossed that channel, there was a track, four miles long, that would take you to Tarbert. The track was rough and tortuous and, for anybody who wanted to see a doctor urgently, the journey was quite daunting. Anyway, my father chose to visit Tarbert by boat and the doctor did finally arrive. Having considered my condition, he concluded that he was not in a position to help as the deformity required surgery. As you might imagine, that prognosis was very upsetting to my parents. Fortunately for me, my father was a strong, determined and religious man and refused to accept that I was destined to lead my life as a cripple. My aunt and other friends in Glasgow were confident that, if I were living near to a major city hospital, a good orthopaedic surgeon would make it possible for me to walk as normal.

Today, we tend to forget that in the 1920s travel between the Outer Hebrides and the Lowlands was so long and wearisome. After sailing from Scalpay to Stornoway, we had to travel by a small steamer across the stormy waters of the Minch to the Kyle of Lochalsh. From there, the passengers travelled by train to Glasgow, a long haul that took many hours. In all, the journey from the Lagan Domhainn to Glasgow took more than one and a half days.

I thank God for giving my father the courage to set off with me, at the age of eighteen months, to seek help at the Victoria Infirmary in Glasgow. My father's faith and perseverance were rewarded. By his God-given skills, an orthopaedic surgeon at the Victoria carried out a procedure that completely altered the shape of my feet, which, for months thereafter, were encased in plaster of Paris. That surgical operation enabled me to grow up as physically active as any of my contemporaries and, by the grace of God, I have remained fit and robust throughout my life.

I clearly remember my first day at school. I was six years old. My older brother took me by the hand and, as we entered the school playground, the other boys came round, examining me and discussing my clothes and haircut as if I were an alien from some distant planet! Perhaps I was a wee bit timid at first, for I remember being overawed by the sight of all those children running about during the interval and swirling about in the playground like a flock of birds. Of course, it didn't take me long to get used to the experience and to join in the fun! At that time, there were 140 pupils on the school roll of Scalpay.

Gaelic was the native language of all the islanders. There were five teachers but they weren't all Gaelic-speaking. Some of them, for example the cookery and the singing teachers, just visited once or twice a week. We were allowed to speak Gaelic within the playground, but I think the schoolmaster would have preferred us to speak in English. Still, none of the staff actively discouraged us or punished us for speaking our native language. In the classroom, all teaching was in English. Of course, that is what the school curriculum demanded but we did have one, perhaps two, half-hour periods a week during which we were taught through the medium of Gaelic. We thoroughly enjoyed the experience of speaking our native language in the classroom. Apart from those short periods at school, our ability to read was further enhanced at Sunday school, where only Gaelic was spoken.

At that time, the population was around 700. Most islanders worked at the fishing and, in fact, I would say that there was full employment throughout the 1920s. My father and his brother managed to save some money and decided to build what we now know as a *taigh-geal* [white-house], a house made of dressed stone and cement with gables, and slates on the roof. They built it together and our two families shared its accommodation. It was the first *taigh-geal* built on the island. My uncle's family occupied one end and we the other. Each family had two bedrooms and a kitchen-cum-sitting-room. So far as I can remember, there was still quite a number of black-houses in Scalpay – that is, thatched houses which had the fire plumb in the middle of the living-room. Although they were black-houses, many of them had stone walls which were bound with cement.

As boys, we always celebrated *Oidhche Challinn* [the Old New Year] on 12 January. We looked forward to that particular evening for it was a high-spirited event that lightened the long hours of darkness. As the great day approached, all the boys rehearsed a special rant called *Duan na Callainn* [Hogmanay Rant], most of the words of which I have long since forgotten. It was a rant that came down to us through the ages and was known to successive generations throughout the Highlands and Islands. As we progressed through the village, we chanted the *Duan* at each house we came to. Having listened to '*Ho-ro bhi-o, na slatan, na slatan*' and so on, each family in turn welcomed us into their living-room. I suppose that originally, the purpose of such a visit was to wish the entire community health and happiness for the year ahead – to bless them, in a sense. However, as boys, we were more interested in the excitement of going through the procedure and getting some little present from each household. As the occasion demanded, every door opened to us and each household presented us with perhaps some baking or confection or, if they had money to spare, they would give us a coin or two. Our haul of presents wasn't really worth a lot of money but it seemed a lot to us. Having visited all the houses, we would congregate in one house and enjoy a small feast there.

Both the boys and girls also celebrated *Oidhche Shamhna* [Hallowe'en]. We did the usual party games such as dipping for apples. There was the pail of water with apples floating in it, and you were blindfolded. And if you touched the pail with any part of your body but your face – perhaps, put your hand in the water – you were in for some forfeit or penalty. You could be sure that there were some awkward moments in store for you if you transgressed the rules!

Scalpay was an excellent environment in which to grow up and my childhood was a happy one, full of fun and laughter. I have very happy memories of the fine people who supported me throughout my childhood. One of my most vivid recollections of my early years is my going out in my father's boat when I was about seven years old. I still remember the pleasure and the wonderment of being far out to sea. We caught seven crans of herring – seven crans that day [200 kg approx]! That's twenty-eight big baskets of herring. You can just imagine the satisfaction of arriving home with all those beautiful 'silver darlings' in the boat! My love of the sea probably began with the excitement of that fishing trip and that love has endured to this day. Throughout my adolescence, I felt that I couldn't wait to become a grown-up and become a fully fledged fisherman!

Fishing helped the community a great deal. The herring was plentiful and there were five curing stations on the island – quite an industrious little community. The barrels of salted herring or cured white fish were exported to Russia and other countries on the Continent, particularly those around the Baltic. From 1920 to 1930, the herring was very plentiful in the Minches, but from about 1930 to 1940, the fishing was very poor. Consequently, the 1930s were lean years for the fishermen and their families. For some unknown reason, after 1940 the fishing improved and so did the earnings of our families.

We were never short of food. Our breakfast was just the usual – porridge and milk, then tea, bread and butter. For dinner, we ate potatoes and herring; salt herring every day except Sunday, when we had meat and dessert. We salted herring in summer to have during winter and the early months of spring. We drank tea at most meals and we also had plenty of milk for most of the year. We ate *aran coirc* [oat bread] and scones and big bannocks of oat bread as well as of flour. The island's output of cereals was far less than the demand so that, in my time at least, we had to buy the oatmeal and flour from the shops. I understand that the shops received a supply of meal every month so that there was plenty on the island throughout the whole year.

My mother kept hens, so we had eggs galore. We also had one or two cows for their milk, cream, butter and crowdie. People whose cows were in milk shared the milk with their neighbours, and families which had poultry were also generous with their eggs. Whenever fish was brought into our home or, indeed, into any of the homes, it was shared out to those who didn't have fishermen in their households. The widows and everyone else who did not have a breadwinner were remembered and were given a share of the fish. There were large families who had to struggle sometimes but, as I said, the people who had food were happy to share with those who were in need of it. The grannies and grandfathers helped their sons and daughters and their grandchildren. There was always a good sense of kindness and neighbourliness. Sharing what they had was something that crofters every-where seemed to have in common.

My father was both a crofter and a fisherman. So, while he worked the land, his main income came from the fishing. Along with the other Scalpay men, he used to go to the East Coast for the summer season working at the herring. Usually, but not always, a crew of four or five men owned a boat and shared the profits equally at the end of the season. If the boat happened to be owned and skippered by one person and there were five men in the crew, the total earnings would be divided into six shares – the owner getting two shares. There came a time when my father and my uncle and three or four neighbours bought a boat, sharing the cost equally between them. That was a big event in our lives – very exciting for me as a lad. The boat was only about thirty feet long but to me it was really huge! After some time, they bought a larger boat – a 35-foot Zulu – and they installed an engine in her. The fishing-boats worked to the north of the island in summer. In winter, they moved round the south of Scalpay to the South Minch.

As I said, there were curing-stations on the island – buildings in which herring was gutted and salted in barrels. When I was a boy, curing herring for export was a very important industry. Sometimes, if the price for herring was better in Stornoway, the fishermen coming back from the fishing-grounds would decide not to discharge their catch at Scalpay but sail north to Stornoway to get the advantage of the better price. More often than not, the Scalpay boats came into the island's own curing-stations. It wasn't only the Scalpay boats that came! I have seen the harbour just packed full of boats from the East Coast – in fact, from all over Scotland. Those were all boats that had been fishing in the Minch. One of the curing-stations on the island belonged to Duncan McIver of Stornoway. Another belonged to a Mr Stewart. Before my time, Kenneth Campbell, a local man, owned another. He was the only shopkeeper in Scalpay. There was yet another one owned by a Mr MacRae from Kyle of Lochalsh.

There were two fishing seasons at Scalpay. That was something that developed over time to exploit the huge shoals of herring which came into the local lochs twice yearly – in summer, and then in winter.

Towards the end of the summer season, the 'Klondykers' would arrive. Those were big cargo ships that came all the way from Germany to do business with the owners of the curing-stations. They anchored in Loch Seaforth and other lochs nearby and bought the hundreds of barrels of salt herring which had been cured on the island. It was wonderful to see seamen from faraway Germany going about their business. After a day or two, the yards of the curing-stations were gradually emptied of barrels, which were destined to be sold on in countries in northern Europe. Of course, the Klondykers' purchase of the herring meant that everybody on Scalpay benefitted. At the height of the season, dozens of people were employed in the curing-stations. They were mostly young women, expert at gutting the herring and laying them neatly in the barrel, layer after layer, with the salt applied between each layer. Most of the able-bodied women on Scalpay found employment there but other women came to our island from all over – but mostly from the Harris mainland. They worked in crews of three – very well organised as gutters and packers.

When I grew up and became a fisherman, I was conscious of the existence of the huge world beyond our own shores. Our boat would fish out at sea, then return to the island, where I usually met only people we knew from the neighbourhood. Certainly, we occasionally travelled to Stornoway but really there wasn't much contact between us and the young folk living there. I must say that, although we were an insular community, the people were all outgoing by nature. We enjoyed meeting people from other places, especially at Communion time when there was an opportunity of meeting people from all over Harris and from Lewis too.

My father was in the Royal Naval Reserve in Stornoway. He sometimes walked all the way from Scalpay to Stornoway, a journey of between thirty and forty miles I'm sure. Because of his being in the RNR, he knew many people in Lewis. And, of course, being fisherfolk, the Scalpay folk were always meeting people from all over Scotland and sometimes from much further afield.

One of the disadvantages of living on a small island is that the young have not a great deal of contact with the outside world and very little opportunities for socialising. Consequently, there weren't many opportunities for boys and girls to meet their co-ages from other parts of the country. There were, of course, the normal romances and marriages within the island community, but most young men and girls born on Scalpay took wives or husbands from the mainland of Harris. I remember one or two marrying spouses from Lewis, but only a few.

When a couple publicly proclaimed their intention to get married, a *rèiteach* [engagement party] was held in the bride's home. It was the custom for the bridegroom to bring a friend, with him to the *rèiteach*. The duties of the friend, or 'best man', were to 'negotiate' with the bride's parents. His job was to make a plea on behalf of the bridegroom. Of course, the parents knew perfectly well what the best man was up to! But it was the custom – the old custom – so every generation used to observe it. The best man would perhaps say to the father of the bride-to-be, 'If you are as generous as they say you are, will you give me your boat?'

The father was bound to reply, 'No, I certainly won't give you my boat.'

And then the best man would go on and ask for the cow, perhaps, or for the father's best ram. The bargaining, such as it was, was all very lighthearted and good-humoured. After a succession of requests had been made and rejected by the father, the best man would, at last, come to the point! 'Well, if you won't give me any of those things, I have a gentleman with me who wants a very special favour from you. This gentleman wants permission to marry your daughter.'

That pleading took place a week before the young couple's big day – the marriage service in church. After the church service, the wedding proper was held in the bride's home – a celebration that sometimes lasted for several days.

It was the custom that islanders bought most of their clothes in Stornoway. The men wore jerseys knitted by the women, trousers bought in Stornoway and also socks and boots. That was their working clothes. On Sunday, they would wear the dark suit – most often a double-breasted jacket, a waistcoat, a white shirt, and collar and tie. The women always wore a hat to church and, in fact, that practice has continued to this day! I remember my aunt and other ladies wore broad-brimmed hats and then a kind of knee-length robe. On their workdays, they went bare-headed, but occasionally some wore a wee beret – but that was only very occasionally. I remember that they sometimes wore thick crossed skirts, perhaps made of Harris Tweed – but of that I'm not certain.

Tarbert is situated where West Loch Tarbert and East Loch Tarbert almost cut Harris in half! Both sea lochs have very good anchorages and, of course, East Loch Tarbert has become the terminal for the CalMac ferries operating between Harris and Skye. In my day, the congregation of Tarbert included the people of Scalpay and, because of that, we used to travel to the church at Tarbert every Sunday morning. In the evening, we had our service in Scalpay conducted by a lay missionary. The islanders were good, religious people. In saying that, I should stress that they weren't *very* religious. No, I wouldn't use the word 'very'. They were sensibly religious and they applied their faith to their daily work. As a child, I could sense that the adults around me were aware of the presence of God in their midst. Yet they didn't talk a great deal about religion, but they enjoyed taking part in simple services, with heartfelt prayers. Family worship was observed in most homes, morning and evening, and also on the fishing-boats. There were many gifted singers in the community and we all enjoyed singing the psalms.

As a young lad, when I was with the fishermen in the boats, I felt the breath of prayer was over the crews, without their advertising that they were religious at all. I sensed their commitment and their constant awareness of their duty as good Christian people. By their manner and their behaviour, you could sense what they felt. It would not be an exaggeration to say that they applied their beliefs in the home to their daily work, to their fishing and to their crofting. They would have some discussion sometimes but, in those discussions, there was no division made between those who were declared members of the Church and those who weren't. They all respected each other and respected other people's opinions.

I cannot say that I remember anyone talking about 'fear of the Lord'. I grew up knowing a God of love and being aware of His presence around me. But we were taught that God was Father in Christ through the Spirit – 'As a father pitieth his children, so the Lord pitieth mankind.' That was what I remember learning of God, as a child. That image of the Caring Father came into my schooling very much and teachers put that concept across in an interesting way. I still remember the stories that were told in school to illustrate that concept. Of course, we learned the Shorter Catechism off by heart. We had a certain kindly minister in Tarbert who came to examine the school and who questioned us closely about parts of the Bible we had been studying. He was very sympathetic to the bright little faces listening to his questions. If a child hesitated just for a second in giving an answer, he himself would jump in with the answer! He was a most kindly person.

Perhaps the absence of a hotel or public bar on the island was why most of the Scalpay men were not inclined to abuse alcohol. Some of the fishermen would occasionally take quite a lot of drink but, as a rule, I would say that the great majority of them were abstemious. I don't think they ever went to sea drunk or under its influence.

Though I worked as a fisherman in the early days, I had a feeling that I should be doing something else. In my late teens, I began to be drawn more and more towards the Church. Our home was surrounded by very kindly people, especially lay missionaries who lived next door to us and influenced my thoughts as I developed into adulthood. My father was an elder, and so our family regularly attended church. When I was a young child, five or six years of age, he used to take me with him to church and seat me in what they called the 'elders' box'. I seemed to sense something deep within me even then and was moved by the mystery of the creation and the beauty of Jesus Christ's teachings. When I was about twenty years of age, I sensed that I was meant for something other than working as a fisherman. There was nothing wrong with being a fisherman, of course, but throughout my teenage years I developed a strong sense of vocation and instinctively knew that I was meant to devote myself my life to the Church.

My formal education had come to an end when I left school aged fourteen. When I decided to study for the ministry, the local headmaster and teachers helped me a great deal. And so also did the parish minister, Dr Duncan MacLeod. He taught me the fundamentals of ancient Greek and influenced me in other ways as well. In due course, I took a course at Skerry's College in Glasgow and sat my 'prelims' – those were examinations aimed at discovering whether I was suitable university material. I studied diligently, passed the prelims and started as a student at the University of Edinburgh. After three years at the university, I went to New College and studied there for a further three years. In other words, I did three in Arts, followed by three in Divinity.

I first met Sophie, my wife, at the home of her uncle, who was the Rev. Murdo MacLeod, minister at Tarbert, Harris. The friendship between us developed gradually over the years. It so happened that she was studying at a missionary college in Edinburgh when I was at New College and we used to meet quite frequently. Though she and I didn't talk about our growing attraction to each other, we instinctively knew that we were meant for each other. Each of us knew that the time would come when we would become man and wife. It was a comforting thought.

As a student, I used my vacations to visit Church of Scotland congregations on the Scottish mainland and throughout the Islands. Sometimes, I was accompanied by individual ministers, but not always. In the end, when I was 'licensed', I was called to the Church of Scotland congregation on the island of Barra. About 85 per cent of the people of that beautiful island are Roman Catholic but I have to say that I found all the people of Barra very friendly and helpful. Sophie and I were very happy during our time there. Most of our neighbours of that time [1950s] have passed away but Sophie and I are still in touch with some of the friends we made there. One of the wonderful things about Barra is that there was complete harmony between the two versions of the Christian religion – the Church of Scotland and the Roman Catholic.

From Barra, we went to a congregation in Argyll – Strachur and Strath-lachlan – and were there for nearly eight years. That was a very different congregation. While we were there, we knew only Protestants. In the congregation, there were lots of incomers who were working with the Forestry. The best-known member of the congregation was Sir Fitzroy MacLean, the distinguished war hero and author. At first, when I discovered that he regularly attended church, I felt quite nervous seeing him sitting before me listening to my sermons. As it turned out, Sir Fitzroy was approachable and kind and proved to be one of the most supportive members of my congregation.

While I was in Strachur I was, for some months, interim moderator of

Lochgoilhead, a small picturesque village which, in those days, was fairly remote. It is less than a dozen miles from Strachur as the crow flies. However, the road linking the two is long and winds through glens which, in stretches, were quite difficult to negotiate as it consisted of a series of hairpin bends – particularly in a narrow pass called Hell's Glen. On the other hand, the scenery in that part of Argyll is quite spectacular.

Lochgoilhead had an ancient church but, while I was interim moderator, the village was without a minister. As a result, I preached there every fourth Sabbath to the Lochgoilhead congregation. Some of the people in that congregation came from little communities as far away as Carrick, which is situated several miles further down on the shores of Loch Goil. I felt very close to my parishioners and I think it would be fair to say that they felt close to me and trusted me to help them as often as they came to me for help. I liked Argyll very much and have often wondered why I ever left it.

It so happened that, at the time, the Church of Scotland was very short of Gaelic-speaking ministers. In Strachur I preached only in English because Gaelic had all but died out in that area. I accepted a call from the congregation of Manais-Scarasta in the south-west of Harris and, with Sophie and our family of three, I spent eight years there. Owing to the fall in the population of the district, the two communities, Manais and Scarasta, had amalgamated to form the one congregation. It was a sign of things to come. There were about 250 in the congregation when I was minister there but the decline in the population has continued, so that the congregation is probably no more than 150 at present.

Of course, Harris has world-famous scenery and is a wonderful environment for children. Apart from that, I enjoyed preaching in my native language and, once more, enjoyed participating in singing the psalms led by a precentor. After eight years in Harris, I returned to Morvern in Argyll. Five years in Morven, then, towards the end of my ministry, I came to Kinloch in Lewis. I was also assisting another chaplain for a year after that.

I am now retired in Stornoway but, until recently, I was working as a hospital chaplain locally. Of course, that is a part-time occupation, but I enjoy going to the wards and meeting all those patients and chatting to them and praying with them. I did two years in the old Lewis Hospital and three years in the new Ospadal nan Eilean [Western Isles Hospital] – about five years in all. I loved it, every minute of it! In fact, I wish that I had done that kind of work from the start.

I have a special affection for the little island of Scalpay, my birthplace. Since the new bridge was built linking it to the mainland of Harris, the island is no longer remote. One even hesitates to call it an island anymore. From the Lagan Domhainn, one can reach Stornoway comfortably within two hours by car. Flying from Stornoway Airport, a person leaving Scalpay, say, at nine in the morning could be in Glasgow by one o'clock in the afternoon. Advances in communications are causing the world to shrink. But whether the world of today is a better or worse world than that in which I grew up is a very difficult question. I don't think that people are as aware today of being members of a community. There isn't the same community sense because people are so much better off. A degree of prosperity allows them to be more independent. When I was young, families in our little island were interdependent. Each household relied for support on the others. The people are still kind and helpful by nature but they tend to live a separate existence, and that inevitably affects the sense of togetherness.

The influx of people who have come from other places and settled in the islands has made a difference to our Hebridean identity, I think. Apart from southern Scots and English, there are many foreign nationalities resident in our islands – Italians, Thais, Pakistanis, Indians, Chinese, Germans and so on. I don't think that is a bad thing. They're people just like ourselves and, so far as I know, they are law-abiding, decent citizens. Some might say, with all those people coming in, that our position as a Gaelic community is being weakened. But really, I don't think language as such is that important at all. I should not wish anybody to think that I am, in any way, against the survival of the Gaelic language, which is, of course, my own native language and, for centuries, has been the language of my forebears. Certainly, I do enjoy singing the psalms in Gaelic and precenting; and yes, I do accept the traditional Gaelic singing is a very beautiful way of expressing one's faith. Nevertheless, I don't think Gaelic should be regarded as indispensable in the life of the Church. I feel that there may be an over-emphasis on the language and striving to preserve it has, in fact, become a kind of religion for some. Our relationship to our Maker – to God – and to each other is what really matters and should be the basis of our thinking at all times. When Jesus was born, he was born into a Hebrew home. The national language was Hebrew but, so far as we know, he spoke Aramaic. But his aim and purpose was to communicate his message of salvation and grace to people everywhere.

The language that one speaks is not what matters. What matters is the character of the person and how that person regards his fellow man and relates to God in Heaven. By that I mean our fellowship with one another and our sense of always being in the Divine presence.

The following verses from two separate poems, are all that have been found of the Rev. MacSween's bardic compositions:

An t-Isean, 's an Tang 's an Todam chas ghruamach
Gu Flathalach, suairce, neo-bhuaireant mar chlann,
Ag innse don t-sluagh a tha tàmh fo am bruaichean
Mu bhuadhan ro-uasal an Tì chuir iad ann.

The Isean, the Tang and the steep dour Todam,
Dominating, impressive, yet as placid as children,
Reminding those who bide in their marches
Of the majesty of Him who placed them there.

Ach 's e foillseachadh Athaireil Dhè ann an Crìosd
Tha toirt brìgh do gach foillseachadh eile,
A cheanglas sinne le spiorad ris Fhèin
'S ri chèile le còrdaibh bhios daingeann is buan.

But it is the revelation of God the Father in Christ
That gives meaning to every other revelation,
That binds us in spirit to Him
And to each other by bonds everlasting.

Kenneth MacLeod (Kenny White)

1916–2001

I was born in 1916 in my grandfather's black-house at No. 11 Port Mholair on the Isle of Lewis. My father was a Regular soldier in the Seaforth Highlanders. After the First World War, we went to live at Fort George.* Our family went to school in Ardersier. When I was a little boy, we used to go home to Port Mholair for our holidays. I remember getting into trouble once when I was telling some of the other little lads in Fort George that my grandfather had a wonderful house. You could climb up on to the top, right on to the roof, and there was no danger whatsoever. You didn't need ladders or anything else. My mother heard me overhead and I was pulled in and I've seldom seen her so angry.

'Don't you tell anybody your grandfather lives in a straw house!' she said.

My father had joined the army to earn enough money to take him to Canada. But then the war broke out and he was called up immediately because he was on the reserve list. And he didn't see anything for it but to stay in the army. It's a good job he did because, in no time at all, he was promoted to sergeant major, which is as high as you can get in the non-officer class. He loved the army.

Our parents were given accommodation in the married quarters in the Fort. Then, after a while, they were allocated married quarters about half a mile outside the Fort. Very acceptable. They were brand new houses with a bathroom, a shower and everything you could think of. Wonderful places to play in. We had never seen these things in our lives before.

We didn't speak Gaelic in the home at that stage even though the soldiers of the regiment were mostly from the islands. There were too many English people around, so that English was the common language.

My father was a PT [Physical Training] instructor. Yes, and a crack swimmer. He always won the lifesaving cup, which was hardly a 'cup'!

---

* Fort George is situated on an isolated spit of land jutting west into the Moray Firth at Ardersier, some eleven miles north-east of Inverness.

It was at least a couple of feet tall. As you can imagine, my father was very athletic and my brother and I were also pretty fit but we didn't shine in anything. Our father taught us to box and to swim very early in life – which was just as well. Both skills came in handy from time to time. After a few years at Fort George we went to live at Ullapool, which was one of our best moves ever. Of course, again we got a brand-new house with bathrooms and toilets and gardens and a huge gymnasium to play in on a wet day.

In those days, Ullapool was like Stornoway, a centre for the Territorial Army. My father was in charge of the Territorial Army on the west side of Ross-shire. He acquired a motorbike, which he needed to enable him to travel from place to place. He was a religious man. I suppose he was, but he was never oppressively so. Every Friday he had his cronies over for a prayer meeting and I used to take the opportunity to go for a spin with the motorbike.

We had to go to Sunday School – no ifs or buts – and we had to go to church but we were allowed to go for a walk on Sunday, provided we didn't bother anybody else. In those days, the population of Ullapool was about 500. And it had nothing going for it at all, just a few fishermen.

In the summertime, Ullapool livened up with tourists. There were people who came there with their families – came year after year. It's a delightful place in the summer. If you notice, it's a sort of a suntrap. With certain winds it doesn't get any cold at all but it gets the heat. And if you look at Ullapool, you'll see that it was in the bay in front of the houses that we did all our boating. And anything we did wrong was noticed right away. Or if we got into any trouble, which never happened really, they could go for us quickly. It was a wonderful place for the family growing up.

I became very interested in boating at that stage and my love of the sea stayed with me throughout my life. When I was aged about fourteen, we came to live in Stornoway where the opportunities for boating were unlimited. Of course, Stornoway was a very different place from what it is now. Very different. For example, you frequently saw steam lorries going down to the pier to collect coal. You saw them putt-putting, just like a train. At that time, there were very, very few buses. We travelled from the Rubha to Stornoway in a gig, which, as you know, is a horse and trap. The gig didn't take very many passengers. It would take the 'invalids', you know – your mother and the younger members of the family. There were a lot of gigs and carts on the roads. Lorries, which were a very important form of transport in the First World War, became more and more numerous in the 1930s. And so did buses.

The Stornoway harbour was full of Zulus and Fifies and every other kind of boat you could think of. Different kinds of sailing boat, fishing-boats. It so happened that my uncle had a fishing-boat and it might as well have been mine for I was never out of it! She was a Zulu – the first fishing-boat in town with a diesel engine. She was very fast for her day and age. And she made a very distinctive noise, like the German bombers. You could tell her a mile away. My uncle had discarded the sails and relied entirely on the diesel. That would be 1923 or '24. But there were at least five big sailing vessels in Stornoway when I was young. The *Monach* still had her sails and so had the *Ichthyology* – by the way, it took us a long time to find out what that name meant! I can't recall how we discovered that 'ichthyology' means 'the science of fishes'. In 1927, 210,000 cran* was landed in Stornoway. That was the biggest catch ever. There was nothing like it ever. Of course, there was a very big fleet of fishing-boats – very big! The 1940s were quite good for herring catches but the '30s were very patchy. I can remember, I was in school then of course, and we used to go down the pier to see if they were getting many herring and, you know, average three cran – that sort of catch. But it improved.

The problem is that they've fished the herring to destruction. I mean, I get the fishing news very often and, goodness me, they're putting ships as long as from here to that house, with every sort of fish-detection equipment and huge nets and ring-nets. Well, they've got a navigating skipper and a fishing skipper. That shows you how sophisticated they are. Even the wee boats that were out from Holm there had their fish-finders. So you can imagine what all-consuming capacity the big fellows had!

I don't think that even my best friends would describe me as a bright spark when I was at school. I passed the exams, that's about all; and was dashed lucky to pass them. Life in those days had plenty of outlets. We didn't spend our time watching TV or listening to the radio. But there was so much to be done. By the time you took in water from the well, brought in the cow, took in the peats and then started to enjoy yourself out in the boat, there was not much time left for study. But we did learn very early that, if you wanted to get on in life, you had to pay attention in school.

We were living in Sandwick then†. At the age of twenty-something, I went to Glasgow University and studied Maths, Science, Geography and English. I doubled in English and doubled in Maths, that is, took the

---

* A cran typically contains abut 1,200 fish but may vary between 700 and 2,500 according to size of herring.
† On the outskirts of Stornoway.

subject two years running. We took Moral Philosophy. We didn't know what Moral Philosophy was! We thought that being from Lewis and understanding these things we'd get cracking marks in Moral Philosophy but it was something quite different. I enjoyed university a lot.

In Glasgow, we knew a lot of Lewis girls from our schooldays and we knew the university girls as well, because we were finding that we had gravitated together. And there were also quite a lot of Glasgow girls who were Glasgow Highlanders. Those girls were very kind to us on weekends, inviting us around to get Sunday dinner and that sort of thing.

At the Central Station in Glasgow, there's a wide bridge that carries the railway over Argyle Street. The shelter that the bridge provided was known, in those days, as the Highlander's Umbrella. When you are under the Umbrella, you're dry no matter what comes down from the heavens. It can snow or it can rain but those under the Umbrella were OK. I don't know whether it was bomb-proof, but certainly nothing ever penetrated it. And the Highlanders congregated there on Friday or Saturday evenings. It was a wonderful place for people going from Lewis for the first time. You're walking along and you suddenly hear your name called. It was home from home. It certainly was.

After I graduated from university, I decided to become a teacher and went to Jordanhill College of Education to train as a teacher. I had just finished the first part of my training when things in Europe began to turn sour.

After the war, I applied for teaching and was sent to Aird Public School. In a sense, I was back to square one! Aird Public School had children coming from five villages, one of which was Port Mholair where I was born. No doubt I was teaching children who were directly related to me but I cannot remember. Of course, with Colonel John MacSween as headmaster, I might as well have been back on Operation Somme because he wanted to know everything that happened to me at sea during the war! But, och, I enjoyed being down there in the Rubha. However, I wasn't there long before I was sent to Ness* – to Lionel School. Oh, the Education Authority didn't want to lose you because there was a serious teacher shortage after the war. Too many teachers were staying down south. So I got a nice job in Ness which I loved. From there, I went to Dun Carloway† as headmaster.

Dun Carloway is a wonderful place. Five minutes and you were over the top of the hill and you could be a thousand miles from home or any place.

* The most northerly parish in Lewis.
† On the west coast of Lewis.

I well remember how wonderful it was. A place you could go to and you could forget everything. Anybody visiting there might regard it as a dreich, barren place, which it undoubtedly is alongside the road. But when you get over the hill there, when you see the lochs in the distance and the grass is green in many parts of the moor – wonderful. And the lochs were full of fish and that was far more important to me than the green grass!

I moved closer to town when I became headmaster at Cnoc Public School, just two miles or so from Stornoway. I was five years there. In 1965, there was a revolution in primary school education. The 'Primary Memorandum', as it was called, allowed teachers to be far more creative in their teaching. The staff and I at Cnoc acquired a great, big aquarium with a volume in excess of a cubic metre, I'm sure. Many of the pupils had fathers, uncles or brothers working on fishing-boats out of Stornoway. All those adults contributed creatures to our sea-aquarium – creatures that they found in their nets and lobster-traps.

The teachers and I learned quite a lot while all this was going on. For example, I was able to tell a fish-farmer, absolutely categorically, 'You're gonna lose the whole lot unless you remove half of your fish out of that tank!' They were putting too many fish into a tank, into too small a space, and it turned out to be true. They got fish disease. We thought, in the tank we had – about as long as that window – we put too many fish in. They started to die and stink. And that very often happened when we started out. When there was a spring tide, we'd go down to the 'Ebb'* with the children and got lots of things, buckets of them. Everybody wanted to put whatever they caught into the tank. Next day, half of them would be dead. There wasn't enough oxygen in the water. Mind you, we got over that by getting an oxygen pump. Oh, we learned quite a few tricks.

The children were very interested. They did all their maths, creative writing, geography, history, etc., based on our sea aquarium. Throughout my career as head, I was very lucky in the staff I had working with me. Every one of them was gifted and enthusiastic.

After Cnoc School, I spent ten years as head of Sandwickhill. Let me show you this – a model that survived from my days at our local school here at Sandwick. This is a Viking longship. The longship was probably one of the first real sea-going ships. She was used by the Vikings for commerce, for exploration, for putting people ashore in different places, you know, emigration and all that. A general-purpose boat but, as a rule, she had two planks at least higher, so she could take to the high seas. Now they were

---

* A large area of sand revealed by the ebbing tide.

magnificent sea boats. Most of the time they were running before the wind because they never left home except with a north-east wind. *Gaoth an ear-thuath*! And if you see the rudder, it's across, it's athwartships. Now the helmsman stood with his back to the sail, watching for the big sea that might swamp them. He also had, at his side, a good reliable man who hadn't got too good a nerve but who was careful. He warned him if there was a sea coming so that he could turn the stern in to take away. They required a lot of care. But with a lot of good seamanship, they could do anything.

We got the plan for a Viking longship from a Mr Ingebreston, a Norwegian who's been married in Stornoway since the Second World War. He was a commander of a mine-sweeper flotilla. At school, the pupils varnished the model and, I think you'll agree, it still looks very nice even though it is thirty years old. And it says a lot for Sandwickhill Primary School that there's nothing wrong with it. I took it home here because I meant to repair the things that I thought might be broken. In fact, there's nothing broken. Now I asked Mr Ingebreston what colour. He says all the ones he ever saw were black and red. So, we immediately changed to black and red and it's quite dramatic actually. Because these were killer boats. You can imagine how interested the boys were in the subject of the Vikings who, in most cases, were ancestors of theirs!

Because I had been in places like Iceland, Faroes, Ireland, France, the Med and so on, during the war, I was able to give the pupils an idea of what those places were like. And I was able to tell them a bit about places raided and later colonised in some cases by the Norsemen. Some of the Norsemen went east right along the Mediterranean into the Caspian Sea. They even went up some of the rivers like the Volga and met some of their kinsmen halfway, coming down from the north. They were the people who discovered North America. They were an amazing people. Now the children found all this very interesting.

When I was at Lionel School in Ness and at Dun Carloway, teaching based on projects had not been introduced. And some people were very slow to start that approach to teaching. They preferred the old 'Open your books page such and such,' where everybody would listen for an hour. Then we'd do some maths and some history – all of it in watertight compartments. But when teaching through projects was introduced, everything came together. You'd do Geography and Maths, History and so on, all at the same time. I had a wonderful time during my teaching years. Just wonderful! As I told you, the clouds of war were beginning to gather while I was at the Jordanhill Teacher Training College. We all came home expecting to get called up. All the army people were getting called up and we came home here and, och, had a glorious time lifting the peats for my uncle, occasionally getting a pound from him. There might have been a bit of gloom amongst the old folk because they could clearly remember the pain of the First World War. I mean, my father was wounded three times in the First World War. I think that meant that you got sent home for a while. One of my uncles had been drowned – two of them in fact had been drowned. And so it went on: relations on all sides had been lost. The army took an awful toll.

Anyway, the authorities took their time calling us up – just as we were beginning to get worried that they weren't sending for us after all. But they did finally send for us in November. We were told to go to Portsmouth. The drill consisted of marching up and down with a few soldiers. Rifle drill, mainly. The training was quite divorced from sailors' duties. Anyway, we went through all the drill and then they threw us on a ship and said, 'You are all sailors now!'

By that time, we had learned how to fire a rifle and how to salute properly. We also learned how to wash our own clothes and to press our trousers – sailors' trousers. You fold them little by little so that when they come out, they're like a concertina. Of course, by that time we knew how to conduct ourselves among strangers and were quite confident! Oh, yes, we had every confidence in the world. It's a good job because I remember one day being late. They had been piped to gun drill and I hadn't heard it. And after a while I noticed there was nobody around me, so I went up to see. And this young lieutenant said, 'Ah, MacLeod, I don't suppose you can understand English.' And I knew what he was referring to because, at that time, many of our lads didn't understand English as it was spoken by some English people. They went away in ships and just spoke in Gaelic because the rest of the crew were Gaels. I says to the young lieutenant, 'Sir, I can understand English and French and Latin and Gaelic.' You know, he was rocked on his heels. He didn't know what the dickens to say! 'Fall in there. I don't want to hear another word out of you!'

So when I went down to the mess, everyone said, 'Good for you, Mac, well done Mac! You showed him!' But I was really annoyed at the fellow. He was an Englishman. Mind you, not all the Englishmen were like that. Some of them were the funniest people I knew.

We were sent to our ship before she was quite ready to go to sea. She was called the *Tynwald*, which is a Norse term meaning 'capital city'. She was built in Norway before the war and, as you know, the Norwegians are pretty good at building ships of all kinds. She had been used as a ferry operating between the Isle of Man and Liverpool. Now she was being converted to act as an anti-aircraft escort vessel.

I arrived in Portsmouth along with the rest of the crew as the *Tynwald* was being armed and provisioned. There again, I fell foul of authority. Perhaps I had been showing that I was perfectly at home on board a ship. Then, one day, the leading seaman said to me in sailor language, 'You're cocky enough in dock, mate, but we'll see what you're like when we get to sea.'

I just looked at him because I had every confidence that, after my experience in the Minch on my uncle's drifter, nothing this ship did would bother me. And sure enough, when we left Portsmouth, we sailed down the Channel at twenty knots in the teeth of a gale. I remember going to report to the leading seaman who had been so dismissive of me while we were in port and there he was sitting down looking very green, as were most of his crew. I said, 'What am I going to do about the rum?'

'Bring it up here. We'll keep it here until we get into calmer waters at the end of the day.'

When I brought the rum up, everybody gave me a little sip – that was the custom. And by the time everybody had got their rum, I had all those sips and I ended up with a pair of wings on! I was flying! It didn't matter to me what happened to anybody, even supposing it was the *Bismark* coming after us! That was the effect of the rum. In all my years at sea afterward, I never saw a ship travelling at that speed – not for all day long anyway. We left Portsmouth in the morning and we were there in Plymouth just when it was getting dark. The year was 1940.

The *Tynwald* was an anti-aircraft cruiser – extremely well equipped. She had two twin four-inches on the fo'c'sle, two twin four-inches on the quarterdeck and also massive pom-pom, you know, multi-barrelled pom-pom. We called the pom-pom a Chicago piano. We also had numerous Orlekon guns along the side. And, what was most important, she had all the very latest radar equipment. We could pick up an aeroplane miles and miles away, even when they were leaving the coast of Germany. In fact, that equipment saved our lives. And we were there with a convoy for that purpose, for early warning. She was a big, stable ship and very comfortable. The *Tynwald* wasn't as agile as a destroyer or anything like it. When she turned round at full speed, you thought she was going to tip everybody over the side as she leaned over. There were two others ships of the same kind and there were Lewismen in their crews. They were called the *Poserika* and the *Paramaris*. They were doing the same duties as we were – protecting convoys. I saw the *Poserika* in Algiers. She had been badly smashed up.

We reached Plymouth and I had two pals in the crew by that time. When we went ashore, one of them said, 'I wish the bloody ground would stop moving!' He was landsick, but after a few hours he got over it. This was the wonderful thing. Men were sent to sea without any previous experience and some of them became very sick. They thought they were going to die. A few weeks later, after they found their sea legs, you'd think they'd been sailing all their lives.

On board ship, we carried on doing exercises for about a month but concentrating on anti-aircraft drills and perfecting the ship's abilities. Above everything, the anti-aircraft. We saw some German aircraft during that period. But they seemed to know about us, so they didn't come near us. After we had gone through all the drills and were used to all the equipment on board, we were committed to convoy duties. Yes, we sailed to the Clyde. Made sure everything was working perfectly.

I was given shore leave and went ashore at Greenock, where I met two Lewis people whom I knew and liked. Unfortunately, they're no longer with us. And we were going to meet them the next day but the *Tynwald* was ordered to pick up a convoy bound for North Africa.

As we were approaching North Africa we did not encounter any enemy aircraft until our last night at sea. Then we were attacked by everything that the Luftwaffe could send against us. To make matters worse, there were U-boats in the area. At one time, you were firing against the aircraft; next you were dropping depth charges. Then all of a sudden, all enemy activity stopped. The reason was that they began to concentrate their attention on what they thought was a convoy. This was the formidable 'Force H' with troop-carriers and British battleships such as the *Nelson* and some of our best cruisers – the best ships we had in the navy, including destroyers which were dashing all over the place. The armada stretched from one horizon to the other. Anybody who tried to attack that fleet was just committing suicide. After all, the ships were full of American soldiers, and if they got hurt, you could be sure that there'd be trouble. So when the aircraft went there looking for trouble, they soon changed their mind and cleared off home!

Enemy activity resumed when the sun went down and kept on throughout the night. Then, at daybreak, we positioned ourselves close to the landing beaches and the soldiers started going ashore in their assault crafts. Landing-troop-carriers I think they were called. Oh, they were huge. They would hold fifty men. Unfortunately, as they were going ashore, the swell increased and most of them were soaking wet. In fact, there were a number of accidents and a few of the soldiers were drowned. The *Tynwald* lay off protecting the big troop-carriers – ships as big as any ship you ever saw in the Minch. Our ship shepherded them to places of safety, getting them as close to the land as possible, so that enemy aircraft could only attack from seaward. And that's what the Germans did. During all this tremendous stramash with bullets and bombs, the *Tynwald* was never hit. She wasn't hit during the landings but later on she went to her doom. That happened a few days later. After we had done all we could to protect the transports, there was no more we could do. They were all on fire anyway, nearly every one of them. They were burning and they would never be any good to anybody.

What happened to the *Tynwald* – the ship, you could say, on which I grew up – is not the sort of occurrence that you can easily forget. I was on the *Tinwald* from the day she was launched as an anti-aircraft vessel till the day she sank. It was an awful sensation to feel the ship you're on sinking. It sort of brings you to your senses and makes you realise how vulnerable you are. We had all thought that, with a ship like that, we were cock o' the walk. We felt confident that the *Tynwald* could fight off anything. Except, of course, that a battleship would have blown us to bits in seconds!

We had been in Algiers for a short time and then we went on to Budjie. I think I mentioned before, I don't know why on earth we went to Bougie. We only had a couple of transports with us. And when we arrived there, we could see an aircraft-carrier in the distance and, to our great delight, we recognised Seafires, which was the navy's answer to the Spitfire – the famous fighter plane. The Seafires had been slightly altered to be flown off the carriers.

But I remember we tucked one ship right under a tall headland, almost like under Tiumpanhead, so that the bombers couldn't get at her at all. The bombers were trying their best but their bombs were arcing past her and falling in the sea. They never got near her. But everything that was in the open and vulnerable was on fire.

On board the *Tynwald*, the radio operators told us that there was something brewing to the north of us. There was an awful lot of, you know, radio messages and that we better look out for ourselves. Skipper took the message and told us. He said, 'We can expect an attack from the north any time. So ship's company will remain at action stations until further notice.' And action stations meant the height of alertness.

I was on a gun, an Orlekon gun, which fires eight-centimetre bullets. Now eight centimetres, as you know, is almost a three-inch bullet. And she could fire the whole sixty in less than a minute. So if you got the whole lot into an aeroplane there was no way that aeroplane could fly away from you.

We went close in to the shore and were quite happy in there, and felt that we didn't have to move the ship anywhere else for better protection. The ship was just more or less idling, moving only a little now and again. And it was the most beautiful morning. Gosh, it really was! A lovely morning in early November, I think it was. We saw as we were watching, we saw to the south of us, lights jinking up and down and seemed to be going in every direction. And we knew then that this was a flight of aircraft coming towards us. They were torpedo-bombers – Savoya 79s, flying very low. And all we really had to do was, when they got within range, fire our four-inch guns at them or rather at the sea in front of us. And if the enemy didn't die in a maelstrom of water they died in a maelstrom of steel. And they did. They never got – well, how far is it from here to Lower Sandwick? They never got as near as Lower Sandwick, quarter of a mile from us here. In fact our short-range weapons didn't open fire at all. They just watched them coming. There were six Savoyas coming at us from the north. The Savoyas were two-engine planes. I don't know where they had been based. It could have been Italy. It could have been some of the other Mediterranean islands.

Those aircraft were probably piloted by Italians – and good pilots they were too. Then the Orly guns opened up, firing into the sea just in front of those six low-flying aircraft. The sea rose to meet them and it was impossible for the pilots to control their aircraft. Those who came through that had to meet the full force of our gunfire. I saw one passing over the bow of the ship. That one had escaped the barrage but not for long. There were two or three men inside her. We could see them bent over as if working inside the plane. The pilot, you could see him where you'd expect him to be but the other two men behind him were working on something, as if the torpedo had jammed or something like that. And she just cleared our fo'c'sle and down she came about as far away as the house down there, 150 yards away from us. And not only did she crash but her torpedo left her and went straight into the breakwater so the whole lot was blown up. Nothing was left. It was an awful noise. The torpedo's a very powerful weapon, you know.

The crew of five of the Savoyas were killed, of course, and when that it was all finished, we noticed that one last aircraft had altered course and tried to escape at the corner of the channel, so to speak, but a four-inch gun had a direct hit on her before she was able to veer away. So that was all six gone. We were all cheering, of course, until we were stopped and the skipper said, 'You have faced the bravest men you'll ever face. These men lie now dead in their machines. We should show every respect for them and may the Lord bless them.'

So that brought us back to our senses. The skipper knew what he was talking about. He was an 'ex' – a retired skipper. He had been on boats before but he was old and superannuated. Well, he was probably about fifty – that's quite old for a skipper in the Royal Navy. After a while, he said, 'Retribution will follow. When the news of this disaster is brought back to headquarters, heads are going to roll! Lots of things went wrong in that attack. The Savoyas should never have been put into such a narrow channel. But they had to follow orders. I don't know how they could get out of it.' But he says, 'Above all, they should have been supported by other aircraft.'

The sensible thing that they should have done against us was to send in fighter-bombers, fast planes that could drop a few light bombs and spray a lot of bullets amongst the weaponry. If they had done that, we wouldn't have been so ready to take on the Savoyas.' For the Italians, it was a terrible disaster. To go there with nobody to help them, it was on a par with the Charge of the Light Brigade. If they had sent ten fighter-bombers, well, ten fighter-bombers to bomb a ship, you can kill everybody on deck! They didn't think about that.

I cannot remember how I felt during or after the Savoyas attack – whether I was afraid or exultant. All I can say is that we were lucky to escape from such powerful machines. And six of them coming against us under normal circumstances should have sunk us. No doubt about it. The thing to remember is that when they were coming at us and managed to drop their missiles, one torpedo was quite enough to incapacitate us for the rest of the war. But they didn't get anywhere near us.

As I said, the skipper warned us. Retribution was soon to follow. We went to action stations. Everybody forgot about nodding off! It was a case of preparing mentally for some form of attack on the following day. We were all on deck anyway, drinking endless cups of tea, smoking endless cigarettes, bread and jam. In any case, we were kept awake all night by the blighters dropping flares. It was just to make sure we were still there. There's no doubt about it, they had us in their sights. The day was ushered in with a beautiful dawn. I'll always remember that dawn. Everything was peaceful at first. And then the peace was shattered. First of all we heard a dull thump. This was a bomb that had gone through the funnel into the boiler house and a torpedo into the engine room. There's a large cavity in a ship and if that's breached, there's nothing on earth will keep her afloat. She's also got weight at the bow and weight at the stern, you know – ropes and ammunition. The ammunition's in the bow usually, but there is also some in the stern. And once that hold is breached, there's nothing will keep her afloat for any length of time. The *Tynwald* started to sink but, like the lady she was, she kept herself afloat until the decks were level with the sea. As she was approaching the end, she sort of slowed down and every able-bodied person on deck was able to get off. There was plenty of escape vehicles. We all got off safely. But the whole crew didn't get off – only those who were fortunate enough to be on deck. Half the men were down below. The torpedo more or less blocked the forward part of the ship from the after part. Those who were forward were all trapped. As with the Italian airmen, the sea is forever their resting place. Fortunately we were less than a mile from land and the sea was warm. It wasn't like an experience I had later on in the Arctic – so bitterly cold, you didn't care whether you were picked up or not.

Our islands produced excellent seamen. They had the sea in their blood. They were used to going out in open boats to their lobster-pots or their small-lines. No engines in those pre-war days – just two pairs of oars or a sail. The Tolsta men and the Ness men were all good rowers, as strong as horses because, when they were fishing in home waters, they were rowing every day for hours on end. The East Coast men too were used to working the sea. In my experience, Englishmen were good sailors, good seamen, but most of them had been on vessels that were motorised pre-war – not so good with the oars. But when it came to discipline and comradeship, they were all good seamen. I saw examples of cowardice all right. But what is cowardice? Perhaps it is what comes of being absolutely terrified. In dangerous situations, you've got to control your fear, otherwise if panic sets in, you're going to lose everything.

I got off the *Tynwald* in a general lifeboat – one that was badly damaged. She had been holed. She had been secured just above where the explosion took place and had been lifted off her cradle and was split. She was no sooner in the water than we knew fine that she wouldn't float all the way to land. But we got into her anyway because all the sailors had caps which they used as bailers! When we got close in to the breakers we just chucked our hand in and got out of her and guided her in to the shore. At that point, we had an unpleasant surprise. A fellow came down waving a pistol at us. It happened that I was the first to reach him. Not that I had said a word to him. He yelled, 'What do you guys think you're doing?' I said, 'Can't you see what we're doing?' 'You should put back to sea and help your comrades,' he shouted.

Then behind me, I heard another voice say, 'Have you got something to say to us? If you have, say it to me. I'm the Chief Petty Officer.' You know the guy cowed down right away! The chief said, 'Go and have a look at that boat. And if you're willing to take her out, you can take her or keep her for yourself if you wish. We're finished with her. She's useless.'

We left the fellow with the wrecked boat and we went up to the village. When we arrived there, we came across Algerian sailors who had come off three big ships. The Algerians were firing up ovens to make meals. I don't know who on earth they were making the food for. It might have been for the locals because the town was getting bombed all the time. When they saw us coming in soaking wet, they started laughing at us. They invited us to take our clothes off and throw them into the oven, promising that they would be dry in a minute! So there we were, half a ship's company going around naked. The Algerians gave every one of us a big, long shirt, like the night-shirt of long ago. I took mine home, actually.

All in all, there were about fifty of us – survivors off the *Tynwald*. About twenty-five were put on to the ss *Glen Strathnaver* – a cruise-ship in her pre-war days. The other half of the men were put on to a destroyer. And, oh, boy, were they happy to get on the fast destroyer that could travel twice as fast as the *Glen Strathnaver*. Unfortunately, that destroyer wasn't an hour outside Gibraltar when she got blown up. The whole lot went down with her. She was holed, so she sank fast, you see – nothing to keep her afloat. But we went on this Noah's Ark, as we called her – the old *Glen Strathnaver*. She was very slow moving, doing only ten leisurely knots! Quite a change from our previous ship and we felt it after being used to a skipper who never went less than twenty!

The *Glen Strathnaver* had been built for comfort and leisure and we had a wonderful time. She was as beautiful as ever. Of course, we weren't used to such luxury. Every man got a sofa for himself to sleep on at night. Someone just woke us up with a cup of tea. The drinks were duty free, smokes were duty free, everything you could think of was duty free and some of the lads made the most of it! I've got to hand it to them, they could fairly carry their liquor. They would have their tot at midday and they would take that and then, just to make things nice and rosy, they'd have another. They were all drinking – it's the first time I ever drank brandy and port together. And it was a lovely drink. I mean, you never knew you were drinking something alcoholic after the first sip.

I don't know why the ship was empty of passengers apart from us. She was probably a reserve of some kind during the landings in North Africa and she was late in arriving. Plodding along at ten knots made her a beautiful target for a U-boat but she was straight out into the Atlantic for three or four days. This was to get clear of anything en route or coming at us from the coast. And, of course, once you're 100 miles from land, aeroplanes don't like it out there unless it's an important target. And the *Glen Strathnaver* was unimportant. Anybody could see we were empty:

our engines were just about played out. Then she turned right – north. After a few days, our amateur navigator said, 'You're now on the same parallel as Glasgow. So, it's obvious where we're going.' And sure enough, we turned towards Glasgow, passing the north of Ireland, which we all knew so well in our younger days. Up the Clyde. It was wonderful!

But I can tell you that the reception we got as we approached Greenock was not as welcoming as what we had got from the Algerians. When we got into the Greenock harbour, we were put on to a little iron drifter. The coldest thing on earth. It had the job of taking the survivors from ship to shore. The *Glen Strathnaver* wasn't the only ship carrying survivors. The drifter travelled from one ship to another, taking a few survivors from one and then a few from the next and so on. We were nearly perished with the cold! You see, we had no clothes except the survival clothes: a shirt, a jersey, a pair of trousers, that's all. The clothes were fine for the North African beach – but for Greenock harbour in the middle of December! By the time we got on to the train we were all right. An officer came round and checked who we were and what ship we'd been on. But there was also a naval police escort, ready for anybody who tried to be funny. As it happened, I knew one of them – from Ness he was. He was about to go back to Lewis on leave, so I asked him to call in and see my father the first time he was in Stornoway, to tell him I was OK. He said, 'I'll do that the very night I arrive in Lewis.'

I think that was in 1942. My mind isn't clear on that. There was so much happening in the first two or three years of the war. From Greenock, we went to Liverpool to get kitted out properly and to get warm clothing on. In Liverpool, they told us we would have to look after ourselves when we came back off leave. But we didn't want to spoil our survivor's leave, which is three weeks, I think. I also got ten extra days for being as far away as Stornoway. The Scots in the group travelled home by train, of course. Things were moving a lot better than they are nowadays. And, of course, we knew every station inside out: to Glasgow, to Perth, then over to the west to Fort William. When we arrived in Kyle, we felt we were home. I'd been there so often in my student days. Four or five times a year.

Those of us going to Stornoway were sent down to the *Hebridean*. She wasn't much bigger than a drifter and her accommodation was one long room about two-thirds the size of the boat. But one nice thing on board that ship that I appreciated, there was a nice bogey fire there – one that we could all sit round and enjoy. I remember us all sitting there having a yarn and a beer to pass the time. The vessel was very slow – no faster than the old *Glen Strathnaver*. But she plodded on and, at last, we were in sight of the Arnish light. Great!

When we all got home, I suppose it was the old story. Some of us went home to bliss and some went home to something that was far from bliss. Others went home to meet again in MacCalum's pub on the following morning! Sad to think how many people did not all go home to bliss. It was not particularly bad here in the Western Isles, but out of here, oh, poor souls! On board ship, we used to feel sorry for them. They were getting what they called 'Dear John' letters by the score. I knew one guy who put lead weights into his pocket and jumped over the stern into the ship's wake. And he was a good swimmer. He had to put those lead weights on, otherwise he wouldn't have sunk.

After the *Tynwald*, I was sent on duty to various other vessels, which occasionally became directly involved against the enemy. We were sent to the United States to join a new ship – a frigate. That was a type of warship that was also referred to as a 'destroyer escort'. Though we weren't there for very long, we had a great time in America, I must say. In Boston, we went downtown and somebody heard us speaking and the next we heard a voice shout, 'You from Scotland?'

'Yes, of course.'

We were told, 'Come home with me.'

Well, the fellow introduced us to his family and they were the nicest crowd. I remember the man saying to his daughter, 'Go down and get some beer.' And she went out and she came back: 'Dad, my car won't start, I'd better have yours.'

When I heard that! The girl of the house, just a young teenager, had a car as well as the father! I could hardly believe how wealthy those people were compared to ourselves back home. And they were by no means unique. They knew where the ship was and came for us. We didn't have to go looking for them. They used to come down to the docks for us every night.

Anyway, just a few days after we arrived in the USA, we were taken down to Boston Harbour and we met our ship for the first time. The frigate was brand new. She was called the *Bickerton* – rigged out with the latest electronic equipment – ASDIC, designed to find U-boats. She was a purely anti-submarine frigate – a good-looking ship. All told, there would have been about 120 in the crew. Our captain was a two-and-a-half-ringer and he had much experience. A 'two-and a-half ringer' means that he was wearing yellow bands on the sleeves of his uniform – two thick ones and a thin one. It showed that he was a lieutenant commander. Lieutenant commanders always called themselves commanders. They forgot about the half ring! Oh, ours was a Scot by the name of MacIntyre – a tough nut. He had been an airman in the Fleet Air Arm but he preferred the sea to that.

We had a lieutenant engineer, Royal Navy, and there were two or three chief petty officers and two or three petty officers. They were all considered tradesmen, you know. Before they would get to engineering on one of these ships, they had to know all the component parts of engines – small and big and how to piece them all together. The *Bickerton* didn't have any sophisticated machinery up top for picking out aeroplanes coming at us with evil intent! In that sense, she was the opposite of the *Tynwald*. We just had the ASDICs for detecting submarines. ASDIC means 'Anti-submarine detection'. They took us round the ship and we met the first lieutenant, who was from Newfoundland. He spoke practically the same as I did – a similar accent, just slightly different. He chatted with me for a while, asking about the place I came from and the lifestyle in the Outer Hebrides. He said, 'Look, Mac, you're a fisherman. I want you to take away the motorboat and see how she goes.' I said, 'Oh yes, I'll do that,' I said. 'I've never taken a boat that size, though.' She was an engined whaler – very robust boat. She had that double skin on her and she also had a huge Deason engine which, in those days, was quite something. But she was a wonderful boat and after the war I often wished that I had one like her.

As the *Bickerton* was brand new, the crew had to learn the ropes – pronto! No time to lose! We did a lot of exercising with her and her sister ships – taking them out and conducting manoeuvres – turning swiftly port or starboard trying to turn them on their side, dropping depth-charges and so on. That way, we all had extensive training before we put to sea. Go here, there and everywhere and do this, that and the other. Learn to lower the boats and get them up quickly, drop the anchor and retrieve it. There was no end to it and, of course, the depth-charge crew were exercising day and night.

When we went looking for submarines in earnest, we operated mostly in the North Atlantic – anywhere between the latitudes of Iceland and of Gibraltar. That's a very big sea area. The Admiralty had a good idea where German submarines were congregating. As we now know, our British boffins had broken the German signalling code and were able to read all the radio instructions sent to the wolf packs. A message would come to us instructing us where to go and sometimes it meant high-speed dashes to places 200 or 300 hundred miles away. Our ship and her sister ships could do twenty-five knots, no matter what the weather was.

When we were out in mid-Atlantic, we were at our most vulnerable. That was the place that was called 'The Gap'. It was known by that name because we had no anti-aircraft protection there. You see, 'The Gap' was beyond the range of our aircraft at that time – aircraft operating from both sides of the Atlantic.

Like most seamen from the Western Isles, Kenneth
MacLeod 'Curro' sailed deep-sea and was familiar
with seaports all over the world

Visitors to 'Curro''s home heard stories of life in
the old crofting community and of encounters and
adventures in distant lands

In her mid-twenties, Mary MacKenzie was
appointed housekeeper to the Adams family,
Glasgow

With husband, Charles Crane, Mary settled into life
in the city

Anus MacLeod ('Ease') with his wife, Annie, in 1987, after receiving the MBE for his work with the Crofters Union

John Morrison, miller, remembers a time when the islanders' staple diet consisted mainly of barley and oatmeal, fish and potatoes

Nowadays, the Garrabost mill produces meal only for local bakeries and supermarkets

Andrew and Gianfranca Cabrelli, equally at home in Lewis and Tuscany

Sandra Ferguson flanked by sisters Maryann Martin (left) and Christina

Alighting from 'bus John Murdo', Maryann Martin arrives home dressed in fashionable city attire

George Smith, member of a 1950s camera club specializing in portraits

George Smith, one of three brothers who owned the Stornoway 'Shoe Shop', venue for the local worthies' 'parliament'

John MacDonald (Iain an t-Saighdeir), crofter–fisherman and war veteran, known for his strong Christian faith

John MacDonald's twin daughters, Catherine and Joan, had to walk three miles to and from school and completed their education with perfect attendance

Iain Crichton, internationally known as one of Scotland's foremost composers of music for accordion and bagpipes

A proud moment: Iain Crichton's achievements were recognized by Comunn Leòdhais 's Na Hearadh Ghlaschu

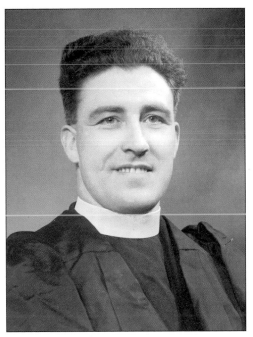

Rev. Norman MacSween's first charge was in Barra, where he and his wife, Sophie, spent some of the happiest years of their lives

Rev. Norman MacSween as chaplain to the Western Isles Hospital

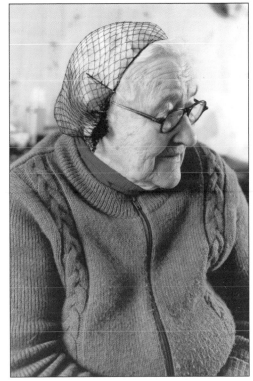

'Kenny White' MacLeod, an inspirational teacher who specialised in environmental studies. Favourite subjects, Norse civilisation and marine biology.

In old age, Màiri Chaluim Alas' 'c Uilleim was a well-known radio performer as a story-teller

Donald MacKenzie ('Sligo)' with his cousin Kate Macdonald, district nurse and well-known folklorist

Born in Canada, Margaret MacMillan's first language was Gaelic

Dolly Murdo in Lacasaigh with the moors of South Lochs as backdrop

As a lad, Donald Alasdair MacDonald first heard about radio in the ceilidh-house

After graduating from Medical School, Aberdeen, Mairi Macleod found employment in the Midlands of England

Baillie Julia Martin Fraser, a forceful member of the Town & County Council

Dr Roderick Fraser, a popular and successful GP, particularly considerate of patients among poor families

Sandy Mòr, a life-long supporter of the Labour movement

Sandy Mòr with Katie-Ann, his wife, in a house designed and built by himself

Duncan MacKenzie (Donnchadh Toggan), crofter, genealogist and local historian

After discussing their genealogy, Duncan MacKenzie identifies a visitor as 'one of my own relations'

Author of *A Kenneth Street Boy*, Dr Allan Campbell regards Stornoway as his 'spiritual home'

The three MacKenzie sisters carried enough beach-shingle on their backs to build this two-storey house

Like most island girls of her generation Mary Crane earned her first wage curing herring
(*Stornoway Gazette*)

Left. Angus Graham, great uncle of John Morrison, was famous for his feats of strength

Below. The Stornoway herring fleet berthed at Bayhead, yards from the Shoe Shop (*Stornoway Gazette*)

Bottom. Iain an t-Saighdeir was born in an earth-house like this

Left. Peat-cutting, a spring-time chore for all crofting families (*Stornoway Gazette*)

Below. The Stornoway Dance Band in which Iain Crichton was an accordionist

Spiritual by nature, the people of the Western Isles were steeped in Bible knowledge. This open-air service said to have been held at Garden Street, Stornoway, in the 1890s (*Stornoway Gazette*)

At an early age, 'Kenny White' went to sea in Stornoway herring drifters (*Stornoway Gazette*)

R.M.S. Mona's Isle.

Top. The launch on which 'Kenny White' was leading seaman is seen rescuing survivors from the stricken *Bickerton* (centre left)

Above. A black-house with a barn converted to house a landless cotter family (*Stornoway Gazette*)

Left. 'Sligo' was a crew member of the *Monas Isle*, the first ship to arrive at Dunkirk to evacuate troops (www.simplonpc.co.uk)

Margaret MacMillan at the Scottish Office, sitting
at the very desk used by Margaret Thatcher

The Lancaster bomber, one of Dòmhnall Alasdair's favourite aircraft, could carry
ten tons of bombs to the heart of Germany (Imperial War Museum BU-005892)

Dòmhnall Alasdair frequently flew on bombing missions to
Germany and Italy (Imperial War Museum A-028244)

In the Antarctic, 'Sandy Mòr' spent nearly two years
employed in the whaling industry

In the early 1930s, the surface of the Stornoway's main
thoroughfares was mostly of clay and stones (*Stornoway Gazette*)

Dr Allan Campbell stood in as locum for Dr John Goodall at the
old Lewis Hospital on Goathill Road (*Stornoway Gazette*)

As you can imagine, the weather out there was sometimes awful but we just got used to it. We had got this idea into our heads that the worse the weather was, the less the likelihood of an attack by a U-boat and that was OK by us! Commander MacIntyre on the *Bickerton* was as keen as mustard. He said to one of the crew one day, 'I'll give a half-crown to the first person who sights a U-boat.' And the guy he said that to got that half-crown. He was from the Rubha – from the village of Flesherin. He sighted a U-boat, just her periscope, and MacIntyre said, 'All right, I'm a Scotsman myself, here's your half-crown.'

Once you turned the ASDIC on to a submarine, you could hold her until you caught her with depth-charges, which was usually the case. Once MacIntyre got hold of a U-boat, there was no escape for her. Whenever a destroyer suspected that a submarine was lurking in the vicinity, she just put on speed and kept the enemy at bay until she got help. To be sure, to be reasonably sure, of defeating a submarine, you needed two destroyers. If you went in on your own, you were taking a big, big risk. When two destroyers worked a U-boat together, they employed different strategies. For example, the submarine knows if it has been 'streeped' because the ASDIC beam seems to hit it like a whip and it knows it is being tracked.

Our duty was to skirt round the U-boats to frighten them off or else to sink them if we could. And we sank quite a lot! Commander MacIntyre was a crack anti-U-boat man. At that time, our five frigates operated together. We travelled with about half a mile between us. I remember one incident that illustrates a typical sequence of events. One of the boats signalled that he had a 'ping' on an enemy submarine. MacIntyre just said, 'Right! Hang on to her. Don't lose her. And the rest of you scatter.'

MacIntyre had the five ships under his command. He was a DC, you see – a destroyer commander. After giving his instructions, our ship would then get a beam on the U-boat and the skipper would know pretty accurately where the enemy was. He would say to our sister ship, 'Pretend you've lost her and I'll come in from the side he least expects.' Then, after doing his calculations to show the enemy's position and the course she was travelling, he would say all of a sudden, 'Right, go in full speed and drop a whole packet of depth-charges round her.'

We came across, dropped the depth-charges and it must have been terrifying for the men in the U-boat. She popped up right away. By this time, we had travelled quarter of a mile beyond her. We wheeled round and, to everybody's surprise, some of her crew rushed along the deck and manned the surface gun and started firing at us. They must have realised that that wasn't going to get them very far. A few shots from our Orly guns soon put a stop to that! We opened fire and the gunners on the U-boat were just blown away. And still more poured out of the conning tower and they were shot down as well. It was cruel in a way. Those who were left of her crew jumped into the sea and we picked them up, of course. Oh, they had good survival gear. We were glad to pick them up, of course. They were just human beings. Some of them were very nice indeed. And they were so much preferred to the French. Our old sailors hated the French and so did the Germans. We liked our enemies better than we like some of our allies. It was a paradox.

You can imagine that having a lot of German prisoners on board could present a bit of a problem. Say you had picked up twenty. Well, you would put about four into each mess and they were watched at all times. They never tried to do anything out of order. They kept the mess nice and tidy and took a cup of tea to you at eleven o'clock. They dished up when you finished eating. They were happy to be out of it. They were prisoners and that was it. Usually, a submarine was detected some time after lunch. I don't know why but the action always seemed to start in the late afternoon, and by the time it was dark the submarine had been sunk – that is, if it was going to be sunk! Then, you'd hear the pipe. 'Hands will splice the main-brace!'

That meant that you got a double tot. You already had a tot at twelve o'clock! So you then got a double tot at suppertime, which is usually some time between six and eight. Supper was always the same – steak, egg and chips. Oh, boy! By the time you had finished that you were ready to discuss the action with everybody around you. There was a sense of elation when we sank a U-boat. I liked the Germans, I must say. I don't know if it was following that particular sinking, but one time, anyway, there was one fellow there whom we picked up all covered in oil. I took him in hand and led him into the hot shower room. It was nearly as big as this room. And he wouldn't go in at all. He thought I was taking him in to torture him, which was far from the case. But, after a while, he went in and he got the oil off him. Oh, they were good on board. You see, they were sailors; they were real sailors. One awful dirty night, I saw one of them, up in the fo'c'sle of all places, playing cards and looking very contented. I says to him, 'Are you not getting sick?'

'No,' he says, 'I'm a destroyer sailor.'

'And you joined the crew of a submarine?'

'Well, it was either a submarine or the Eastern Front fighting the Russians.'

That's a real example of Hobson's Choice! I remember the boys became very fond of the Germans on board and when we arrived in port, we were all at the gangway wishing them goodbye and good luck. Would you believe it! The blinking RAF military police started shouting at us, 'Let them go. Don't fraternise!' 'Leave them alone,' shouted some of our crew. 'They're good blokes! They're just as good as some of you probably and better!' Well, if they did, the military police were furious, it was very nearly a stand-to. Our prisoners had our protection as far as the gangway, but they found a different attitude waiting for them once they were ashore.

As I told you there were five frigates working together at first – I could still remember the names if I tried – joined together to form an anti-submarine escort group working round the south of England. I don't know how long our ships worked together but, one by one, we lost three of our sister ships in the English Channel. What a horrible place for shipping at that time! I'll tell you about a convoy we were escorting. We were operating as before with several hundred yards between us. Our ship was up front with two others flanking and astern of us. Well, one of our sister ships signalled our captain saying, 'I have a contact.' I heard the captain say, 'Go in and have a sniff.'

Well, he went in and the next thing I knew there was a huge explosion. One of the cargo vessels disintegrated into nothing. It gave us quite a fright because we got the impression that the submarine that fired the torpedo knew exactly what he was about and singled out the ammunition-ship. Oh, she just disappeared. There was nobody picked up from her. In fact, the incident frightened the skipper and he wasn't very easily shaken.

The *Bickerton* and one other frigate were together for a while, and then, something went wrong with our companion and he also had to go into port. So we were on our own. Gosh! You don't know what loneliness is until you are the only one of a flotilla left like that in the English Channel! Nerve-racking! But just as it was getting dusk, we saw two huge shadows coming up on our side, winking at us. Two big destroyers coming to protect us till morning – to 'put us to bed'. Oh, the Channel was pretty grim.

After a spell of duty, we went to have a boiler clean and the engine looked after. But we weren't there very long when we were told to join a convoy which was to take war materials to the Russians. It was a high-powered convoy going to the far north with escort vessels galore. The crew didn't really know what was happening, but of course you only found out on the way. I should mention that this all happened after D-Day and the war was well and truly turning against the Germans. The battles were raging on land, but the action was also still going on relentlessly at sea.

So, you've got two aircraft carriers, you've got a battleship in the offing, you've got cruisers in the offing and you've got destroyers. It's a wonder they don't sink themselves, there's so many of them! Of course, all were under complete control. The admiral knew where they all were. They had to be a very brave U-boat crew to go in amongst that lot! But then, things were getting desperate for them. The ships of the convoy mustered off the coast of Northern Ireland. You know, there were some Point boys there. 'Sligo'* was there, so was Iain ('Skurrik') MacDonald from Flesherin in the Rubha. I often came across him ashore, you know, in different places. He was on one of the aircraft carriers. Moving north into the open waters of the Atlantic, our ships steered a course that kept them well out of reach of German aircraft. We weren't very frightened of submarines because the convoy had plenty of escorts against them. At that time, the Russian armies were pressing Germany from the east but were short of supplies of aircraft and bombs.

The crews of the ships in the convoy didn't really know where they were bound for. You only found out on the way. There was plenty of attention from U-boats on the voyage north but, with destroyers and frigates constantly herding the ships, they were finding it difficult to do their dirty work! The convoy got to its destination all right but ships didn't have to go into a Russian port to deliver the goods! The planes flew ashore from the aircraft carriers with their loads of bombs.

Now, we were on our way home thinking, or rather hoping, that all was well. We continued our journey home following the same arc well clear of the land and right up in the Arctic. It's funny how quickly the weather can change in those latitudes. From lovely, cool, dry weather it can change overnight so that, next morning, the wind could be howling and white seas breaking over the ships!

Disaster struck when we were 120 miles north-west of the North Cape. That's right at the most northerly landfall of Norway. Luckily, the weather was not too bad. The *Bickerton* was torpedoed and she started going down. The torpedo hit her very near to the screws and broke her back. The propellers were in bits. She couldn't move her pumps, so that the sea just poured in. She was sinking fast. Destroyers are very flimsy ships, you know.

You might be surprised that a submarine hunter like the *Bickerton*, with all our detection equipment on board, would be caught out like that – the hunter hunted by a U-boat and caught by her. Well, there were so many other warships there it's possible that our guys had just got careless. On the other hand, maybe it was the detection equipment that let us down. I'll tell

* See pp. 159 and 179.

you what I mean by that. We were far north in the Atlantic, and into the Arctic, just edging up towards the cold from time to time. The further north you go in the ocean, the more unstable the ocean conditions become. You get different layers of water. You find a cold layer, then a warm layer so that it is possible that our ASDIC beam was bent – a bit like refraction, I suppose. Our boys may not have been getting a correct reading. I think that might have had something to do with it. By hitting the *Bickerton*, you could say that the Germans were evening up the score. We had sunk at least twelve U-boats before we were caught off guard – at least a dozen, perhaps as many as twenty.

When we were hit, nearly everybody down aft was lost – the stokers and the depth-charge crew. That was a large part of our crew, the depth-charge crew and the stokers. Those of the crew who were unfortunate to be there were all killed – between thirty and fifty men. That's directly underneath the depth charges. I remember I went down because there was a fellow there who looked awfully like Donnie, my brother. Somebody told me that he was dead and I went down to have a last look at him. I remember feeling very sad.

I had commandeered a prisoner's footwear and, if I hadn't, somebody else would have! That's a price that the prisoners had to pay in return for our saving their lives and treating them with kindness and courtesy. I had a lovely German jacket on and leather sea boots. The leather was like what you see in the very best shoes or boots nowadays – supple and fur-lined. I used to go around there like an undercover Fuehrer! But on the day we were torpedoed, the boots came off mighty quick and I put on my Wellington boots again. I didn't want any German ship to find me with German boots on. As I said, there were several destroyer escorts with the convoy. One was the *Kent*. I remember her because when the *Bickerton* was torpedoed the *Kent*, which was only a few hundred yards away, went off like a blinking motorboat. Oh, yes, she left us. They couldn't afford to leave the battleship, cruiser and aircraft-carriers unprotected.

In this book *The Buckley Class Destroyers*, there is a photograph of the *Bickerton* in her death throes. I'll show you exactly what happened as she was sinking and we were leaving her. See, her stern is right under – the guys who were working the depth charges were, by this time, in the sea. We were lucky that the depth charges didn't go off, too. But she had smoke canisters there and as soon as they touched the seawater they started smoking heavily. When the photo was taken, the smoke seems to have cleared there but we had an awful job at first. It was choking us. You can see there's a sort of swell, but the weather is not too wild. Her stern is under water. And she's listing slightly to starboard. And there's some of the survivors waiting patiently to be taken off. See, they're beside the bridge. Now this crowd waiting here beside the funnel, there's the motorboat down there, waiting for to take them.

Just a few minutes after that, the ship slid down until the sea was up to her funnel. As I and other members of the crew were lowering the launch into the sea, one of the officers, much to his discredit, decided he would take charge, although he had no right to. Evacuating the survivors was up to me and the crew who were assigned to working the launch. The officer took a load of survivors to another ship, came back and shouted to me, asking if I would take her now! He went to the bow and I went to the stern. His action was not too difficult to interpret. He had made sure that 'number-one' got off the sinking ship. But the skipper was watching him. He never got any promotion after that, I can tell you. These things happened. Not very often but they did happen.

The ship was in such a state that she couldn't be towed to any harbour. With two propellers and two rudders smashed up and a cracked stern, you'd never get her to harbour. She'd be yawing and veering all over the place, you see. If they were nearer home we might have tried it, but it was 120 miles north of the North Cape. You would have had another hundred to do to get to the Faeroes, and goodness knows how far to get to Liverpool. Too big a job to tow. She was finished off with a torpedo from a fleet destroyer. I forget her name. As you can imagine, we were all conscious that the U-boat couldn't be all that far away from us. Indeed, she wasn't very far away because she was sunk before nightfall. Yes, she was sunk by a destroyer before we got on to our survivor ship.

When we had taken all the survivors off the ship, we were ready to go for home. We were told to abandon the launch. I was so fond of her that I hated to see her go free. What a waste! Before we headed off the scene, somebody on an Orly pumped a few shells into the launch and that was her finished. That was done, of course, in case the Germans got hold of her. I dearly wished I could have taken her home and left her somewhere off Bayble as we were steaming up the Minch! If I had been in a position to take her, I would have been more than happy to keep her. Her engine was about half the size of the table! She could go like the wind. Wonderful. You see the engine was heavy, it wasn't like an outboard motor with the stick on the stern. This was deep down. It was ballast. And, as you know, a decent engine can keep on going forever.

While the *Bickerton* was in trouble in the Arctic, her four sister ships met a similar fate off the south coast of England. Aye, they bought it after

D-Day. Fortunately, we'd been on foreign service and missed the action in the Channel on D-Day. After our misfortune in the Arctic, we were all due leave anyway. Of course, in choosing to tell about what it was like on warships in the Mediterranean and in the Arctic, you should know that everybody who spent four or five years in the thick of it had similar experiences.

I clearly remember my homecoming after the sinking of the *Bickerton*. I happened to see a naval policeman whom I knew in the station when we were getting on a train down south. You happened to meet people from home in all sorts of unexpected places. I once saw 'Sligo' – Donald MacKenzie from Bayble – standing on the deck of a warship that our top brass were visiting. I shouted to him, '*An ith do sheanmhair rionnaich?*' [Does your granny eat mackerel?] The top brass who were with me in the launch must have thought I had taken leave of my senses!

I remember being in Stornoway a couple of days later and a bloke shouting across to me, 'Are you enjoying your survivor's leave, then?'

I shouted back, 'Yes, how did you know I'm on survivor's leave?'

'We sank your ship!'*

As I said, Lewismen turn up in the most unexpected places!

* *The Bickerton* was scuttled by a torpedo fired from HMS *Vigilant*.

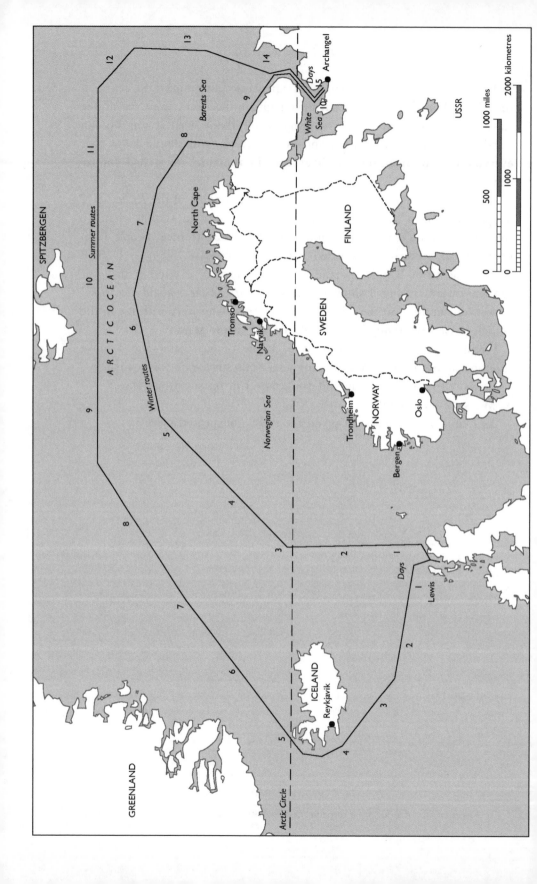

Màiri Chaluim Alas 'ac Uilleim

1896–1984

Obair an eòrna? Mo mhallachd aigesan – falbhadh esan! Falbhadh a' chruach-eòrna às mo shealladh, agus mi gha coimhead ann an cliathaich an t-sabhail! Nuair a gheibheadh sinn mo mhàthair a-mach às an t-sabhal sìos a dheas-achadh biadh . . . Thighearna, bha clach mhòr ann an cliathaich an t-sabhail agus bhiodh sinn a' slaisigeadh nam badan ris a' chlach gus am falbhadh na diasan. Ach, a ghràidh, thigeadh mo mhàthair air ais: "Nach sibh a bha cliobhar na bha an sin a bhuthaidean a dhèanamh bho dh'fhalbh mi!"

Cha robh fios aicese nach robh sinn idir air a bhith frasadh nan diasan air a' chlach mhòr a bha siud. Bhiodh mo mhàthair a' dol tron a h-uile bad a bha sin, gam fosgladh agus a' glanadh nan diasan a bha staigh nam broinn far nach ruigeadh a' chlach mhòr orra. Ach, a ghràidh, nuair a sguireadh sinn dhan a' chruach, bha an dùn mòr dhiasan a bh' ann an sin a' feitheamh rinn airson am bualadh sìos le dà shùist ròp . . . sinn a' toirt dhaibh. Dà shùiste mhòr ròp (mar buidhe-ròp long-chogaidh) gam bualadh air a h-uile clàr a leigeadh sinn sìos. Nuair a dh'fhalbhadh a' chalg dhiubh, dh'fheum-adh sinn an cur a thaobh, air falbh bhon an dùn mhòr ghrànda eile bha seo ann an cliathaich an t-sabhail. Leigeadh sinn sìos clàr mar a bha sinn a' dèanamh . . . agus bhiodh ise (mo mhàthair) a' tighinn a dh'fhaicinn na rinn sinn ceart e. Mo mhallachd mòr aig na calgan a bha siud.

Bhiodh sinn a' sàbhalachadh sìol-cura a-mach às a h-uile càil a bha sin. Sìol-cura gha chur air leth a-mach às a h-uile càil a bh' ann an sin. 'Air a fhrasadh tu an sìol – coirc no eòrna – dh'fheumadh an sìol-cura a bhith air leth airson gum biodh e agad airson na h-ath-bhliadhna a-rithist. Bha obair gu leòr fhathast ri dhèanamh air. Ach bha sinn a' faighinn tòrr feum às an obair ud ged a bha sinn air ar sàrachadh aice. Bhiodh iad a-nis a' cur sin ann an pocannan. 'Air a thigeadh latha brèagha tioram bha iad a' dol a-mach ga fhrasadh – agus bha a' chalg sin a' falbh às an t-sìol agus, 'air a bhiodh sinn deiseil, bha sinn a' dol dhan an àth leis is gha bhrùthaigeadh air braisteach. Leis a' bhùrn a bhiodh anns an eòrna agus anns an t-sìol choirc, chitheadh tu ceò a' falbh às air a' bhraisteach mar gum biodh e dol na theine aig a' bhùrn a bha falbh às an t-sìol, gus an deigheadh an sìol cho cruaidh ri brisgean.

Agus bha thu an uair sin, nuair a gheibheadh tu seans a dhol dhan a' mhuilinn, bha thu falbh le cairt leis a h-uile poca sìl a gheibheadh tu mach às an arbhar – bha thu falbh is gha bhleith airson min. Is mathaid gum biodh ceithir pocannan sìol eòrn' ann, no dà bholla min-choirc dha gach seòrs', 'eil fhios agad. Nam biodh tòrr dhaoine a' feitheamh, dh'fheumadh tu fuireachd ann gus am faigheadh tu do thurna dhan a' mhuilinn. Nuair a thigeadh do thurna, gheibheadh tu cothrom sgilidh anns an spot. Bha iad a' sgileadh an t-sìl sin anns a' mhuilinn.

Bha dà dhrabhailt ann – tè ann an sin, anns an robh thu cur an t-sìl, is bha scoop a-mach bho bonn an drabhailt far an robh i a' bleith an t-sìl gu bhith na mhin. Bha scoop a' tighinn a-mach aig bonn an drabhailt gu h-ìosal fon staidhre, is bha thu dol le poc' agus ga chur air dà dhubhan, 's a' mhin a' tighinn a-mach às an scoop sin.

Bha sinn a' dol dhan mhuilinn tron an latha, ach dh'fheumadh sinn fuireachd, is mathaid, fad' na h-oidhche, a' tighinn dhachaigh tron an fhionnairidh agus a' falbh suas anns a' mhadainn a-rithist airson, nam biodh feadhainn romhainn, gum faigheadh sinn ar turna airson bleith an t-sìl.

Nise, dè an seòrsa pàighidh a bhiodh sinn a' toirt dhan a' mhuillear? Uill, bha e a' toirt dhà na trì de mhiotraichean sìl às an drabhailt – sin am pàigheadh a bha e a' gabhail. Na h-uimhir de mhiotraichean sìl gha thoirt às gach drabhailt, gha chur ann an ciste mhòr a bh' aige ri taobh an drabhailt. Bha nise ciste mhòr ri taobh a' bhalla. Bhiodh e a' toir nan sgupaichean sìl agus gan dòrtadh dhan a' chiste sin airson am probhaid fhèin a dhèanamh. Bhiodh sin aca às dèidh dha na daoine sgur a bhleith. Gheibheadh sinn trì bollaichean min, agus uaireannan trì gu leth, no trì is dà chlach de mhin. Bha feadhainn ann na b' fheàrr na sin, a bhròinein, a rèir an t-sìl a bhiodh agad.

Bha ceithir fichead ruisg – 's e 'ruisg' a chanadh tu ri bad eòrna: à ceithir fichead ruisg gheibheadh tu . . . 's mathaid gur e trì bollachan mine a gheibheadh tu à trì fichead no trì fichead 's a deich. Bha e a rèir an robh sìol bochd orr' no an robh sìol trom orr'.

Nuair a ruigeadh sinn dhachaigh leis a' mhin, bha sinn gha cur ann an ciste – gha stampadh ann an cist'. Mura gabhadh a' chist' i, bha sinn gha stampadh is gha cur ann am baraill. Fuine, is mathaid, dà bhreacag no trì a h-uile latha gus an deigheadh a h-ith air a' cheann bho dheireadh. Cha bhiodh luchainn a' faighinn gu càil dhan a siud – Oh, no, a ghràidh, cha deigheadh gin a luch dhan a' chiste nuair a bhiodh a' mhin dùint' ann an cist'.

B' e siud am biadh eile bha sinn a' cur mu seach airson a' gheamhraidh:
min-choirc. Bha sinn a' faighinn dà bholla min-choirc no dà bholla gu leth
de mhin-choirc, buntàt' is iasg no buntàt' is sgadan, fad a' gheamhraidh
airson diathad; agus uaireannan bhiodh e againn gu ar suipear. Bho àm gu
àm, bhiodh sinn cuideachd ag ithe feòil. Bhiodh iad uaireannan a' ceannachd ceathramh mairt de dh'fheòil airson a shailleadh. Bhiodh iad a'
marbhadh crodh an uair ud – ceathrar againn a' dol timcheall air bò.
Bhiodh ceathramh an duine aca. Bha feadhainn a bhiodh a' ceannachd
crodh. Gheibheadh tu an crodh, an uair ud, air sia notaichean, seachd
notaichean. Is bhiodh tu marbhadh bò eadar crowd. Ceathrar na coignear
aca, is na h-uimhir aig a h-uile duine gha fhaighinn, a' dèanamh roinn air
a' chorp aice agus gha gearradh sìos na pìosan – agus a h-uile duine a' falbh
is a' tighinn gha shailleadh agus a' dèanamh pìosan dhan a sin; potato soup
chun na suipearach na chun na diathaid, a rèir dè am mood anns am biodh
tu airson a dhèanamh.

Smaoinich air an ullachadh a bha sinn a' dèanamh air an fhearann mus
tòisicheadh sinn a' cur. Uill, a Thighearna, is math gun dh'fhalbh e! O, a
Chruthaidheir! Is mi bha sgìth de bhàrr a' chladaich le feamainn is le clèibh!
Chan iongnadh ged a thigeadh mo ghlùinean gu bhith lag! Bha luchd an
todhair againn cho beag . . . dh'fheumadh sinne a bhith a' cur a-mach an
todhair a h-uile ceann trì mìosan, is cha leigeadh mo mhathair no m' athair
dhuinn biod a chur a-mach gun feamainn a bhith na cheann, ag ràdh gum
biodh am bùrn a' toirt an neairt às an todhar na aonar. Dh'fheumadh layer
feamainn a bhith eadar a h-uile fichead cliabh todhair – ochd clèibh de leud.
Tha cuimhn' agam aon latha is mi cur sìos an todhair còmhla ri mo
mhathair – Thighearna, leis cho fad' 's a bha mi a' faireachdainn an todhair,
nach robh e tighinn a-nuas air an talamh . . . bhiodh mo mhàthair a' cur
nan sreathan cho dlùth ri chèile. Is ann a bhithinn-sa air cùl mo mhàthar
. . . bhithinn a' tarraing mo chliabh a-nuas bìdeag. Tà, nuair a thigeadh ise
nuas le cliabh fhèin, theannadh i sìos an cliabh sin na b' fhaisge dhan an
fhear aice fhèin a-rithist. Dh'aithnicheadh i mar a bha mi leigeil an
sraonadh dhan an dà shreath bho chèile, dh'aithnicheadh i . . . Theireadh
i, "Tha thusa toirt an dà chliabh sin ro fhada bho chèile, is chan fhàs càil
anns an talamh mar a tha thu a' leigeil an talamh bàn le dìth mathachaidh!"

Nuair a bhios mi a' cuimhneachadh air an obair a bh' againn ga
dhèanamh air mullach an taighe – O, mo mhallachd air! A Thighearna,
nuair a bhiodh sinn a' tughadh an taighe, dheigheadh sinn na mhullach. Bha
againn ris an t-seann thughadh a thoirt dheth agus bha sinn làn dhan an
t-sùith. Bhiodh tu air do ghànrachadh. Agus nuair a thilleadh tu nuas
bhiodh an sùith air feadh a h-uile càil a-riamh air feadh an taigh.

Bha thu gha bhuain . . . a' buain an eòrna leis a' bhun-dubh, ga tharraing às an talamh. Nuair a bhiodh tu ga cruachadh bhiodh dà fhireannach a' sgathadh, a' gearradh dheth a' bhun-dubh. B' e sin an rud a bhiodh a' dol air a' mhullach aig'. 'S e sin a-nise – mo mhallachd aig a' bhun-dhubh a tha sin! Mo mhallachd eile aige – bhiodh tu ga shriopaigeadh mar sin, agus an aghaidh agad fèidhear mar miner, aig stuth nam badan-dubha. 'S e sin a-nis a' chonnlach a bha dol air an taigh-dubh. Is 'air a dheighinn suas gu cùl an taigh a chur tughadh gu mo mhàthair – is 's e iad fhèin (am bodach 's a' chailleach) a dh'fheumadh a bhith càradh an tughaidh – brèagha nam beachd fhèin – bho sail gu sail. Nuair a shealladh tu suas mar shin, bhiodh e cho brèagha coimhead, ach bha thu air do mhallachadh mus fhaigheadh tu air glanadh na bha shìos air 'deic a' bhàta'! O, Thighearna, bha deic a' bhàt' – cha robh càil nach robh cur fairis le tughadh agus sùith!

Bha againn an uair sin ri dùn sùith a dhèanamh. Nuair a gheibheadh sinn latha brèagha, bha sinn ga chur na eallaich air ar muin sìos dhan lot airson a chur ris na barran anns an sgrìob-bhuntat'. Is mo mhallachd aig cearcan Uilleim Roisilinn! Bhiodh iad a' tighinn a-nuas bhon a' Chreag a sgrìobadh air falbh a h-uile càil a bha sin. Bhiodh iad ris an dol-a-mach sin dhà is trì a dh'uairean anns an latha. Ach nuair a thàinig Iain Torachan às an Eilean Sgiathanach, mhaoidh e air Bean Thorcaill: "Dia orm, mura cuir thu na cearcan agad fo ghlas, cuiridh mise am peilear dhan a h-uile gin aca air do bheulaibh!"

Is rinn iad sin – an glasadh. Bha iad a' cumail obair rinn – na bugairean! Bha iad cho lìogach, a bhròinein. Thighearna, bha iad cha lìogach . . . cha tigeadh iad a-nuas fhad 's a bha sinn anns an lot ag obair. Ach, a Thighearna, bha iad a' tighinn a-nuas (bha iad glaist' shìos bho tòin taigh Thorcaill fhèin), a' tighinn a-nuas aig bonn na Creig mar sin gus an tigeadh iad suas an stioghaidh fhad 's a bha sinne a' gabhail sìos a dh'iarraidh na feamainn . . . far am biodh Aonghas a' togail na gainmhich a bha shìos fo bonn na lot againn ann an sin. Taobh taigh Uilleim Roisilinn dhan an Lèig – far am biodh na sìtheanan buidhe a' fàs as t-samhradh. Chuir Torachan stop air na cearcan an uair ud. Is, gu sealladh Dia ormsa, fhuair sinne faochadh. Cha robh biod sùith a bhiodh againn ri na barran – 'n dèidh fàd an latha a thoirt a' cur an t-sùith sin ris a h-uile sreath bharran a bhiodh ann an sin, bhiodh a h-uile biod sùith a bha sin cho fada bhon an t-sreath is a tha am mat sin bhon an stòbha, aig na donais air a reubadh air falbh. Ged a bha an sùith salach, 's e obair chàilear a bh' ann a bhith 'g obair anns na sgrìoban-bhuntàta. Ach bhiodh tu le do dhruim crom fad an latha.

Dhèanadh an sùith am buntàta càilear nuair a bhiodh tu ga fheuchainn aig deireadh an t-samhraidh: buntàta agus spealtragan sgadain. Bhiodh fàileadh brèagha – chan fhairich thu fàileadh brèagha air a' bhuntàta an-diugh ann – aig buntàt' ùr. Agus as t-fhoghar, chan fhaic thu ùbhlan air barran a' bhuntàta an-diugh mar a chitheadh tu an uair ud.

Bha 'n obair bu truime a' tòiseachadh aig toiseach an earraich, nuair a bhiodh sinn a' tòiseachadh as t-earrach san Dimàirt às dèidh nan Ordaigh-ean. Dh'fheumadh sinn tòiseachadh leis na spaidean nuair nach fhaigheadh sinn each a threabhadh an talamh dhuinn. Bha sinn a' dèanamh dà thionndadh dhan a h-uile talamh a bha sinn. Nam beachd fhèin, chan fhàsadh càil le aon tionndadh! Dà thionndadh – is mo mhallachd mòr aig a' chliath. Cliath an duine againn gha tarraing às dèidh a chèile le ròp a bha cho fada ri feist nan each ann an sin. Mu ar h-amhaich a' slaodadh an dà chliath. Is dheigheadh iad an uair sin a chur an t-sìl, nuair a chliathadh sinn an talamh, an dèidh dà thionndadh a thoirt dha. Nuair a bhiodh sinn a' cur a' bhuntàt' dh'fheumadh sinn dà thionndadh a thoirt dha agus a chliathadh airson a dhèanamh mìn romhainn mus fhaigheadh sinn air an sgrìob-bhuntàt' a dhèanamh rèidh airson am buntàt' a chur. Is nuair a bhiodh am buntàt' a' tighinn ris anns an talamh, dh'fheumadh sinn a ràcadh, le ràcan le ceann fiodha. Cas bruis le ceann ràcain agus "fiaclan ann mar fiaclan bò-mhara", mar a thuirt Iain Beag 'Ain Bhàin! Fiaclan fiodha ann airson a bhith pronnadh nan cnapan a bhiodh air an talamh romhainn.

A Thigheana, mar a thachair mo latha rium, nam èirigh an-àirde! Chan iarrainn, O, chan iarrainn a-chaoidh . . . Ach thàinig caochladh air an t-saoghal a bh' againn nuair a thòisich an Cogadh Mòr. Dh'fhalbh an saoghal a bh' ann. Everything is away.

Chan aithnicheadh an ginealach a th' ann an-diugh cò air a bhiodh tu bruidhinn. Nam b' ann mu dheidhinn Pagastan, thuigeadh iad tòrr na b' fheàrr cò air a bhiodh tu bruidhinn na thuigeadh iad an èirigh suas a bh' againne. Dh'fhalbh siud nuair a thòisich an Cogadh agus a thòisich daoine a' leigeil dhiubh nan lotaichean.

Às dèidh an Dàrna Cogaidh, sguir iad a chur sìos eòrna is coirc is buntàta nuair a thòisich daoine a' faighinn donations, benefits, peinnseanan. Sguir a h-uile càil dhan a siud. Chan fhaic thu an-diugh talamh buntàta anns na bailtean. Thug sin caochladh mhòr air beatha dhaoine.

Uill, tha aon rud: tha rest aig na boireannaich a bha ga dhèanamh. Chan eil guth ac' an-diugh gu robh leithid a riamh ann. Cha dèanadh iad an-diugh e ged a bhiodh aca ri dhèanamh. Chan eil an neart unnta. Ach cha dhèanadh an ginealach a th' ann an-diugh e bharrachd – cha bhodraigeadh iad. Dh'fhalbhadh iad dha na hotels; dheigheadh iad gu deasg, bhon a bhiodh sgoil aca. Dhèanadh iad sin – ach no aig an taigh work.

Cha robh càil na mo bheath' ach eallaich! Mura biodh eallaich mòine, bhiodh eallaich feamainn. Mura biodh eallaich feamainn, bhiodh eallaich fodair le coirc is eòrna. Is mura biodh sin ann, 'air a sguireadh eallach a' mhòine ga tarraing às t-samhradh, dh'fheumadh cruach mhòr talmhainn a bhith againn gha dèanamh dhan a' chrodh airson bedding a dhèanamh dhaibh tioram tron a' gheamhradh. Cha robh càil ach eallaich na mo bheatha – all my life. Taing do Dhia gun dh'fhalbh e.

Bhiodh eallaich mhòr againn a' tighinn bhon an t-slèibh mhònach . . . làn a' chlèibh agus m' àirde fhìn os cionn beul a' chleibh. 'S bhiodh sinn a' fighe fhad 's a bha sinn a' coiseachd . . . a' fighe agus a' toirt dhachaigh na mònach, agus bhiodh an diathad deiseil nuair a thigeadh sinn dhachaigh aig mo mhàthair. Is dh'enjoyaigeadh sinn an uair sin ar diathad, air sgàth bhith muigh is a' toirt dhachaigh na mònach agus a' fighe agus a' dèanamh gheansaidhean no socks aig a' cheart àm. Bha sinn a' dèanamh an dà obair còmhla. Dh'fhàg sin làidir sinn – up till now. Cha tug mi latha riamh tinn anns an leabaidh le tinneas-cuirp gus na thòisich mo dhà ghlùin a' fàill-igeadh. Ach is beag an iongnadh aig na h-eallaich a bha mi a' dèanamh an toiseach mo bheatha.

Na faighnich dhomh dè an aois a tha mi! Thighearna, cha bheag sin! Cha bheag an aois a tha mi! Chan eil mi gu bhith 'g innse! Tha twenty-three! Uill, chaidh mo bhreith ann an 1896, cha chreid mi. Tha sin ceithir fichead bliadhna is a ceithir. Oidhche Challainn. Sin agad e dhut! Cha robh mi latha riamh tinn. Cha bhithinn a' faighinn preusantan aig àm mo bhirthday. Cha robh sgilligean ann.

Nuair a bhiodh Oidhche Challainn ann, 's ann a bhiodh na balaich a' dol timcheall air an t-slabhraidh a' gabhail Amhran na Callainn. "O-ro bhith o, O-ro bhith o." Dè mar tha siud a' dol? "Ho-ro bhith o, na slatan, na slatan . . . " Bhiodh bonnach coirc againn air a dhèanamh le siùcar, poca air a dhruim, fear eile a' gabhail an Amhrain. Bhiodh sinn a' toirt bonnach coirce dhan an fhear a bhiodh leis a' phoc' . . . no ìm, no siucar, airson gun dèanadh iad fhèin teatha nuair a sguireadh iad a ruith air feadh nan taighean. Tron fhionnairidh.

Bhiodh na balaich a-nis, às dèidh na suipearach – bha iad a' dol a-null an rathad agus suas gu stacaichean Sheonaidh Aonghais Uilleim, agus bha bean Aonghais Uilleim ag radh nuair a bha i beò, bhiodh i ag ràdh, "Tha na blaigeardan grànda ud a' tighinn a chluich a' cheòl ud a h-uile oidhche, gar cumail-inn bho chadal. Nach eil iad dìreach mar a tha na cait – a' caithris na h-oidhche agus a' cadal an latha."

Bhiodh iad an uair sin, fear an siud is fear an seo, a h-uile fear a' dol gu a roghainn fhèin a shuirghe fad na h-oidhche dhan an leabaidh-àrd, man tuirt iad. Na bi ag innse mo chòmhradh-sa dhaibh ann an Glaschu air do bheath'!

Sin agadsa mar a bha an t-suirghe an uair ud. Cha b' e cuairt an rathaid a bhiodh iad a' gabhail. Ist, cha deigheadh iad (a' chlann-nighean) cuairt an rathaid an uair ud ann le eagal am beath'. Ach cha b' e càil a dh'eagal a bh' oirre gun tachaireadh duine riutha a mharbhadh iad ach eagal aca ro na balaich. Cha robh iad idir cho forward ri clann-nighean an là an-diugh, a thèid air holiday dha na taighean aca mìosan mus . . . Theicheadh iad bho na balaich nam biodh iad a' tilgeil orra nam balach . . . theicheadh sinn air falbh gus nach tachaireadh iad rinn leis an nàire a bhiodh againn riutha. Ach bhiodh sinn ga enjoyaigeadh – an t-suirghe oidhche. Dh'enjoyaigeadh sinn oidhche nam biodh iad a' tighinn a dh'iarraidh 'rùm' oirnn!

Bhiodh sinn gan leigeil a-steach air an daras. O, a ghràidh, b' ann air an daras; bhiodh na fir a' tighinn a-steach air an daras. 'S bhiodh leabaidh-àrd aig a' chlann-nighean shìos aig an teine far am biodh na fir a' stad airson bruidhinn riutha. Bhiodh na bodaich is na cailleachan shuas anns a' chùlaist – anns a' cheann a bha shuas. Bho dheigheadh iad a chadal, cha bhiodh gnothaich aig a' cheann a bha shuas ris a' cheann a bha bhos! Cha bhiodh am bodach agus a' chailleach a' cluinntinn càil. Bhiodh na balaich a bhiodh a' tighinn a-steach air an oidhche . . . fear a thigeadh a-steach – cha bhiodh duine a' tighinn a-steach ach an aon duine a bha a' dol a shuirghe air an nighean, a bhiodh a' tadhal oirre. Cha bhiodh duine a bha shuas a' cluinntinn sin. Bhiodh e a' tighinn a-steach mar mèirleach a bhiodh a' tighinn a ghoid. Ma bha cùisean a' còrdadh ris an dithis, dh'fhuiricheadh am fear a thigeadh a-steach airson greis mhath . . . Uill, gu ceithir uairean sa mhadainn, eadar sin is às dèidh ceithir, mus tigeadh an latha. Dh'fhàgadh e mus tigeadh an latha is nach fhaiceadh daoine e a' falbh.

Bhiodh na balaich a bh' anns a' bhaile sa a' falbh suas an sgìre a shuirghe air clann-nighean ann an ceann shuas an Rubha. Bhitheadh, às a seo suas do Phabail is à Pabail a Gharrabost, à Garrabost chon a' Chnuic . . . is air feadh Leòdhais gu lèir . . . all over Lewis. Chan eil mi cinnteach an e droch rud no rud math a th' ann gun deach sin às an fhasan. Mar a tha iad an-diugh, 's ann a tha iad a' dèanamh na suirghe aig na dannsan, tighinn às na pictures – a' gabhail chàraichean, busaichean dhachaigh, no a' dol cuairt le càraichean. Fear aig a bheil càr, bidh e a' toirt an girlfriend a-mach dha na pictures no cuairt anns a' chàr.

Tha mi a' meas gu robh e na b' fheàrr anns an latha anns an robh mi fhìn òg. Saoilidh mi gu robh sinne ga enjoyaigeadh na b' fheàrr. Cha robh an còrr ann dhuinn! Cha robh 'n còrr ann. Cha robh càr againn ann an uair ud. Nuair a bha cùisean a' tighinn gu buil agus a bha cupall a' dol a phòsadh, bhiodh rèiteach beag aca gha dhèanamh is bha rèiteach mòr aca às dèidh sin. An uair sin, bha banais mhòr aca gha dhèanamh. Is bha a h-uile duine ag ullachadh cearc airson a dhol gu taigh na bainnse – ga marbhadh is ga bruich. Bhiodh banais mhòr aca agus danns anns an t-sabhal fad na h-oidhche.

Nise, an seòrsa còmhdaich a bhiodh oirre – bhiodh còmhdach, uill, a rèir an fhasain a bh' ann. Bhit' a' dèanamh blobhsa le broilleach sìoda air. Agus gùn an aon seòrsa, sgiort an aon seòrs' ris a' bhodhaig agus rud ris an canadh iad ceipichean lios agus bonaidean beaga cruinne mu an ceann. Cha b' ann geal idir a bha an t-aodach a bh' air a' bhean-phòsaidh. Cha b' ann, ach gorm no slate-coloured – any colour you would choose.

Air an fhireannach, cha bhiodh air ach deise shrianach – deis' is tàidh. O, bhiodh fireannach all right, cha bhiodh air ach briogais co-dhiù. Cha b' urrainn dha a chur air ach briogais, mar a bh' air a sheòrsa fhèin, agus seacaid, tàidh is ad chruaidh. Tha cuimhn' agamsa a bhith dol gu pòsaidhean a Gharrabost. Bhiodh na cupaill a' dol suas an rathad mar gum biodh iad air tiodhlaiceadh, a' dol suas gu ruigeadh iad Garrabost, a' leantainn cupall a' phòsaidh. Càil ach "Hurrah! Hurrah!" aig a h-uile duine ac' ag èigheachd; a h-uile duine, a h-uile cupall, feidhear mar tiodhlaiceadh. Is bha bràtaichean a-mach aig a h-uile duine air slatan, a' sealltainn gu robh pòsadh anns an astar. Bhitheadh! Bha feadhainn ann a bha cur suas flagaichean airson sealltainn gum biodh pòsadh anns an àite, ach cha robh a h-uile duine cur suas flagaichean idir.

Chanainn gur h-e latha sona anns an robh sinn beò nam òige. A ghràidh, bha e sona gu leòr gus na thòisich an Cogadh Mòr. Thug an Cogadh Mòr air falbh na balaich – a dh'aon oidhche. Na balaich a bha dhan enjoyaigeadh fhèin an uair ud. Thugadh air falbh iad a dh'aon oidhche dhan a' Chogadh agus cha do thill a' chuid bu mhotha aca riamh. Mharbh sin a h-uile càil a bh' ann. Mharbh e, cha mhòr, an enjoyment a bh' aig an generation a bh' ann an uair sin. Mharbh e cha mhòr a h-uile càil. Shèinsig an saoghal gu lèir an uair sin. Tha barrachd enjoyment aig an fheadhainn sinn an-diugh air na bh' againne. Cha robh enjoyment againn ann. Cha robh hàllaichean-dainns ann, càil ach uireas 's a dhèanadh iad ann an sabhal air banais no aig na balaich a bhiodh a' danns fada dhan an oidhch' . . . gu dà-reug agus, an uair sin, a bhiodh a' sgapadh bho chèile is a' falbh a shuirghe chon a' chlann-nighean a bhiodh iad a' ruith às dèidh dà uair dheug. Bhiodh iad a' falbh an siud is an seo. Ach an-diugh 's e a tha agad suirghe an rathaid, suirghe ann an càraichean, dol gu dannsan ann a hàllaichean-dainns, dèanamh appointment agus a' falbh mar sin.

Anns an là ud, bha an Soisgeul air a chumail ceart. Tha cuimhn' agamsa nuair a bha mi ag èirigh an-àirde – dh'fheumadh buntàta na Sàboind a bhith air a nighe lem athair a h-uile oidhche Shathairn, for dinner Sunday, airson nach biodh càil ri dhèanamh air Latha na Sàboind ach na soithichean a nighe a bhiodh agad às dèidh do bhiadh. Ach an-diugh, chì thu na fireannaich a' dol a-mach leis na coin a dh'obair air na caoraich . . . mach ann an sin dhan an t-Siùmpan. Bha Latha na Sàboind air a chumail cho quiet an seo ri meadhan na h-oidhche. Chan fhaiceadh tu càil a' gluasad, na nonsense sam bith a' dol air adhart air Latha na Sàboind – Oh, no! Chan e an aon seòrsa dòigh a th' anns an generation an-diugh is a bh' againne nuair a bha sinn òg ann. Eadar-dhealaichte anns a h-uile dòigh. Chan e an aon dòigh a th' unnt' ann an dòigh sam bith. Tha iad eadar-dhealaichte. Chan urrainn dhut bruidhinn riutha. Tha iad a' toirt dhut cheek air ais ma bhruidhinneas tu riutha. Ann an dòigh, shaoileas iad gu bheil thu gha mhionaigeadh. Ach nuair a bha sinne ag èirigh an-àirde, cha robh sinn a' tionndadh ri duine mar shin a bhruidhneadh rinn airson ar math fhìn.

Bhiodh ar pàrantan air a bhith a' toirt rabhadh dhuinn nam biodh sinn a' dol a-mach às an taigh: bhiodh m' athar ag ràdh rinn, "Cuimhnichibh a-nise, ma thèid sibh a thaigh dhuine dha na tha timcheall: ma chì sibh prìne air an làr, cuimhnich nach cuir sibh nar h-aodach fhèin e. Cuimhnich gun toir sibh seachad e do bhean an taigh. Agus nuair a dh'fhàsas sibh nas aosta, nuair a thòisicheas sibh a' dol dha na bùithtean, bidh rudan brèagha air na cuntairean agus feuchaibh mus cuir sibh bhur làmh air agus nach coisinn sibh nàire dhòmhsa."

Mary Ferguson MacKenzie

1896–1984

I hated working on the barley. I curse even the memory of the cornyard stack and the pile of harvested barley that used to be waiting for me in the barn! Sometimes my mother left us working, while she went back home to prepare a meal. O my Lord, there was a big stone standing there by the wall of the barn against which we had to thresh the barley sheaves. That was done to dislodge the grain from the sheaf. But, gosh, when my mother would return, she would inspect what we had done and, with justifiable suspicion, say, 'You seem to me to have been mighty quick going through all those sheaves!'

We had been hoping that she wouldn't twig to the fact that we hadn't been at all thorough in threshing the sheaves! Unlike us, she was meticulous in getting all the grain off the barley to the extent that she used to open each sheaf to get at any ears of grain that were hidden within and had been unaffected by our threshing.

But, my dear, when at last we had threshed the whole of the barley-stack there was a huge pile of bearded grain waiting to be given the next bashing, but this time using flails. Our flails were two lengths of ropes as thick as hawsers from a battleship! With those, we hammered away at the batches of bearded grain until the beards came off. When that was successfully done to one batch, the treated grain was carried away so as to be clear of the mountain still waiting to be done. Before the next batch was brought on to the floor, my mother would come to inspect our work and make sure that everything was to her satisfaction. A thousand curses on barley beards!

It was important to set aside enough grain for us to plant in the following spring. But plenty of work remained to be done after the flailing. Although we were exhausted by the demands of the cereals, we certainly benefitted from the effort. The grain that was to be reduced to meal was shovelled into sacks. When a good, dry day came, it was taken out to be winnowed. In that process, all the extraneous material was discarded and, after that, the grain was ready to be taken to the kiln. The grain was heated over a strong heat and you could see smoke [vapour] rising from it as if it were on fire. It would gradually become as hard as the root of the silverweed.

When you were allocated a place at the Garrabost mill, you went off with a horse and cart loaded with all the sacks of grain that you wished to reduce to meal. You'd take enough of barley and oats to give you two bolls [290 litres] of each. If there was a queue at the mill, you just had to wait your turn. When you were called, you prepared to have the 'shelling' done at once [i.e. removing the husks of the grain].

There were two hoppers. Into the one hopper your grain was poured, to trickle down between the grinding-stones. A scoop protruded at the foot of the stairs and you had to go down there and hang a sack on two hooks to receive the meal.

We went to the mill, four miles from our home, during daylight hours and had to stay there, perhaps, all through the night. Sometimes, if there were others in the queue in front of us, we came home in the evening and went back in the early morning to get the job done.

The miller was paid for his work in this fashion. He took for himself three measures from each hopper. That was the pay he received – so many measures taken from each hopper. Now, he had an enormous chest against the wall. He used a scoop to pour his share into the chest. What was in the chest was his. That was his reward, after the customers' milling was done. We would come away with, perhaps, three bolls, or three and a half, or three bolls and two stones of meal. Some people came away with far more than that but, of course, that depended on the amount of grain they brought to the mill.

You might arrive with eighty barley sheaves. From that much, or from sixty or seventy sheaves, you might expect to get three bolls of barley-meal. It all depended on whether the barley grain was light or heavy. On arriving home with the meal, we would pour it into a chest and stamp it down as tight as possible. If the chest couldn't contain it all after stamping it down, we would put the excess in a barrel. Then baking – perhaps you'd bake two roundels of bread every day until the whole lot was eaten. Of course, the meal was safe from mice as they could not possibly get into the chest.

Oats was the other cereal we sowed to provide us with food during the winter – oatmeal. We used to get two and a half bolls. Potatoes and fish or potatoes and herring all through the winter for our afternoon meal and, occasionally, for our supper. From time to time we also ate meat. Some-times, they purchased quarter of a beef carcass, which they salted. At that time, they used to slaughter cattle. You could purchase a cattle beast for £6 or £7. A cow was slaughtered to be shared between a crowd – perhaps four or five people – with everybody taking a certain amount, backwards and forwards taking chunks to be salted – for potato soup at supper, perhaps. It all depended on the prevailing mood when, during the day, you wished to have a meal which included soup.

Consider the amount of preparation there was before we could sow or plant the seed in the ground. Well, my goodness, I'm so glad it's all behind us! O Lord, how tired I was of the drudgery of hauling seaweed on my back over the lip of the cliff [at the foot of the croft]. Is it any wonder that my poor knees are now so weak! The amount of farmyard manure we had was not great. We had to carry it [to the fields] every three months. My mother and father would not allow us to put any manure on the fields without its being augmented with seaweed. They used to claim that rainwater washed the strength out of the manure. It required a layer of seaweed to be deposited on the ground between each twenty creel-loads of manure arranged in rows eight creel-loads wide.*

I remember one particular day my working with my mother on the manure. My goodness, I was seeing our advance down the field so slow that I began to cheat my creel-loads slightly further down than was the norm. My mother used to have the rows of creel-loads too close for my liking, so I thought I could establish a new routine. However, when she tumbled to what I had been up to, she would deposit her own to conform to the 'correct' pattern and proceed to pull mine into line! She knew at a glance what I had been trying to do. She'd shout, 'You have deposited your creel-load so far apart from the last one that you are going to leave untreated gaps in the field, with the result that nothing will grow there because of the lack of fertiliser!'

Then, when I remember the amount of work we had to do [annually], servicing the roof of the house. Oh, curses on it all! When we set about thatching the house, you'd go up on to the thatch and end up covered in soot. You'd be absolutely filthy. Then, when you came back down, you'd find soot all over the inside of the house.

The barley was reaped with the roots still on the plant.† During the process of making a barley-stack in the cornyard, two men were employed to cut the 'black-end' half from each sheaf. The lower part of the barley

---

* The fields were parallel strips, each about four metres wide and about 150 metres long. They were on a gentle slope and terminated at an eroded boulder-clay cliff, four metres high, overlooking the foreshore.

† Unlike oats, which were harvested by scythe or sickle, the barley crop was harvested by pulling the plant out of the ground by the root.

plant was used to thatch the top of the stack. I hated those black-ends. Because of all the soil that was bound to come off them, your face ended up as black as a miner's. The black-ends were also used to thatch the house. I used to go up top to pass the new thatching materials to my mother. Of course, she and my father were the ones who carried out the repair of the thatching – 'immaculately', according to themselves – and going from one pair of rafters to the next. When you looked up at the completed work, it certainly was very neat and tidy. However, when you began to clear up the 'ship's deck', that was quite a different story. What a mess! The whole of the 'deck' – the floor of the house – was full of thatch and soot.

When the house had been thatched to our parents' satisfaction, we had to make a soot-mound [consisting of the old sooty thatch]. When a good dry day came, we had to creel all that sooty thatch on our backs down on to the croft where it would be deposited in the rows, against the young potato shoots. Curses on Uilleam Roshilin's poultry! His family's chickens used to sneak up from the shore and scrape away all the sooty thatch that we had done in the field. We had to chase them away three or four times a day. Relief came when Iain Torachan, a Regular soldier from the First World War, came from the Isle of Skye to live beside us. He went to Mrs Torquil [daughter of Uilleam Roshilin] and said to her, 'If you don't lock up your chickens, I'll shoot every one of them right there in front of you!'

As a result of that outburst, Mrs Torquil did lock them up. You see, the chickens had been keeping us on the hop. A gang of vandals! You wouldn't believe how cunning they are. They wouldn't sneak up on to the field so long as we were working in the croft. But while we were down on the shore collecting seaweed, just down where Angus used to collect sand by the patch where the marsh marigolds grow in summer, they would sneak up from the shore by way of the cliff-path. Torachan put a stop to those hen-raids and what a relief that was! All our hard work putting soot against the potato shaws had been good for nothing through being consistently scraped away. But although the peat soot was dirty when we were working with it in the potato field, it wasn't really unpleasant work even though you had to be bending down all day.

At the end of the summer, when you ate the potatoes, you found that the peat soot had given them a lovely taste. Potatoes and fried herring, what a treat! Actually, the potatoes of today don't have that sweet smell we used to enjoy. Furthermore, when the potatoes are growing in today's fields, you won't see the crop bearing 'potato-apples' – the fruit of the plant.

The hardest work of the year began at the beginning of the spring. The first Tuesday after the Communion was the signal to commence. When there wasn't a horse available to do the ploughing, we had to start tilling the ground with the spades. We had to do the spadework twice over. People believed that the crops which grew from one turning of the soil would be very poor. Just imagine it: two tillings of the one field!

Curses upon the implement called the harrow. After the field had been tilled, two of us would be allocated a harrow each which by means of a stout rope, we had to pull over the ground. To pull the harrow properly, you had to hold the rope across the chest. After the harrowing, the seed would be sown and then, the field would again be harrowed.

When we were planting potatoes, we used to harrow the ground after the two tillings. That was to ensure that the ground was evened out in front of us as the planting of the potatoes progressed along the ground in straight rows. When the potato shoots began to appear, we had to rake the ground. The rake had wooden teeth on it 'like the teeth of some sea-monster', to quote Iain Beag's description! Wooden teeth, they were, for the purpose of breaking up any lumps of earth that may have been in our path as we progressed with the planting.

O my Lord, when I recall how exhausting were the demands on my stamina in my formative years! I would never wish for those days to return. But the world was transformed by the First World War. The world I knew in my childhood just vanshed. Everything is gone. Today's generation would not know what I was talking about. They would have more idea of life in, say, Pakistan, than they would have of the demands made on the young of this island at the start of the First World War. It was at that time in our history that people began to turn their backs on the crofts.

When, after the Second World War, people began to receive government donations, benefits and pensions, they began to forsake the routine of sowing barley, oats and potatoes. Everything of that nature gradually came to a standstill. Today, you can't see one field of potatoes in the villages around about us. Abandoning the crofting ways of the past brought about a great change in the way people lived their lives.

One thing is for certain: the women who had to do the work are now able to rest. Today, they have no idea that, at one time, what I've described was the lot of their forebears. Of course, the women of today would just refuse to do it even if it were to fall to their lot. The fact is that they do not have the physical strength to do it. Today's generation would rather take off to work in hotels or take desk jobs for which they have the appropriate qualifications. That's all very well, but who is there at home to do the housework?

Bearing loads on my back is the story of my life! If it wasn't loads of peats, it was loads of seaweed; if not seaweed, then manure or oats or barley. As if the amount of peat-carrying we did in summer had not been enough, we had to start straight away making a stack of earth, which would ensure that we would have dry bedding for the cows in the byre during the winter. Load after load all my life. Thank God, it's all gone.

Such big loads we carried when transporting peats from the peat moor – loads my own height of peats stacked in my creel. As we walked along with the creels on our backs, we knitted ganseys [jerseys] or socks all the way and, when we'd arrive home, my mother would be there waiting for us with our dinner. We'd really enjoy our dinner because of what we had accomplished, doing two forms of work at the one time – carrying peat-loads and knitting. The result is that I have been physically strong up till now. Until my two knees began to yield, I was healthy and haven't been ill in bed through any physical illness. But no wonder my knees are in this sorry state when I consider the loads they had to bear from my very early days.

Now, whatever you do, don't ask me to tell you how old I am! O Lord, I would have to say that I'm no spring chicken! I refuse to say, but what I will tell you is that I was born in 1896, I think. Hogmanay night is when I was born. There! I've told you. I wasn't in the habit of receiving birthday presents. There weren't any pennies to spare.

At Hogmanay, the boys used visit all the houses. They used to come and go round the cooking-chain* reciting the Hogmanay Rant, saying the 'Oro vi-o, Oro vi-o.' For the occasion, we used to make oat bannocks spiced with sugar which we presented to the lad carrying a sack; either that or some butter or sugar so that they would enjoy making tea after they had visited all the houses in the evening.

After supper, it was customary for the young men to walk along the road to the stone steps at the end of the store belonging to Johnnie MacLeod, the merchant. Old Mrs MacLeod [Johnnie's mother] used to complain, 'Those blaggards come nightly to play their music, keeping us from getting our night's sleep. They behave like cats, caterwauling all night and sleeping all day!'

After the road dance, the boys would disperse, each going this way or that to woo whichever girl he fancied. A couple did their courting in the *leabaidh-*

* In black-houses, a cooking-chain, with a hook on the end of it, was suspended from the rafters, plumb above the centre of the fire. Some of the revellers used to take hold of the chain (usually caked with soot), as they circled clockwise.

àrd [box-bed] as it was called. Be sure now not to give out my description to folk 'in Glasgow' [i.e. furth of Lewis!]. That, then, is how courtship went in those days.

Walking the roads was not the way of courting couples in those days. At that time, girls would not venture on to the road. They weren't 'forward' like today's lot who won't hesitate to go 'on holiday' to the boys' homes. In my young days, we would even avoid individual boys if, in people's minds, our names were associated with them. We'd avoid individual boys in that way because we were so self-conscious. However, we'd enjoy a night's visit from such a fellow if he were to approach us! We would allow them in by the main door. The visiting lad wouldn't enter by a window as none of our windows could open. In houses which were attached to large barns, a visiting lad might enter by the *toll-fhasgnaidh* [winnow hole].*

As I was telling you, young men usually entered by the main door. The girls' box-beds were located down by the fire in the living-room, where the visitor might chat them up. The old folk would be sleeping in the *cùlaist* [bedroom] in the 'up end' of the house. Once they retired, they would have nothing to do with the 'down end' and would not hear anything. Only one boy would be allowed to visit and that was the one who wished to court the girl and he would be as quiet as a burglar who had come to steal! If both the boy and girl got on well, the boy would stay for some time. He would probably stay until four in the morning but, at the latest, he would depart some time before daybreak. He had to be sure that people would not see him going.

Young men from this village used to go courting all through the parish, visiting girls as far as the other end of the Point peninsula. Yes, they did, to Pabail and from there to Garrabost and on to Cnoc – in fact, all over the Isle of Lewis. I cannot decide whether it's a good thing that the custom has now disappeared. Today's generation do their courting at the dances, coming away from the cinema and using cars. The young man who has a car of his own can take his girlfriend to the cinema or just take her for a spin.

All in all, I think things were better when I was young – that we enjoyed ouselves more. The range of entertainment we had was very limited. No cars in my day! When matters were progressing so well with a young couple that they decided to marry, they would have a *rèiteach beag* – a wee

---

* Immediately above the wall of the barn, there was a small gap left in the thatch by which sheaves of oats or barley were passed from the stack in the cornyard. During wet weather, the wind blowing through that gap allowed winnowing to be done indoors.

engagement party. Following that, they would have a *rèiteach mòr* – a big engagement party.* After all that ritual, they had the wedding proper. All the families round about prepared a chicken to go to the 'wedding-house' – killing the bird and preparing it and then sending it on. There was always a dance in the barn and that went on all through the wedding night.

The bride and groom were dressed in accordance with the fashion of the day. The bride wore a blouse which had a silken front and also a matching gown. The girls attending the bride wore skirts of the same material tied at the waist, along with capes and little bonnets. White was not in vogue as the colour for the bride's dress. Her dress was either blue or slate-colour or, perhaps, some other colour of her own choosing.

The groom wore just a striped suit, shirt and tie. Oh, the groom would look well. He'd wear the usual style of trousers and jacket and a hard hat. I well remember going to weddings and being in the procession as we followed the couple all the way to become wed at the Garrabost church. All the way, people were shouting, 'Hurrah, hurrah!' as we progressed along the road. There were flags flying from fishing-poles at many of the houses to show that there was a wedding in prospect.

In spite of all the hard work, I'd describe the days of my youth as happy times. Happy enough until the Great War came. The Great War took the young men overnight. The young men who had been so enjoying themselves. They were taken away to fight and most of them never returned. That killed off the customs that that generation enjoyed. It killed off almost everything and changed the world out of all recognition. Today's young people have more choice of leisure-time activities. There weren't any dancehalls in my day, so that you danced indoors [in barns] only when there was a wedding.

The Gospel was very influential. I remember how, in my formative years, my father insisted that even the Sunday potatoes had to be washed on Saturday night so that nobody would do any work on the Lord's Day – no work except that we were allowed to wash the dishes used at our Sunday dinner. Nowadays, you see men with dogs working at their sheep out there at The Siùmpan [the tallest of local hills]. The Sabbath Day used to be kept here as quiet as it is in the dead of night. You wouldn't see any activity or nonsense taking place on the Sabbath Day. Oh, no! The present generation is so different in that regard. Different in every way. Today's attitudes are different. They will not allow an adult to show disapproval or,

---

* The purpose of the *rèiteach* was to allow members of the families of prospective bride and groom to get to know each other and to celebrate the union in prospect.

particularly if it's an older person, to chastise them for their bad conduct. In my young days, you wouldn't dream of giving cheek to an adult who was trying to correct your behaviour.

Our parents used to warn us whenever we went out. My father would say to us, 'Remember when you visit the neighbours' houses, if you see as much as a pin on the floor, do not take it for your own use. Remember always to hand it to the woman of the house. And when you grow up and begin to go shopping, never be tempted to take any of the lovely things you will see on the counters and cause me to feel ashamed.'

Donald J. MacKenzie ('Sligo')

1921–

I was born on this croft, 15 Upper Bayble. When I was about a year and a half, my father died and my mother took me down to Shader – the village a couple of miles to the north of us. I was taken there to stay with my grandmother, who was staying on her own in the black-house which had been my grandfather's.

I remember a particular incident that took place while I was down there living with my grandmother. I was refusing to eat my food. I didn't have an appetite to eat the food that had been laid out before me. I was sitting between my grandmother and my mother. The food was there and I wouldn't eat it. Why that was I cannot tell you but children do that sometimes to draw attention to themselves. What came stalking in the door but a huge cockerel. To me, as a young child, it looked as big as an ostrich. Suddenly, it flapped its wings and stretched itself and crowed: 'Cock-a-doodle-doo!' I asked my grandmother, 'What is the cockerel saying, Granny?' And she said in Gaelic to me, 'Are you not eating, Donald?'

Well, without another word of complaint, I ate the food on my plate – potatoes and herring – until not an ounce of it was left! Yes, potatoes and salt herring, what else! The usual menu! It was a staple diet in those days. Now perhaps I might have got a wee bit fed up of that continuous potatoes and salt herring but, in the presence of the big cockerel, my lack of appetite vanished pretty quick!

In my day, teachers were very strict. Corporal punishment of pupils was an everyday occurrence. For the least thing, you'd be hauled out to the front of the class and given hefty strokes on your hands with what they called the 'Lochgelly tawse'. That was a two-foot piece of stiff leather about a quarter of an inch thick, if not thicker. The end of the tawse, which was the end which inflicted the punishment, was parted so that it had two spokes on it. And when those two spokes came down on your hand, you felt real pain. I believe it was effective in making the children to be obedient to the teachers. That was OK so long as the teacher was fair in his or her treatment of the pupils.

In my experience, the headmaster, Mr John MacSween, was a very nice man and rarely, if ever, used corporal punishment on the children. He was enthusiastic and helpful so far as the education of the children was concerned. He took great pride in his school, especially in the teaching of navigation. Being a seafaring generation, we as young lads were all interested in that subject. We all wanted to go to sea and it was natural that we wanted to learn the science and skills that made it possible for men to sail their ships round the world.

Navigation was a great subject. We all liked it, along with the other related subjects: Morse code, semaphore, boxing the compass, and so on. When they went into the RNR [Royal Naval Reserve] or Royal Navy, his pupils benefitted from Mr MacSween's teaching. Many of them passed their navigation examinations first-class because they had already had the rudiments taught them in their schooldays. So, all in all, although there was very, very strict discipline in the school, our schooldays were very happy days and excellent preparation for when we left school.

I was in the RNR before the [Second World] war started. We used to go up for six weeks training in gunnery – small arms and heavy guns. We did a month of small arms, squad drill and down at the heavy gun-battery for six-inch guns and various calibres. And then we had a fortnight in a naval ship to give us the feel of what it was like being in a ship of the Royal Navy. Then, of course, we came home after the six weeks with the intention of going every second year for a refresher course down to Portsmouth, Devonport or Chatham in the south of England. At that time, those were the main naval ports. That was the normal routine but, of course, the Second World War interfered with all that.

I was aged eighteen and, in fact, was called up even before the war started. Because I was in the Royal Naval Reserve, I was mobilised and was plunged straight into the hostilities.

To start off with, I was ordered on to an armed boarding vessel. She was HMS *Mona's Isle*, a steamship which before the war was used as a ferry between the Isle of Man and Liverpool. In 1939, she was commandeered by the Royal Navy. She was one of three of those ferries belonging to the Isle of Man Steamship Company which were taken by the Royal Navy. I remember that one of those, the *Mona's Queen*, was sunk at Dunkirk and a report came back to this country 'regretting' that the vessel sunk was ours. It led to some consternation back home before the mistake was corrected.

The *Mona's Isle* had an interesting history. She had sunk at one time but was raised from the seabed and refurbished. There were eight Lewismen aboard her. I was there for two years and the first bit of action that we saw was at Dunkirk. What a sight that was – the repatriation of the remnants of the British Expeditionary Force sent to France to resist the advance of the all-conquering German armies in Europe. Well, we did what we could at Dunkirk. We brought back to England thousands of men. Of course, the English Channel was full of boats of every imaginable size bringing our soldiers back home. Those who made it back lived to fight another day. The Germans conquered the whole of Western Europe but they stopped at the Channel and decided not to invade the UK at that time. Thankfully, they turned their attention to the east and invaded Russia.

Dunkirk was an experience that cannot ever be forgotten by anybody who was there. As you know, there were thousands upon thousands of our soldiers waiting on the shores of France hoping to be rescued before the advancing German armies forced them to surrender. Along with hundreds of other craft, our job was to embark as many of our soldiers as we could and transport them back to England.

The *Mona's Isle* was equipped with three guns – two four-inch guns, one forward and one aft. The third was an anti-aircraft, high-angle gun, a twelve-pounder.

Approaching the French coast we saw fires burning everywhere, as far as the eye could see. Big blazes from fuel tanks which had been hit. We proceeded towards the French coast and went in at Gravelines, a small port between Dunkirk and Boulogne. I remember that there was a large buoy which, I believe, marked the boundary of a minefield. As we approached the buoy, shells began to scream in our direction, some of them straddling us, some in front and some aft. The Germans had advanced to positions overlooking Gravelines and had got our range. Our ship began to take evasive action so as to steer out of harm's way and we thought we were going to escape unscathed. Suddenly, we were hit by three shells, one after the other. Mercifully, nobody was killed though a number of our men were wounded. Funnily enough, a shell had gone through the donkey-man's cabin and famously destroyed the man's uniform! I should tell you that the donkey-man was responsible for greasing the winches and keeping that sort of machinery in good trim. Our donkey-man was about sixty years old and had come to the *Mona's Isle* when the navy took over the ship. He had been very proud of his naval uniform which the Germans had reduced to tatters!

When we arrived at Dunkirk, the bombardment did not seem to be quite as intense. We entered the harbour and, as soon as we berthed, hundreds of our soldiers began to pour on board. You can imagine the scene. More than 300,000 British soldiers were being driven back by the Germans and were being herded into that area of the French coast, constantly under enemy fire. We left Dunkirk with perhaps between 1,500 and 2,000 men on board. We were much relieved to get away from Dunkirk but we weren't out of harm's way yet. The ship suddenly came to a halt. The main steam-pipe to the engine had been severed by one of the shells that had hit us at Gravelines. We sighted seven aircraft approaching – fighters they were, and somebody remarked that they were a squadron of Spitfires sent to escort us home. The first lieutenant told us different. 'They're Messerschmitt 109s. Get ready to fire!' he cried.

He was right, of course. The Messerschmitts came in low, firing at our guns. I was in the gun crew on the twelve-pounder, which was of 1912 vintage. It proved a very cumbersome weapon. Against the German fighters, it was like running a Clydesdale horse against a thoroughbred. My job was to supply the ammo but the gun's rate of firing was poor. We just couldn't compete. They sprayed us with their machineguns time after time. After a few passes over the ship, the seven-man gun crew were told to take shelter behind steel shields. The Messerschmitts killed a lot of soldiers and wounded many more. Of the seven-man gun crew, three or four were wounded including the sub-lieutenant, who had a string of bullets through his thigh. I can only guess but I estimate that between fifty and a hundred men lost their lives to the German machineguns.

Only one member of the *Mona's Isle* crew was killed, a seaman by the name of Bushnell whom I knew well. The destroyer *Ivanhoe* took us in tow and, in the end, a tug towed us into Dover. What a voyage that was! The decks were awash with blood and the cries of the dying ringing in our ears. At Dover, trucks were waiting for us to take the dead to mortuaries. Ambulances were there as well, of course, to rush the wounded to hospital. Repairs to the ship took two days and then we set off to bring more men home.

As I said before, I was a member of the gun crew but, my second duty was as a lookout. As I looked through my binoculars I saw, in the middle distance, an object that looked like a ship in trouble. I reported to the bridge, 'Object bearing red 10!'

As we approached, we saw that it was a French coal-burning vessel lying on her side with hundreds of men in the water, many of them dead. They had been machinegunned by a German aircraft – a terrible sight. Our engines were stopped and the first officer ordered the whaler to be lowered. When that was done, he ordered me to leave my position with the gun crew and join half a dozen of our men in the whaler. As it happened, all of them were stokers. I quickly went down 'the falls' into the whaler and the whaler moved off, over to the crippled ship. On the approach, survivors began to cling to the gunwale. I believe we managed to rescue them all. We noticed two wounded soldiers, one British and one French, standing beside the bridge and the petty officer suggested that I go on board and bring them down. We both knew that the ship could blow up any time. However, you don't think of the danger when people are dead and dying all around you. I clambered up and took the British soldier and carried him to a place where I could hand him down to the men in the whaler. The Frenchman got the same treatment. As soon as we took the two off, the crew began to row as quickly as they could towards the *Mona's Isle*. I can tell you that it really brought home to us the full horror of the war, seeing all those many dead men lying face-down in the sea. It wasn't long after we reached our own ship before the French vessel blew up and sank.

We re-entered Dunkirk and managed to berth at the mole [a pier or breakwater] there without mishap. Again up to 2,000 men embarked and we set off for Dover. On that voyage, we were attacked by Stuka bombers but escaped with less damage and loss of life than on our first mission. The whine of the Stukas was frightening at first but you sort of got used to them. Plenty of bombs exploded around us but no hits. We were fortunate in that we escaped with comparatively few casualties. Of course, if the Stukas had done as much damage as the Messerschmitts had done on our first venture, it would have been a different matter.

I have to say that the Germans were a formidable enemy. Militarism is in their blood and had been for generations. They were very well disciplined and were aggressive and fearless wherever they were required to fight. I saw one incident that demonstrated how inhuman man becomes when he is fighting for his life. A Stuka had been brought down and the pilot had managed to bail out. As you can imagine, the soldiers and sailors who had been on the receiving end were in a state of anxiety and anger – you might say that they were at boiling point. When they saw that enemy pilot hanging there in the air, descending in his parachute, they reacted with ferocity. Everywhere, guns began to blast away and the German was riddled with bullets long before he hit the ground. Man's inhumanity to man.

My memory of my experience of the *Mona's Isle* was not a very happy one. It's true that her carrying thousands of soldiers from France was a spectacular achievement and nobody can deny that. Unfortunately, a member of our crew, one of our fellow islanders, was a TB carrier and a number of our lads went down with the disease. It was a very worrying time for everybody on board. Fortunately for me, I was not one of those who succumbed.

After the *Mona's Isle*, I went on to serve on a modern frigate, HMS *Cotton*. That type of vessel was known as a 'destroyer escort' and was under the command of Lieutenant Commander Beloe. While at sea, the ship's duty was to escort convoys and that required our constantly searching for U-boats. Our task was to protect convoys of merchant ships transporting cargoes from North America to Britain and Russia. Sometimes we sailed as far south as Freetown in South Africa to meet ships which had rounded the Cape of Good Hope. It was arduous work which took us not only into the North and South Atlantic but also into the Arctic. The ship's tally against the enemy was three U-boats sunk and at least one other severely damaged. You can imagine that when we destroyed a U-boat, the crew of HMS *Cotton* felt a great sense of relief and achievement. On the other hand, I'm sure that few of us were without a feeling of sadness as we watched the grey steel tube of the enemy submarine sinking to the depths of the ocean with its crew of brave men going with her.

After the war, I came home. Having been six years at war and every part of your nerves keyed up, you found 'civvy street' too slow. I found the life on Lewis too easygoing and found it hard to settle down. I met James MacDonald, a friend of mine who was in the class with me in school, and we decided to go and join the Glasgow police. We believed that that would provide us with excitement enough! James said, 'Well,' he says, 'you go and try it and when I finish this voyage I'll join the Glasgow police as well.'

Sad to say, James's ambition wasn't to be realised. He was killed after coming ashore at Liverpool. The accident happened when the crew were settling the derrick on its crutches. It slipped the winch and hit James on the head and killed him.

I was two or three years in the police force in Glasgow before I met my wife, the fair Mary! During that time, Glasgow became home from home for us. Like all big cities, Glasgow at that time was a rough, tough place – quite a change from Lewis, I can tell you! And I enjoyed it very well. Though there were gangs, the problems facing the police were different from those they have to deal with today. Drugs and drug addiction were mostly among foreigners down by the docks. A certain number of policemen patrolled the docks on foot and they, also, had motor-patrols. But generally, drugs weren't a problem among the public. At that time, alcohol was the curse.

Even when I was at school, I was very tall. I'm six-foot-two and my wife, Mary, is nearly as tall as myself – well, not quite. At the age of twenty, I weighed fifteen stones, fifteen-seven. During the war, I did a little boxing which I enjoyed. Not that my boxing was too skilful, but I carried a fair dig at the time. During my time in the Glasgow police in the early '50s, I was in the athletic team participating in the heavy events and got quite a few prizes throwing the hammer. And of course we were also, a group of us, in the tug-of-war team which became Scottish champions and champions for the North of England and the Midlands. I enjoyed athletics.

Patrolling Glasgow streets on foot brought you face-to-face with all kinds of people and, occasionally, with situations which were dangerous. A friend of mine, Constable John MacLeod, who was well known to me and, originally, came from just a couple of miles away from here [Cnoc], was killed by a young bank clerk who had embezzled money and armed himself with a gun. While off duty and walking in the West End of Glasgow with a colleague, John recognized the villain and approached him. That cost him his life. The second policeman was also shot but survived.

The most dangerous situation I encountered was on a day in July 1952. I was on foot patrol in Castle Street. I happened to glance back and saw smoke pouring through a tenement window. I called for the fire brigade and ran up the stairs. In the flat, the smoke was dense and the fire raging. I could hear children screaming in a bed – the typical tenement hole-in-the-wall. With a wet cloth over my head, I got hold of the three children in my arms and carried them out of harm's way.* The children's mother was rescued by other officers who arrived along with the fire brigade.

I decided to come back to Lewis because my wife had an experience in Glasgow and her nerves were shattered. I decided to come home away from it. Well, Mary had become quite nervous in the city and was frightened whenever I left her on her own. That nervousness followed an incident during which a stranger accosted her – a pervert.

We came back in the mid 1950s. As soon as we came home, I started looking for work. I think I was home for about a month or two when they started laying the piped water down to the villages of Point. We tend to forget what a wonderful development that was – getting water from the tap in the house, rather than drawing it from a well some distance from the home. Of course, well water was good and beautiful to drink but what an inconvenience it was when, in dry weather, the level of the water in the well became low. In the 1950s we got not only piped water but also electricity – hydroelectric power. And what a splendid development that was. Prior to

* For this act of bravery, Constable MacKenzie was awarded the Glasgow Corporation Medal for Bravery.

the Second World War we didn't have domestic electric light in Lewis. We just relied on 'Tilley lamps' and the old-fashioned two-wick lamps, all using paraffin as their fuel.

What a huge advance also in housing conditions. On the crofts, the old black-houses were abandoned as soon as white-houses were built to replace them. Most of those new houses were funded with grants and loans from the Board of Agriculture. Just imagine how people felt in the rural villages as they moved from the black-houses of ancient design and learned to relax in modern homes in which electric lights and heat, bathrooms, vacuum cleaners and all modern conveniences were there at the throw of the switch!

For a number of years, I was a lobster-fisherman, working the shores from Seisiadar to Suardail. We made quite a good living though the weather was wild at times. The lobster is in prime condition in winter and, of course, that is when the gales are most frequent and the seas running wild. On one occasion, when I was with Kenneth MacKenzie [Coinneach Dhòmhnaill a' Phìobaire] – just a two man crew –we found ourselves in a wee spot of difficulty. We were to the north of here, down by Sheshader. We had just pulled our creels when the westerly wind began to stiffen against us. We only had the outboard engine and the oars, of course. We hadn't made much progress on our homeward journey when the wind really blasted at us. As we had only a limited supply of fuel in the tank, we decided to run before the wind. We put into the shelter of the bay of Norabhaig. Of course, there aren't any houses anywhere near Norabhaig. No mobile phones in those days! We had no way of telling them back home that we were safe and sound. Kenneth and I pulled the boat ashore as best we could, then carried the outboard home with us across the moor. Where we had left the boat is about two miles from here. Just a wee adventure that comes to mind. But that was an unusual situation. We seldom had any difficulty in returning to the beach here at Bayble, even when there was a heavy sea running. Watching out for us, Mary used to set off to meet us with tea and a bite to eat whenever she saw us coming into sight at Eilean a' Chàis. She decided to discontinue the practice after her seeing us beating our way through the billows on a particularly wild day!

I had inherited the croft at No. 15 Upper Bayble and that provided us with a sound base at which to make our home in Lewis. We decided to build a modern house and we stayed in Shader for a while until the house was complete. Once we established ourselves on this croft, we got animals. I started a flock of sheep of my own and my wife started getting poultry. We also began to cut peat for fuel. Indeed, we still cut peats, one of the few families in the village which continues to do so.

At that time, the population of Stornoway and the rural communities relied on small shops. In the crofting villages, the little shops stocked more or less everything the customers needed: meat, cheese, sugar, salt, treacle, school jotters, scythes, boots – most of the things you wanted. A sort of Paddy's Market! In Stornoway, there were one or two large shops like Lipton's, where you could buy all your groceries but, apart from Lipton's and the Co-op, there were many little shops which specialised in certain goods – tobacconists, drapers, confectioners, cafés and so on. The whole thing has changed now. Few of the villages have village shops and almost all the little shops in Stornoway have disappeared. All that business now goes through the tills of the two superstores – the Co-operative superstore or Safeway. There was nothing like that in my young days.

Since I was the age of thirty-eight or thirty-nine years I became a member of the Free Church of Scotland and began to become involved in the work of the Church. You might well ask why the Free Church and not the Church of Scotland? Well, there is actually not much difference between preaching of the Gospel in the two Churches in Lewis. Until 1843, there was only the Church of Scotland. Unfortunately, the Church of Scotland in those days was governed and controlled by the landowners and ministers were appointed by them. Ministers said from the pulpit what the land-owners wanted them to say – the very landowners who were driving the people off the land. That, of course, was the era of the Clearances, a time of great hardship for the people of the Highlands and Islands. Our oppressed people at that time decided to form their own church – the 'Free Church of Scotland'. The Declaratory Act established that the Free Church was separate from the Church of Scotland. From the time of the Reformation, the Westminster Confession of Faith was the standard doctrine of the Church of Scotland until such time as this Declaratory Act came into place. But to hear the ministers of those two separate churches preach in Lewis, the same Calvinist doctrine underlies the preaching in both. The important thing is that when God intervenes in the way you lead your life, you accept that he is the author of the transformation. But God never refused any man who truly and humbly asked to be saved. Most often, man lacks the humility to do that.

Most of the island churches are moving away from the use of Gaelic in their services. Most native Gaelic-speakers whom I know find the Gaelic service more acceptable; English is a language which has travelled far from its original Anglo-Saxon form. It has borrowings from French, German, Latin, Greek, Italian – even from Gaelic. It borrows from all other languages and that gives it huge power and scope. But as long as we live, Gaelic will not be ousted in our church, no matter what!

My own three daughters are fluent in Gaelic. Two of them, Marisa and Chrisella, live close to us here with their husbands and families. But many of today's children in Lewis refuse to speak our ancient language. When I ask some local children a question in Gaelic, they answer me in English even though they understand my question perfectly well. My eldest daughter, Etta, lives in Inverness. Now, my grandchildren in Inverness are a different kettle of fish! They speak Gaelic very well. When I address them in Gaelic, they'll respond in Gaelic and that really pleases me. I hope that, as they grow up, all my grandchildren will continue to recognise the value of our language and treasure it as much as I do. Of course, I'll continue to love them whatever language they choose to speak.

Mairead B. Mhic a' Mhaoilein

Thàinig mo chuideachd à Dùthaich MhicAoidh – ach 's fhada bhon uair sin. Tha mòran dhan chinneadh againn anns an Rubha càirdeach do chàch-a-chèile – air a thighinn a-nuas bhon chiad fhireannach leis an ainm MacAoidh a thàinig dhan dùthaich sa. Bha esan a' fuireachd ann an Aiginis agus bha e aithnichte air an ainm 'an Caoidheach Mòr'. B' e sin an t-ainm a bhiodh aca air Alasdair MacAoidh, am fear bhon tàinig na Caoidhich againne. Bha dà bhean aige. B'e Nighean a' Bhàillidh a' chiad tè a bh' aige, agus sin an fheadhainn bhon robh 'Stiù' ann an Siadar 's na daoine sin. B' e Màiri Thormoid 'Ain Thormoid an dàrna bean a bh' aige, agus sin an fheadhainn bhon robh m' athair-sa.

Bha Alasdair MacAoidh – an Caoidheach Mòr sin – ag obair air an taca ann an Aiginis, ach b' ann aig 28 Garrabost a bhàsaich e. Bha a mhac, Alasdair Alas' 'c Aoidh, ri ar taobh ann an seo, agus 's e Uilleam a bh' air mo sheanair. Thuilleadh air sin, bha Coinneach ann agus Iain agus Ruairidh. Bha teaghlach mòr ann.

Nise, mar a thubhairt mi, b' e na Caoidhich cuideachd m' athar. Ach b'ann do Chlann Choinnich a bhuineadh mo mhàthair. Bhuineadh i dhan a' bhàrd ainmeil, Uilleam Dhòmhnaill 'ic Choinnich. Tha mi cinnteach gu bheil deagh fhios agad air an leabhar aige: *Cnoc Chùsbaig*. Faodaidh tu bhith cinnteach gu bheil a h-uile duine a bhuineas dha uailleil às a' cheangal a bha againn ris. Ach chan fhaca mise Uilleam a-riamh. Chunnaic mi am 'Poidhleat', a bhràthair. Bha e pòsta air na Lochan agus bhiodh e a' tighinn a-nall agus bhiodh e a' fuireachd uaireannan an Steòrnabhagh air Newton Street còmhla ri Oighrig, a nighean. Sin gus na bhàsaich e. Bha Oighrig pòsta aig fear de Thomsonaich Àird Thunga. Tha deagh chuimhn' agam air, gun tàinig e a-nall, agus bha feusag mhòr gheal air sìos air a bhroilleach. Anns an là ud, bha feusag air a h-uile fireannach a bha air a thighinn gu latha. Ach tha cuimhne agam air feusag a' Phoidhleat, gu robh i sìos gu a mheadhan. Nuair a bha e na dhuine òg, bha e na 'chuipear-in' ann an Sgoil na h-Àirde.

Cha robh muinntir Gharraboist a' dol do Sgoil na h-Àirde idir. 'S ann a bha sinne a' dol gu Sgoil Phabail. Bha am ma'-sgoile a bh' againne iomraiteach. B' esan Maighstir Thomson, athair Derick Thomson am proifeasair – Ruaraidh MacThòmais, bàrd ainmeil eile. 'S ann an Sgoil Phabail a dh'ionnsaich sinne a' Ghàidhlig cheart. Chan fhaodadh sinn 'beó' no 'ceó' a dh'ràdh mar a bhios muinntir Phabail – O, chan fhaodadh, ach 'beò' agus 'ceò' agus 'seòladh', chan e idir 'seóladh'. Chanadh muinntir Phabail 'seóladh', agus bha a h-uile duine ann am Pabail leis a' bhlas sin air an cuid Gàidhlig – tha chon an là an-diugh. Seall mar a tha muinntir na h-Àirde fhèin. 'S e 'Màilead' a chanas iad nuair a bhios sinne ag ràdh 'Mairead'. O, ged a bha an gnàth cainnt a bha sin aig muinntir na h-Àirde, bha ma'-sgoile math aca anns an Àird cuideachd. B' e sin Iain MacSuain – Colonel MacSween. Rugadh esan an seo ann an Garrabost, dà thaigh suas oirnn an seo.

'S e a' chuimhne as òige a th' agamsa air Garrabost nuair a thàinig an teaghlach againn dhachaigh à Canada – mi fhìn aig aois nan ceithir bliadhna. Tha cuimhn' agam air a bhith a' tighinn air a' bhàta. Thàinig sinn gu Grianaig. Chan eil dad de chuimhne agam air trèana na air càil. Tha cuimhn' agam air a thighinn air bàta gu tìr an Steòrnabhagh. Bha na càirdean gar coinneachadh agus bha an rud cho annasach leam – gu h-àraid an taigh-dubh a bh' aig m' Antaidh Sìne. Nuair a chaidh mi a-steach ann an toiseach, cha bhreithinn air làimh oirre air chor sam bith. Bha mi air a thighinn gu saoghal a bha caran iongantach leam, 's mi ceithir bliadhna dh'aois!

Bha sinn air a bhith ann am Fort William, Ontario. Tha cuimhn' agam air an taigh againn cho math ri càil, agus innsidh mi dhut cionnas. Bha seilear shìos air cùl an taighe anns am biodh iad a' gleidheadh a h-uile càil. Anns an là ud, 's e taighean fiodha a bh' ann. Bha sinne ann an taigh fiodha – taigh-còmhnaidh math seasgair – agus tha cuimhn' agam gu robh stòbha ann. Bha Dena, mo phiuthar, na suidhe ann a high-chair mu choinneamh na stòbha agus bha mise air sèithear air a chùlaibh 's mo chasan air cùl a' high-chair 's mi ri seinn – nam bheachd fhìn. Siud, 's ann a thiopaig mi an sèithear air an robh Dena, agus bhuail a ceann air oir na stòbha. Abair thusa èigheachd agus rànail! Aig an àm, thurchair gu robh mo mhàthair ag iarraidh rudeigin shìos anns an t-seilear agus thàinig i na ruith a-nuas. Tha cuimhn' agam air sin cho brèagha ri càil. O, fhuair mi mo chruaidh-fhortan!

Nuair a thigeadh duine a-mach à Leòdhas – às an Rubha co-dhiù – 's ann ann thugainn a thigeadh iad. Ach cha robh iad a' fuireachd againn ach gus am faigheadh iad lodgings iad fhèin. Bha Peigi Chaluim Iain à Sìadar a' fuireachd againn; agus cuideachd Mairead Dhòmhnaill Bhig, gus an d' fhuair iad fhèin taigh. Tha cuimhn' agam orra nuair a gheibheadh iad am pàigheadh, iad a bhith a' tighinn dhachaigh thugainn le loiliopopan air cùl an cluasan. Nach mìorbhaileach an rud a chumas tu air do chuimhne?

'S i a' Ghàidhlig a bh' againn am broinn an taighe ann an Canada. Thì, 's i a' Ghàidhlig! Ma-thà, 's i! Cha robh trioblaid sam bith againn a' tighinn dhachaigh an seo, oir bha sinn fileanta gu leòr nar cànan fhìn. B' i a' Ghàidhlig a bha a h-uile duine a' bruidhinn an seo an uair ud.

Bha m' athair na foreman anns an elevator agus bha m' uncail Knox na shuperintendent, ach ghluais esan a-mach gu ruige Bhancùbhar. Nuair a thigeadh duine às ùr gu Fort William, bha càch a' faighinn obair dhaibh; bha, a h-uile duine. Bha iad còir ri chèile. O, bha! Bha iad a' cuideachadh a chèile. 'S ann anns an elevator a bha a' chuid mhòr aca ag obair. Cha robh duine an siud ach Caoidhich ag obair.

Chan eil dad a chuimhne agam dè an seòrsa biadh a bhiodh againn an Canada. Tha mi a' creidse gu robh sinn ag ithe nan rudan a bha iad ag ithe aig an taigh. Cha bhiodh sgadan saillte againn ach, bho thàinig sinn dhachaigh a Leòdhas, bha gu leòr dhan sin againn – sgadan is cudaigean 's h-uile seòrsa iasg – you name it! Sgadan saillte agus pailteas dheth! Bha gu deimhinne. Bhiodh iad cuideachd a' sailleadh na feòla.

Tha cuimhn' agam air a' bhoireannach a bha ann an taigh a bha ri ar taobh. 'S e Mrs Teasdale an t-ainm a bh' oirre. Bhiodh i uaireannan gam thoirt a-steach dhan taigh aice. Nach eil e funny na rudan air an cùm thu cuimhne, seadh, rudan a thachair nuair a bha thu dhà na thrì bhliadhnaichean a dh'aois. 'S iad sin as treasa a chùm mise air mo cuimhne. Bhiodh am boireannach ud gam thoirt suas an staidhre 's a' sealltainn dhomh an obair a bha i a' deanamh. Bhiodh i a' dèanamh tòrr crochet agus embroidery 's rudan mar sin, agus bhiodh an t-aodach sin aice sgaoilte air uachdar na leapa. Tha crochet hook agam ann an sin – bone crochet – a thug i dhomh 's mi nam leanabh airson nuair a dh'fhàsainn mòr gun ionnsaichinn an seòrsa fighe sin. Agus rinn mi sin. Dh'ionnsaich mi mar a bhiodh tu ga dhèanamh. Bha Leadaidh Miseanaraidh ann an Eaglais an Aonaidh, 's bhiodh sewing-class aice agus dh'ionnsaich i an dà chuid dhomh: crochet agus embroidery.

Nise, Mrs Teasdale a bha sin – 's e a' Bheurla a bh' aice, ach feumaidh e a bhith gum b' e a' Beurla a bha mi a' bruidhinn rithese. Tha sin mar gum biodh e a' dearbhadh gu robh an dà chànan againn – agam fhìn agus Dena. Feumaidh e bhith gu robh. Nis, a' tighinn air ais a Steòrnabhagh an seo: tha fhios agam gun tàinig sinn sìos a Gharrabost ann a bhan. Thàinig sinn sìos anns a' bhan gu taigh mo sheanmhar. Bha an teaghlach anns a' cheann shuas agus a' bhò anns a' cheann shìos. Chì thu anns a' phioctar seo an seòrsa taigh a bh'ann. Bha pìos dheth geal agus pìos dheth dubh. Tha mi a' creidse gu robh e uaireigin dubh bho cheann gu ceann, ach bha am pìos ud anns an robh an teaghlach a' còmhnaidh aca air a dhèanamh geal. Dheigheadh a' bhò a-steach gun dàil air an daras agus thionndaidheadh i gu a làimh chlì gu a h-àite fhèin. Bha an sabhal ceangailte ris an taigh.

Nise, nuair a bha na h-òrdaighean ann, bhiodh an taigh làn luchd-tadhail is bhiodh sinne nar glòraidh agus seidichean air an làr anns an t-sabhal! Bhiodh an taigh cho làn! Bha e cho faisg air an eaglais. Bha sinne a' smaoineachadh gur e rud mìorbhaileach a bha sin, na bha siud de choigrich a bhith tadhal oirnn.

Agus rud eile a bha mìorbhaileach leinn, 's e an rud a bhiodh m' athair a' dèanamh dhuinn. Bha esan air fuireachd ann an Canada a' cosnadh beòshlaint is bhiodh e uaireannan a' cur dhachaigh baraille ùbhlan. 'S am fàileadh brèagha a bha an siud! O, dh'fhuirich esan an Canada. 'S ann a bha mo sheanmhair ann an Gharrabost na h-aonar, oir chaidh balaich leatha a chall anns a' Chogadh agus bha i na h-aonar. Uill, thòisich i a' pliodaigeadh ri mo mhàthair a thighinn dhachaigh. Agus, an ceann sreath, dh'aontaich mo mhàthair. Seach gu robh e cho sealbhach s' gu robh e a' faighinn tuarastail fad bliadhnachan an Depression, bha e 1934 mus tàinig m' athair dhachaigh thugainn.

Nis, cha robh ach an dà nighean anns an teaghlach againne. Cha robh bràithrean againn idir. Tha mi a' tuigse gu robh duine cloinne aig mo mhàthair romhamsa agus gur e balach a bh' ann agus gu robh e marbh a' tighinn dhan t-saoghal. Ach cha bhiodh iad uair sam bith a' bruidhinn air. 'Eil fhios agad, bha iad an uair ud cho private a' bruidhinn. Chan eil cuimhn' agam cionnas a fhuair mi fios air sin. Ach 's iongantach mur ann gun fhiosta a thuit e bho cuideigin!

Fhad 's a bha m' athair ann an Canada, 's e 'Mairead Màrdaidh' a bhiodh ac' orm air sgàth mo mhàthar. Bho thàinig m' athair dhachaigh, 's e 'Mairead Dhòmhnaill Uilleim' a bhiodh ac' orm. Cluinnidh tu feadhainn fhathast ag radh 'Dena Màrdaidh', agus feadhainn eile 'Dena Dhòmhnaill Uilleim'. Ach thuigeadh iad cò sinn air ainm seach ainm.

Cha robh fada againn ri choiseachd airson an sgoil a ruighinn – Sgoil Phabail. Gheibheadh sinn an uair ud air a' mhòinteach a choiseachd nam biodh sìde mhath ann. Bhiodh sinn a' dol tarsainn na buaile. Cha robh feansaichean ann. Anns an là ud, bha duine snog ann a bha lìbhrigeadh nan litrichean le Bhan a' Mhèil, agus nam biodh droch shìd ann, bhiodh e a' toirt dhuinn lioft. Ach bha greigh againn ann. Bha teaghlach 'Stiù' is teaghlach nan Caimbeulach air an taobh eile. Donnchadh Caimbeul. Beileag 's Ceitidh Mary agus Iain agus Sandaidh, bha iadsan an sin cuideachd. Bha poball mòr ann.

Bha cliù aig na tidsearan anns an latha sin gu robh iad gu math cruaidh air a' chloinn. O, bha iad cruaidh gun teagamh. O, an tè a bh' aig a' chlann bheaga, cha robh i sin idir cruaidh: Annag Mhurchaidh a' Bhac. Bha a piuthar, Ciorstag Mhurchaidh a' Bhac, anns an Àird. Bha an uair sin an ABC agus Part 1 agus Part 2 anns an rùm mhòr. Bha thu an uair sin a' dol gu Standard One. 'S e an Leadaidh Liath a bh' againn ann an sin: Miss MacKenzie. Bha Miss MacDonald aig Standard Two – nighean Dhòmhnaill Gheàrr. Agus Miss MacKay, 's ann bho na Lochan a bha i, aig Standard Three. Agus Miss MacLeod à Àird Thung aig Standard Four, agus Miss MacIver a bh' againn aig Standard Five.

Nuair a chaidh sinn dhan an sgoil an toiseach b' i a' Ghàidhlig a bhiodh Annag Mhurchaidh a' Bhac a' bruidhinn rinn. Air sgàth sin, fhuair sinn cothrom air seatlaigeadh sìos. 'S e a' Bheurla a bh' aca ga teagaisg anns an sgoil, ach bhiodh sinn a' bruidhinn na Gàidhlig a' cluich a-muigh. Ach nuair a bha thu a' fàs na b' aosta, bha iad airson gum biodh tu a' bruidhinn na Beurla. Mar a bha iad gad ionnsachadh, cha robh rian nach dèanadh tu adhartas. Cha mhòr nach robh iad 'one-to-one' – an tidsear agus an sgoilear. Sèithrichean beag agus bòrd beag mar seo.

Bhiodh iad ag ràdh gu robh na balaich anns an linn ud gu math borb nan dòigh – feadhainn aca co-dhiù. O, bha. Bha muinntir Phabail na bu mhiosa na an fheadhainn a bh' ann an Garrabost. Dheigheadh balaich Phabail a shabaid an-còmhnaidh! Tha cuimhn' agam Dòmhnallan Liosg – tha esan beò fhathast – nuair a bha sinn air Part 2. Bha sinn ann às deidh an ABC. Bhiodh tu a' toirt leat pìos an uair sin dhan an sgoil. Dè bh' agamsa ach aran eòrna a bha mo mhàthair air a dhèanamh agus ìm ùr às a' bhiot air, agus dh'fhaighnich e dhomh dè bh' agam, agus bidh mi an-còmhnaidh a' tarraing às nuair a thachras e rium. "Tha," arsa mise, "ice cream." Thòisich e ag iarraidh pìos dheth. Thuirt mi ris nach toirinn dha mìr. Ach, a bhròinein, nuair a chunnaic e an rud a bh' ann . . . O uill, thàinig gnùig air an aodann aige leis an tàmailt.

Bha an Leadaidh Liath, bha i a' fuireach ann an taigh Anna Ailein. Bhiodh sinn a' dol chon na h-uinneig aice a phiopaigeadh a-steach. Bhiodh i an-còmhnaidh a' cur ola a' chroinn-ola orra fhèin. Bhiodh sinn a' fàtha-daireachd oirre. Nach sinn a bha crosd! Bho thàinig sinn a-nuas an seo – chaidh an taigh sa a thogail ann an 1934, agus bhiodh m' athair a' marbhadh nam beathaichean anns a' bhàthaich. Bhiodh na carcais aige crochaichte an sin. Bhiodh tu gan ithe fresh. Chops is na rudan sin. Ach a-nis, nuair a bha e a' dol seachad air chops, bha an fheòil a' dol dhan tuba am bogadh ann am picil. Bhiodh iad a' cur pìos ann, ga theastadh an robh am picil làidir gu leòr, 's nan seòladh am pìos feòla, bha sin ag innse gu robh am picil cho làidir 's a dh'fheumadh e bhith. Bha an fheòil ga sailleadh mar sin. Bhiodh iad ga togail a-rithist 's ga cur ann an salainn tioram. Nuair a bha thu a' cur feum air an fheòil, mìos no dhà às deidh sin, bha agad ri ullachadh eile a dhèanamh oirre. Mus bruicheadh tu i, dh'fheumadh tu a cur am bogadh airson latha. Dh'fhàsadh an fheòil geal. An ath rud, bha thu a' dèanamh potato soup. Bha potato soup againn gun abhsadh!

'S an t-aon rud leis an iasg. Bha rud aig m' athair man triangle a bhiodh e a' crochadh an-dràsta air taobh muigh an t-sabhail ann an sin. Bha e airson iasgan a bhiodh e a' sailleadh a thiormachadh. Anns an latha sin, bha na h-iasgan a bh' aca mòr, brèagha – liùthan is langannan is adagan. Ach cha bhiodh e a' tiormachadh an truisg idir. Chan eil fhios agam dè bu choireach, ach bhiodh e an-còmhnaidh a' tiormachadh na liùth as t-samhradh. Gan crochadh ann an sin.

Nuair a bha mi òg, bha geàrran air a' mhòintich, ach chan eil fhios agam an robh iad shìos an seo anns an Rubha. Bha pailteas robaidean an seo shìos ann an earball na lot againn. A bhròinein, bha air Tuill! Agus a-nall chon an uillt – Allt Choinnich Bhig. Làn robaidean. Chan eil gin ann an-diugh. Bho thàinig am myxomatosis a bha siud, cha mhòr gum faic thu robaid. Chì thu feadhainn a-muigh taobh Hòil. Bidh an cat agam fhìn a' toirt a-steach iseanan robaid an dràsta 's a-rithist. Sin Hòl, an cnoc a chì thu a-muigh air cùl an taigh-sgoile.

Tha fhios agad far a bheil na Tursachan, tha mi creids. Sin an t-ainm a th' orra: na Tursachan – na seann chlachan a tha nan seasamh a-muigh faisg air Hòl ri taobh Cnoc Bhail' an Roth.* Bhithinn a' cluinntinn mo mhàthair ag innse eachdraidh nan clachan sin. Tha an-diugh an riasg air fàs agus tha tòrr dha na clachan air a dhol fon talamh. Bhiodh iad a' cumail a-mach gum biodh iad, bho chionn mìltean bhliadhnachan, ag ìobradh na cloinne aig na Tursachan. Bha còrnair ann far am biodh iad ag ìobradh chloinne dha na diathan a bh' aca. Faodaidh tu bhith cinnteach nach robh rim linn-sa! Bha siud anns na linntean bho chian. Ach leis an fhìrinn innse, chan eil fhios againne an robh am fasan ud ann riamh, ged a bha siud air a ràdh rinn. Co-dhiù, tha e air a radh gu bheil iad a' dol a dhèanamh rathad a-mach gualainn Hòil chon nan Tursachan. Agus a' chlach eile a tha an sin – a' Chlach Ghlais a chanas iad rithe. Tha i aig Allt na Muilne, mach ris an allt. Bhiodh iad ag innse dhuinne anns an sgoil gur e saighdear ainmeil air choreigin a thuit ann an sin agus gur e sin as coireach gu bheil a' Chlach Ghlais anns a' mhòintich mar chuimhneachan air. Cha eil e duilich faighinn thuice idir. Tha rathad ann a bheir

---

* Chan eil cinnt air litreachadh an ainm seo.

thu chon na Cloich. Gabh an rathad a chì thu eadar an eaglais agus taigh nighean an Lòlaich. Tha e a' leantainn a-mach ann an sin taobh Allt na Muilne, a-mach dhan mhòintich.

Bha seòrsa de phort againn ann an Garrabost uaireigin, agus bha eathraichean ag obair a-mach às bho chionn fhada – suas gu linn mo sheanar. Chì thu fhathast an cidhe a bh' ann, shìos fon a' Mhansa. Seann chidhe – chan eil ann ach ablach a-nise. Bhiodh eathraichean an sin gu bho chionn beagan bhliadhnaichean. 'S ann a bhiodh an eathar a bh' aig na balaich againn fhìn. Ach leis an eathar a th' aca a-nis, tha e nas fhasa dhaibh a dhol leatha a-mach à Pabail. Bidh iad ga tobhaigeadh a-null leis a' chàr.

Tha cuimhn' agam air m' Antaidh Sìne. Bha i mu ar coinneamh air taobh eile an rathaid. Bhiodh na balaich aicese, Seonaidh agus Murchadh, a' dol a-mach air an eathar. Nuair a bha dùil riutha dhachaigh, bhiodh Sìne a' falbh sìos chon a' chladaich airson an coinneachadh. Cho luath 's a ruigeadh iad air tìr, bhiodh i a' càradh an sgùil na cliabh deiseil airson falbh leatha dhachaigh air a druim. Ach cha b' e uireas na bh' aice de dh'eallach. Bhiodh an sgùil aice agus cuideachd an earrainn a gheibheadh na mic aice dhan iasg. Bha a h-uile càil a bha sin aice air a druim. Nuair a thigeadh i an uair sin dhachaigh, ghoileadh i an coire 's bhiodh i deiseil le dà mhias ach an nigheadh iad an casan. Bha i a' deanamh sin mus fhaigheadh iad fuachd. Anns an là ud, bha na màthraichean a' milleadh nam balach. Bha iad spoilt. Bha iad air am milleadh.

Nise, carson a bha na màthraichean cho frionasach a' dìon nam balach? 'S mathaid gu robh na màthraichean a' dèanamh dhaibh seach gu robh aig na balaich ri dhol dhan na cogaidh anns am biodh nàimhdean a' feuchainn ri am marbhadh no am bàthadh. Agus bha aig na balaich ri sin a dhèanamh gun teagamh. Tha mi a' creidse gur e sin a bha cosnadh dha na mnathan a bhith mar a bha iad. Chaill mo mhàthair dà bhràthair anns a' Chiad Chogadh. Chailleadh Coinneach agus Murchadh.

Nam bithinn air a bhith òg an-diugh, 's dòcha gu robh mi air a dhol dhan a' cholaiste no dhan a' university. Bha mi air toiseach air càch anns a' chleas fhad 's a bha mi am Pabail – a h-uile bliadhna ach aon. 'S bha mi Dux air a' bhliadhna mu dheireadh a bha mi innte, ach cha robh mi airson a dhol na b' fhaide na sin. Bha mi airson a dhol a dh'obair. Anns an latha bha sin, cha robh cùisean cho farasta 's a tha iad an-diugh. Air an làimh eile, 's mathaid gu robh, ach mar a thurchair, cha robh duine agam gam spiorsaigeadh. Tha cuimhne agam air Mgr. Thomson, am ma'-sgoile a bh' againn ann am Pabail, cho dèidheil 's a bha e air na balaich a chur tron fhoghlam. Bheir mi dhut eiseamplair air sin. Bha Calum, an duine agam, gu math comasach nuair a bha e na oileanach anns an sgoil. Tha cuimhn' agam air an Tomsanach a thighinn gu athair Chaluim agus gu a mhàthair airson gun sguireadh iad a bhith ga chur a dh'obair gan bhùth a bh' aca. Thuirt e riutha gu robh iad a' dèanamh call air a chuid foghlaim – gur ann bu chòir do Chalum aghaidh a chur air a chuid leabhraichean agus a dhol air adhart anns an fhoghlam. Ach, O, cha robh Calum ag iarraidh sin idir. Och, bhiodh esan a' draibhigeadh nam busaichean 's e gu math òg. Cha robh e an aghaidh an lagh dha a bhith dèanamh sin anns an là ud. Cha robh teastaichean ann anns an latha sin.

Co-dhiù, chaidh mise a dh'obair dhan Mhans againn fhìn an seo an Garrabost nuair a bha mi gu math òg. Chòrd e rium a bhith ag obair còmhla ri teaghlach a' mhinisteir. 'S cha b' e sin an teaghlach beag. Feumaidh mi a ràdh gur e sin a' ghràin a th' agam air iarnaigeadh an-diugh! Cha chreideadh tu na bh' agam de dh'iarnaigeadh ri dhèanamh, gu h-àraid aig àm nan òrdaighean. Bhiodh uiread de dhaoine a' tighinn air aoigheachd chon a' Mhans 's gu robh na bha siud de bhedrooms loma-làn. Nuair a bha mi òg, bha na ministearan aig na daoine air pedestal.

Cha robh laundry idir anns a' Mhans. Cha robh na bloigh! Bha pailteas de bhùrn anns na h-uillt. Ceart gu leòr, bha tobair ri taobh an uillt agus bha pump ann airson a bhith ga obrachadh nuair a bha feum air a bhùrn anns a' Mhans.

Cuideachd, bha toilet agus bathroom anns a' Mhans. Bhiodh napkins agus a h-uile càil eireachdail air a' bhòrd agus a h-uile pilleag a bha sin ri iarnaigeadh nuair a bha am biadh seachad. Bha sinn a' nighe na bha an sin de dh'aodach le ar làmhan. Cha robh dad an uair sin nach fheumadh tu iarnaigeadh. O, mo chreach! Nach sinn a bha èasgaidh anns an là ud! Agus a-rithist, nuair a smaoinicheas tu air na bha siud de dh'aodaichean leapa. Bha againn ri dhol leotha dha na tubaichean as t-samhradh. Bhiodh sinn air ar casan luirmeachd a' stampadh nan aodaichean. Ach aodach nan òrdaighean: cha bhiodh iad a' nighe nam plaidichean 's nan cuibhrigean; cha bhiodh iad a' nighe sin a h-uile bliadhna idir. Cha bhiodh iad gan iùsaigeadh ach ann an April agus ann an November. 'S cha robh an luchd-tadhail agad ach weekend. 'S bha na siotaichean aca gan chur seachad gu cùramach deiseil airson a thighinn a-mach a-rithist aig àm nan ath òrdaighean. O, mo chreach, a bhròinein, bha an obair ud cruaidh. Ach 's ann dìreach mar sin a bha tachairt anns na taighean-còmhnaidh fhèin an Garrabost. Aodach nan òrdaighean ga chàradh air ais dha na dràthraichean cho luath 's a bha na h-òrdaighean seachad.

Nise, cha b'e a-mhàin gu robh ùpraid ann aig àm nan òrdaighean. Bha crodh aig a' mhinistear cuideachd. 'S i bean a' mhinisteir a bhiodh ri bleoghan a' chruidh. 'S i. B' ise a bhiodh a' bleoghan a' chruidh. Fhios agad, bha mi air a bhith a' leantainn na h-eaglais bhom òige, agus mar sin bha mi na mo ghlòraidh anns a' Mhansa. Chan eil fhios agam carson a bha sin. Bha e diofaraichte. Bha clann a' mhinisteir agam an uair sin agus agam ri coimhead às an dèidh 's ri a bhith dèanamh dhaibh. Bha a h-uile bad aodaich a bhuineadh dhaibh agam ri nighe agus ri iarnaigeadh.

Bhiodh Màiri, an nighean aig an Urr. Lachaidh MacLeòid, còmhla rium. Bhiodh sinn anns an sgoil còmhla agus bha sinn a cheart cho eòlach ann am Mans na h-Eaglais Shaoir 's a bha sinn anns an Aonadh. Bha, an aon rud. Anns an latha sin bha Lachie MacLeòid na mhinistear anns an Aonadh. 'S ann an sin a dh'ith mi a' chiad oven scones a dh'ith mi a-riamh. Dh'ith mi sin le homemade strawberry jam a chaidh a dheanamh anns a' Mhans. Bidh mi fhathast ga chur ann an cuimhne Màiri.

Nuair a bha mi òg, bhiodh dannsa an rathaid ann ach, leis an fhìrinn innse, cha robh mise a-riamh aig dannsa an rathaid bho dh'fhàs mi mòr. Bhiodh danns aca ga chumail aig ceann rathad Phabail nuair a bha sinn anns an sgoil, agus bhithinn a' dol a dhannsa an sin còmhla ri mo chomhaoisean. Ach chuir mi cùl ris na dannsan nuair a dh'fhàs mi mòr. Thòisich mise a' dol dhan an eaglais a' bhliadhna mu dheireadh a bha mi anns an sgoil ann am Pabail, agus tha cuimhn' agam a' chiad Dhiardaoin ('s ann a' rùdhadh na mònach a bha sinn) agus thuirt mo mhàthair gu robh sinn a' dol dhachaigh tràth airson na coinneimh. Thuirt mi ri mo mhàthair gu robh mi airson a dhol còmhla rithe dhan a' choinneimh. Cha b' e Latha na Sàboind a bh' ann, cumhnich, ach Diardaoin. Theab i fanndaigeadh! Bha fhios aice gum bithinn a' falbh nan coinneamhan. Aig an àm ud, bha an dà eaglais a bha an seo ann an sgìre an Rubha, bha iad mar aon. B' e sin Eaglais an Aonaidh agus an Eaglais Shaor. Bha a h-uile duine am measg a chèile, gun sgaradh eatarra. Cha robh duine a' cur umhail air a chèile. Agus tha cuimhn' agam aon oidhche 's mi a' dol dhan a' choinneimh a Shiadar. Bha mise fhathast anns an sgoil. Bha m' Antaidh Sìne air taobh thall an rathaid. Thàinig i a-nall far an robh m' athair is thuirt i ris, "Tha a thìde agad Mairead a chumail am broinn an taighe. Tha i a' falbh a h-uile h-oidhche sìos an sin, agus cionnas a tha i dol a sheasamh ris?"

Cò-dhiù, thuirt m' athair rium an oidhche sin, "Nise, chan eil thu a' dol a-mach air an daras a-nochd. Chan eil mi airson thu dhol a-mach." Bha bòrd againn ann an sin ris an uinneig agus thug mise an oidhche nam shuidhe an sin, a' coimhead nan daoine a' dol sìos seachad air an taigh againn, agus bha mi a' sileadh uisge mo chinn. Co-dhiù, làrna-mhàireach thuirt e, "Cha dèan mise siud gu bràth tuilleadh. Ma tha thusa ag iarraidh a dhol ann, thèid thusa ann."

B' ann às dèidh sin a-nis a bha sinn a' rùdhadh na mònach agus a dh'innis mi dha mo mhàthair gu robh mi a' dol còmhla rithe, agus chaidh mise còmhla rithe an là ud. Tha cuimhn' agam gu robh Calum gu math òg ag obair anns a' bhùth aig an àm ud, 's bhiodh na balaich a' cruinneachadh anns a' bhùth. Bhiodh a h-uile duine aca dìreach gobs-macked gam fhaicinn a' dol sìos dhan a' choinneimh air Diardaoin còmhla ri mo mhàthair.

Às dèidh dhomh sgur a dh'obair anns a' Mhans, chaidh mi a dh' obair a Shiabost. An sin, bha mi a' coimhead às dèidh clann òg. An uair sin thill mi nall a Steòrnabhagh a dh'obair ann an taigh Aonghais a' Chailidh. Bha mi riamh dèidheil air còcaireachd agus fhuair mi mo leòr dheth an siud! Thug mi an ath cheum a-mach gu tìr-mòr, mi fhìn agus Dena agus Katie Ann agus Calumina NicAoidh. Fhuair sinn obair aig Oilthigh Dhùn Èideann, anns na Halls of Residence. An ath rud, fhuair mi àite ag obair nam housekeeper do chupall aig Ravelston Dykes. Bha esan à Inbhir Nis agus ise à Sussex. Bha esan air a bhith anns na h-Innseachan còrr is deich bliadhna fichead ag obair dhan Riaghaltas. O, chòrd Dùn Èideann rium. Bha mi air mo dhòigh ann.

Aig an àm sin, cha robh eòlas agam air Calum ach dìreach tro bhith anns an sgoil. Bhiodh sinn dìreach a' coinneachadh ri chèile agus nuair a thigeadh e a-nuas a chèilidh, agus cha robh duine a' cur an aghaidh dha bhith dèanamh sin. O, bha a dhòigh fhèin aige air a bhith gam tharraing! Bhiodh e a' tighinn a-nuas an seo 's bhiodh e a' toirt thugam Liquorice Allsorts. Bha mi uabhasach dèidheil air na Liquorice Allsorts. 'S iad a b' fheàrr leam na seòclaid. Nuair a thòisich e a' draibheadh a' bhus, bhiodh e a' coinneachadh rium nuair a dheighinn suas am baile. Mu dheireadh, dh'fhalbh mise a-mach gu tìr-mòr a dh'obair ann an Dùn Èideann, agus thòisich Calum a' sgrìobhadh thugam fhad 's a bha mi an Dùn Èideann.

Nise, cha bu mhi an aon chaileag air an robh Calum measail. Duine mòr brèagha a bh' ann agus bhiodh e fhèin agus Aonghas Lì a' dol chon a' Bhac,'s bhiodh iad a' dol dhan an Àird 's a Shiadar. Nuair a bha e leis a' bhus, bhiodh e a' dol a Phabail a shealltainn air 'Bibi' an Tàilleir. Bibi chòir. Phòs i 'Pods', duine gasta snog far a' Bhac. Bliadhnaichean an dèidh sin, bhiodh Pods a' tarraing à Calum: bhiodh e ag radh ris, "Rinn mise a' chùis ort, a charaid! Rinn mise a' chùis ort glan!" Och, 's minig a bhiodh sinn a' coinneachadh ri Bibi agus Pods anns a' bhaile. Dibhearsain gu leòr eadar Calum agus Pods.

Nuair a thòisich sinn a' suirghe dha-rìribh, bhiodh mise agus Calum a' caithris na h-oidhche fhad 's a bhithinn air holiday. Bhiodh e a' tighinn a-nuas chon an taigh an seo a chaithris na h-oidhche. Bha mi aig an taigh air holiday, agus 's ann aig an àm sin a chuir sinn an ceangal air a chèile. Bha mi aig an àm sin ag obair anns na University Halls, 's bha sinn a' faighinn dhachaigh aig àm na Càisg 's aig Christmas. Ach airson holidays an t-samhraidh, cha robh sinn a' faighinn dhachaigh chionn 's gum bhiodh conferences aca a' dèanamh airgid dhan Oilthigh. Co-dhiù, thàinig mi dhachaigh aig àm na Bliadhn' Ùir, tha mi smaoineachadh, agus phòs sinn as t-earrach. Fhuair sinn triùir bhalach 's aon nighean. Chaidh Alex Dan, am balach as sine againn, bho Sgoil Phabail do Cholaiste a' Chaisteil. B' ann ag ionnsachadh saorsainneachd a bha e an sin. An uair sin lean e air dhan Esk Valley College ann an Dalkeith, deas air Dùn Èideann. Tha e an-diugh ag obair anns a' Scottish Office ann an Dùn Èideann na Mhaintenance Manager.

Nis, lean Calum air bho Sgoil Phabail do Cholaiste a' Chaisteil, ach b' ann ri engineering a bha esan. Fhad 's a bha e anns a' cholaiste a' dèanamh engineering, bha e cuideachd ag obair ann an Eilean na Cothail. Bha iad a' lorg feadhainn airson trèanadh ann an sin còmhla ri bhith a' dol dhan Cholaiste. Mar sin, rinn e marine engineering agus a-nis chaidh e sìos gu tìr-mòr às dèidh sin. Rinn e weldeadh cuideachd, agus tha e ag obair a-nis ann an Àrnais.

Nis, an nighean againn, Marina, chaidh ise gu Robert Gordon's. An toiseach, chaidh i steach airson a bhith na Domestic Science teacher, ach an ceann beagan bhliadhnaichean dh'fhàg i sin, oir bha ùidh a-riamh aice ann an nursadh. B' e sin a roghnaich i a dhèanamh. Bha i gu sònraichte ag obair le euslaintich aig an robh trioblaid dhubhagan. Nach e 'renal' an t-ainm a th' ac' air rud a tha co-cheangailte ri dubhagan? Agus chaidh i an uair sin sia mìosan a-null a North Carolina a dh'obair còmhla ri clann, agus nuair a thàinig i air ais chaidh i sìos a Shasainn dhan an Royal Marsden a dhèanamh cancer nursing. An uair sin Health Visiting, agus tha a h-uile càil a tha sin aice nise fo a sgèith. Tha i a-nis ag ullachadh airson PhD a dhèanamh,* 's nach bi sin pailteas!

Ach a-nis Donaidh. Fhuair e Higher National Diploma ann an Colaiste a' Chaisteil. Bhiodh P&O a' tighinn a dh'iarraidh bhalach, agus dh'fhalbh dhà na thrì aca còmhla. Bha Donaidh aca airson ochd bliadhna na engineer.

---

* Cheumnaich Marina le PhD an 2005.

Shiubhail e an saoghal còmhla riutha. Bhithinn-sa a' cur a' *Ghasait* thuige, agus nuair a bha e thall ann an Japan 's ann a chunnaic e advert airson Ospadal nan Eilean ann an Steòrnabhagh. Uill, chuir e steach air a shon air an Eadar-lìon, agus nuair a thàinig e dhachaigh aig a' Bhliadhn' Ùir thàinig litir tron an daras thuige airson interview. Bha e àraid. Agus chaidh e airson na h-interview agus fhuair e an obair. Bha sin dìreach cho freagarrach dhaibh, airson bha iad air leanabh fhaighinn aig an àm sin. Bha e cho freagarrach. Ach a dh'aindeoin sin, b' fheàrr leis a bhith aig muir. Ach tha na seòladairean dualtach a bhith mar sin, oir tha an sàl a' ruith nan cuislean! Nan seòladairean, tha iad a' faicinn àitichean nach biodh iad a-chaoidh air fhaicinn: suas gu ruige Alasga, thall ann an Astràilia 's New Zealand 's a h-uile h-àite a tha an sin. Feumaidh gu bheil na daoine againn uabhasach siùbhlach nan gnè!

Bha na seòladairean Gàidhealach a-riamh a' dèanamh sin. Ach cha b' ann mar sin a bha beatha nan clann-nighean nuair a bha mise òg. Cha robh uiread de sheòrsaichean obrach ann airson ar samhail. Dh'aindeoin sin, bha aig a h-uile tè ri togail oirre agus a dhol a-mach a choimhead airson tuarastail. Ach ge air bith càite an tèid fear no tè, tha grèim aig fearann Gharraboist oirnn – fearann na dùthcha far na thogadh sinn. Tha, tha! Tha a h-uile duine a dh'fhàg seo air a bhith coimhead air ais gu Garrabost. Tha am fear as sine againne an sin, agus a h-uile turas as urrainn dha, bidh e aig an taigh.

Tha mòran Shasannach ann air feadh an àite. Nuair a thèid thu tron a' phone-book chì thu na sloinnidhean neònach a th' ann. 'S e droch rud a th' ann ann an seagh – gu bheil uiread aca ann. Ann an àitichean, tha feadhainn aca a' feuchainn ris an dòigh aca fhèin a stèidheachadh air còraichean nan croitearan. Ach chan eil a h-uile fear no tè mar sin. Bha tè ri ar taobh à Yorkshire – boireannach gasta, modhail. Cha robh fiù 's nach robh i a' cantainn rium seo: "Chan eil mise," ars ise, "airson dad a dhèanamh an seo a thaobh na Sàboind ach mar a tha muinntir an àite." Ars ise, "Chan iarr mi air falbh à seo."

Chan iarradh i às a' bhad sa. Ach thug am bàs às i. Bhàsaich i le cansair. Chaidh a tiodhlaiceadh ann an Sanndabhaig. Dh'fhuirich an duine aice greis anns an Àird ach tha e a-nis air a dhol air ais a Yorkshire. Chan fhuilingeadh ise a ràdh gur e Sasannach a bh' innte ach gur ann à Yorkshire a bha i! Bha i ag ràdh gu robh muinntir na siorrachd sin na bu dàimheil ris na h-Albannaich na bha iad ri muinntir Shasainn. Ach tha Sasannaich ann às a h-uile ceàrnaidh de Shasainn a tha glè ghasta, agus nach fhaod sinn a ràdh gu bheil iomadach Leòdhasach ann an Sasainn cuideachd. 'S mathaid gu bheil feadhainn dhiubhsan nach eil a' còrdadh ris na nàbaidhean acasan ann an sin!

Canaidh mi seo mu dheidhinn na dòigh-beatha a th' againn an seo ann an Eilean Leòdhais. Is caomh leamsa i. 'S caomh leam na daoine agus an dòigh-beatha a th' againn gu h-iomlan. Tha a' Ghàidhlig – cànan nan daoine – co-cheangailte ris an dòigh-beatha a th' againn. Is caomh leam a' Ghàidhlig 's a h-uile rud traidiseanta a th' againn, 's cha bu chaomh leam càil dheth a chall. Chan eil càil dheth gun luach. Chan eil càil.

Margaret MacMillan

1924–

My folks originally came from Sutherland – but that was a long time ago. A lot of my relations are scattered throughout Point, descended from the first MacKay to come to the district. He was Alasdair MacKay, known as 'Big MacKay'. He was married twice. The first wife was the bailie's daughter and 'Stew' in Shader was their descendant. The second was Mairi, daughter of Tarmod, son of Iain, son of Tarmod. My father was descended from that union.

Alasdair MacKay – Big MacKay – worked on Aiginis Farm but he died at 28 Garrabost. His son [Alasdair, son of Alasdair MacKay] lived beside us here and his son William was my grandfather. Besides him, there were John and Roderick. There was a big family.

As I said, my father's folk were MacKays but my mother's people were MacKenzies. They were related to Uilleam Dhomhnaill 'ic Choinnich [William MacKenzie], the famous bard. You are sure to know his book *Cnoc Chùsbaig*. You may be sure that everybody who was related to him is proud of their connection to him. I never saw him but I did see 'Am Poidhleat', his brother, who was a postman and who sometimes came across and stayed with his daughter Effie at Newton Street in Stornoway. He used to do that until he died. I well remember him with his white beard. In those days all the men of mature years wore beards. The beard of Am Poileat was extra long as it came right down on his chest. When he was a young man he was 'whipper-in' of the Aird School.

Garrabost children didn't attend Aird School. They went to the Bayble school. Our headmaster, Mr Thomson, was very well known. He was the father of Professor Derick Thomson, another famous bard. At school, we weren't allowed to pronounce the words 'ceò' and 'seòladh' as the Bayble folk do – ceó and seóladh!*. All Bayble folk have that difference in their pronunciation. Look even at how differently the Aird folk pronounce some

* ò as in 'awe' as opposed to ó as in 'woe'.

of their words. Instead of 'Mairead', they say 'Màilead'. Oh, that was certainly true of the Aird folk's Gaelic. Of course, there was also an excellent headmaster in Aird School – Colonel John MacSween, who was born in Garrabost, just a short distance from here.

My earliest memory is of the time when our family returned to Lewis from Canada. I was four years of age and I can recall the voyage to Scotland on the steamer. We arrived at Greenock. I can't remember the train journey* but I do remember the voyage.† The relations were all out to greet us that evening, and what was so very strange to me was that my Auntie Jean was living in a black-house! When I first entered her house, I refused to shake hands with her. At the age of four, I had entered a very strange world!

We had been living in Fort William, Ontario. The houses were of wood in those days. We were living in one of those and I remember there was a stove in ours. I remember the house we were living in very clearly and I'll tell you why. At the back of the house there was a cellar in which they kept all sorts of odds and ends. My sister Dena, who is younger than I, was sitting in a highchair opposite the stove. I was behind her, also sitting on a chair and swinging as best I could. Suddenly, I tipped the highchair forward, pitching Dena headlong so that her head hit the stove. Much weeping and consternation followed. My mother, who had been in the cellar fetching something, came bounding up. Oh, yes! I remember the incident all too well. I was given such a row!

When anybody from Lewis arrived in the district – and particularly, if they were from Point – they all made straight for our house. They only stayed with us until they found suitable lodgings. Peggy MacKenzie [Peigi Chaluim Iain] from Shader was living with us temporarily at one time and so was Màiread Dhòmhnaill Bhig. They were waiting to get a home of their own. I remember that, when they received their pay, they used to arrive at our home with lollipops fixed behind their ears! Amazing what little details stay in one's memory!

My father was a foreman in an elevator and my uncle Knox was a superintendent. However, Knox moved off out to Vancouver. Whenever anybody arrived from home in Fort William, the others tried to find work for him. Everybody did! Most of them worked in the elevators. There was hardly anybody around there but was related to the MacKays! They were all very kind to each other. Oh, yes, they were out to help one another.

---

* From Glasgow to Kyle of Lochalsh.
† Across the Minch to Stornoway.

I cannot remember much about our diet in those days. I suppose we ate the kind of food they ate back home in Lewis. We ate very little salt herring in Canada but we more than made up for it when we came back home to Lewis, where we ate herring, cuddies [small saithe, pollacks, etc.] and fish of every kind. You name it, we ate it! Of course, in the old days here, the people here used to salt lots of meat to have that over the winter.

I remember, when we were in Canada, being in the home of our neighbour, Mrs Teasdale. She used to invite me in. Funny, what I remember of those days – events that took place when I was aged two or three. Those are vivid in my mind. Mrs Teasdale used to take me upstairs and show me the work she was doing. She used to have lots of her crochet and embroidery spread out on her bed. I still have the bone crochet hook she gave me so that, when I'd grow up, I'd learn how crochet was done – and I did just that. I learned how to do crochet at a sewing class organized by the lady-missionary of the Church of Scotland. She also taught me how to do embroidery.

But let me tell you about that Mrs Teasdale whose language was English and, that being so, I must have been able to express myself in English as well as in Gaelic. Of course, Gaelic was the language of our home in Canada. What else but Gaelic! Consequently, we had no trouble at all in adapting back here in Lewis. Our being able to communicate with Mrs Teasdale suggests that both Dena and I were bilingual. That must have been the case. Anyway, when we reached Stornoway, we were transported to our granny's house in a van. In her style of house, the family lived in the 'up end' and the cow in the 'down end'. You can see in this photo the kind of house it was. One half of it was white [with a gable] and the other half black [thatched]. I believe that, originally, it was black from end to end [i.e. with the fire on an open hearth in the middle of the living-room]. On entering the house through the main door, the cow used to turn to her left and proceed to her own stall, people turning to the right to go to their quarters. The barn was attached to the house.

When the Communion was under way, we used to have lots of visitors to our house – a very busy time as we were, in accordance with custom, providing 'shake-downs' [floor-beds] in the temporary sleeping quarters, namely, the barn. Our house was so close to the church, you see. Dena and I used to think it was a wonderful thing that so many people came to visit us. A more wonderful thing still was what our father was doing for us. He stayed behind in Canada and used to support us from there. He occasionally sent us a barrel of apples. What a lovely smell when it was opened. You might wonder why we came back to Lewis from Canada. Well, my grandmother was living alone and she pleaded with my mother to come back home. In the end, my mother acceded to her wishes. As he was fortunate to be employed during the Depression years, my father didn't come back to us until 1934.

Our family consisted of two girls, my sister Dena and myself. We didn't have any brothers. Reading between the lines, I believe that my mother had a boy before she had me but he was stillborn. I cannot remember how I got that information. In those days so much of what was said was said privately. No doubt it was a snippet of information that was dropped by someone unwittingly.

While my father was in Canada, I was known as 'Mairead Màrdy' – Margaret, daughter of 'Màrdy', which was my mother's nickname. Since my father came home, I was known as Mairead Dhòmhnaill Uilleim – Margaret, daughter of Donald, son of William. Some knew my sister as Dena Màrdy, others as Dena Dhòmhnaill Uilleim – Dena, daughter of Donald, son of William. Both nametags were in common usage.

We didn't have far to go to reach Bayble School. At that time, there weren't any fences, so that we were able to cross the moor quickly if there was good weather. At that time, there was a kind postman who had a mail van for delivering letters. When there was foul weather, he sometimes gave us a lift. The problem was that there was a big crowd of kids all hoping for a lift – a big squad!

The teachers of my childhood had the reputation of being hard disciplinarians. Oh, they were hard without question. But the teacher we had in the Infants, Annie Murray [Annag Mhurchaidh a' Bhac], was the exception. Her sister Christina [Ciorstag Mhurchaidh a' Bhac] was the infant teacher in the Aird School and she was in the same mould. Wonderful teachers. In the infants' class Miss Murray spoke to us in Gaelic. That made it easy for us to settle down. English was the language used to teach us but, in the playground, we spoke Gaelic. Their method of teaching made it easy for us to learn. The method they used was, more or less, one-to-one – the teacher and the scholar close together. The pupils sat on little chairs each with a little table. In those days the ABC [Primary 1] was in the same room as Primary 2. When we went to Standard One [Primary 3], our teacher was Miss MacKenzie – the 'Leadaidh Liath' [The Grey-haired Lady Teacher]. Miss MacDonald [daughter of Dòmhnall Geàrr] had Standard Two. Miss MacKay from the district of Lochs taught

Standard Three. Miss MacLeod from Àird Thung taught Standard Four and Miss MacIver taught Standard Five.

It was said that the boys of my generation were very rough diamonds; some were. Certainly, the Bayble boys were much rougher than the Garrabost boys. I remember 'Doilean Liosg', who's still with us . . . I remember him when we were in Part 2. He and I were both quite bright pupils and were seated at the back of the class. The clever ones were also seated at the back, you see! In those days, we took a 'piece' [snack] with us to school. It so happened that my piece on this occasion was barley bread smothered with fresh butter newly out of the churn. He [Doilean Liosg] asked me what I had to eat. 'Oh!' says I, 'I have ice-cream.' He began to pester me for a share of the ice-cream but I told him that he would have none of it. I knew that he was planning to take some of my ice-cream by hook or by crook but when he saw what I had for my piece . . . well, his face dropped with disappointment.

The Grey-haired Teacher was staying at Anna Allan's house. We used to go to her window and peep in. She was in the habit of massaging herself with olive oil. We used to eavesdrop. Little mischiefs!

Our 'white-house' here in Garrabost was built in 1934. Since coming to live down here, my father used to butcher animals in the byre and their carcasses were hung from the rafters. We ate the meat from those animals while it was fresh – chops and that kind of thing. But, apart from the chops, the rest of the meat was preserved in a strong pickle in a tub. After a time, the meat was lifted and, when dry, was preserved in dry salt. You left it for a month or two, and after that, when you had need of it, you had to give it further treatment. Before you could cook it, you had to soak it in fresh water for twenty-four hours. The meat would then turn white – excellent for making potato soup. We ate potato soup forever!

Fish was treated in the same way. My father had a wooden triangle which was hung outside of the barn there. It was constructed with hooks on it so that salt fish could be hung on it to dry. The fish were the large varieties – pollack, ling and haddock. I don't know why they didn't dry cod but they certainly went for the pollacks – hanging them in that fashion.

When I was young, there were lots of hares on the Lewis Moor but I don't know if there were any here in Point. Plenty of rabbits down here, though. At one time, the foot of our croft was overrun with them. Burrows everywhere, right over as far as Coinneach Beag's Stream – full of rabbits. There's not one there now. Since myxomatosis, I've scarcely seen one. Mind you, you may catch sight of one out towards Hòl. Our cat occasionally brings in a young one. Hòl is the hill that's out there on the moor, behind the Bayble school.

There are standing stones on Cnoc Valero near to Hòl and it is rumoured that a road is going to be built to the stones which are known as Na Tursachan. That is the name by which they were known since long ago. Today, some of them have sunk so that they are hidden underground. I used to hear from my mother that children used to be sacrificed there. According to folklore, there is one corner in which children used to be sacrificed. But, to be truthful, although that was the case according to folklore, we haven't got any proof that that custom ever existed here.

Now, there's another monolith standing on its own out there. It is known as the Clach Ghlas [Grey Stone] and is situated at Allt na Muilne [Mill Stream] – just out by the stream. We used to be told at school that a famous soldier was slain there and that that was the reason why the Clach Ghlas was erected on that spot, as a memorial to him. It is quite accessible for there is a path that will lead you to the stone.

At one time there was a kind of harbour at Garrabost and boats used to operate from there up until my grandfather's generation. You can still see the quay seaward of the manse. The old quay is now dilapidated. My own sons used to berth their boat there but with the kind of boat they have now, it is easier for them to launch it out of Bayble. They tow it by car over to Bayble pier.

I remember my Auntie Jean on the other side of the road. Her sons, Johnnie and Murdo, used to go out to fish. When they were expected to arrive back, she used to set off down to the shore to meet the boat. As soon as they beached the boat, she would get hold of their *sgùil* [a wooden or wicker tray for carrying baited small-lines] and place it in her creel and she would prepare to set off on her homeward journey. In her creel she carried on her back not only the *sguil* but also the boys' share of the catch. By the time the boys arrived home, she would have boiled the kettle so that they could bathe their feet. In that generation, the boys were pampered. They really were spoiled. Cosseted!

Now, why were mothers so inclined to spoil their sons? Perhaps it was because it was the boys who had to go to war to be killed or drowned by their enemies. It's undeniable that boys could be placed in that kind of danger. I personally believe that that was one reason why mothers fussed like that. My mother, for example, lost two brothers in the First World War – Kenneth and Murdo.

*

If I were young now, I would most likely go to college or university. While I was at school in Bayble, I was ahead of the rest of the class every year except for one. In my last year, I was Dux but I didn't wish to continue further than that. Problem was, I was anxious to go out to earn a wage. At that time, living conditions were not as favourable as they are today. On the other hand, some might argue that they were. In any case, I didn't have anybody in the background encouraging me to continue. There wasn't any encouragement for girls to continue their education. I well remember how enthusiastic Mr Thomson, the headmaster, was that the boys should advance their education. I'll give you an example. Calum, my husband, was quite a clever pupil. Mr Thomson came to his parents asking them to stop making their son work in their shop. He told them that they were damaging his schooling and that he should be giving all his attention to his books and progressing with his education. However, what the headmaster advised was against what Calum himself wanted. Och, he was driving buses from a very young age. In those days, it was not illegal for him to be doing so. At that time, drivers weren't tested.

Anyway, I went to work in the manse. I enjoyed working in the company of the minister's family. In terms of numbers, it was not a small family! To be honest, my experience of working in the manse caused me to have a scunner of ironing clothes to this day. You wouldn't believe the amount of ironing I had to do – particularly at Communion time. There were so many people coming as guests that the many bedrooms were full to the gunwales! In my young days, ministers were greatly respected as if they were on pedestals.

There was no laundry in the manse, not at all. There was plenty of water in the stream. There were both a toilet and a bathroom. Piped water could be pumped into the building from a well which was beside the stream. At the Communion time, there used to be a cook and a table-maid, and napkins and all the paraphernalia were set out on the dinner-table. After the meal, every one of those pieces of cloth had to be washed by hand and then ironed. Hard to believe that we were so industrious in those days. In the summer, we got the tubs out and had to wash the bedclothes by stamping them with our bare feet. However, the bedclothes used at the Communion were exempt. Those weren't washed every year because they were used only in April and November. On those occasions, the visitors stayed at the manse, only at the weekend. The dishes were washed, of course, and stored away and brought out after each Communion. It was all very hard work. It was just like what happened at ordinary family homes like our own.

Communion clothes were washed and ironed and stored away in drawers in anticipation of the next occasion.

Now, quite apart from the programme of work at Communion time, there was the ongoing, never-ending chores attached to the minister's cattle. The minister's wife was in charge of milking the cows but, of course, there were the other duties such as feeding the animals, cleaning the byre, driving them to the pasture and so on.

You know, I was interested in religion since I was very young and, while I was at the manse, I was very happy. I cannot explain why that was so. It was just such a different existence. At one time, I was looking after the minister's children. I had to wash every stitch of clothes they wore – and also iron it!

Màiri used to be with me; that is, Màiri who is married to Alasdair Crichton. We were just as familiar with the Free Church manse [as with the manse of the Church of Scotland]. They were very similar and we often visited that manse when we were young. In those days, Lachie MacLeod was our minister. It was there that, for the very first time, I ate oven scones. I ate those along with homemade strawberry jam made at the manse. We were used enough to baking griddle scones but we couldn't make oven scones for the simple reason that we didn't have an oven. Strawberries were grown behind the house and the minister's wife made strawberry jam – wonderful to eat it. Those two items put together were food for the aristocracy! To this day, scrumptious scones remind me of Màiri.

When I was young, there used to be the road dancing but, truth to tell, I never attended such an event since I grew up. In my schooldays, there used to be a road dance at the Bayble road-end and I used to go there with my school pals. Since I grew up, I used to attend church meetings. My father was against our going to dances and I was never in a dancehall. In those days, the two Point churches at Garrabost [Church of Scotland and Free Church] were as one with each congregation mixing with the other. Nobody looked askance at anybody else. Whether they were Church of Scotland or Free Church, it didn't matter a hoot which you attended. One evening, I was going to a church meeting at Shader. I was still at school and my Auntie Jean who lived across the road from us, came in and said to my mother, 'It's high time that you put your foot down and kept your daughter indoors. She goes off every night down there. How can she keep on doing that without suffering the consequence?'

Anyway, my father said to me that evening – by the way, this was before I started attending evening church services – he said, 'Now you are not going out of doors tonight. I don't want you to leave the house.' We had a winged table over there with drawers at each end, and I sat there all evening weeping as I watched people walking up and down past the house. Anyway, on the following day, he said to me, 'You will never have to suffer that kind of restriction again. If you want to go out, you may do so.'

I started going to church in my last year at Bayble School. And I remember my first attendance on a Thursday, a day on which we were out 'roo-ing'* the peats. My mother said that we were going to knock off early so that she could attend the evening church service. I said to her that I would come with her and she very nearly fainted! She was aware that I used to attend meetings on my own before that.

Calum, my husband, was employed in his parents' shop from a young age and lots of boys used to congregate at the shop. Everybody was gobsmacked whenever I was sighted going off to the church meetings with my mother on Thursday evenings.

For a time, I was employed in our own church manse and after that I went to Siabost where I was looking after children. I always enjoyed cookery and I went to work in Taigh Aonghais a' Chailidh.† Following that, I took off for Edinburgh along with my sister Dena and Katie Ann and Calumina MacKay. We were employed at Edinburgh University Halls of Residence. Next, I became cook-housekeeper to a couple at Ravelston Dykes. He was from Inverness and she from Sussex. He had served for thirty-one years in a government post in India. Oh, I enjoyed Edinburgh. I loved it.

It so happened that Calum also sometimes went to the cinema, but as I was not in the habit of going we didn't have many opportunities of meeting except when he sometimes came up to the house for a wee ceilidh. When he did so, he always came with a bag of Liquorice Allsorts. I was awfully fond of Liquorice Allsorts. I was also fond of chocolate. When he started driving the bus, we would occasionally meet when I was a passenger travelling to Stornoway. In the end, when I left the island to work in Edinburgh, Calum and I started writing each other.

Now, I wasn't the only girl in whom my Calum was interested. Of course, he was a big, strapping, good-looking fellow. Along with Angus

---

* Lifting blocks of cut peat into small pyramids so as to allow them to be dried by the action of the wind and the sun.
† Now the Clachan Bar.

Lee, he used to go 'visiting' to Bac, to Aird and to Siadar. When he was driving the bus, he used to go to Bayble to see 'Bibi an Tàilleir'. Lovely 'Bibi'; she married 'Pods', a nice chap from Bac. Years afterwards, Pods used to tease my husband with the boast, 'I took her from you!' We often met Pods and Bibi in the town and whenever we did, there was always a lot of good-humoured banter between Calum and Pods.

When we began to see each other as 'a couple', Calum and I engaged in *caithris na h-oidhche* [night courtship]. He used to come up to our house and spend the night in my company. That happened when I came home on holiday in 1950 and our relationship developed. At that time, I was employed at the University Halls and was given leave to come home at Easter and Christmas. At the university's summer vacation, I wasn't allowed home because of the number of academic conferences being held at that time of the year. When we started courting in earnest, Calum and I used to engage in *caithris na h-oidhche* whenever I came home on holiday. I came back home to marry in 1951. We were blessed with three sons and a daughter.

After Alex Dan, our eldest son, left Bayble School he went to Lews Castle College to study carpentry and joinery. After graduating from there, he went on to study at the Esk Valley College at Dalkeith near Edinburgh. He now works in Edinburgh as a maintenance manager at the Scottish Office.

Calum, our second son, also went from Bayble School to the Lews Castle College and graduated with a degree in engineering. He served an engineering apprenticeship at Goat Island, Stornoway. He learned welding at the Arnish Prefabication Yard and then went off to work on the mainland.

Our daughter, Marina, did domestic science after leaving the Nicolson Institute, then went to Robert Gordon's University. She loved teaching primary-school children but wasn't so happy teaching senior pupils. In any case, she decided to leave teaching and go in for nursing. In the early years, her main interest was in nursing 'kidney patients'. After six months' training in paediatric nursing in Carolina, she went over to nursing cancer patients in the Royal Marsden Hospital in England. After that, a stint as a health visitor. Occasionally, she travels to Birmingham, Perth or Dundee to deliver lectures on subjects in her area of expertise. She is now working for a PhD degree.* Surely that should be enough!

Our son Donnie did his Higher National Diploma in the Lews Castle College in Stornoway. P&O officials came to the college and chose two or

* Graduated PhD in November 2005.

three lads and he was one of them. He spent eight years with that company and, in that time, travelled all over the world. He certainly did. When he was over in Japan, I used to send him the [*Stornoway*] *Gazette*. In one of the issues, he saw them advertising a post for an engineer at the Western Isles Hospital. Well, he applied by e-mail and, when he came home at the New Year, there was a letter waiting for him inviting him to come for interview. It was so unusual! Anyway, he got the job. Now, that suited him down to the ground. In spite of that, he sometimes wishes he were back at sea. Sailors have that problem in that they have seawater in their veins! It seems that, on board ship, they had such wonderful conditions and, on top of that, they had such opportunities for seeing places that they could never have visited otherwise. Calum visited places from Australia and New Zealand to the coasts of Alaska. Our island people have a natural wanderlust!

Our young men have always been on the high seas. Girls did not have that kind of opportunity when, even when I was young, we each had to launch out to earn a wage. And wherever in the world we happened to find ourselves, the mother earth of Lewis keeps a hold of us! This is absolutely true. Everybody who leaves Garrabost looks back to his birthplace. Our eldest comes back home at every opportunity.

Many English people are now living here. When you look in the phone book, you see lots of unfamiliar surnames. In a sense, it is not a good thing that they are so numerous. In some places, they try to impose their own culture. They are not all like that by any means. There was one lady living close to us from Yorkshire but she wouldn't allow you to suggest that she was an English woman at all! She used to claim that the people of Yorkshire were more akin to the Scots than they were to the [southern] English. Actually, there are people from every part of England who are very nice. Also, we must remember that there are many of our own fellow islanders who are living in England and it is quite possible that some of them are not all that popular with their neighbours. Unfortunately, the Yorkshire woman died of cancer. She used to say, 'I don't wish to do anything on the Sabbath Day, except as is done by the locals. I never wish to leave here.' She was a lovely person. She was buried at Sandwick Cemetery. For a time, her husband continued to live in Aird but has now gone back to Yorkshire. I like the people and everything that belongs to our island lifestyle. The Gaelic language is part of that lifestyle. I love our language and all our traditions and I wish to preserve them in every aspect. No part of it is worthless. Absolutely none.

Doilidh Murdo MacFhearghuis

1922–

Bha mise ceithir fichead bliadhna 's a h-aon ann am May a chaidh, agus tha mi fhathast fallainn gu ìre, agus taingeil airson a h-uile latha a gheibh mi. Chaidh mo bhaisteadh air an ainm Dòmhnall Murchadh, ach chan aithnich mòran mi air an ainm sin an-diugh. Thugadh dhomh ainm eile nuair a bha mi gu math òg agus lean e rium. 'S e sin 'Doilidh Murdo'.

Thàinig Clann Fhearghuis dhan eilean goirid an deidh do Chlann Choinnich Eilean Leòdhais a thoirt bho Chlann 'IcLeòid. B' ann mar sin a thachair. Thàinig mo shinnsirean a-steach a Cheòs, nach eil ach trì mìle air falbh bho mo dhachaigh an seo. Thàinig iad bho chionn faisg air trì cheud bliadhna agus cha do ghluais sinn mòran air falbh bho na tulaich a bh' aca bho thoiseach. 'S fìor am facal, 'Is binn guth an eòin far na ghuireadh e.' Co-dhiù, fhuair mo sheanair àite ann an Lacasaidh an seo – aig ceann shuas a' bhaile. Cha b' e croit a fhuair e idir. 'S ann a fhuair e pìos fearainn airson gum biodh e a' sealltainn às dèidh nan caorach. Cha robh feansaichean ann anns an là ud. B'esan (mo sheanair) an 'Cuairtiche' a bha ann an Lacasaidh – am fear a bhiodh a' cumail nan caorach bhon a' bhaile. Bha aige ri sin a dhèanamh bho toiseach an earraich gu deireadh an fhoghair fhad 's a bha an coirc 's an t-eòrna 's am buntat' a' fàs anns na h-imrichean. Faodaidh tu bhith cinnteach nach robh an cuairtiche a' faighinn mòran cadail fad nam mìosan sin. Saoilidh mi gu do rinn an cuairtiche – mo sheanair – a dhleastanas, oir thugadh dha am pìos talmhainn seo. Bhiodh timcheall air trì acairean ann.

Às dèidh dha mo sheanair sin a bhith aige, fhuair m' athair am fearann. Ach seach nach b' e croit a bh'ann, cha robh còir againn air taobh a-muigh gàrradh a' bhaile. Cha robh còir sam bith againn air cùl a' bhaile – mar a chanadh sinn, anns a' 'Chommon Grazing'. Ach le gean-math a' bhaile, bhiodh m' athair a' cumail bheathaichean.

Co-dhiù, aig an toiseach, cha robh eadhon numbar-taighe againn anns a' bhaile. Airson leigheas fhaighinn air a sin, chaidh fear dha mo bhràithrean agus cuideigin eile timcheall a' bhaile airson gum faigheadh sinn numbar-taighe agus gum biodh sinn a' pàigheadh màl mar a bha daoine eile. Agus fhuair sinn sin. Fhuair sin Numbar 30 agus bhiodh sinn a' pàigheadh rent air mar a bha càch. Dh'aindeoin sin, cha robh cuibhreann againn air taobh a-muigh a' bhaile.

Rugadh a' chiad leth dhan teaghlach againn ann an Dail Beag, faisg air Càrlabhagh. An uair sin bha am baile sin na thac. Bhiodh a' chlann bu shine a' dol dhan sgoil ann an Càrlabhagh. Agus bhiodh m' athair a' sealltainn às dèidh nan caorach agus às dèidh a' chruidh. Bha a' chlann ag obair cuideachd, an fheadhainn bu shine aca. Bha sin mus do rugadh mise. Chaidh an uair sin mo phàrantan leis an teaghlach a bh' aca a Lacasaidh. Chaidh, air ais a sin, agus thog iad bothan beag dhaib' fhèin. Taigh beag dubh ann an seo ann an Lacasaidh. Rinn iad sin a-mach à ceann an t-seann taigh a bh' ann – taigh mo sheanar. Rugadh an fheadhainn mu dheireadh dhan an teaghlach an seo anns an taigh-dhubh. Bha teaghlach mòr ann. Bha deichnear ann gu lèir, agus cha robh sin furasta anns an latha sin. Cha robh goireasan ann agus cha robh cùisean idir furasta dha na boireannaich gu h-àraid. Bha an abhainn ri ar taobh agus bha sin feumail airson nighe-adaireachd. Dhà no trì thurais anns a' bhliadhna bhiodh iad a' dol sìos dhan an abhainn le aodaichean 's le gnothaichean – tubaichean is praisean 's mar sin air adhart airson na nigheadaireachd.

Tha an t-ainm Lacasaidh a' ciallachadh 'Lag a' Bhradain'. Sin a' Ghàidhlig cheart a th' air. Ach am facal 'Lacasaidh' fhèin, tha mi a' creidse gur e an cànan Lochlannach a tha sin – no Beurla Lochlannach, mar a chanas iad. Co-dhiù, faodaidh tu bhith cinnteach gum biodh na fir a' dol dhan abhainn airson iasg a thoirt aiste. O, abair fhèin e! Abair fhèin e! Ach bha barrachd èisg ann na th' ann an-diugh. Ged a bha pailteas bhradan anns an abhainn, cha robh e ceadaichte do dhuine bha seo a dhol air an tòir. Cha robh idir, idir. Dh'aindeoin sin, bha e nàdarrach gum biodh muinntir a' bhaile a' dol a dh'iarraidh an cuid dhan tiodhlac a bha tighinn a-steach às a' chuan saor agus an-asgaidh. Cha robh na geamairean cho teann orra an uair sin 's a tha iad an-diugh. Cha robh duine anns na bailtean mun cuairt a' reic an èisg airson prothaid no càil mar sin. Bha iad a' toirt an èisg às an abhainn dìreach airson an teaghlach a bheathachadh. Fhios agad, bha biadhan fallain ann nuair a bha sinne òg. Cha robh duine math dheth ach an dèidh sin bha sinn a' tighinn troimhe glè mhath.

Cha robh anns na taighean-dubha mar bu tric' ach dà rùm: rùm-cadail agus 'aig an teine'. Bha sinn greis ann an sin gus an do thog sinn taigh eile. Bha ceathrar nighean agus sianar bhalach ann an teaghlach mo phàrantan. Bu mhise am fear a b' òige dha na balaich. 'S mathaid gu robh e duilich do phàrantan anns an t-suidheachadh sin rian a chumail air teaghlach cho mòr.

Air an làimh eile, bha sinn air ar togail modhail agus gasta ri càch-a-chèile. Cha bhiodh an deichnear chloinne anns an taigh còmhla idir. Cho luath 's a dh'fhàsadh iad suas, thogadh iad orra agus chuireadh iad cùl ris an dachaigh. Le sin, bhiodh an fheadhainn a bu shine air falbh an ceann an cosnaidh.

A' dol dhan sgoil, bhiodh sinn uile glè thric casruisgte. Nam biodh càil idir air an tìde, bhiodh sinn a' dol air ar casan lomnochd deireadh April agus bha sinn a' dèanamh sin gu saor-thoileach. Ach uaireannan bhiodh dìth bhrògan ann cuideachd. Cha robh an t-airgead ann.

Tha cuimhne agam aon latha 's mi anns an sgoil. Bha an aimsir math anns a' mhadainn nuair a dh'fhalbh sinn dhan sgoil. Bha mi òg an uair sin. Cha robh mi barrachd air còig no sia. Co-dhiù, tron fheasgar thàinig an sneachd agus am fuachd, fras chruaidh de shneachd, agus sgaoil an sgoil. Uill, bha mise an sin gun bhròg. Mar a thachair, air an là ud bha fear dha na balaich mhòra a' dol seachad orm 's mi air an t-slighe dhachaigh a' rànail. Bhiodh esan mu chuairt air dusan no trì bliadhna deug. Chan eil an duine còir sin beò an-diugh. Uill, chuir mi uimhir de thruas air agus gun do chuir e air a mhuin mi. Chuir e mo chasan na phòcaidean, pòcaidean na seacaid a bh' air, agus chaidh sinn dhachaigh mar sin. Bha lathaichean cruaidh ann an uair sin, ach bha càirdeas ann an gnè nan daoine agus bha a h-uile duine anns an aon rèir, gun bheartas agus gun mòran de chùl-cinn. Dh'aindeoin sin, bha aran gu leòr ann agus, uaireannan, maragan gu leòr. An uair a dheigheadh beathach a mharbhadh, cha robh mìr dheth nach robh gu feum. Dheigheadh an ceann a dhathadh airson deagh bhrot a dhèanamh agus, nam b' e rùd a bhiodh ann, dheigheadh na h-adhaircean a chumail airson làmhan chromagan. Air an làimh eile, cha robh càil againn dha na rudan spaideil annasach a th' aig clann an-diugh.

Tha cuimhn' agam aon uair aig àm Christmas, chaidh sinn a chadal – bhiodh sinn a' dol a chadal cho tràth co-dhiù aig an àm ud – ach cha b' urrainn dhomh cadal leis an fhadachd a bh' oirnn airson na madainn-bha sinn air ar stocainnean a chrochadh – agus leis an fhuireachd a dh'fhaicinn dè bha dol air adhart shìos aig an teine. Eadar deich 's aon uair deug chaidh mi sìos 's sheall mi ciamar a bha cùisean. Tha cuimhne agam fhathast gu robh greideal aig mo mhàthair agus m' athair air an t-slabhraidh os cionn an teine agus bha mias air a beul fòidhpe air a' ghreideal. An seòrsa mias tiona a gheibheadh tu an uair sin, bha oir oirre a bha tighinn a-mach mun bheul aice. Uill, bha a' mhias a bha sin 's a beul fòidhpe am meadhan na greideil agus bha an frìom a bha mu a beul làn de dh'èibhleagan dearga. Bha m' athair 's mo mhàthair ann an sin gu cùramach a' frithealadh an rud a bha iad a' deasachadh. B' e m' athair a' thermostat! 'S esan leis a' chlobha a bha

cumail èibhleagan dearga timcheall na mèis, mar a bha an fheadhainn eile a'
dol dubh. Ach ann an ceann ùine, chunna mi mo mhàthair a' togail na mèis
far na greideil. Abair thusa sealladh! Bha cèic mhòr àlainn ann an sin, cho
brèagha ri cèic a chunna tu a-riamh, agus b' e pìos dhan chèic sin a fhuair
sinn nar stocainnean anns a' mhadainn – sin agus orainsear no ubhal. Bha
sinne cho toilichte le sin an uair sin 's ged a bhiodh sinn air magaid
fhaighinn a bhiodh iad air a cheannachd ann am bùth.

Nuair a bha mi ag èirigh, cha robh mòran feòil a' dol, ach bha iasg gu leòr
againn, gu h-àraid sgadan agus adag agus bradan. Tha cuimhn' agamsa
sgadan a bhith a' tighinn air tìr ann an seo air cladach Lacasaidh. Bha
bodach a' fuireachd ann an taigh shìos an sin aig a' chladach. Aona latha 's e
na shuidhe a' gabhail a' bhiadh, 's ann a thàinig an cat a-steach agus sgadan
aige na bheul. Ruith am bodach sìos chon a' chladaich agus cha mhòr gun
creideadh e an sealladh a bha roimhe ann an sin. Bha an tràigh geal le
sgadan. Thòisich e gan tional agus gan slaodadh a-nuas, gus an robh, mu
dheireadh, càirntean dhan sgadan aige air a thogail. Abair thusa sealladh!
Bha an adag cuideachd pailt anns an loch sa. Bhiodh iad a' dol a-mach ann
an sin leis na h-eathraichean agus a' tilgeil nan dubhanan a-mach 's cha
leigeadh a leas biadh a bhith orra. Bha iad cho pailt ri sin. Bha iad a' glacadh
nan adag gun bhiathadh idir air na dubhanan.

Nise, cha robh na daoine a bha seo idir ris na fèidh. Cha bhitheadh ann
an seo anns a' bhaile sa. Bhiodh sin a' tachart nas fhaide thall, taobh na
Pàirce ann an sin. Cha robh duine a bha seo an sàs ann an Aimhreit na
Pàirce. Cha robh, cha robh.

An uair a bha sinn nar balaich bhiodh sinn a' cumail Oidhche Challainn is
bhiodh sinn a' dol timcheall nan taighean le 'Duan na Callainn'. Bhiodh peilid
caorach air druim fear dha na balaich – timcheall a ghuailnean. Chuireadh
sinn trì caran mun taigh fhad 's a bha sinn ag èigheachd an duain:

> Thàine sinn an seo gur n-ionnsaigh
> a dh' ùrachadh dhuibh na Callainn . . .
> Bha i ann bho linn mo sheanar . . .

Tha mi air tòrr dha na facail a dhìochuimhneachadh. Ach tha deagh
chuimhn' agam cho toilichte s' a bhiodh sinn an uair a thigeadh bean an
taighe a-mach le annlan a dh'itheadh sinn – rudan math milis. Nise, 's e
Oidhche Shamhna a bh' aig a' chlann-nighean. Ach ann an tòrr de
dh'àitichean air an Taobh Siar, bhiodh na balaich 's a' chlann-nighean
còmhla air Oidhche Shamhna. Tha mi smaoineachadh gu bheil iad fhathast
mar sin.

Cha robh Beurla againn nuair a bha sinn òg. Bhiodh facal no dhà againn ceart gu leòr a bhruidhneadh sinn ri coigreach a thigeadh à Glaschu no badeigin eile mu dheas. Ach bha mise air fàs mòr mus robh mi gu ìre fileanta. Bha mi air an sgoil fhàgail agus air an eilean fhèin fhàgail. B' ann an uair sin a thòisich mi ri bruidhinn na Beurla. Ann am broinn na sgoile, cha robh càil ach a' Bheurla. Cho luath 's a bha sinn a' faighinn a-mach a chluich, cha robh againn ach a' Ghàidhlig. Ach chan ann mar sin a tha clann an là an-diugh. Tha a' Bheurla a' fàs nas treasa agus tha mi a' smaoineachadh gur e an telebhisean as coireach ri sin. Shios ann am Bail' Ailein bha a' chlann a' tionndadh chon na Beurla fada mus robh iad mar sin an seo. Bha am maighistir-sgoile dhaibh airson a bhith leis a' Bheurla a-muigh mar bha iad a-staigh. Bha a bhuil. Tha pàrantan aig a bheil an dà chànan a' dèanamh call mòr le bhith a' cumail comas anns an dà chànan bho an cuid chloinne. Bithidh a' Bheurla aca co-dhiù.

Bha mi fhìn uaireiginn ag obair aig Tawse. Bha mi mu sheachd deug nuair a thòisich an cogadh agus bha mi ann an cuaraidh Tawse an uair sin. Bha i dìreach air fosgladh an uair sin. Uill, cha robh càil ann an uair sin ach . . . an t-òrd mòr agus gràpaichean airson a bhith a' lìonadh làraidhean. Abair obair chruaidh. Bha suas gu trì cheud duine aig an uair ud ag obair ann an cuaraidh Tawse. Anns an latha ud, cha robh ann ach aon crusher mòr. Dh' fheumadh na clachan a bhith air am briseadh leis an òrd mus deigheadh iad dhan chrusher. Bha an uair sin a' chlach mhìn a bha tighinn às a' chrusher ga giùlain air falbh airson rathaidean a dheanamh agus cuideachd an aerodrome air Machair Mhealaboist. 'S e contract mhòr a bh' ann an contract na h-aerodrome. Bha mi greis ann an sin agus chaidh mi an uair sin sìos chun an drome fhéin. Bha sgaorr dhaoine againn ag obair shìos ann an sin. Bha fear às an Rubha ann, tha mi a' creids gun aithnich thu gu math e – 'Hodan'. Bha e ag obair ann le each leis fhéin. 'S e each glas a bh' aige an uair ud. Mus do phòs mi, bhithinn a' dol chon nan consartan 's nan cèilidhean – an àbhaist am measg nam balach. Dh'fheumadh sinn an cur-seachad againn fhìn a dhèanamh. Bhiodh dannsan agus consartan 's rudan dhan t-seòrsa sin againn. Ach cha robh mòran chur-seachadan dhan t-seòrsa sin agam bho thòisich mi ag obair 's mar cheannard teaghlaich.

Chaidh an dà bhràthair a bu shine a bh' agam dhan Arm timcheall air 1928 no '29. Rinn gach fear trì bliadhna anns na Seaforths, agus an uair sin thàinig iad dhachaigh agus bhiodh iad ag obair a-muigh ris an obair-latha, timcheall aig rathaidean agus rudan dhan t-seòrsa sin. Bha am fear bu shine ag obair aig Stèisean nam Muc faisg air Àird Àsaig ann an ceann a tuath na Hearadh. Fhuair m' athair obair an sin cuideachd. Aig an àm ud, bhiodh bàtaichean-seilg a' siubhal a' chuain a' marbhadh nam mucan-mara agus gan slaodadh air an cùlaibh a-steach chon na Stèisein. Bhiodh na bàtaichean sin a' sealg cho fada a-muigh ri Hiort – eadar leth-cheud agus trì fichead mile muigh anns a' chuan. Bha pailteas de mhucan ann anns an là ud agus bha luchd-obrach na Stèisein air an cumail gu math dripeil a' gearradh nam beathaichean agus a' leaghadh na saill.

Dh' fhalbh dithis eile dha mo bhràithrean dhan an Arm agus thug iad sin seachd bliadhna ann, agus nuair a thàinig iad dhachaigh bha an Dàrna Cogadh an ìre mhath gus tòiseachadh. Cha robh iad aig an taigh ach mìos no dhà gus an d' fhuair iad teachdaireachd tilleadh a-mach anns a' bhad. Nise bha bràthair eile agam, Dòmhnall Fionnlagh, am fear a b' fhaisg' orm fhin san teaghlach, bha esan cuideachd anns na Seaforths. Anns a' cheann thall, bha a h-uile duine againn anns a' Chogadh. Bha triùir thall anns an Fhraing, 's chaidh dithis dhuibh a ghlacadh aig St Valery. Bha iad nam prìosanaich airson còig bliadhna aig na Gearmailtich. Fhuair Alasdair, an treas bràthair, a-mach às an Fhraing. Thàinig esan dhachaigh tro Dhunkirk. 'S mise an duine mu dheireadh a chuir cùl ris an dachaigh. Chaidh mi dhan an RAF an toiseach. Bha sin ann an 1942. Chuir mi greiseag seachad an sin agus fhuair mi an uair sin transfer dhan an Arm. B' ann anns na Seaforths a bha mise mi fhìn cuideachd. Sianar bhràithrean anns an aon rèiseamaid. Bha mi shìos ann an Sasainn agus cuideachd shuas ann an Sealtainn. Aig deireadh a' chogaidh, bha mi anns a' Ghearmailt. Man a dh'innis mi dhut, bha ceathrar pheathraichean agam agus bha triùir dhiubh sin nan nursaichean an Glaschu aig àm a' chogaidh. Dh'fhuirich an tè a b' òig' aig an taigh. Le sin, faodaidh tu a radh gu robh naoidhnear a-mach às an deichnear air falbh anns a' Chogadh. Bha mo phàrantan beò aig an àm ud agus cha robh am beatha idir soirbh dhaibh. Àm duilich a bh' ann dhaibhsan agus dha gach pàrant eile aig an robh teaghlach air falbh a' sabaid ris an nàmhaid.

Chaidh mo bhràthair Iain a mharbhadh aig àm D-Day. Bha esan air a bhith còmhla ris an 8th Army thall anns an Èipheit. Air chùl sin, bha e anns an Eadailt. Ach mu dheireadh chaidh e dhan Fhraing air D-Day. Bha e air Bren-carrier. Fhuair e air tìr ceart gu leòr, ach chaidh rudeigin ceàrr air a' Bhren-carrier – air an track – agus thàinig orra stad airson sin a chur ceart. B' fheudar dhaibh an uair sin falbh le sgoinn airson gum beireadh iad air a' chòrr dhan a' chonbhoidh. Gu mì-shealbhach, bhuail e ann an craoibh. Chaidh an rud thairis 's chaidh mo bhràthair a ghlacadh fodha. Chaidh a mharbhadh ann an sin.

Às deidh a' Chogaidh, thòisich mi ag obair aig contractors ann an seo fhèin. 'S e Tawse am fear bu mhotha a bh' ann aig an àm. Dh' fhalbh mi an uair sin gu sgeamaichean a' Hydro timcheall air 1948–49. Tha mi a' creids gun tug mi faisg air còig bliadhna deug ris an obair sin, air ais agus air adhart, a' faighinn tuarastal aig na sgeamaichean a bha sin. Bha mi aig Canaich agus bha mi aig Loch Luicheart. Bha mi cuideachd aig sgeama eile anns an Eilean Sgiathanach – Loch an Stòir. Dh'fhàg mi sin agus chaidh mi sìos a Shasainn a dh'obair aig Windscale, far a bheil an nuclear-stèisean mhòr. Sellafield an t-ainm a th' aca air mar as tric' an-diugh. 'S e Windscale am pìos mu dheireadh a chaidh a dhèanamh dheth. 'S ann aig na cranaichean a bha mise ag obair, a' deanamh thogalaichean. Bha mi ann nuair a bha 'scare' uabhasach ann timcheall air 1957 no '58. Chaidh fear dha na similearan na theine. Abair thusa ùpraid! Cha chreid mi nach deach duine no dhithis a mhilleadh gu dona ann aig an àm ud. Bha am fallout – an dust radioactive a bha sin – aca ga thogail cho fada deas ri Lunnainn. Tha cuimhn' agam aona làraidh a bh' ann is i aca air a lodaigeadh le gnothai-chean. Bha i a' dol suas a Ghlaschu gu Babcock & Wilcox. Ghlac iad i mus deach i a-mach air a' gheata agus rinn iad tests oirre agus bha i làn dhan a' fallout.

An ath rud a chunnaic sinn, chaidh falbh leis an làraidh agus a cur fo ghlas am badeigin. Chan eil mi ag ràdh nach deach a cur ann an dump. Thàinig daoine le deisichean geala agus masks agus chladhaich iad an-àirde an rathad air na dh'fhalbh i – rathad concrait – 's chuir iad a h-uile mìr a bha sin ann an pocan canabhais, 's dh'fhalbh iad leis na pocan sin agus thiodhlaic iad iad. Feumaidh e bhith gu robh stuth an rathaid a bha sin gu math cunnartach. Bha am fallout a bha siud air na bonaidean againn 's air ar làmhan 's a h-uile càil. Tha mi a' smaoineachadh gur e Sir William Penny am fear a b' àirde aig an robh uachdaranas aig Windscale. Thàinig esan a thoirt lecture dhuinn ag innse dhuinn mar a bha air tachairt agus gar misneachadh. 'S chaidh a h-uile duine againn a thoirt a-steach an sin airson tests. Co-dhiù, chon seo, cha do rinn a bhith ag obair aig Windscale cron sam bith ormsa. Cha robh e ceadaichte bainne a' chruidh òl – am bainne a bha tighinn bho na tuathan anns na sgìrichean ceithir-thimcheall Wind-scale.

Mar tha fios agad chaidh ainm ainm ùr a thoirt air Windscale. B' e sin Sellafield. A rèir eachdraidh, tha iad fhathast a' cur a-mach cuibhreann dhan sgudal dhan a' chuan. Chan eil fhios dè na tha a' dol a-mach dheth an-diugh. Ach an uair ud bha trealaich mhath. Bha pìoban a' dol dhan a' mhuir 's bha na h-uimhir ga leigeil às an ceann a h-uile tìde agus bha rud, mar a chanadh iad fhèin, an 'Graveyard' – togalach mòr concrait, cha robh uinneagan no càil air, 's bhiodh an skip a' tighinn leis an sgudal 's a' dol an-àirde taobh an togalaich. Bha e ga fhalamhachadh fhèin anns an togalach sin. Ach bha na h-uimhir dheth a' dol a-mach air a' mhuir tro na pìoban an-dràsta 's a-rithist. Cha robh còir aig duine iasgach anns a' mhuir ann an astar chòig mìle deug bhon stèisean. Chan fhuireadh an t-iasg a-mach às a' phìos mara a bha sin agus dheigheadh an t-iasg sin a ghlacadh ann am pàirtean eile dhan chuan. Mar a thuigeas tu, chan eil fhios agam cò ris a tha Sellafield coltach an-diugh, ach b' ann mar siud a bha e aig an àm ud.

Co-dhiù, theàrn mise agus thàinig mi dhachaigh an uair sin. Agus b' ann an deidh sinn a rinn mi an ceangal ris a' bhoireannach a tha seo! Bha Seònaid a' fuireachd ann an Calanais. O, chan eil an t-slighe idir fada nuair a tha an òig' agad. Bha tractar agam an uair sin agus bhithinn a' dol a shealltainn oirre leis an tractar a-null a Chalanais. Abair tuirilich ann am mòinteach Leòdhais! Abair sin. Bha fhios aig a h-uile duine anns a' bhaile gu robh coigreach a' tighinn dhan bhaile! Bha sinn a' suirghe airson còrr air bliadhna co-dhiù. Ghabh i an fhàinne bhuam agus thug sinn bliadhna leis a' cheangal sin mus do phòs sinn.

Bha banais-taighe ann an toiseach. Bha sin againn anns gach àite – an Calanais an toiseach agus ann an seo ann an Lacasaidh. Àbhachdas gu leòr le dannsa an t-sabhail le pìobaire agus meileòidian. Bha mo bhràthair fhìn – Aonghas – math air a' phìob. Nis, chan eil cuimhn' agam an robh esan ann. Cuideachd, bha fear againn ann am Bail' Ailein a bha math air an fhidheall. Ceòl math dannsa co-dhiù.

Fhuair sinn còignear chloinne – aon bhalach agus ceathrar nighean. Tha Sandra a chunnaic thu a-staigh ann an seo. Tha tèile pòsta anns an dachaigh a bh' aicese ann an Calanais. Pòsta aig fear à Fife. Tha tèile, Seonag, tha i shìos ann an Sasainn: Shropshire. Tha i pòsta aig fear ann an sin. Agus tha Donna, an tè as òige, tha i ann an Obar Dheathain. Tha i a' nursaigeadh ann an sin. Agus tha i pòsta aig fear à Ùig – sgìre Ùige. Tha iad air feadh na fìdhle.

Nise, tha am balach againn anns an t-seann làrach shuas. Anns an t-seann dachaigh. Thog e taigh ùr ann an sin. Tha e a' fuireach an sin. Tha e ag obair; tha sguad aige. Chan eil fhios agam dè an t-ainm a th' air a' firm an-diugh: tha iad ag atharrachadh an ainm cho tric. 'S e John Fife a bh' oirre o chionn greis. Tha e ag obair ann an sin air sguad na tearra.

Bho dh'èirich mi an-àirde ann am bliadhnaichean, dh'fhosgail an Sois-geul mo shùilean agus thàinig obair na h-eaglais a-steach na mo bheatha. Carson a tha sinn anns an eaglais againn (an t-Aonadh) seachad air a h-uile eaglais eile? Uill, 's e ceist a tha sin. Ach leis an fhìrinn innse, chan eil mise ann an dòigh sam bith an aghaidh na h-Eaglais Shaoir no eaglais eile anns a bheil ùmhlachd ga toirt do Dhia tro Shoisgeul Iosa Crìosd.

Bha mi aon uair ag obair ann an Sgalpaigh, agus 's e an Eaglais Shaor as treasa a th' anns an eilean sin. Mar a thachair, bhiodh an t-seirbheis ann an Eaglais an Aonaidh a' tòiseachadh aig sia uairean feasgar ach cha bheirinn oirre air sgàth gu robh mi ag obair. Anns an t-suidheachadh sin, bha mi gu math toilichte a' dol dhan an Eaglais Shaoir, oir cha robh mise a' cur umhail gu robh dealachadh sam bith eadar na seirbheisean anns an dà eaglais sin. Bha e dhomh anns an Eaglais Shaor dìreach mar gum bithinn anns an eaglais againn fhìn.

Tha eadar-dhealachadh de dh'eaglaisean ann, agus bha bho riamh. Ach 's e tha cudromach gu bheil iad uile fon aon mhaighstir, agus 's e sin Crìosd. Sin an rud a tha cunntadh. Tha mise a' creidsinn a' Bhìobaill, agus lem uile chridhe tha mi a' creidsinn Chrìosd nuair a tha e ag radh rinn, "Cha tig aon neach a chum an Athar ach tromhamsa." Tha Crìosd ag ràdh sin rinn, agus 's e sin a' bhunait air a bheil mise air mo thogail agus leanaidh mi orm a rèir mo chreidimh fhìn cho fad' 's as beò mi. Sin mar bu choir dhuinn a bhith – a' toirt ùmhlachd do Dhia agus, cho math 's as urrainn dhuinn, a' leantainn na slighe a tha air a soillseachadh dhuinn anns an t-Soisgeul.

Thàinig atharrachadh mòr air cùisean bho àm a' Chogaidh mu dheireadh. Cha robh wirelessan no telebhisean no càil againn roimhe sin. Cha chreid mi nach b' e sinn fhìn a fhuair a' chiad wireless anns a' bhaile sa – tè bheag, 's cha mhòr gun cluinneadh duine càil oirre! Uill, thòisich cùisean ag atharrachadh an uair sin às dèidh a' Chogaidh. Thàinig wirelessan agus telebhisean agus thòisich magaidean eile agus innealan a' tighinn dha na taighean. Thàinig a' washing-machine, an deep-freeze agus rudan dhan t-seòrsa sin. Gun teagamh, thàinig tòrr de rudan math a-steach, ach cuideachd thàinig cleachdaidhean nar measg nach eil idir a' leasachadh ar dòigh-beatha. Dh'fhalbh an latha anns am biodh smachd ga chumail air a' chloinn. Tha mi cuideachd dhan bheachd nach eil mòran dhan òigridh cho modhail 's a bha an òigridh nam latha-sa. Dh'fhaodte nach eil iad air an oideachadh chon na h-aon ìre 's a bha sinne. Cuideachd, chan eil mi dhan bheachd gu bheil uiread de smachd air na h-oileanaich anns an sgoil. Nuair a bha sinne anns an sgoil, gheibheadh sinn stràic nam biodh sinn a' dèanamh crostachd no mì-mhodalachd, agus bha sinn feumach air, tha mi creidsinn.

Cuideachd, tha mòran Ghall is eile air a thighinn a chòmhnaidh dhan eilean. Cuid dhiubh a tha glè mhath nan dòigh agus a tha a' dèanamh feum, ach thàinig feadhainn eile le dòighean ùra nach eil idir math. Tha mise a' smaoineachadh gu robh tòrr dha na cleachdaidhean a bh' againn fhìn ceart agus feumail anns a h-uile dòigh – samhail a bhith a' cumail na Sàbaid. Tha tòrr dhan a sin a' falbh oirnn agus is mòr am beud.

Donald M. Ferguson

1922–

I was eighty-one years old last May. I remain quite well and grateful for each day I am spared. I was christened Dòmhnall Murchadh [Donald Murdo] but not a lot of folk would recognize me by that name now. From the time I was very young, they started to call me 'Dolly Murdo' – and that is what they still call me.

The Fergusons first came from the mainland to the village of Ceòs in Lochs, Lewis. That's where they first got houses. They came here from the Black Isle in Inverness-shire. I believe that they were blacksmiths to trade and were brought to Lewis by MacKenzie of Seaforth when he took the island from the MacLeods.

That was the way of it. My forebears settled at Ceòs, which is only about three miles from us here at Laxay [Lacasaigh]. That was about three hundred years ago and we, their descendants, continue to live quite close to the sites they occupied long ago. As the Gaelic proverb says, 'The bird sings sweetest in the place where it hatched.' Be that as it may, my grandfather got land here at Laxay – at the upper end of the village. He was given that after he accepted the position of *Cuairtiche* for the village. As such, he was responsible for keeping the sheep out on the rough grazing from about mid March until November – in other words, from when the potatoes and oats were planted until the crops were safely harvested. During those months the *Cuairtiche* never got more than a few hours of sleep at night. He was kept pretty busy all summer and autumn, for the sheep will always want to raid fields where the oats and vegetables are growing. They can cause a lot of damage in a very short time. Well, my grandfather worked hard at his job and, in recognition of his diligence, he was given about three acres of land within the village itself. Even so, his holding wasn't recognised as a croft. It was just a concession given to him by grace and favour.

After my grandfather, my father inherited the land but, as I said, it wasn't a croft and, because of that, he had no right to the Common Grazing outside the village boundary. However, with the goodwill of the local crofters, he was allowed to have sheep on the Common Grazing.

Our holding didn't even have an address – I mean a number by which our place could be identified. That was inconvenient, so one of my brothers and a friend of his went round the village to ask if they would object to our having a number. Of course, my parents wanted to pay rent like the rest of the crofters. Well, we did get a number – No. 30 – and, from then on, we paid rent for the land like everybody else. Even so, we didn't have shares of the Common Grazing .

The first half of our family were born in Dail Beag on the west coast of Lewis near Carloway. At that time it was a tack [farm]. In fact, the older children went to school in Carloway. My father looked after the sheep and cattle. And the older children also worked. That was before I came on the scene! After Dail Beag, my parents moved to Laxay here with the first of their children. The younger members of our family were born and raised at No. 30. My father worked as a shepherd and a grieve on the farms. Being a grieve meant that he had to turn his hand to all sorts of work around the farm. For a while, he worked on Teedy's farm, down in Melbost on the other side of Stornoway. In Laxay, he built a black-house – out from the end of the old house that was there – my grandfather's house. The last of the family were born there. There were ten in our family. As you can imagine, raising such a large family wasn't easy in those days. Everything was very basic. Difficult for the women especially. The river was nearby and that was a help. It was very handy for washing. Two or three times a year they carried clothes such as blankets and other bedclothes down to the river with tubs and pots and washed them there.

The name of the village is Laxay, which, in the Old Norse tongue, means the Hollow of Salmon. So there must have been Norse families living here at one time. In my father's time, the people here took the occasional salmon from the river. No doubt about that. Of course, at that time, there were more fish in the river than there are today. Though there was plenty of salmon in the river, nobody living locally was allowed to go for them. Not at all. In spite of that prohibition, it was natural that village folk went for a share of the bonanza that came to us freely from the ocean. The game-keepers were not as strict as they are now. In those days, no one sold salmon taken from the river for profit. Just to feed the family. You know, there was a healthy diet when I was young. Nobody was well off but, in spite of that, we were managing to win through.

Black-houses usually had just the two rooms – a bedroom and the living-room. We were living in the black-house for a while until we built another house. My parents had four daughters and six sons. I am the youngest of the sons. I suppose it was difficult for parents in that kind of situation to keep a semblance of discipline in a family so large. The fact is that we were raised to be well-mannered and generous to one another, Now, I have to point out that it would be wrong for you to think that my parents and their ten children were crammed together in the two rooms of the black-house. You see, the older ones were grown up and were away earning a living elsewhere.

As children we often went to school on our bare feet. If the weather was at all good, we would go barefoot. All the boys of my generation did that from the end of April and up to the summer holidays. I did that of my own free will. Yes, there was a lack of shoes too, for there was little money available. I remember being in school one day. It was a good day when we left home. I was young then, no more than five or six. In the afternoon, the snow came. A hard shower of snow and the school broke up and there I was, bare-footed. It so happened that one of the older boys was passing me as I was making my way home weeping. Well, I've never forgotten the kindness of that boy who was twelve or thirteen years old. He felt so sorry for me because I was crying with the cold that he put me on his back. He put my cold feet in his jacket pockets, and we went home like that. Those were hard days but generosity of spirit was in the nature of the people. Yes, everyone was in the same boat – poorly off. Yet, we lacked for nothing when it came to food. Plenty of bread and, sometimes, plenty of puddings and sausages. Every part of a slaughtered animal was put to good use. The head was singed and excellent soup made of it. The horns of a ram, say, were kept and made into the crooks of walking sticks. On the other hand, we had none of the luxuries and the good things that children get today. I remember one Christmas Eve, we went to bed full of hope for what the morning might bring. As a rule, we used to go to bed early. After hanging up our stockings, I couldn't sleep for impatience. I wanted to see what was going on down at the fire where my parents were sitting. I got up between ten and eleven and I stole down to have a look. I still remember it. There was a griddle on the hook-and-chain above the fire and there was a tin basin – one of the ones you got then with a projecting lip on it. The basin was placed upside down in the middle of the griddle and round the rim was full of red-hot embers. My father was the thermostat! Whenever the embers lost their heat and turned to black my father, using the tongs, quickly replaced them with more red-hot ones. I watched as all this went on and, in the end, when my mother took the basin off the griddle, there was a big cake, the nicest you ever saw. And that's what went into our stockings that Christmas – chunks of that beautiful griddle cake wrapped in pieces of clean white cloth. A piece of cake, along with an orange or apple, made us all happy – as happy as we would have been if we had been given a shop-bought toy.

In those days, there wasn't much meat but plenty of fish – herring, salmon, and haddock. The herring were so plentiful in the loch; I remember herring coming ashore here. There was an old man down at the shore having his dinner one day in his house when the cat ran in with a live herring in its mouth. He ran down to the shore and the beach was alive with jumping herring – herring even covering the seaweed. He started gathering them up and brought home loads of them. And there also was plenty of haddock in this sea loch. Oh, yes, plenty. They would go out there in their boats and cast their lines into the water with no need for bait – they were so plentiful that they caught the haddock with bare hooks. Yes, with no bait on the hooks.

There were plenty of deer in the park to the south of here but the people of Laxay weren't given to poaching of the deer. They were not involved with the famous Park Deer Raid in the 1880s. We had nothing to do with that.

As boys, we celebrated the Old New Year. We went from house to house reciting 'Duan na Callainn', the New Year rhyme. One of the older boys with a sheepskin over his shoulders would enter the house and go around the fire three times. We boys would be reciting the traditional rhyme in Gaelic, of course:

> We have come tonight to renew the New Year,
> As has been from my grandfather's time . . .

I don't remember the words, but I do remember very well that once we had said the rhyme, the housewife would give us something to eat – perhaps a bannock or something tasty. Now, the girls celebrated 'Oidhche Shamhna' – Hallowe'en. But in a lot of places on the West Side, the boys and girls were together at Hallowe'en. They are like that even today, I think.

We didn't have English when we were young. Maybe we would say a word or two if a visitor came from Glasgow or somewhere away; we would try a few words. I was quite old before I became fluent in English – after we left school, I suppose, and started going off the island. That's when we really started speaking English. They taught us English in school but as soon as we got into the playground we spoke only Gaelic. Today's children are not like that, though. I suppose about thirty years ago English started coming in strongly. Television was responsible for the change. Up in Bail' Ailein* the children were turning to English earlier than that. There, the headmaster was very keen for them to speak English all the time, even when they went out into the playground. It took root more quickly there than in other villages. Parents who speak both Gaelic and English are making a big mistake if they don't encourage their offspring to master the two languages. Today's children will be fluent in English come what may.

Aged about seventeen, I went to work in Tawse's Quarry. That's the big quarry on the Lochs road as you come to the outskirts of Stornoway. There were up to three hundred men at that time working in the quarry. I got to know all about breaking rocks while I was there! The quarry was opened just about the time that the Second World War broke out. Well, at that time, the workers only had sledge-hammers for breaking rocks and graips for loading the lorries. Very hard work. In those days, they had only one big crusher. The big stones had to be reduced with the sledge-hammers before they could be fed into the crusher. The metal from the crusher was carried away for road-making and for building the aerodrome at the Mealabost machair.† I worked for a time at the quarry and then went to work at the 'drome' itself. There was a big crowd of us there. There was one fellow there from the Rubha whom you probably know well – Hodan MacDonald. He was working there with his own horse – a grey one at that time. We had a lot of fun there. We made our own entertainment – just the usual amongst boys. In those days we were all fond of dances and concerts and the like. From the time I married and became the head of a family, I haven't had much time for that sort of pastime.

My two oldest brothers went into the army with the Seaforth Highlanders. After three years there, they came home and were employed making the roads and labouring-work like that. The eldest got work at the whaling station at Àird Àsaig in Harris. Then my father also got work there. In those days, whale-hunters roamed the ocean killing whales and towing them to the station. They hunted as far out as St Kilda, between fifty and sixty miles to the west of Àird Àsaig. Plenty of whales in those days and the workers at the station were kept busy cutting the animals and rendering the blubber.

Later another two brothers joined the army round about 1928 or '29 and served for seven years. When they came home, the Second World War was just about to start. They were back for only a couple of months before they

* A two-mile-long linear township in the south of the island.
† Now Stornoway Airport.

were recalled urgently. Next, Donald Finlay, the fifth brother who was nearest to me in age, he also went into the Seaforths. In the end, all six of us were in the war.

Three of my brothers were in France and were captured by the Germans at St Valery* and spent five years as prisoners of war. Alasdair, a third brother, managed to get back to Britain through the port of Dunkirk.

Now, Donald Finlay, a fifth brother, next to myself in age, was also in the Seaforths. I was the last one to go; that was in 1942, two years after the war began. I joined the RAF first and, while I was in the air force, I worked on car maintenance. I was there a while and was then transferred to the army. So, in the end, we six brothers were all in the Seaforth Highlanders. First, I was stationed down in England and then up in Shetland. When the war ended, I was stationed in Germany. At that time, three of my four sisters were nurses working in Glasgow. The youngest was allowed to stay at home. My parents were alive and living through the war was a worrying time for them. Difficult for them and for every other parent whose families were away fighting the enemy.

My brother Iain was killed shortly after D-Day. He'd been with the Eighth Army fighting over in Egypt. After that, he was with the invasion of Italy. On D-Day he got ashore in France OK. He was in a Bren-carrier. Unfortunately, something went wrong with the track or something came adrift which forced the vehicle to stop. The crew had to get out and fix it. After a time, they managed to get the Bren-carrier going again and they speeded up to catch up with the convoy. On the way, they hit a tree. The carrier capsized and everyone was thrown clear except my brother, who was caught under it. Iain was killed in the accident.

After my demob I started working with contractors locally. Tawse was the biggest at the time. But then, I went away to work on the mainland, in Inverness-shire, to the hydro schemes. That would be round about 1948–49 and I suppose I took about fifteen years at that, back and forth. I was at Cannich, and Contin, and Loch Luichart, and at Loch an Stòir in Skye.

My next move took me further afield. I went down to England to the big nuclear power station at Windscale. I was employed on cranes building the station. I was there at the time of the big scare when one of the chimneys caught fire. That was round about 1957 or '58. I think a couple of people were injured there. The radioactive dust came through the chimney and rose into the sky and spread all over. They were finding nuclear fallout as far south as London. Milk was cancelled in a two-mile radius. People weren't

---

* St Valery en Caux on the Channel coast near Dieppe

allowed to drink the milk. In fact the radioactive dust was all over our hats
and our hands and everything. There was a lot of commotion. I remember
there was a lorry. It was loaded up with stuff. It was on its way to Glasgow,
to Babcock and Wilcox. They caught it before it got out of the gate and did
tests on it and it was full of fallout. And the next thing we knew, the lorry
was taken away. It might well have been put in the dump, and they put the
debris in canvas bags and they took them and buried them. People came
with white suits and masks and everything and they dug up the road that
the lorry had driven on – a concrete road. The debris from the road must
have been pretty dangerous. That fallout stuff was on our caps and hands
and everywhere. I think the most senior scientist there was Sir William
Penney. He was quite famous. He gave us a lecture to give us confidence
and he seemed a man who knew what it was all about. All of us were
brought in for tests and I'm pleased to say that working there didn't do me
any harm. Milk produced by dairy farms in the area surrounding Windscale
was pronounced unfit for human consumption.

As you know, the name of the station was changed from Windscale to
Sellafield. It is still spilling pollution out into the sea. Who knows how
much of it goes out, but at that time there was quite a bit. Pipes went down
to the sea and so much waste was released every so often. There was a big,
concrete building they called the 'Graveyard' which didn't have any
windows or doors. A skip would come with the waste and went up to
the side of the building and emptied itself automatically into the building. A
proportion of that waste went out to sea through pipes, so much every now
and again. Nobody was supposed to fish near there. I think there was a
fifteen-mile area, or something like that, where fishing wasn't allowed.
Nobody told the fish to stay out of there! Fish wander about the sea and
could be caught outside the fifteen-mile limit. Of course, I don't know how
Sellafield is today but that's what it was like then.

Anyway, I survived hale and hearty and I suppose I felt it was time for me
to settle down. I began to see Seònaid here who is now my wife – and has
been all those years. I was courting Seònaid for more than a year and we
were engaged to be married for just as long as that. She lived in Calanais,
away on the west side of the island. I used to go all the way there with my
tractor. Och, it's not really far at all when you are in love! What a din I
made crossing the Lewis Moor. In my day, coming into a village to court a
girl was regarded as a secretive business, done without advertising the fact
to the whole community. But arriving on a tractor – what a racket! There
was no way of hiding my courtship of Seònaid. Everyone in the village knew

when I was about! Our courtship lasted for at least a year. She accepted the ring from me and we were engaged for a further year before we married. We had the 'house-wedding' first. In fact, we had that in both places – first in Calanais and then here in Lacasaigh. Plenty of fun at the barn dance with a piper and melodeon player. When at last we got married, we held the wedding in the bride's house, which was the traditional way. Oh, everyone had a house-wedding at that time. We had two nights of celebration in each of our homes – hers and mine, in Calanais and here. We had a barn dance – I mean a dance in the barn with bagpipe music. My own brother, Angus, was a good piper. Now, I don't remember if it was him but there was also a melodeon. But there was also a man from Bail' Ailein who was a good fiddler.

We have a family of five: one boy and four girls. There's Sandra, whom you saw here. Another is married to a man from Fife and she is in the house she had in Calanais. Our daughter Joan is married in Shropshire. Donna, the youngest, is a nurse. She's married to a man from Uig and is living in Aberdeen. They are scattered all over. Our son has built a new house on the site of the old house here in Lacasaigh. He works with a tar squad for the company we used to know as John Fife. They changed the name to something else a while ago.

I was getting on in years before the Gospel entered into my life. Why have I chosen to be in the Church of Scotland rather than some other church? An interesting question. To tell you the truth, I have nothing against the Free Church or any other denomination which worships God through the Gospel of Jesus Christ.

When I was working on the Isle of Scalpay in Harris, I discovered that most people there go to the Free Church. Now, our own church service in Scalpay started at six in the evening. Because I was working, I couldn't make it for six o'clock, so I just went to the Free Church. I didn't notice any difference between their service and the service I was used to in my own Church of Scotland. Many a time, I would find myself walking along the road with friends from the Free Church. Then we would have to part at the crossroads to go to different buildings in which the same Gospel was being preached.

There's a variety of denominations within the Christian Church and there always will be. What is important in all of that is that they all recognise Christ as the master. As for myself, I believe the Bible and whole-heartedly believe what Christ has said, 'No-one comes to the Father but through me.' That is His message and that is the foundation on which my belief is based and will continue to be so for as long as I live. That is how we should live, acknowledging God and, as well as we are able, following the road that is illuminated for us by the Gospel.

Things changed here a lot since the war ended. We didn't have wirelesses or televisions or any of those things before then. I think it was our family that got the first wireless in the village – a wee one and you could hardly hear the sound coming out of it! Well, things started changing then, after the war. Wirelesses and televisions came in, and lots of gadgets appeared in houses, like washing machines, fridges and deep freezes and things like that. Lots of things came in but lots of customs that were not so good came in that are not improving our lives. Gone are the days when children could be disciplined. In my opinion some of the youngsters are not as courteous as were the co-ages in my young days. The reason for that may be that they are not taught in the way we were. In the school we received corporal punishment for misbehaving or being cheeky and I believe we certainly deserved that degree of correction.

Different kinds of people have come to live on our island. Some of them are an asset to the community. Others are less so, for they introduce their own ways which are contrary to our traditions. I'm thinking particularly of the way we like to observe the Sabbath. A lot of that is dying out, I'm afraid, and that is regrettable.

Dòmhnall Alasdair Dòmhnallach

1919–2003

Rugadh m' athair ann an 1883, tha mi a' smaoineachadh, agus mo mhàthair an 1880. Bha i beagan na b'aosta na am bodach. Tha mise mi fhìn dìreach ceithir fichead 's a trì.

Tha deagh cuimhne agam air mo sheanair. Tha mi creids gun do rugadh e anns na 1850s. 'S e Aonghas Beag a bh' air athair mo mhàthar agus bha e far a bheil 10 Garrabost an-diugh; far a bheil 'Donnchan' 's na daoine sin. 'S e sin taigh mo sheanar agus bha taigh mo sheanar eile na b'fhaide shìos anns a' bhaile. Bhàsaich Aonghas Beag dìreach mus deach mi dhan sgoil agus tha cuimhne mhath agam air an oidhche a bhàsaich e. Chaith e bliadhnachan ag obair san Talamh Ùr. Cha chreid mi nach ann a' briseadh chlachan a bha e. B'e sin an obair a bh' aige – rudeigin dhan t-seòrsa sin.

Ach, nise, mo sheanair eile, Dòmhnall (athair m' athar), bha esan cuideachd anns an Talamh Ùr, ag obair aig a' Hudson's Bay Company. Co-dhiù, chan eil cuimhn' agam air mo sheanair Dòmhnall. Bhàsaich esan, tha mi a' smaoineachadh, aig àm a' Chogaidh Mhòir.

Bidh mi gu tric a' smaoineachadh air an t-seòrsa beòshlaint a bh'aca ann an Garrabost anns an latha ud. A rèir eachdraidh, cha robh ach beagan bìdh a b' urrainn dhaibh a chur air a' bhòrd aig amannan àraid dhan bhliadhna. Ach ri mo chiad chuimhne 's e an t-iasgach a bha gan cumail a' dol – an t-iasgach agus obair na talmhainn. Aig àm dhomhsa dhol dhan sgoil, cha robh òirleach de Gharrabost nach robh fo phòr; eadhon suas gu doras an t-sabhail. Bha an t-iasgach an uair sin na mhàl. Bha iasgach an sgadain ann an Steòrnabhagh agus bhiodh a' chlann-nighean a' falbh chon an iasgaich. Bhiodh mo mhàthair a' bruidhinn air mar a bhiodh iad a' dol gu Cullivoe. Nis, 's ann ann an Arcaibh neo ann an Sealtainn a tha sin. Agus bhiodh iad eadhon a' dol deas gu ruige Yarmouth. Agus na bodaich, bhiodh iad, mura robh bàta-iasgaich aca fhèin, bha iad a' dol nan làmhan ann an criutha bàta gu iasgach an Taobh an Ear – Ceann Phàdraig agus a' Bhruaich. Cuideachd, bha iasgach eile aca – iasgach nan giomach.

Bha m'athair air eathar-ghiomach. Bha sin anns a' gheamhradh. Giomaich mhòra bhrèagha a bhiodh iad a' faighinn anns an latha sin. Airson an glacadh bha sgùilean aca – sgùilean no 'clèibh' a their cuid riutha.

Bha na sgùilean a' dol gu grunnd na fairge, faisg air bodhaichean far an robh na giomaich ag ionailt am measg na feamad. Chuireadh iad am biadh dhan an sgùil-ghiomach – mar bu tric rionnach saillt. Nise, bha dà tholl anns an sgùil far am faigheadh na giomaich a-steach a dh'ithe a' bhìdh. Ach cha robh de chiall aig a' ghiomach a dheigheadh a-steach dhan sgùil na gheibheadh aiste.

Bha 'bucas' aig na h-iasgairean anns a' chladach le clachan mòr ceithir-thimcheall air airson a chumail sàbhailt air dhòigh 's nach fhalbhadh am muir leis. Cha robh giomach a ghlacadh iad air latha anns na sgùilean nach robh a' dol dhan phrìosan sin! Smathaid gum biodh iad an sin airson seachdain mus deigheadh duine air an tòir airson an reic. Bha am muir-làn ag iathadh a' bhucais agus a' cumail nan giomach beò. Mus cuireadh iad giomaich dhan bhucas, bhiodh iad a' ceangal nan ìnean aca, tha mi a' creids gus nach marbhadh iad càch-a-chèile. Cho fada 's as cuimhne leam, cha bhiodh iad a' cur biadh dhan a' bhucas idir. Cha bhitheadh. Bhiodh na giomaich gan reic air Billingsgate ann an Lunnainn.

Bha bodach anns a' bhaile againn ris an canadh iad Coinneach Thorcaill. Nach eil fhios agad far an robh a' bhùth air a' chòrnair ann an siud. Uill, 's e taigh Choinnich Thorcaill a bha ri taobh sin, agus bha gig aige. 'S e sin an tagsaidh a bh' ann anns an latha ud.

Bhiodh Coinneach Thorcaill a' ceannachd nan giomach a h-uile ceann tìde nuair a bhiodh rud air an robh 'lot' aca. Bha 'lot' a' ciallachadh grunn mhath ghiomach, dhà na trì dhusain. Bhiodh e a' tighinn ga iarraidh agus gha cheannach bho na h-iasgairean. Chuireadh e an 'lot' air falbh gu Billingsgate. Bho àm gu àm, bhiodh e ag ràdh ris na h-iasgairean gun do bhàsaich tòrr dha na giomaich air an t-slighe. Uaireannan eile, chanadh e nach gabhadh na ceannaichean na giomaich seach gun robh a' mharcaid air 'floodaigeadh' le bananas. Tha cuimhn' agam na h-iasgairean a bhith ag ràdh gur e leisgeul a bh' aig Coinneach Thorcaill gus an cumadh e a' phrìs a bha e a' pàigheadh dhaibh ìosal.

Chan eil fhios agamsa an robh Billingsgate a-riamh air a fhloodaigeadh le bananas ach tha e furasta gu leòr a chreidsinn gum biodh cuid dha na giomaich a' bàsachadh air an t-slighe. Bhiodh Coinneach Thorcaill a' cur nan giomach air falbh air an t-*Sheila*, am bàt'-aiseig a bha ruith eadar Steòrnabhagh agus an Caol. Cho luath 's a ruigeadh iad an Caol, dheigh-eadh na giomaich a chur air trèana gu ruige Glaschu. Dheigheadh iad à sin air trèana eile a bheireadh iad a Lunnainn. Bho dh'fhàgadh iad Garrabost bheireadh iad eadar dà latha agus a trì mus ruigeadh iad Lunnainn.

Dh' fhaodte gu robh feadhainn dha na giomaich a' bàsachadh air an t-slighe ceart gu leòr. Ach tha mi creids gun robh am bodach airson prothaid a dhèanamh às air dhòigh no dhòigh air choreigin. Chan eil fhios agam dè bu choireach nach robh na h-iasgairean iad fhèin a' cur nan giomach air falbh gu Billingsgate. Tha cuimhn' agamsa nach biodh na h-iasgairean a' faighinn ach deich tastain airson dusan giomach! Ten shilling note, airson dusan giomach. Pàigheadh bochd airson an saothair. Ach b' e sin an obair a bh' aca – an t-iasgach agus obair na talmhainn. Bha beatha chruaidh aca.

Tha cuimhne mhath agam air muileann Gharraboist. Tha cuimhn' agam a bhith innte nam bhalach agus iad a' tìreadh a' ghràn. Anns an latha sin, bha a' mhuileann air a h-obrachadh le cumhachd an uisge a bha sruthadh à Allt nan Gall. Ach tha ùine mhòr bho leig iad às a bhith 'g obrachadh na muilne le cumhachd an uisge. 'S e diesel a th'aca an-diugh. Nise, chaidh muileann Gharraboist a thogail bho chionn faisg air ceud bliadhna. Roimhe sin, tha mi 'n dùil gur ann leis a' bhrà a bhiodh muinntir an Rubha a' bleith an t-sìl. Cha robh an còrr ann a b'urrainn dhaibh a dhèanamh airson an sìol a bhleith ach a chur tron bhrà.

Anns an latha sin, bha obair shònraichte ann do dh'fhireannaich agus obair eadar-dhealaichte do bhoireannaich. Chan fhaodadh fireannach dèan-amh an rud a bha air a chur a-mach do bhoireannach. 'S mar an ceudna, chan fhaodadh boireannach a bhith a' dèanamh an rud a bhiodh fireannach a' dèanamh. Bha iad mar gum biodh an riaghailt sin air a bhith air a cur a-mach dhaibh bho thùs. Chan eil cuimhn' agamsa air duine riamh – ach m'athair- a bhiodh leis a' chliabh a' giùlain eallaich air a dhruim. B'e siud obair bhoireannach! Obair bhoireannach a bhith le clèibh air an dromannan fad am beatha – clèibh mònach, clèibh feamad, clèibh todhair 's mar sin air adhart. Tha cuimhn' agam a-nis, agus tha mi a' smaoineachadh gum b'ann aig àm an Dàrna Chogaidh a bh' ann 's mi aig an taigh air lìobha, mi bhith a' faicinn, aig cruach-mhònach àraid, boireannach a' tighinn a-mach leis a' chliabh agus i ga lìonadh le fàdan gus an robh cnuachd mhòr mhònach air. Thàinig am bodach a-mach 's a phìob na bheul agus a làmhan na phòcaidean agus thog e an cliabh air a druim. Dh'fhuirich e ann an sin gus an tàinig am boireannach air ais a dh'iarraidh eallach eile. Lìon e an cliabh còmhla rithe agus thog e sin a-rithist air a druim. Cha robhas a' saoilsinn càil dhan dol-a-mach sin.

Their cuid gur e bu choireach ris a' chleachdadh sin gu robh boireannaich, gu ìre, a' dìon nam bodach airson gur ann aig na fir a bha ri dhol gu muir ann an cunnart am beatha. Gun teagamh bha e fìor gu robh uiread de bhàthaidhean ann anns an latha ud. Agus nuair a thigeadh cogadh gum b' ann aig na fir a bha ri dhol a shabaid ris an

nàmhaid. Bha uiread de dh'fhireannaich gan call aig muir agus tro
chogaidh gun teagamh, agus, a rèir aithris, b'e sin an t-adhbhar gum
biodh na boireannaich a' dèanamh dhaibh. Uill, chan urrainn mise innse
an robh sin mar sin, ach nam bharail-sa, cha robh ann ach fasan a bha air
èirigh tro na linntean. Droch fhasan! Bha na fireannaich dòigheil gu leòr
leis na mnathan a bhith, nan sgalagan anns an dachaigh. Bha tòrr de
dhroch fhasanan ann. Nuair a bha mi fhìn òg, cha leigeadh mo mhàthair
leam nighe nan soithichean. Fhios agad, cha robh annam ach balach! Ach
leigeadh i le mo phiuthar na soithichean a nighe! Bha e uabhasach
neònach. 'S e obair bhoireannach a bh'anns na soithichean! Rud boireann
a bh'ann. Seall an-dràsta, chan fhaiceadh tu chaoidh fireannach a' fighe le
bioranan. Chan fhaodadh iad. Dh'fhaodadh e fighe le beairt ach chan
fhaodadh le bioranan; 's chan fhaodadh iad fuaghal le snàthad. Nam
biodh toll air a chuid aodaich ri a chàradh, dh'fheumadh a bhean a
chàradh dha. Agus chan fhaiceadh tu boireannach a-chaoidh le briogais
oirre ach chitheadh tu fireannach le fèileadh tric gu leòr.

Cha robh e ceadaichte, 's chan eil fhathast, do bhoireannach a bhith na
ministear. Nuair a bha mis' òg, cha smaoinicheadh duine air gum b' urrainn
do bhoireannach a dhol a shearmonachadh. Ach dh'fhalbh na nòsan sin
agus, an-diugh, chan eil mòran ann nach fhaod boireannaich a dhèanamh.
Uaireannan 's ann a tha e duilich faithneachadh cò tha fireann 's cò tha
boireann! Chan aithnich thu air an fhalt neo air an còmhdach.

Nuair bha mi nam leth-bhalach, thàinig plèan aon là gu far a bheil port-
adhair Steòrnabhaigh an-diugh. Dh'fhalbh mise agus balach eile, casruisgte 's mar a bha sin, suas ga faicinn. Mus do ràinig sinn buileach,
chuala sinn an ràn aice agus i ri falbh. Dragon Rapide a bh' innte ach cha
d'fhuair sinn ach sealladh oirre a' dol à fàire san adhar. Ach cha b'e an ùidh
a bh' agam ann am plèanaichean idir a chuir mise dhan an RAF. Cha do
rinn sin ach an ùidh agam ann an rèidio.

Bha mi anns an RAF beagan ùine mus do thòisich an Dàrna Cogadh. Ach
cha robh fada. Cha robh eòlas sam bith agam air rèidio ach chuala mi mu
dheidhinn anns an taigh-chèilidh. Thog mi ùidh anns a' chuspair sin – rud a
bha gu math ùr anns an latha sin. Ghabh e grèim air m' inntinn, agus bha
mi airson eòlas fhaighinn air mar a bha an rud ag obrachadh. Ach nuair a
thàinig an cogadh dh'aontaich mi dhol dhan an Air Training School airson
an dà chuid ionnsachadh: rèidio agus gunnaireachd.

Nuair a bha mi ag èirigh suas, cha chreid mi gun robh fios againn gu
robh leithid de rud ann ri 'homosexuals'. Bha mise aosta mus do thuig mi
gu robh daoine ann dhan t-seòrsa sin. Agus cha do thachair dad dhan
t-seòrsa sin rium a-riamh gus an deach mi dhan RAF. Ach bha mi dà uair

no trì an làthair aig Court Martial anns an robh casaid air feadhainn airson sin. 'S e eucoir mhòr a bh'ann anns an Air Force aig an àm sin. Chan eil fhios a'm an saoil iad càil dheth an-diugh.

Ach sin mar a chuala mise gu robh a leithid de dh'fhireannaich ann agus cuideachd tro leughadh mu dheidhinn. Chan eil dad a chuimhn' agam duine dhan t-seòrs' a bhith còmhla rinne nar balaich. Bha feadhainn ann nach biodh a' cluiche football, 's bha feadhainn ann nach biodh a' dol a shnàmh, na rudan a bha sinne a' dèanamh gu nàdarrach a h-uile samhradh, fad an t-samhraidh. 'S mathaid gur ann liùgach a bha iad airson a dhol a shnàmh. 'S mathaid gur ann, oir bhiodh sinn a' snàmh lomnochd gun nàire sam bith gu robh sinn gun aodach. Cha bhiodh brèid air duine againn an uair sin. 'S e rud a bh' ann nach robh a' cur dragh sam bith oirnn.

Thàinig an cogadh is b'fheudar dhomh, ann an lùib rèidio, dreuchd eile ionnsachadh anns an RAF. B'e an dreuchd sin gunnaireachd. Bha agam ri dhol an sàs ann an gunnaireachd fhad 's a bha mi an sàs ann an rèidio, an dà chuid còmhla. Leis an t-seòrsa phlèanaichean a bh'ann anns na làithean sin bha e iomchaidh agus deatamach gum biodh eòlas aig an radio operator air gunnaireachd cuideachd.

Cha robh balaich anns na plèanaichean aig an àm ud ach balaich a bha annta gu saor-thoileach. Cha robh duine ag iarraidh ort a dhol annta. Leis an fhìrinn innse, cha robh e furast' faighinn annta. Bha agad ri faighinn tro dheuchainnean. Bha agad ri dhol tro leth-dusan deuchainn aig dotair airson gum biodh iad cinnteach gu robh thu cho slàn ri fiadh! Anns an latha ud, cha robh dad a' cur dragh ormsa. Aig naoi bliadhna deug a dh'aois, bha mi tapaidh, fallain agus dà eòrlach fo na sia troighean. Cha deach m' àird a thomhais a-riamh gus an deach mi dhan Air Force. Chan eil mi smaoin-eachadh gu robh mòran Ghàidheal anns an Air Force aig an àm ud. Bha a' mhòr-chuid dha na Gàidheil ri seòladh no anns an Arm. Bha cunnart gu leòr far an robh iad! Co-dhiù, cha tàinig mi tarsainn air duine ach dithis no triùir. Bha dithis à Steòrnabhagh ann agus caraid dhomh – Rodaidh MacLeòid à Bràigh na h-Aoidhe. Ma bha feadhainn eile ann cha tàinig mis' tarsainn orra.

'S e Dragon Rapide a' chiad phlèan anns an robh mi riamh. 'S ann oirre bha mi an toiseach nuair a thòisich an nàimhdeas ann an 1939. Bha an Dragon Rapide math airson a bhith a' teagasg luchd-ionnsachaidh. Às dèidh sin, chaidh mo chur air Hampden Bomber. 'Flying Coffin' a bhiodh aca air an t-seòrsa sin, oir bhathas a' call a leithid de chriutha oirre. Cha robh ach ceathrar anns a' chriutha aice. An toll anns an robh mise, bhithinn ag ràdh nan cuireadh tu muncaidh ann an-diugh, gun cuirte dhan phrìosan thu! Bha stòl beag air an làr, ceangailte ris an làr, airson leigeil dhut suidhe.

Air mo bheulaibh, bha radio receiver agus transmitter, agus air muin sin bha rud ris an canadh iad cupola, uinneag a ghabhadh fhosgladh. Nan seasadh tu le leth do chuirp tron uinneig, ruigeadh tu air dà ghunna. Bha aodach oirnn a bha mòr, trom, glè choltach ris a' chòmhdach a chì thu air spaceman an-diugh. B'e sin 'Z coat' agus 'bomber jacket'. Nise, bha paraisiut aig a h-uile duine a bha air bòrd. Cha robh e idir ceadaichte dhòmhsa am paraisiut a bhith agam air mo dhruim. Bha m' fhear-sa ri mo thaobh deiseil airson a chur orm nam biodh sinn ann an cunnart. Bha aig a' phàidhleat ri bhith na shuidhe air an fhear aigesan. Ach bha adhbhar math air a' pharaisiut a bhith aige fo a thòin. Nam biodh èiginn chabhagach air a thighinn oirnn, cha bhiodh cothrom aigesan air an rud a thogail bho a thaobh agus a cheangal uime air a bhroilleach mar a bhiodh agamsa. B'e am pàidhleat an duine mu dheireadh a dh'fheumadh leum a-mach às a' phlèan.

A h-uile uair a dh'fhalbhadh sinn air iteig, bha agam ri dà chalman a thoirt leam. Shaoileadh daoine gum b' e fealla-dhà a bha sinn a' dèanamh. Bhiodh an dà chalman againn ann am basgaid. Bha e caran neònach a bhith cluinntinn an dà chalman a' dorghain an shiud leotha fhèin fad na h-oidhch', 'Chan e mo chuideachd thù! Chan e mo chuideachd thù!'

Taing do shealbh nach robh agam ri leum a-mach às a' phlèan riamh. Cha robh agus 's math nach robh, oir dh'fheumadh tu a bhith àrd os cionn na talmhainn mus robh e sàbhailt dhut leum. Cha do leum ach chaidh mi gu math faisg air! Aon uair, bha an rud ceangailte agam air mo bhroilleach deiseil airson leum aiste. Leis na Hampdens, bhiodh sinn a' dol a-null dhan Roinn Eòrpa cho fada ri Berlin. Seadh, ach mus dèanadh sinn sin, bha againn ri iomall de thancaichean a bhith againn − tancaichean ola − ceangailte fo na sgiathan. Tha e anns an logbook agam. Bha sin bliadhna no dhà a-steach dhan chogadh eadar 1940 agus '41. Cha robh na Gearmailtich idir dòigheil nuair a chluinneadh iad sinn a' gnùsdaich os an cionn! Tha fhios nach robh! Cha robh iad a' cur fàilte sam bith oirnn ach leis a' ghunna! Bho ruigeadh tu costa na h-Òlaind gu ruigeadh tu Berlin, bha na gunnaichean aca a' losgadh oirnn. Bhiodh sinn a' feuchainn − neo bhitheadh an fheadhainn a bha gar cur ann − a' feuchainn ri cùrsa thoirt dhuinn, a stiùireadh sinn eadar na h-àiteachan bu chunnartaiche. 'S ann air an oidhche a bha sinn a' dol a-null ach cha b'e am am plèan againne a-mhàin a bh' ann a' toirt ionnsaigh orra. Och, bhiodh suas ri ceud plèan ann. 'S cha b'ann bhon an aon stèisean a bha na bha sin a' falbh idir. Bha plèanaichean a' falbh bho iomadach stèisean ann an Sasainn. B' ann air an oidhche a bhiodh sinn a' dol a-null agus, glè thric, chan fhaiceadh tu gin dha na bomairean eile. Bho àm gu àm bha corra phlèan a' srucadh ann an tèile − rud a bha gu math cunnartach, ach cha robh sin a' tachairt ach ainneamh.

Bha a mionaid fhèin aig a h-uile bomair airson an targaid a ruighinn agus a ghnothaich a dhèanamh. Cho luath 's a bha sin agad air a dhèanamh – an uair sin, bha thu mach à sin man an radan! Bha agad ri bhith cinnteach gu robh thu anns an àite cheart aig an uair cheart, oir bha bomairean os do chionn cuideachd. Nan leigeadh iadsan às na bomaichean agus tusa fòdhpa, bha thu ann an cunnart do bheatha nam bualadh 'am meall' ort. Bha plèanaichean fodhad cuideachd agus bha iadsan ann an cunnart bhuatsa anns an aon dhòigh. Dh'fheumadh a h-uile plèan a h-eallach a leigeil às aig a' mhionaid a chaidh a chomharrachadh dhi.

A' sealltainn sios air a' bhaile a bha sinn a' sgrios, bha e cianail a bhith smaoineachadh gu robh daoine mar sinn fhìn am measg nan lasraichean. Bha e na Ifrinn air thalamh! Chì thu air an teilidh neo anns an cinema iad a' feuchainn ri sealltainn cò ris a bha e coltach. Ach 's e an rud mu dheidhinn sin nach eil e comasach air sealltainn dhut ach meud an fhearainn a tha sùil a' chamara a' toirt a-steach ann an aon frìom. Le ar sùilean, bha sinne, a bha fichead mile troigh os cionn na talmhainn, a' coimhead ceud mìle fearainn timcheall oirnn air a h-uile taobh dhinn. Chitheadh sinn, an siud 's an seo, bailtean nan teine agus bha an t-adhar e fhèin làn teine cuideachd. Cha chaill mi cuimhne gu bràth air na h-uabhais a chunna mi fhad 's a bhiodh sinn thall os cionn na Gearmailt – sgrios theine. Bha dà sheòrsa lasair a' tighinn thugainn dhan adhar. B'iad sin light flak agus heavy flak. Mar bu tric', cha ruigeadh na gunnaichean beaga a bha losgadh oirnn seach gu robh sinn cho fada shuas os an cionn. Air an làimh eile, bha heavy flak gu tric a' ruighinn seachad oirnn. Chitheadh tu an t-adhar làn de bhurstaichean – burstaichean ceòthaidh gun theine idir – agus, ged a bha dìon agad air do chluasan agus tu ann am broinn a' phlèan, chluinneadh tu na burstaichean sin ceithir-thicheall oirnn; agus bhithinn uaireannan a' gabhail iongantas dè mar a fhuair na seilichean suas seachad oirnn gun ar bualadh. 'S e bu choireach ri sin nach b' ann suas a bha tòrr dhan sin a' tighinn idir. 'S ann a bha iad a' tighinn bho fad' air falbh; bho, can, deich mìle romhainn no deich mìle bho ar cùlaibh. Glè thric, chluinneadh tu bragadaich shrapnel air slige a' phlèan.

Tha cuimhne agam a bhith nam sheasamh san rud air an robh an astrodome air mullach a' phlèan, a' coimhead a-mach airson night-fighters. 'S ann ormsa bha an t-uallach a bhith coimhead a-mach airson plèanaichean Gearmailteach a bhiodh an tòir oirnn. Nam faicinn nàmhaid gar leantainn, bhiodh fhios agad nach b'e coibhneas a bha air aire! Gun dàil, bha agad ri èigheachd ris a phàidhleat, 'Left!' neo 'Right!' Tha cuimhn' agam air oidhche àraid, 's mi nam sheasamh ann an sin anns an astrodome agus nuair a bha sinn a' smaoineachadh gu robh an cunnart seachad 's a shuidh mi air ais far an robh an rèidio agam, chunna mi gu robh cnap flak air a dhol tron t-suidheachan agam. Bha toll anns an dearbh bhad san robh mi dol a shuidhe. Gu fortanach cha robh mi nam shuidhe nuair a bhuaileadh sinn. Nam bitheadh, cha bhiodh sgeul orm an-diugh!

B'e siud a' chiad tour air an deach sinn anns an Hampden. Chaidh sinn an uair sin gu training unit airson rud air an robh 'Rest' aca. Agus bha thu a' faighinn dhà neo trì mhìosan an shin airson ar teagaisg. Ach mar a bhiodh iad ag ràdh ris gach buidheann a thigeadh thuca às ùr, cho luath 's a ruigeadh sinn, 'You've come here for a rest – from being shot at! It's the only kind of rest we can offer here.'

Aig toiseach a' chogaidh – suas gu 1942 – bha agad ri dhol suas anns na plèanaichean le pàidhleat nach robh ach air ùr-ionnsachadh mar a bha am plèan ga h-obrachadh. Seach gu robh pàidhleatan cho gann anns an RAF aig an àm sin, cha robh e idir ceadaichte do dhà phàidhleat a dhol suas innte. Bha tòrr luchd-ionnsachaidh a bha a' call am beatha aig an ìre sin. Chunnaic mi statistic a bha ri sealltainn gun do chailleadh còig mìle mus do ràinig iad squadron. Cha robh thu faighinn cothrom fuireach anns an leabaidh idir no bhith a' gabhail fois. Mus sealladh tu riut fhèin, bha thu a' dol suas a theagasg chuideigin eile. Anns an latha ud, bha mise nam air gunner agus radio operator. Bhiodh navigator anns a' chriutha cuideachd. Bha esan anns an aon shuidheachadh. Bha aig an navigator ri dhol suas còmhla ri pàidhleat anns nach robh earbsa sam bith aige. Rud cugallach a bh' ann ach cha robh an còrr a dhòigh air.

Nuair a thàinig an Lancaster Bomair thugainn, bha seòrsa de chomhartachd na broinn nach robh idir ann a Hampden. Dh'fhaodadh dà phàidhleat a bhith oirre. Bha i cho mòr 's agus gum faodadh tu coiseachd air àird do dhroma na broinn. Mòr 's mar a bha mi, sheasainn fhìn anns a' fuselage aice. Bha cuideachd seòrsa de lavatory innte – peile! Le mo chuimhne, 's e 'Elson' an t-ainm a bh' aca air a' pheile sin. Bha aon rud nach robh cho math mu dheidhinn an Elson a bha sin. Bhiodh iad ag ràdh, nan suidheadh tu air an Elson aig fichead mìle troigh os cionn na talmhainn, gun reothadh do thòin ris a' pheile. Bha aon leabaidh innte – leabaidh airson duine air bòrd a dheigheadh a leòn. Bhitear ag ràdh gum biodh cuid a' sadail bhotal falamh a-mach às a' phlèan. Rèir eachdraidh, bha na botail sin a' dèanamh fead uabhasach air an t-slighe sios – glè choltach ri fuaim bom a' tighinn gu làr. Chan eil fhios an robh facal fìrinn an sin. Cò-dhiù, cha do shad mise botal a-mach a-riamh.

Bha cuid dha na h-airfields ann an ceann a deas Shasainn, mar a shaoileadh tu a bhiodh iad, ach bha sinne aig toiseach tòiseachaidh ann a

Yorkshire. Nuair a fhuair sinn an Lancaster, chaidh ar suidheachadh ann an Lincolnshire. Cha robh an dà àite glè fhada bho chèile. Leis an Lancaster, thòsich sinn a' dol air iomadach raid a-null dhan Roinn Eòrpa. Bho àm gu àm, chunna sinn plèanaichean Gearmailteach a bha shuas gar lorg airson ionnsaigh a thoirt oirnn. Cha d' fhuair iad air sin a dhèanamh. Dh'fheumadh tu esan fhaicinn mus fhaiceadh esan thusa. B'e sin an t-uallach a chuireadh ormsa anns an astrodome. Ach 's ann air an oidhche a bhiodh sinn ann agus mura biodh gealach mhath ann, chan fhaiceadh sinn dad dhan t-seòrsa sin shuas far an robh sinn. Thachair gun robh night-vision mhìorbhaileach agam. Chuir iad sin dhan an logbook agam, 'exceptional night-vision', agus chithinn rudan anns an adhar fada mus fhaiceadh na gunnairean iad. Cha robh duine dol a' losgadh air nightfighter an toiseach, oir dh'innseadh sin dha càite an robh thu. Bha agad ri fuireachd gu 'n tigeadh e cho faisg 's gu robh fios agad gu robh e air d' fhaicinn. Cho luath 's a thachradh sin, bha agad ri èigheachd ris a' phàidhleat, 'Go! Go! Go! Ann am priobadh sùla, thòisicheadh esan a' dèanamh rud air an robh corkscrew aca – a' dol sìos mar sin agus ag èirigh suas. Nuair a bhiodh am plèan a' dol sios dh'èireadh tu a-mach às do shuidheachan, agus nuair a bhiodh i a' dìreadh suas, chan fhaigheadh tu air carachadh às.

Cha robh agamsa riamh ri losgadh air fighter. Cha robh. Anns an Lancaster cha robh gunna agam. Ach bha gunnaichean gu leòr oirr dh'aindeoin sin! Bha feadhainn anns an deireadh aice agus air a mullach agus na toiseach. Bha trì turrets oirre agus anns an deireadh bha ceithir gunnaichean. Shuas gu h-àrd bha dhà, agus anns an toiseach cuideachd bha dhà. An aon àite bha gun dìon idir, 's ann shios foidhpe. Ach bha i air a deagh chòmhdach le gunnaichean agus, gu sealbhach, bha i luath. Cha robh plèan eile dha samhail ann aig àm a' Chogaidh. Cha robh dad coltach rithe anns an adhar! Thàinig na Liberators agus na Fortresses agus Super-fortresses às a dèidh ach cha robh dad a choltas aca ris an Lancaster. Bheireadh an Lancaster deich tonna a Bherlin aig 25,000 feet, agus cha toireadh an Liberator no am Fortress ach leth sin. Agus cha deigheadh iad sin idir a-mach air an oidhche. Day bombers a bh'annta. Cha do dh'ionnsaich iad a-riamh night navigation. Chaidh mi dhà na trì thursan ann an Lancaster tarsainn air na h-Alps airson ionnsaigh a thoirt air an Eadailt.

Nuair a thàinig Mussolini dhan chogadh, chaidh sinn tarsainn gu Genoa, 's Turin, 's Milan. Chaidh sinn an sin a thoirt sgleogan dhàsan! Agus rinn sinn sin gun teagamh. Fhuair Mussolini a-mach gu robh cogadh ann! Cha chreid mi nach e duine gun bhrìgh, gun thoinisg a bh' ann. Ach cha b'e esan a dh'fhuiling ach sluagh na h-Eadailt.

Mar a fhuair a h-uile duine eile, fhuair mi demob goirid an deidh a' chogaidh. Chuir iad fios orm agus dh'fhaighnich iad dhomh an robh mi deònach coimisean eile a ghabhail. Fhuair mi an uair sin gu ìre Flying Officer agus, anns a' cheann thall, ceum gu Flight Lieutenant. Agus b' e sin a bh' agam nuair a thàinig mi a-mach aig deireadh a' chogaidh. Chuir iad fios orm a dh'fhaighneachd dhomh an gabhainn a-rithist trèis airson peinnsean fhaighinn, agus cha robh an còrr ann a b' urrainn dhomh a dhèanamh. Cha robh dreuchd eile ann a bheireadh a leth uiread de phàigheadh dhomh 's a bh'agam nam Flight Lieutenant. Chaidh mi air ais, agus thug mi naoi bliadhna eile ris an dreuchd sin – còig bliadhna deug uile-gu-lèir. Nuair a bha na còig bliadhna deug seachad bha iad ag iarraidh orm fuireach agus tuilleadh a dhèanamh. Ach nuair a bha sin seachad, bha iad ag iarraidh orm fuireach dà bhliadhna eile. Dh'fhaighnich mi dhaibh dè an t-àrdachadh a bheireadh iad dhomh sa pheinnsean mu choinneamh an dà bhliadhna sin. Thàinig fios air ais bhon Air Ministry, 'Five shillings a week'. Thug mi dhaibh taing airson a bhith cho fialaidh 's a bha iad, 's thuirt mi riutha gun robh gu leòr agam ri dhèanamh aig an taigh. Aig an dearbh àm ud, bha mi air tòiseachadh air taigh a thogail ann an Garrabost. Dh'fhàg mi an Air Force ann an 1955 nuair a bha mi sia bliadhna deug thar fhichead a dh'aois. Cha robh mi fhathast air pòsadh. Bha mi dà fhichead bliadhna 's a ceithir nuair a phòs mi.

Bha beatha agam anns an Air Force a bha annasach agus a chòrd rium ann an iomadh seagh. Às deidh a' chogaidh cha b'e an aon seòrsa Air Force a bh'ann. Cha robh càil air aire dhaoine ach faighinn air adhart le promotion! Cha robh dad a choltas aige ris an dàimh a bha eadarainn rè a' chogaidh – eadar mi fhìn agus a' chòrr de chriutha a' phlèan. Bha ceangal mòr eadarainn agus tha sin cinnteach. Chan eil duine beò aca a-nis ach mi fhìn 's am pàidhleat.

Tha mi creidsinn gu bheil e a' cur seachad na tìde mar a tha mi fhìn a' sgrìobhadh no a' dèanamh drungan de dh'obair anns an leas. 'S caomh leam a bhith ri bàrdachd Ghàidhlig. Thàinig leabhar* leam a-mach bho chionn beagan bhliadhnachan. Chan eil fada bho thàinig dithis nighean às an t-Suain a shealtainn orm, agus iad ag ràdh gun robh ùidh mhòr aca ann am mion-chànanan na Roinn Eòrpa. 'S ann ag ullachadh prògram a bha iad air a' chuspair sin. Bha camara aca agus thug iad orm pìos bàrdachd a leughadh dhaibh ged nach robh iad a' tuigsinn smid dha na bha mi ag radh. Nochd am pìos bàrdachd sa anns an leabhar agam, agus tha e air cuspair a tha gu math dlùth dha mo chridhe, 'O, Nam Faicinn Alba Saor!'

---

* *Bàrdachd Dhòmhnaill Alasdair*, Acair Ltd.

O, nam faicinn Alba saor
Mus tuit a' chraobh sa dhan talamh,
Bu shuarach agam g' eil mi aost';
Dh'fhàsainn aotrom is fallain
O, nam faicinn Alba saor!

Dhèanainn sùgradh 's dhèanainn ceòl,
Sheinninn òrain mar ghille,
Lìonainn glainne 's dhèanainn òl,
'S shaoilinn gu robh m'òig' air tilleadh –
O, nam faicinn Alba saor!

Chan eil Albannach cho truagh
Nach bi buadhmhor is sona
Nuair a choisneas sinn a' bhuaidh,
Nuair a chì ar sluagh an solas –
O, nam faicinn Alba saor!

Coma leibh bhith sireadh maoin,
Biodh ur smaointean air Uilleam:
B' fheàrr dhuinn a bhith beò air taois
Na bhith air an taod fo bhuillean –
O, nam faicinn Alba saor!

Tha rìoghachdan a-bhos is thall
Ag iarraidh slabhraidhean a ghearradh –
'M beil ar riaghladh fhìn cho dall
'S gun ceus iad sinn le ball is spearrach?
O, nam faicinn Alba saor!

Chuala mi aig sruth a' chaoil,
Aig a' ghaoith 's allt a' ghlinne,
Gu bheil an aimsir air ar taobh
'S gu bheil an t-Aonadh fo thinneas –
O, nam faicinn Alba saor!

Nuair a bhios ar dùthaich saor,
Thèid am fraoch fhèin na lasair;
Bidh gach beinn is allt is craobh
'G èigheachd 'Saorsainn bho Shasainn' –
O, nam faicinn Alba saor!

An là sin sgaoilidh sgàil is sgòth,
Buille 's beò thig na cuisil,
A fèin-mheas tèaraint' is a pròis
Mar a bha i 'n dòrn a' Bhrusaich –
O, nam faicinn Alba saor!

Donald A. MacDonald

1919–2003

My father was born in 1883 and my mother in 1880. I'm aged eighty-three.

My grandfather, my mother's father that is, was called Aonghas Beag [Angus Junior]. He had spent years working in the New World and, when I was young, he lived where No. 10 Garrabost is now – where Duncan MacLeod lives. I think my grandfather, Aonghas Beag, was employed breaking rocks, probably for road-building. Something like that. He died just before I went to school. I well remember the night he died.

My other grandfather, Donald, lived further down the village. He also had been working in the New World – working for the Hudson's Bay Company. I don't remember him at all. In those days, a lot of men had to go abroad to earn money to support their families – to keep food on the table. Very often, there was only very little on the table! For as long as I can remember, most people earned a living by fishing and by croft-work. At the time when I went to school there was not a square foot of our Garrabost crofts that wasn't planted. There was herring fishing in Stornoway and the girls would go off fishing. My mother used to talk about Cullivoe. That was in Orkney or maybe Shetland. They also used to go to Yarmouth. The men, if they didn't have a fishing boat of their own, they would go as crew to the fishing on the east coast, to Peterhead, and there was also lobster fishing.

In winter, my father was on the lobster boats. In those days, they caught lovely big lobsters. You would pay a fortune for them nowadays. There was a large storage box on the shore, with big stones placed all around it to anchor it. The sea covered it with each high tide – that is, twice a day. The fact that the box was immersed like that kept the lobsters alive. Each man in turn would store away what he had caught that day. They tied the lobsters' claws with string to stop them from killing each other. As far as I know, it was not thought necessary to put food in the storage-box.

The fishermen started work early in the morning to set their lobster-traps in places along the shore, usually close to the reefs. The traps, which some called 'creels', were cleverly designed. Bait such as salted mackerel was tied inside the trap, which had two holes wide enough to allow the hungry lobster to enter from the top. It was easy for the lobster to enter but it did not have the intelligence to figure out how to escape. I composed a song about it!

When they had enough lobsters to make it worth their while, the fishermen arranged to have them sent to be sold at Billingsgate in London. There was a man in the village called Coinneach Thorcaill [Kenneth, son of Torquil], who acted as middle man. He owned a shop and also a gig, a small horse-drawn buggy. The gig was the taxi we had when I was a lad!

Coinneach Thorcaill bought the lobsters whenever there was a suitable amount of them, two or three dozen, say. He would come to collect them, buy them from the men and then send them away. Sometimes he told the fishermen that a lot of the lobsters had died on the journey. I remember at one time the locals saying that the Billingsgate buyers wouldn't take the lobsters because the market had been flooded with bananas!

I cannot say whether Billingsgate was ever flooded with bananas, but it is quite feasible that some of the lobsters died en route. They travelled on the old SS *Sheila* from Stornoway to Kyle of Lochalsh, then by train to Glasgow and thence to London. It was a long journey which took a long time for the lobsters to reach market. The journey would have taken at least two days. On the other hand, it is possible that Coinneach Thorcaill told the fishermen tall tales about the difficulties of getting the lobsters to Billingsgate so that he would continue to make a profit from his enterprise. I don't know why the fishermen themselves didn't organise the marketing, but I do remember that they got little in return for their labours – sometimes as little as ten shillings for a dozen lobsters.

Fishing was important to the crofters' livelihood. The other activity that took up the rest of their working lives was the croft-work. They grew crops such as barley, oats and potatoes and raised cattle and sheep. Of course, we shouldn't forget that they got their year's supply of fuel for the fire out on the moor – fuel in the form of dried peat.

Living by crofting and fishing was hard. The mill that served the crofting communities of the Point district was situated in our village, less than a mile from where I grew up in Garrabost. I remember being in the mill at a time when they were drying the grain. 'Malting' is the official term for that process. They were upstairs in the mill, malting both oats and barley. There were men with shovels on each side turning the grain, which was slowly roasting. As boys, we would be sitting around, watching. After it was completely dry, the grain went into the mill – the huge stone rollers which ground it. The roasted grain travelled between the rollers and when it emerged from those wheels, it went pouring downstairs by a chute. On the ground floor two men were there waiting with open sacks. In those days, the machinery was worked by water-power. The reservoir for the mill was up on the moor at Swordale and had been created when Allt nan Gall [The Strangers' Stream] was dammed. After a time, the mill owner abandoned water-power after installing a diesel engine.

Before 1900, when the mill was built at Garrabost, the crofters had to grind their grain by means of a quern. That's what the crofters of my grandfather's generation would have used to make their oatmeal and barley meal.

In my young days, women had a very hard life and, in my view, carried a heavier burden that the men did. There was a clear line drawn between work for men and work for women. Men were not allowed to do the things that women did and women were forbidden to do the things that men did. I have no memory of any man – apart from my father – ever carrying loads on their backs with the creel. Every woman had a *cliabh mònach* – a peat creel. That's just how it was. I saw a perfect illustration of this ridiculous job-demarcation at one time, probably when I was at home on leave during the war. This is what happened: a woman came out to a peat-stack with a creel and proceeded to fill it with a huge pile of peats. Her husband had followed her to the peat-stack, with his pipe stuck in his mouth and his hands in his pockets. When the woman indicated that the creel was fully stacked, the man lifted the load on to the woman's back. After performing that demanding task, he waited there at the peat-stack until his wife came back for another load. For the second load, he actually helped her fill the creel before lifting the load on to her back! None of the neighbours would have thought anything strange in that kind of behaviour.

Some might say that through the generations, the women had developed an instinct that made them try to protect their husbands because it was the men who had to go to sea at a time when there were so many drownings. Also, of course, the men had to fight in the wars. I don't buy that explanation! Giving the women the privilege of doing most of the hard work was just an age-old custom and, in my view, just a bad habit. There were many such customs that, today, seem ludicrous. When I was young, my mother wouldn't let me wash the dishes because I was a boy. She would let my sister wash them, though. Demarcation existed in quite a few areas of responsibility. Cooking was the woman's job. Nor would you ever see a man knitting. It was OK for men to weave with the loom but not to knit with knitting-needles nor to sew with a darning-needle. Attire was another area in which there were strict taboos. You would never see a woman wearing trousers. You would see a man in a kilt often enough, though.

Those distinctions have been done away with. Today's Lewis woman does whatever kind of work she wishes to do and wears whatever form of dress appeals to her, including trousers. Sometimes it's difficult to make out who are men and who are women. In some cases, you can't tell by either their clothes or their hairstyle.

When I was young, there were just boys and girls. When we went into the sea for a swim, all the boys went naked. None of us wore trunks – probably because we had no such thing to wear! Our nakedness wasn't something that bothered us at all and we would never dream of swimming when there were girls present. We were two separate entities. But I was completely unaware that there was a kind of male person who was a homosexual. The term 'gay' had not been invented. I was old before I realised that there were other than heterosexuals. I didn't meet any 'gay' until I went into the RAF. I attended at courts martial three or four times when men were accused of being practising homosexuals. At that time, conduct of that nature was regarded, in the Air Force, as being a very serious offence. They probably don't think anything of it nowadays.

My father was in the First World War and I in the Second. Though the danger was ever present in both wars, my father's experience and mine were very different. My father was in the navy, on the cruiser, HMS *Galatea*, which took an active part at the Battle of Jutland. I remember a big picture he used to have called 'Night Action at Jutland'. It was about that big and I really wish that I had it today, but the old man built a barn and wanted glass in the window, so he took the glass out of the picture and used it in that. He was at sea all through the war. He had been in the Royal Naval Reserve, and as soon as war broke out, he was conscripted. A lot of the local men were in the RNR. Good sailors and fishermen and the Navy was very pleased to have them. When war broke out, they snapped them up.

My experience of war was quite different. During the war – the Second World War – I was in the Royal Air Force. When I joined, I was a young lad and had never even been near a plane. I remember that when I was in my early teens, my pals and I heard one day that a plane had come to the Machair, the level stretch of ground where Stornoway Airport is now. We were all barefoot, but we took off at the trot and, having covered the three miles to the Machair to look at the plane, were disappointed to hear it taking off as we approached. It was a Dragon Rapide and we just got a glimpse of it as it disappeared into the sky.

I had been in the Air Force for a while before the war started in 1939. Before I went into the RAF, I knew very little about radio apart from what I had learned in the ceilidh house! But I was interested in radio and it was my fascination with radio that made me go into the RAF. It was a new medium at that time and I was keen to learn how the signal was transmitted and how it was received.

When the war started, I agreed to go into the air training school. There were tests, half a dozen medicals to pass. At that time, nothing bothered me, though. I was only nineteen. I never measured myself to find out how tall I was until I went into the Air Force. Anyway, I was five foot ten.

Like all the other young men, I was sent on courses of training designed to make me an effective member of an air-crew. I had to learn not only how to be an effective radio-operator but also to be familiar with the skills of gunnery.

During the war, I flew on different types of aircraft. In fact, the list is as long as my arm. I don't think there were many Gaels in the RAF during the war, but I did meet two or three – two boys from Stornoway and a friend of mine, Roddy MacLeod, from Branahuie. If there were others, I didn't come across them.

I started off in a Dragon Rapide, which was a plane used for training air-crew. Once I got some experience, I was transferred to a Hampden Bomber. So many men were killed flying that kind of aircraft that it became known as the 'Flying Coffin'. There were four of a crew on it. In the hole where I used to be, you would be put in prison nowadays if you confined a monkey there! There was a little stool tied to the floor for me to sit on. Everything was tied down. In front of me, there was a radio receiver and a transmitter and above that there was what we called a cupola, a window that could be opened, Two guns pointed out of the window. We wore a coat and a bomber jacket that were so big that we were made to look like the spacemen of today. We were provided with parachutes. Mine was always placed beside me. I certainly couldn't have worn it as part of my flying-kit. I didn't, but the pilot did. His wasn't the same type of parachute as I had. The pilot had to sit on his because in a dire emergency he wouldn't have had time to lift it and put it on. If the plane was damaged and beyond control, he would have been the last person to jump.

On bombing missions at night, I had to take two pigeons with me. Ground crew used to think we were pulling their leg when they saw us boarding the plane carrying a basket housing two cooing pigeons. It is no exaggeration to say that the pigeons spent all night cooing in their basket!

Today we might think it strange that we didn't have to practise jumping with the parachute. Thank goodness for small mercies! Many people lost their lives making parachute jumps from planes. To be safe, you had to be high enough above the ground to allow the thing time to open. If the plane was damaged and plunging towards the ground, you just had to take a chance. I never did have to jump with a parachute, although one time I came very close to it. On that occasion, I had it buckled on my chest ready to jump but the emergency passed.

Even in those 'Flying Coffins' we flew far into Europe sometimes as far as Berlin. Yes, we flew the Hampdens that far but, to do so, we had to have special fuel tanks tied under the wings. It's all in my logbook. That was in 1940–41. Of course, the Germans always gave us a very warm welcome! From the time we reached the coast of Holland till we reached Berlin, they were shooting at us. The people who sent us out there tried to plot a course for us, supposedly avoiding the most dangerous areas, but, whichever course we followed, there was always flak. We always went at night and we never went alone. Sometimes we went with a few aircraft and sometimes with as many as a hundred. Not all those aircraft came from the same station in England. Though we knew they were there, there were occasions when we couldn't see any of them.

It was amazing that some of the bombers didn't crash into each other more frequently. It did happen, but not very often. You had your own time slot to be at the target; do your business; and then get out of there. Apart from flak and enemy night-fighters, there was a danger from your own side – from other RAF bombers. Because there were planes flying up above you, there was a danger that they would drop bombs which might hit you. Timing over the target was of utmost importance. Only if every aircraft dropped its load at the appointed time would accidents like that be averted.

You sometimes see an impression of a war-time bombing-raid on television and in the cinema. It is impossible to show or to describe what an aircrew witnessed on a bombing-raid. The picture on the screen shows only what can be encompassed within the eye of the camera. From 20,000 feet what we were seeing was very different. We could see 100 miles around and the sky was full of fire. There were two kinds of gunfire coming at us from the ground – heavy flak and light flak. Normally the smaller guns couldn't reach us, but if there was heavy flak, the sky would be full of shell-bursts which exploded in smoke. Although you had something covering your ears, the crack of each shell-burst was quite audible. When shells burst above us, I was sometimes surprised that the flak had come up past us without hitting us. The reason for it missing us was that it wasn't up from below! It was sometimes coming at us from, perhaps, ten miles away. The flak used to come at us from every angle. Quite often you would hear bangs on the shell of the plane.

I used to stand at the astrodome, looking out for night fighters and reporting what I could see. If they were following you, then you knew that they were chasing you, and you would tell the pilot to go right or left. I remember one night I was standing there, and when I went back to my seat where the radio was, I discovered that a lump of flak had gone through the seat. There was a hole as big as my fist. Lucky that I wasn't sitting down at the time or there would have been no sign of me today. You never forget an experience like that.

Well, we went on the first tour in the Hampdens and then went to a trainee unit for what they called 'a rest'. You stayed there for two or three months undergoing rigorous training. As they said to you when you arrived, 'You've come here for a rest – from being shot at! It's the only kind of rest we can offer here.'

In the beginning and up until 1942 you had to go up in the planes with an untrained pilot, two pilots were not allowed to go up in the one plane. I imagine that was just as dangerous as going over to Germany. Many lost their lives. I saw a statistic saying that 5,000 lost their lives before they even reached the squadron.

You didn't get to stay in bed in the mornings. Once you got the hang of things, you had to go up to teach someone else. Trainees weren't allowed to go up without a staff operator or a trained operator. When I went up on exercises, I went as an air gunner and radio operator. There had to be a navigator on board as well, but he was in the same situation as I was – quite new to the game. He had to go up with a pilot in whom he had no faith. It was always a dodgy situation but there was nothing else for it.

Now, when the Lancaster Bombers arrived, there was some kind of comfort. In fact, a lot of comfort, for there could be two pilots on board. The Lancaster didn't have a bowling-alley or a jacuzzi! It had something that was far more useful – a bed for anyone who had been wounded. And it was possible to walk inside the plane. The space inside was tall enough to allow a person as tall as myself to stand upright in the fuselage. Better still, there was a type of lavatory – a pail which, I think, was called an Elson. But it wasn't a perfect luxury. It was said that if you sat on it at 20,000 feet, your bottom would stick to it because of frost.

It is said that empty bottles made a terrible noise when thrown from a great height. Apparently, some airmen threw bottles out when they were over German territory. The idea was that the Germans might have thought they were some kind of bomb. Anyway, I never threw one out.

Many of the airfields were in the very south of England, but at first I was stationed at one in Yorkshire. When we got the Lancaster we were in Lincolnshire. The two places weren't too far apart.

We did see Messerschmitt fighter planes during the day but, fortunately, not close up. At night, if there wasn't a strong moon, we couldn't see anything like that up where we were. That's where the danger lay. You had to see him before he saw you, and that was the job I had as a look-out in the astrodome. It happened that I had excellent night vision and that was recorded in my logbook. I could see things in the sky long before the gunners could. However, nobody was going to shoot at a night-fighter first, because that would let him know exactly where you were. You had to wait until he came so close that you knew he could see you. Then you would shout: 'Go! Go! Go!' to the pilot. Then he would do something they called a corkscrew, diving down sharply and then rising into the air again. When the plane was going down we would rise up out of our seats as if we were floating, and when the plane was rising we were pinned to our seats. I never had to shoot at a fighter. I didn't have a gun in the Lancaster, though it was equipped with plenty of guns – fast-firing guns. There were three turrets with four guns at the back, two on top and two at the front. The only area which wasn't protected was underneath – the belly of the aircraft, as you might say.

Overall the Lancaster was well fortified and was a fast plane. Nothing else came close to them at that time. There was nothing in the sky like them. After that came the American Liberators and the Fortresses, but they were nothing like the Lancasters. The Lancaster would take ten tons to Berlin at 20,000 feet, but the Liberators and the Fortresses could only manage half that. They didn't go out at night either; they were day-fighters. They never learned night navigation. That was how they operated after coming over here. I flew, in the Lancaster, over the Alps to Italy two or three times.

When Mussolini joined the war, we visited Genoa, Milan and Turin, but not as tourists. We went there to give Mussolini a pasting! He soon discovered that war was not a game and, of course, the Italian people were the unfortunate ones who suffered. In my view, Mussolini was something of a clown.

I spent the early years of the war as a pilot officer, which was a low rank. I got a commission in 1942. I was promoted to Flying Officer, then to Flight Lieutenant, and that was my rank when the war ended. When the war was over, I was demobbed like all the other service men and women.

After the war, life in the air force wasn't the same. There was nothing on anyone's mind but getting promotion. Nothing remained of the bond that used to be between us – between me and the rest of the aircrew. When we were fighting the enemy, we had to rely on each other.

Anyway, after the war, the RAF asked me if I was willing to take up another commission. They said that, if I wanted to go back, I could receive a pension. There was nothing else I could do, nothing else that would pay me half as much as I could get as a Flight Lieutenant. So I went back and spent nine years there. That was fifteen years altogether. When the fifteen years were up, they wanted me to stay for another two years. I asked them how much of an increase I would get in the pension for those two years. The Air Ministry sent word back saying, 'Five shillings a week.' I just thanked them for their generosity but said that I had plenty of things to keep me occupied at home.

I left the RAF in 1955 when I was aged thirty-six. Getting used to life as a civilian, I decided to build a house in Garrabost. Of course, I wasn't married then. I was forty-four before I got married.

I've kept in touch with my old RAF comrades, but the numbers are dwindling. The only ones now left are myself and the pilot. The pilot, a Londoner, still writes to me. He's a year and a half older than I am and lives in Devon – in Torquay is it?

In my spare time, I do a bit of writing and enjoy composing *bàrdachd*. Recently, two Swedish girls visited me while they were making a radio programme about European minority languages. They had a video camera, and they invited me to read a piece of my *bàrdachd* even though they couldn't understand a word of it. This is the poem I chose – a piece that is particularly close to my heart. It is in the book of poems that I published a few years ago.

> *If only I could see Scotland free*
> *Before this tree falls to the ground,*
> *I'd have little care for age;*
> *I would grow light and strong*
> *If only I could see Scotland free!*

> *I would make sport and I would make music,*
> *I would sing a song like a young lad,*
> *I would fill a glass and drink*
> *And think my youth had returned*
> *If only I could see Scotland free!*

> *There is no Scot so pitiful*
> *That he will not be victorious and jolly*
> *When we gain the prize,*
> *When our people see the light –*
> *If only I could see Scotland free!*

Forget about pursuing wealth,
Turn instead your thoughts to William:
Better to be alive on leaven
Than to be bound by force –
If only I could see Scotland free!

There are countries far and near
Wishing to cut chains –
Are our own rulers so blind
That they will crucify us with ball and fetter?
If only I could see Scotland free!

I heard it from the filling tide,
From the wind and from the stream in the glen,
That the elements themselves are on our side,
And that the Union is suffering sickness –
If only I could see Scotland free!

When our country becomes free,
The heather itself will be ablaze,
Each hill and stream and tree will shout
'Freedom from England' –
If only I could see Scotland free!

On that day shall cloud and shadow disperse,
Pulse and vigour will fill her veins,
Her self-worth and her pride secure
As they were in the fist of Bruce –
If only I could see Scotland free!

Mairi MacLeod

1926–

I was born in Portvoller, 14 August 1926, the second of three children born to John MacLeod and Mary Jane Elizabeth Fraser JP [Justice of the Peace]. My first language was English. My mother was not a native Gaelic speaker although she did assimilate it as time went on. By the time we went to school, we spoke Gaelic.

My days in the Infants School at Aird Public School with Miss Christina Murray were delightful. The Murray sisters were from Shader: Christina teaching at Aird and Anne, the Infants mistress at Bayble. They were remarkable women. You couldn't have had anybody kinder than those two teachers and what a job they had instilling the new language into Gaelic-speaking infants, often from scratch. In those days, the class sizes were pretty big.

The class photographs of the early '30s show children well enough dressed and certainly shod but they would have been poor by modern standards. I can well remember that, at dinnertime, the teachers undertook to make cocoa for each class in a big pan on the fire – hot, black and delicious and so different from the milky stuff we got at home! We may have taken our pieces with us, although it would have been possible for some of us to run home for dinner.

Two years with Miss Murray were happy indeed before going up to Primary 1. So much so that, to my everlasting embarrassment, I found myself on the first day back, after the dinner interval, at the head of the queue going into the Infants and not into my new Primary 1 class. That big girl must have looked very much out of place among the new infants!

I loved school and had many years of perfect attendance, a very unwise practice if you happened to be unfit to go to school. There was the mile to walk to school in all weathers.

The teachers were good, some very strict. There was Miss Annie MacSween, who gave my brother Angus a very hard time of it and made his life very difficult. It was no good complaining about it at home; the teacher was sure to be right and she did all the hard work with us. We had Alec John MacLean, later headmaster, who had us in the qualifying class and gentle Miss MacLean from Laxdale in Secondary 1. Angus and I went to the Nicolson Institute in 1938. It was in the year that my brother Iain got killed by a bus on the Shore Road. We went into Class 2, me in 2a and Angus in 2b, staying with my grandmother Julia at the Old House, Sunday to Friday.

We would have had a small amount of pocket money for the week. The first job (on Sunday evening) was to go off to Maggie York's down on Point Street to buy a bar of plain York chocolate and we could still afford one night at the 'pictures'.

I cannot remember a lot about homework although it must surely have needed doing. Life at the Nicolson was good for me. I enjoyed it all, while Angus did not find it so easy and was glad to leave after the 'Lowers'. Those were the early war years. At that time, much came to a dead halt, particularly in games – no hockey or netball or tennis; probably no football either.

We took the first lot of Highers in Class 5 and stayed on for further Highers in Sixth Year. By this time, many of the older boys were old enough to be called up to the forces and most of them left just after fifth year. In 1943, I was dux of the school but, really, the competition was that much less with the exodus of so many of the boys. Then it was off to the medical school in Aberdeen for seventeen terms to enjoy student life in the Granite City. After graduating, I gravitated to Sheffield, where my uncle Iain Fraser was in general practice.

Following years of working in different parts of England, I settled in Derbyshire. I married a farmer, Richard Sterland, and continued working in general medical practice, producing three children: Jane, Angus and Iain. Jane got a First Class BSc in Textile Design and Technology at Manchester; Iain was at Leeds and has a degree in Econometrics; and Angus now runs the farm and does agricultural contracting – big toys for big boys! All three live close to and work close to home in a lovely part of rural Derbyshire – a mini-Scotland in many aspects. The call of the island is still strong and they all prize their time up in Portvoller when work allows, and they value their island birthright.

My mother's father was William Brown Fraser, who was headmaster of Sandwickhill School [in the outskirts of Stornoway], having started as a pupil-teacher, as one did in the latter part of the 1800s. His father, Finlay Fraser, had come from the east coast of Scotland to work as a shipwright on the slipway in Stornoway. My grandmother was Julia Martin Fraser, daughter of Roderick Martin who was the tacks-man at Crobeg Farm. They brought up nine of a family, one dying as a young child of diphtheria, which was blamed on bad drainage at school, another having nearly succumbed to the disease.

Julia was ahead of her time. In her teens, she went out to Canada to visit a relative and began to train as a nurse in the Johns Hopkins Hospital in the United States. All went well until she was visited by a fellow islander who gave her bad news about her father's health. She had to come home post-haste to see him alive. As it happened, he was on the quay meeting her off the boat. She would have turned back if she could, after realising it was a 'put up job'!

Living in Sandwick, Julia was involved in the aftermath of the *Iolaire* Disaster but, in my experience, she never spoke of that. When they retired in the early 1920s, Julia became involved in local politics on the town and county council. In those days, county council meetings were held in Dingwall, involving frequent trips across the Minch, so that she became well known throughout the Highlands and Islands. The story goes that a letter reached her addressed to 'Julia Martin Fraser JP, Scotland'.

I can remember her arriving home off the boat, late evening, exhausted and looking forward to a meal of potatoes and salt herring. She was then up in her seventies. I should mention that she was a supporter and friend of Lord Leverhulme. She was one of the two baillies of Stornoway Town Council, but it was only at the end of her career that she was offered the provostship – a position she couldn't accept because of her ill health. She was often at odds with her fellow councillors and used to get very irate with them. I am sure that the *Stornoway Gazette* accounts of those meetings bear that out. Because of her sex and outspokenness, she had little honour in her own land.

Jim Grant, editor of the *Gazette*, didn't say a lot about her in his articles but he did class her as one of the most able of the councillors. She believed in education. I well remember the regular weekend issue of Arthur Mee's *Children's Newsletter*, which she always took and which she shared with us. There's a story of her rebellion against authority as a child: in school, in Crobeg, the boys were allowed to enjoy their playtime while the girls stayed in the classroom with their sewing or other household duties. Julia felt that the discrimination was not to be tolerated. One day, she led the rest of the girls across to a tidal island and managed to get them all marooned! Her mother was worldly and busy with a large family and didn't have any patience with schooling for girls. Her father – whose favourite Julia was – colluded with her in encouraging her in her lessons. He found her a cave by the shore where she could be out of reach of her mother's demands for work on the farm. She was adamant on the necessity of education for her own children, who, in their careers, became teachers, nurses, doctors, an accountant and a pharmacist.

In the 1914–18 era, my mother, the eldest, did teacher training in Aberdeen. She taught at Lochs and Bayble before she married and had her three children but, to her great regret, was never able to return to teaching. In those post-Great War days, once you left teaching to marry, you were never employed in the profession again.

Next came Roderick Martin, who was with the Ross Mounted Battery in the war and was wounded at Gallipoli. Peace having been declared in November 1918, he was one of the host of servicemen languishing in Kyle of Lochalsh, awaiting passage across the Minch on New Year's Eve 1918. He was one of the fortunate ones who were allocated a place on the slow-moving *Sheila* and not on the ill-fated yacht *Iolaire*.

As a mature student, Roderick took his degree in medicine at Aberdeen. Like so many Lewis graduates in medicine, Roderick spent his early years in practice in the Midlands, a hard training ground for them all before finding practices of their own. He did come back to Lewis, treating patients in the Back and Point areas as well as in the town. Sadly, Roderick died in his early forties from a post-operative haemorrhage. His youngest brother, Iain Fraser, also an Aberdeen graduate, did his service in the Second World War on a hospital-ship in the Far East; afterwards working briefly in Stornoway and Leverburgh [in Harris] before settling in general practice in Sheffield.

The other boys, Gordon and Thomas ('Tossie'), were both in the Royal Artillery during the Second World War. Tossie was an accountant. Gordon was through the Desert Campaign.* I remember that I had a weekly job of going down to draw their Army Allowance for their mother – something like 8s 6d for Gordon and umpteen shillings for Tossie, who had 'a stripe'! I understand that if a soldier making 'an allowance' were to be killed in action the parent would receive a pension. After the war, Tossie remained in accountancy and, after his demob, Gordon established the Stornoway Drycleaners.

Of the Fraser girls, Phyllis, for some years before her marriage, was a district nurse in Acharacle in Argyll. Jean was theatre sister in Eye Surgery. Sheila, after a brief nursing career, came home to assist her

---

* During the Second World War; the British fought the armies of Germany and Italy in Egypt and Libya.

mother with the running of the private hotel business at the Old House. Ethel, the last of the girls, was reputedly able to read at the age of three and a half. She was one of the Nicolson school-leavers who were persuaded to go out to Montreal to seek their fortune and make their mark with the TB MacAulay Sun Life Assurance Company. It would have been about 1926–27 – something of a confidence trick. Ethel returned disillusioned.

I can remember the family going down to the quay at the usual eight o'clock night-berthing of the *Loch Ness* to meet Ethel. She completed her teacher training at Aberdeen and taught until her retirement in Nairnshire, spending the war years [while her husband was in the army] teaching in a one-teacher rural school and managing to bring up her four children single-handed – no mean feat! Later on, she taught disadvantaged children in Nairn. She was a born teacher.

My paternal grandfather was Angus MacLeod who was born in 1838 and died in 1920. I think that, when he was young, my grandfather was working in the castle grounds the large area of woodland and flowerbeds in which Lews Castle is situated. The grounds were then in the making with soil being brought in from elsewhere. According to hearsay, my grandfather worked after that at the chemical works at Garrabost and lived with his brother, Kenneth, who lived in Clay Park and was employed at the nearby brickworks making bricks and roof tiles. The outhouses, and certainly the byre, at Portvoller had those red tiles on the roof. Some of the tiles were preserved in the Stornoway Museum after the byre was demolished about twenty years ago

Angus MacLeod settled in Portvoller from the family home at Vatisker and set up his business as merchant and fish-curer. Well known as Angus Portvoller, he became successful. His marriage to Annie MacKenzie [Anna Mhurchaidh 'Ain 'ic an Lèigh] produced ten children. They married in Glasgow. We have an entertaining letter, dated 1930, from a Portvoller emigrant to Australia,* sent to my father recounting the couple's return from honeymoon.

I remember your father and mother. I do remember them both very well. I well remember the afternoon upon which they arrived in Portvoller after their marriage in Glasgow and I got my share of the wedding also. Your father was not the kind of man to forget the boys on such an occasion. We, the boys of Portvoller and Portnaguran, after leaving school, were seriously engaged in a game of marbles on the road just

* Roderick MacDonald, formerly of No. 6 Portvoller.

about midway between his shop and old Donald Martin's house when we heard Duncan's [the horse's] smart step coming home with your father and mother in the gig. We picked up our marbles quick and stepped aside to let them pass. Very soon afterwards we saw the shop door being opened and your father came out with a large bottle of 'conversation lozenges' in his hand, He just said one word, 'Boys!' and immediately he was surrounded by a swarm of boys and began to throw the lozenges for us to scramble . . . and Mother, who had heard the noise, came to the door and, when she saw the game in full swing, she also had a hearty laugh . . .

His South African granddaughter, Isobel MacRae, remembers my grandfather as a very kindly man.

My grandmother, Annie MacKenzie, was a very capable character and used her gifts both in business and in service to the community. It seems that she had inherited the talent of the 'Lèighe' tradition in dispensing medicines and treating the ill.

The business prospered with the shop and big catches of ling and cod, the fish-curing business, the salting-houses and fishing-boats that they owned. Annie was a competent tailoress and her handsome family of girls were dressed in style and in the height of fashion. They were a good-looking lot and would have made an impression driving into Stornoway in the gig to visit their friends. I seem to remember that their friends at the Commercial Hotel were the MacIntyres and the Croziers.

There was always competitiveness between the town versus the country scene, with a lot of town snobbery and, often, unkind mockery. There was the occasion of the tennis tournament when my father was heavily handicapped but won the final match. His first prize was six tennis balls, while the runner-up carried off the silver-mounted cane!

Angus was the eldest son, a graduate in medicine from Edinburgh University. He died at the age of twenty-eight. He had a fulminating illness while in practice in St Ives and died in Glasgow at his sister Molly's home having been unable to make it home to Lewis. Incidentally, he had been going to marry the daughter of Dr Ross who was, of course, the mother of Iain MacLeod MP and Foreign Minister,* who was a prominent Tory politician in the 1950s and '60s.

The next in the family was Mary Ann ('Molly'), who married Norman MacKenzie from Bernera, a sergeant-major in the marines. They settled

---

* (1913–1970) He was in fact Colonial Secretary and later Leader of the House of Commons. He died a few weeks after being made Chancellor of the Exchequer.

in Bayble. The Bayble shop at Burncrook, which was their business, was originally built by her parents. There they brought up a family of seven.

Christina and Maggie ('Meg') were both nurses. Christina became matron of a field hospital during the First World War. While out there, she met her husband, Walter Rees, who was a captain in the RAME. After the war, they settled in Hampstead. Walter was in general practice and acted as an obstetrician at the Hampstead General Hospital, now called the Royal Free. For her work, Christina was awarded the Royal Red Cross. In Hampstead, she continued to be active on many committees and 'wearing many hats'.

During the Second World War, their only son, Ivor, who was a pilot in the Fleet Air Arm, was lost when his plane was shot down over the Mediterranean.

Meg, trained in nursing in Edinburgh and married to Walter Gilmour, a pathologist, settled in New Zealand. Both their sons were killed in the First World War: Dr Lewis while operating in his field hospital in North Africa; and Angus while training with the New Zealand Air Force.

At the age of seventeen or eighteen, John ('Jack'), my father, went off to the Second Boer War as a trooper. Having survived the war, he joined the police for a five-year period and afterwards went to work in the gold mines. Meanwhile, his father was getting old and unwell, and asked my father to return home. So, about 1911 or '12, Jack came home to run the business. His father died in 1920, aged eighty-two.

Katherine ('Kate') settled in South Africa. Her husband, William, joined the Post Office and was eventually head of the Stamp Department in Pretoria.

Of Angus Portvoller's other two children, Isobel is still going strong at the age of ninety-four. Angus died in Jo'burg a few years ago. Both of them had spent a lot of their young lives at Portvoller and attended Aird Public School. Angus continued to be able to speak the Gaelic that his mother had taught him. Both he and Isobel revisited Lewis on several occasions. The close bond with South Africa survived the years with regular correspondence. Letter-writing was, usually, a Sunday night ritual.

Another family visitor, on more than one occasion, was John MacLeod, son of 'Kenneth Garrabost' [Clay Park]. He was a lovely man who became no less than the Chief Inspector of Schools in Natal. His three sons, Kenneth, Angus and Norman, survive him in South Africa; a more handsome trio would be difficult to find.

Accompanied by a lad from Flesherin, Willie John emigrated to Canada. He settled in Saskatchewan and was in charge of a grain silo on the prairie.

He married Murdina MacIver, daughter of Donald MacIver, the Bayble headmaster. They had five of a family, very much of an age with me and my brothers. They had a hard life, marooned for long winters in isolation. Herself a teacher, Murdina taught the children. Both parents were very religious – extremely devout – so life for the kids would have been pretty serious.

The youngest daughter was Jessie, the beauty of the lot. She travelled the world and created havoc wherever she went! She had been at home, helping in the shop and post office, but when the first [World] war started, decided to go off and drive an ambulance at the Front in France. She upped and she went, became a VAD [Volunteer Aid Detachment], unpaid, subsidised by my father, who took a dim view of it, left high and dry by himself and, thus, not easy.

So from there, Jessie travelled the world. She could turn her hand to anything. She was very able. She ran hospitals, homes – nothing daunted. She worked in New Zealand, South Africa, Burma, India and, eventually, settled in London. I remember visiting her in London, where she kept house for Augustus John's sister, and spending an evening with her at the Overseas Club. Eventually, she acquired a house of her own in Streatham and died at the ripe old age of ninety-one.

Ten years after Jessie, Ivor came along, the last of the family. In the First World War, he served in the Ross Mounted Battery and survived the war. He trained in engineering in Glasgow, still supported by my father. He joined Burmah Oil and was out in Rangoon for most of his career. When the Second World War broke out and the Japanese invaded the country, he found himself, a civilian, in the rearguard of the retreat. He was one of the last out of the country, blowing up oil installations, just ahead of the Japanese advance. His wife, Chris, managed to get out, a passenger in a light aircraft, and spent the rest of the war years teaching in a school in Delhi. Ivor served the rest of the war fighting in Burma, ending it as a major in the army. When the war ended, he did a further stint with Burmah Oil. He and Chris retired to establish a fruit orchard in Suffolk, where, after a few years, my brother Angus joined him.

It is obvious from what I've told you that, through the generations, our family members inherited a kind of wanderlust that causes us to travel abroad and discover different parts of the world. In most cases we have found places that have been particularly suited to our temperaments and have chosen to settle there. In my own case, I have found my niche in Derbyshire, and together with my late husband, Richard, built up a little clan there – a wee enclave! My sister-in-law lives just up the road. My daughter lives about twenty yards further down. Then thirty yards further down is the farm where number three child, number two son, is living. Some time in the future, number one son is probably going to live there as well. So it's a nice little enclave, yes.

People ask me why I come back to Lewis and to Portvoller in particular. Well, I am not the only one who, as a native Hebridean, is drawn back to my native heath – rain or no rain! Don't we all feel the irresistible call to come back? All of us have this desperate feeling of belonging to the island. This is home. There is no other place like it, really. It's downright stupid of course, when you compare the life here with the easier life people have in other parts. Where I live in England is very pleasant and the weather is much better and life has more variety. But nevertheless, it's nothing like here. For me, there is, and always will be, the everlasting call of the Islands – an everlasting bond.

Alexander MacLeod ('Sandy Mòr')

1915–

Well, when I was at school we used to walk, of course. No buses in those days! Of course, we really didn't have far to walk – just across the fields of the crofts. And there were 300 pupils in Bayble School in those days and with nine teachers. Although our language was Gaelic, we were taught in English. I didn't have a word of English when I went to school and that was the first thing we learned, was English. We only got Gaelic when I went into the secondary school. It was not teaching through the medium of Gaelic. We were taught a little about how to read and write in our own language. Our headmaster was Mr James Thomson, who was very interested in the language and composed some Gaelic songs and poetry. He was father of Derick Thomson, the Gaelic scholar and poet.

He was quite a good headmaster. He compiled a Gaelic book with the name *An Dìleab*, which means 'The Legacy'. He also composed a song under that name and that also was the name of the first song in the book. When I left school I could read and write Gaelic but I wasn't strong in these subjects. Perhaps I had not been given enough grounding in writing, for, not long after I left school, I found that I couldn't write fluently. I could read Gaelic but couldn't write it.

In my young days, the social conditions in Lewis were very primitive. There were pupils much older than me, from Bayble and from Garrabost, going to school barefoot both summer and winter. That was in the 1920s and early '30s. I left school in 1931. I think I was six or near seven before I went to school. So that would be 1921 when I went to school.

Somebody writing for the Ordnance Survey around 1850 described Bayble and Garrabost as 'a cluster of huts of primitive appearance. The walls made of peat sods. The roof lightly thatched with straw and very incommodious and unhealthy.'

They suggest that it was difficult to see how anyone could live in those houses. Well, I can tell you that, between then and my going to school, housing conditions had changed very little for the better. No, not all that much. There was quite a lot of the black-houses in the village long after I left school. The people were poor but they tried their best to keep their families clean and decent. They struggled to keep their homes clean. But they lived by manual labour and they didn't have a public supply of water coming to the house. It is impossible to keep the house clean and everything nice and hygienic if you don't have tap water. In the good weather especially, everybody was out working from morn to night. Yes, both young and old. If you could at all, you had to work to make it possible for the family to survive. Everybody had to do their bit. Although conditions were hard, it's amazing the amount of people living in the black-houses who lived to a good old age. They must have been very, very healthy!

There was always something to do in every season of the year. The peat-cutting season started in the early spring. The peats were cut out on the moor, of course. Each family had their own peat-banks and once the peats were cut and dried by the sun and the wind, you had to get started on the crops – planting the potatoes, sowing the oats and barley. In the spring, the people of the district were busy carrying seaweed off the shore in creels and spreading it on to the croft for fertilizer.

Every bit of the croft was tilled when I was going to school in the 1920s and for a good while after I left school, every square yard. But one thing that still amazes me was that nobody was planting any vegetables. The potato was the main root vegetable. The cereal crops were barley and oats. The grain was taken to the mill less than a mile from here, just at the end of the village. There the grain was ground into meal.

There was no threshing mill in those days. So the crofter family separated the grain from the stalk by using an implement called a *sùist* [flail]. That was a kind of double rod with which the workers continuously struck the sheaves of barley or oats.

As I said, everybody worked hard in those days. Most of the men were fishermen and they were at sea most of their lives. The men had a hard life but it's women who were doing most of the land work. The women had a hard life as well as the men. Men were lost at sea.

Consumption was the scourge in Lewis when I was young. There was hardly any families or house that didn't have one consumptive patient at one time or another. That was a terrible time for many families. But there were happy occasions too. They had to make all their own entertainment. Especially anybody getting married did so at the end of the harvest. The whole community contributed to the wedding feast. Chicken was the main meal. The women of the village gathered together and the chickens were killed and plucked and cooked. Boiled. Everything was boiled. No oven! And I think that was a great saviour, the way the food was cooked. Everything was boiled, well cooked, and it didn't matter how contaminated it might have been, the cooking was killing most of the bugs. The wedding feast consisted mainly of soup, chicken meat, potatoes and bread (which they mostly baked themselves). If the house didn't have a barn, they would get the neighbour's barn for the dance. The dancing went on all night and the wedding itself kept going for a week anyway. And, of course, there was drink. They got a tipple at a wedding or, say, on market-day in Stornoway – special occasions like that – New Year, Christmas, but during the rest of the year, there was no drinking at all going on. They may have made homemade whisky in the old days but in my time there was nothing like that. No, there was nothing like that, no!

For some considerable time I was active in politics. That was when I was younger, of course. Now, I'm in my mid eighties and I am not so energetic! Although I was keen, I was not high profile. Some journalist referred to me as a 'king-maker' but that was because I helped Labour candidates get into Parliament. The first Labour MP to take over the Western Isles was Malcolm K. MacMillan. He was our MP from 1935 to 1970. He was there for thirty-five years. On his campaigns, I was his driver, just driving the car. His agent was himself! He was his own election agent. For his election address, he did all the preparation himself. He was a good MP – a genuine man. He was the friend of the island people – the crofters. He was also hot on the subject of pensions and welfare. He was always on top of that. He tried to get as much as he could for the people of the islands. I am also an admirer of the young man who is our present MSP – Alasdair Morrison. His home is just along the road from ourselves and I know him and his family very well.

At one time Garrabost was quite a thriving community. It had factories. Of course, I just heard about that. It had finished before my day. The factories and their industries were finished a long time before I was born. They were centred at the *Buaile Chreadha* – the Clay Park. There was a big clay quarry there and it supplied the clay for bricks, roofing tiles, yes, and drainpipes. They were turning out 36,000 bricks per week in the 1850s. That is when Sir James Matheson was the proprietor of the island. He had made his fortune in the Far East. He was a merchant in the opium trade.

I don't know why the company went bust but I think there were big problems with transport. That was the age of sailing ships. Transport became easier as the ships got better with engines instead of the sail. Beside the brickworks there was a chemical factory making paraffin from peat. It's surprising that that factory also went bust, especially when you consider that there was plenty of peat available. There was a big demand for paraffin at that time because the lamps in all the houses used paraffin for fuel. Again, there probably were problems with transport.

In our village here – Garrabost – there was overpopulation. Well, it was a problem all over the island. When the crofts were set out, families were given about four acres each. The croft here, the one we're on just now, it has only three acres. But on the other side of the road it has four acres. That was all right for the first tenants and that was about some time in the nineteenth century. But, latterly, there would be two or three families on each croft. Well there would be two, anyway. Of course, in addition to the two or three acres, the crofters had grazing rights on the common, the moorland belonging to the village. The people depended on the land for their living and every inch of the ground, whether it was the Common Grazing or not, was made use of. When my uncle married, he extended the house on the croft he was living on, but he wasn't allowed to cut peats on the Common Grazing. The grazing was that valuable. They could only have one fire on each croft – one fire to two or three families. Even supposing there were two houses or three houses on a croft, they were allowed to have a total of one fire per croft. Now that was tough. My uncle, you see, was a young man – a fisherman – fishing out of Stornoway. He got married and built a home for himself and his wife. But his home was only an extension to the old house with the thatched roof and all that. But he was for quite a while in it and he couldn't get peats for a fire. He couldn't afford to buy coal. There was no coal going around anyway. There was no proper transport to carry coal except the horse and cart and that was not viable. You can imagine the problems that were caused by having two families sharing the one fire for the cooking.

That law was in force for many years until later on the people began to agitate and let their voices be raised in protest. You see, the people demanded that this law, imposed by the estate, had to be done away with.

I built this house at twenty-one years of age. Every house here built in the first half of the twentieth century was built of poured concrete, which is shingle and cement mixed together with water. The shingle was mixed with cement and water and poured between shutters specially constructed to shape the walls.

For days, I was out on the beach there on the Bràigh getting shingle. And we used to put seven shovels of shingle into a hessian sack, which was supposed then to weigh a hundredweight. And we had to put that on our back right up to the lorry on the road. It was just a grass verge that was alongside. In those days, there was no concrete embankment or anything like that at the Bràighe, as there is now. A grass verge was all along the beach there and we had to climb the slippery slope with the load on our backs, which wasn't easy. All the neighbours that were building a house – and there were quite a few – would be along with me, seven of us. On the following day, I would be with them, taking the shingle for their own house. That's the way the neighbours helped one another. Building these new white-houses was a communal activity. Oh, yes, it was a communal activity.

Nowadays, crofters live in modern houses with every convenience that people enjoy in the cities. Once the Western Isles Council was formed, and with the advent of the Labour government, generous grants from the central government, all the houses were improved, you know, by improvement grants. Once you got your clean, modern house built, you then got all modern conveniences and all that. But the improvements didn't happen overnight! When the oldest of my family was born, there was no running water in the place. We still had to go to the well to get water and bring it home in pails. Although the house was very nice compared with the old one, we still didn't have running water. But once we got the main water supply our housing conditions improved no end. We got bathrooms and toilets drained to septic tanks. Then the sewerage system came along and that did away with the septic tanks. Now that happened after the Second World War – in the 1950s.

In my young days I was a bus-driver. Some people called the type of bus a 'charabanc'. I just started with the 'chara' in 1935 and I was just twenty-one years of age then. I travelled the eleven-mile route from Port nan Giùran to Stornoway several times a day – up and down that road past my own home here in Garrabost.

Now it was fully three years after that the war came on and I went away to the ships, to the merchant navy. I worked on deck as a seaman. Of course, when I went there first, I didn't know how to be a deckhand. After all, my experience had been as a bus-driver. But that didn't bother me. I just picked it up. Well, you had to start at the bottom. You had to go as an ordinary seaman. Then the next step on the ladder was an able seaman, then quartermaster, or whatever level you wanted to attain. You were learning in stages like that, aboard the ship. I was at sea throughout the war.

I was in Algiers when the invasion of Sicily and Italy took place. But I was at the invasion of Algiers when they landed with their patrols there and got ashore and there was no resistance at all at Algiers. The Vichy French were in charge of most of the ports. Of course, the Americans were there as well as the British. I was on a meat-boat and we had to supply the troops. So we left Sicily at the time of the Anzio beachhead and travelled along the coast of Italy to Taranto. That was the nearest port to the Anzio beachhead.

While I was in the Med I didn't see any action, though. The only action I saw was during the Battle of the Atlantic. I was for a year there going across the Atlantic on cargo ships. This was the early part of the war. The German submarines could only go 300 miles west of Ireland. That was their range then. When you were outward bound, the destroyer escorts left you when you were 300 miles west of Ireland. They left and you just went on your own then. But coming back you had to put into Halifax in Nova Scotia to become one of the ships in a convoy. A merchant armed cruiser accompanied the convoy till we were picked up by the destroyers west of Ireland. Well, one night, we had thirty-two ships in the convoy. And this night the armed merchant cruiser left us just as it was dusk. At midnight, the first ship was torpedoed. Then shortly after that the next one was torpedoed. We were supposed to pick the destroyers up in the morning. So when the Germans realised that we were without escort, three of them surfaced and, well, in the end, they must have run out of torpedoes, otherwise they would have wiped out the whole convoy.

There was no way of firing at the U-boats. Every merchant ship carried a four-inch anti-submarine gun and quite a powerful anti-aircraft gun. But it was pitch black. We couldn't see any target. And that was the thing. The Germans put one of their U-boats at the back of the convoy. They shot flares over us and lit up the convoy as bright as day. Our ships were sitting ducks. Thirty-two ships left Halifax in convoy and fifteen were gutted. That was in 1941. As you can imagine, there was terrible loss of life.

It was wonderful when peace was declared – victory in Europe in 1945 and then victory over the Japanese in the Far East a year later. I was at home for a while after I was demobbed and trying to fit into civilian life. My next move took me into foreign parts! Like a lot of Lewis boys of my generation, I decided to go whale hunting in Antarctica. Life was hard down in the Antarctic. Hard work and not much comfort, but you got used to the conditions. In those days, everybody was working hard even at home.

The first year I went down in Antarctica, I went down on a tanker with oil for the factory ships. Salvesen, the Norwegian company, had two factory ships working the whales. On the island of South Georgia, there was a whaling station there. So I went down on the oil tanker with the oil supplies and we oiled the fleet, cleaned the ship out and filled her with whale oil off the factory ships and off the island. By that time the season was over and quite a few of the boys stayed for the winter in South Georgia, so I also applied to stay for the winter. I did that season and I did the following winter before I came home – very near two years.

I made good wages while I was there. But the wage and the hours and conditions weren't that much different from what you might get elsewhere. The only thing was, you couldn't spend it. You had it saved up till you came home and got paid by cheque. You had to cash it at the bank. That's the reason people thought there was a lot of money.

There was a bit of drinking going on in South Georgia but the lads used to make the drink themselves. It was homemade hooch. There was big jars that used to come down to Antarctica with some kind of acid, I don't know how many gallons, and once these were emptied, the boys used the jars for the hooch. They called it 'the brew'. It fermented in the jars. But also 'the brew' was distilled in stills. The barracks in which we lived were built on a hillside and there was a high foundation under every one. Underneath that were the central heating pipes. Every building was centrally heated from the one central boiler situated underneath these foundations. Well, believe it or not, the boys connected the stills to the heating system.

I believe that 'the brew' had a terrible kick! I never tasted it but a lot of men drank it, especially the Norwegians. They'll drink anything! Quite a few of them anyway. Sometimes, you would see them walking a bit unsteady on their legs. When I saw the effect the hooch had, I decided never to taste it. But every fortnight we were getting a tot of rum. Saturday was the night you were getting the tot of rum – your sort of half-day. As soon as you got the tot of rum, the people who operated the illicit still took out their drink and continued the partying. That's the way it was. There was a Customs point and we were told that their officers were quite strict. We were told that if you were caught under the influence of the hooch you were heavily fined and sent home immediately. Anyway, that wasn't one of my worries! I think there were 1,000 Norwegians there and 800 Britishers. It was a great experience for me. It was.

Like so many of our islanders, I've been in a lot of places in different countries. During the war, I visited the United States, South America, South Africa, India, Australia, New Zealand and Thailand. I was all over the Mediterranean, well most of the Mediterranean. I am now eighty-two years of age [1998] and I have seen huge changes take place in Lewis in my lifetime. The most obvious change is the improvement in housing. That has improved a lot and it has improved the lot of our people. Transport also has been transformed. Even the change from the horse and cart to the bus, as I was mentioning before, was a big step forward. Then, it's now from the bus to the private car. But the way things are now you can have your breakfast here and have high tea in New York or Rome. That's the most amazing thing. And now what I see with the Internet, the improvement in communications, it's beyond belief for the likes of me how that is happening.

I must not forget to mention the impact of television and radio. That's the other form of communications I'm talking about. Instead of having to depend on, say, reading about an incident, you can often see it as it is happening. Before television, you often wondered if what you were reading was true or not. Seeing events as they happened on the television has an amazing effect. It doesn't matter what part of the world an event takes place in, you can still see it in your own living-room.

I'm still very interested in politics. I have been a red-hot Labour supporter throughout life, from my very early days. Nowadays of course, there is no red-hot Labour. That's true.

When they changed Clause 4,* the way I looked at it was, I was only three years of age when Sidney Webb created Clause 4. Time changes everything. The world doesn't stand still. In fact, it keeps speeding up! As I mentioned before, I compared it to the horse and cart going to Stornoway. The first time I went to Stornoway was in the horse and cart and it took me a full hour. And now the airport's only 2.5 miles from me and, as I said before, I can have breakfast here and high tea in New York. Well, when Tony Blair's government changed Clause 4 I thoroughly approved of his doing so. I saw Clause 4 as obsolete, completely obsolete.

We had a meeting about it and this is exactly what I told them. But the new Clause 4 should be for the benefit of the many and not the few. And sure enough, on the new form, these exact words are in it. So that's the way I am with politics. I changed with the times. But, I have to say that I see other changes in the society of our island that are not improving the quality of life here. There was neighbourliness in the society into which I was born. Little of that left now. No neighbourliness, just everybody for himself. As you might say, there is a lot of greed in this day and age. The most appalling thing is the behaviour of the youth of today – the way they're influenced by drugs. Some of the young people let down the reputation of the island.

In my young days, the word 'Gaelic' was pronounced 'Gay-lick'. Of

---

* Clause 4, adopted by the Labour Party in 1917, stated, 'To secure for the workers by hand or by brain the full fruits of their industry and the most equitable distribution thereof that may be possible on the basis of common ownership.'

course, I understand that nowadays people refer to the Irish language as 'Gay-lick' and to our Scottish version as 'Gaa-lick'. In any case, it is obvious that our language is decaying. To survive, Gaelic needs to be spoken in the home first and foremost. And now what I see with my grandchildren, I'm afraid, is not very encouraging. Those of my grand-children who are in faraway England, they speak Gaelic, whereas those in the island, they won't. Life in our island homes is swamped by television.

The influence of the Church has waned as well. Is that a good or a bad thing, I wonder? Well, I reckon it's a bad thing. It doesn't matter how much I disagree or anybody disagrees with the Church, it was a good teaching morally to keep you on the straight and narrow, from doing wrong. But when the worldly inventions came along, they seemed to change the character of the people, in a sense. As children we were taught that if you were regular in going to church, and behaved as good Christian boys, you would go to Heaven – that God and the angels were up in the Heavens above. Now, when the Russians and Americans landed on the moon that killed that part of religion. The astronauts saw no Heaven and no angels! There was one empty space. So that's the way I looked at it, anyway. But the moral teaching of the Church was a good influence. It kept us on the straight and narrow. Sadly, we have nothing to replace what has been lost. Certainly, films and television plays don't do anything to show what it means to be Christian and well behaved.

Donnchadh MacCoinnich

1924–2007

'S mise Donnchadh MacCoinnich agus tha mi 'n-dràsta nam shuidhe nam dhachaigh fhìn ann an Tolastadh a' Chaolais. Aithnichidh a' mhòr-chuid mi air an ainm 'Donnchadh Togan'. 'S e 'Togan' am far-ainm a bh' aca air m' athair, agus 's ann air Togan a tha an teaghlach againne air fad air an ainmeachadh. A rèir aithris, b' e am ma'-sgoile a thug air m' athair an t-ainm is e na bhalach beag anns an sgoil. Chan eil cinnt carson, ach tha fiù mo nephew a thàinig à Sasainn aithnichte air an ainm sin. Tha e a' fuireach ann an seo a-bhos. Chuir mise seachad mo bheatha anns a' bhaile sa a' croitearachd agus ri fighe. Innsidh mi dhut a' chiad chuimhne a th' agam air mo bheatha an seo. Tha thu a' faicinn na tobhta sin shìos ri taobh an rathaid an sin. Uill, bha dà sheana ghille a' fuireachd anns an taigh a bha sin nuair a bha mise nam bhalach beag, ach tha fìor chuimhne agam air màthair nam fireannach sin. Chì mi i mar gum bithinn ga faicinn ann an aisling. 'S iongantach gu robh mi barrachd air trì bliadhna.

Tha mi sia troighean 's dà òirleach a dh'àird agus tha mo phiuthar Anna an seo gu math àrd cuideachd. Daoine mòra a th' ann an cuideachd m' athar: Clann Choinnich. Dh'aindeoin sin, cha robh m' athair fhèin mòr idir. Cha robh ann ach beagan is còig troighean is ochd òirlich. 'S e bu lugha a bh' anns an teaghlach dha na balaich. Ach bha bràth'r mo sheanar anns na Geàrrannan – bha ochdnar mhac anns an teaghlach, agus bha iad ag ràdh gu robh sia troighean anns a h-uile fear aca. Bha aona bhràthair-seanar agam na phoileas ann an Glaschu agus bha bràthair-seanar eile agam agus triùir mhac aige nam poilis timcheall Ghlaschu. Ann an teaghlach mo sheanar, taobh m' athar, 's ann a chaidh na mic a bh' ann a-null a dh'Ameireaga. Chaidh triùir aca a-null an sin. Fhios agad, ann an linn m' athar, bha na taighean làn dhaoine. Ach dh'fhalbh na daoine sin agus tha na taighean sin a bha làn dhaoine an-diugh falamh. Chan eil duine a-mach bhuapa a' fuireachd anns an àite. Tha e smaoineachail!

Bitear a' faighneachd dhomh dè a' chiall a th' aig an fhacal *Tolstadh*. Uill, bha sinn a' cluinntinn a-riamh gur e a' chiall a th' aige 'Dol A-steach an

Caolas'. Ged as e àite iomallach a bha seo uair, tha pailteas eilthireach an ceann a deas Shasainn a tha air lorg fhaighinn oirnn. Cha mhòr nach eil uimhir de choigrich anns a' bhaile agus a tha de dhaoine a bhuineas dhan àite. Tha iad an seo às gach seòrsa, ach cha chuir iad dragh air duine co-dhiù. Ach chan eil cleachdaidhean nan daoine a tha an seo aca idir. Cha tig iad a dh'obair nar measg. Tha daoine ann an seo a' dol a dh'obair aig tractar is làraidhean 's faingean, is fuirichidh na h-eilthirich aca fhèin. Tha mòran dhiubh a thàinig dhan bhaile le airgead air an cùl. Tòrr aca ag obair taobh an ospadail 's Comhairle nan Eilean. Air an làimh eile, tha a' chuid mhòr de luchd a' bhaile sa ag obair an ceann an cosnaidh ann am badan air falbh às an eilean. Chan eil mòran òigridh an seo ann: tha iad ag obair a-mach à seo ann an ceàrnaidhean eile.

'S e na beairtean a bha a' cumail an àite seo a' dol bhon sguir an Cogadh – agus eadhon ron a' Chogadh. Cha mhòr gu bheil duine a' fighe an-diugh. 'S e sianar anns a' bhaile an àireamh as motha a tha ris. Bha an fhighe air a dhol chon na bochdainn bliadhnaichean ann an siud. Bhiodh duine mìosan gun chlò aige. Tha triùir air na beairtean mòra a cheannachd. Seadh, triùir. 'S e mo nephew-sa an trìtheamh fear, ach tha e ga leigeil seachad. Fhuair e obair aig a' Chomhairle. Tha sin nas fhasa dha. Tha e cinnteach às gu bheil e a' faighinn cosnadh a h-uile seachdain.

Ann an 1851, dh'fhalbh na daoine às a' bhaile sa – deich teaghlaichean – a-null a Chanada. Chaidh iad gu àite air an robh an t-ainm Bruce County. Bha sin ann an Ontario. 'S ann an dèidh dha na daoine sin falbh à Tolastadh a' Chaolais a thàinig na daoine dham buin mise a-steach ann an seo. 'S e fear John Young a thàinig dhan chroit a bh' ann an seo. Tha mi 'n dùil nach e Gall a bh' ann idir. Cha b' e. Ach 's iongantach mura h-e a thighinn a Leòdhas a rinn athair. Mus tàinig e an seo, bha e air a bhith ann an àite shuas ri taobh Locha Ròg – suas ris a' chladach taobh Sgealascro. 'S ann an sin a bha e a' fuireach an uair ud. Uill, phòs e nighean Ùigeach, nighean Dhòmhnaill MhicLeòid, agus thugadh dhaibh aon dha na croitean anns a' bhaile sa.

'S e croitean mòra tha seo, ach tha tòrr chnuic annta. Tòrr chnuic. Tha iad a' ruith a-null taobh na mara. Tha faisg air fichead acair anns na croitean a tha an sin. Bharrachd air sin, tha cùl baile againn cuideachd – pìos mòr fearainn.

Bha mòran fearainn air àiteach anns a' chroit sa. Bha trì teaghlaichean air an lot seo uaireigin. Ach bha mise a' gabhail uabhas dha lotaichean an ceann a deas a' bhaile. 'S ann orra a tha mi a' smaoineachadh a bha an talamh a b' fheàrr a bh' anns a' bhaile. Bha na croitean aca a' dol bhon an loch, sìos fon an rathad, tarsainn an rathaid chun na mara, agus cha mhòr nach robh a h-uile ploc a bha an sin air àiteach. Bha iad a' buain pholl-mònach a-muigh faisg air far a bheil an cladh, agus anns a h-uile làrach puill bha iad a' dèanamh fheannagan, a thuilleadh air na bh' aca a-staigh anns a' bhaile. Abair thusa arbhar anns an latha sin. Anns an latha bha siud bha na daoine bochd, taca ris mar tha sinn uile an-diugh. Ach an dèidh sin bha iad fhèin glè riaraichte le an crannchur. Aig tòrr aca cha robh cus ach na dhèanadh iad às a' chroit, 's cha robh sin mòran. Thuilleadh air sin bha beagan stoc aca: caoraich agus crodh.

Nuair a bha mise òg, bhiodh corra fhireannach a' dol a-mach gu tìr-mòr nuair a bha na tunailean mòra gan cladhach tro na beanntan. Bhitheadh, 's bhiodh iad a' dèanamh cosnaidh greiseag ann an sin. Bha siud nuair a bha iad a' dùsgadh nan tunailean tro na beanntan airson rathaidean chàraichean agus slighe dhan rèile. Chan eil mi a' smaoineachadh gu robh a' Hydro air tòiseachadh aig an uair ud. Bha siud greis ron a' Chogadh. Bha feadhainn dha na balaich a bhiodh a' dol a sheòladh. 'S ann a' seòladh a bha m' athair. Seòladair a bh' ann bho riamh. Bha feadhainn eile a dheigheadh chon an sgadain. Na boireannaich co-dhiù. Clann-nighean mhòra a bha sin nuair a bha mise òg. Bha na ceudan ann, tha mi a' creidse, a' falbh ann a h-uile bliadhna à Leòdhas, mura robh na mìltean, a' leantainn an sgadain bho Stronsay gu Yarmouth agus Lowestoft, a' dol dha Leverburgh 's dhan a' Bhruaich 's a h-uile àite san robh sgadan. Bha an seusan toiseach samh-raidh. Le seusan a' gheamhraidh, bhiodh iad shìos ann an Sasainn. Tha cuimhne agam air piuthar mo mhàthar a bhiodh a' dol sìos a Yarmouth 'son an sgadain. Aon bhliadhna thug i dhachaigh dà chù – an seòrsa a chitheadh tu ann an tòrr thaighean. Bhris aon dhiubh agus chan eil fhios agam càite an deach am fear eile.

Nuair a bha mise òg cha robh balach faisg orm, ach bha balaich gu leòr a-staigh tron a' bhaile. Dh'aindeoin sin, bha an taigh againn na thaigh-cèilidh. Thigeadh na fireannaich a chèilidh is bheireadh iad an oidhche gheamhraidh a' bruidhinn air taibhseachan 's air buidsichean 's air a h-uile càil a b' eagalaiche. Bha crith nam chnàmhan gu robh taibhse air taobh a-muigh an darais a h-uile uair a dheighinn a-mach. Nuair a dh'iarr mo mhàthair orm a dhol air tòir mòine dhan a' chruach-mhònach, bhithinn a' smaoineachadh gu robh taibhse gu bhith romham. Nuair a dheighinn a-mach agus a dh'fhosglainn an daras, sheallainn a-mach ris a' bhalla an robh gin an sin! Ach nuair a bha mi dusan bliadhna dh'aois, dh'fhalbh feagal nan taibhsean asam 's dh'fhalbhainn an sgìre air an oidhche gun eagal. Bhithinn a' dol a Chàrlabhagh chon nan dannsan. Bha talla ann, bha Drill Hall ann aig na Territorials. Sin far am biodh na dannsan nuair a bha mise òg.

Bha bainnsean math ann cuideachd nuair a bha mise òg. Tha mi a'
creidse gur e an aon seòrsa a bhiodh an seo 's a bhiodh sa h-uile h-àite air
feadh an eilein. Sin nuair a bha mi òg, ach timcheall air 1950 thòisich luchd-
bhainnsean a' dol a Steòrnabhagh. B' fheàrr leam a bhith dol gu bainnsean
anns a' bhaile seo fhèin. Nuair a bha banais ga dèanamh anns a' bhaile sa,
bha obair mhòr, mhòr ann. Bha tòrr ullachaidh ann. 'S e na boireannaich a
bhiodh a' dèanamh a' chuid mhòr dheth. 'S e am fasan a bh' ann a' chuid
mhòr dha na càirdean air feadh na sgìre a bhith a' tighinn chon na bainnse.
Bhiodh na boireannaich anns a h-uile taigh a' bruich aona chearc. Aig
feadhainn dha na bainnsean, chan eil mi ag ràdh nach biodh ceithir fichead
cearc air am bruich airson a h-uile duine a riarachadh. Abair thusa gu robh
obair aig na boireannaich ri dhèanamh. Bhiodh na cearcan rim marbhadh 's
rin glanadh 's rim bruich – obair trì latha ron a' bhanais. Agus dheigheadh
mult no dhà a mharbhadh aig fear aig am biodh stoc. Bha aran aca ri fhuine
agus ìm agus uachdair agus gruth ri ullachadh. Leis an ìm, bhiodh na
boireannaich a' dèanamh bàllaichan beaga agus gan cur grinn air truinnsearan. Bha balach beag a chaidh gu banais an seo (bhiodh e mu aois chòig
bliadhna), agus nuair a chunnaic e na truinnsearan ime, bha dùil aige gur e
siùcaran a bh' air na truinnsearan. Abair thusa tàmailt nuair e chuir e fear na
bheul!

Airson bainnsean baile, chleachd iad a bhith ag ullachadh nan sabhlaichean. Bhiodh iad a' cur siotaichean orra san àite sam biodh am biadh, 's
bhiodh iad a' crochadh decorations an-àirde air a' mhullach, man a bhios aig
Christmas. Bhiodh a-nis sabhal dainns ann. Glè thric bhiodh dà shabhal
dainns aca. Bhiodh iad sin aca air an ullachadh gu grinn le siotaichean
geala air cliathaichean nam ballaichean 's gam fuaigheal ri chèile. Uill, a'
dèanamh greimeannan le snàthad 'son an cumail ri chèile. Bha iad aca gu
math snog.

Bhithinn-sa a' gabhail uabhas nuair a bha mi a' smaoineachadh air cho
cumhang 's a bha na taighean 's na sabhlaichean a bh' ann an uair sin. Nuair
a sheasas mi an-diugh aig tobhtaichean nan seann taighean, 's iad a'
coimhead cho caol, bidh mi a' smaoineachadh leam fhìn: dè man a bha
na bh' annta de shluagh beò ann an taigh cho cumhang? Bha planca fiodha
air an taobh dhan an t-sabhal far an robh daoine a' suidhe nuair nach biodh
iad a' danns, 's cha robh a bheag de leud eadar sin agus cliathaich eile an
t-sabhail. Chan eil mi a' tuigse fo shealbh dè man a bha iad a' dol a dhanns
ann.

Bha dà bhodach thall an seo, fear a' fuireachd air gach taobh dhìom, 's
bhiodh iad a' danns. Bha sinne gam faicinn mar bodaich, ach cha robh iad
cho aosta ri sin. 'S e rud ris an canadh iad fhèin Highland Schottische is

Two-Step a bhiodh aca – ruidhlichean 's Eightsome Reels. B' iad sin na dannsan a bhiodh aca. O, bha a h-uile duin' òg ag ionnsachadh danns. Bha drochaid air a' cheann a deas, 's bhiodh na ginealaichean romhamsa a' dol an sin sa gheamhradh airson danns an rathaid leis a' mheileòidian. Sin far na dh'ionnsaich an òigridh danns nam latha-sa. 'S e am meileòidian an t-inneal-ciùil a bh' ann. Cha bhiodh càil de cheòl eile aca. Ach aig banais, bhiodh fear ann le pìob. Bha an-còmhnaidh cuideigin ann aig an robh ealantas.

Choinnich mi ri seann dhuine aig ceann a deas a' bhaile a bha air a bhith fuireachd an Èirinn, 's bha e ag innse dhòmhsa gun deach a thogail greis aig ceann a deas a' bhaile sa. 'S thuirt e gu bheil cuimhne aigesan a bhith ann an Tolastadh nuair a bha iad a' dèanamh bonfire Armistice aig deireadh a' Chiad Chogaidh. Bha an teine aca air mullach a' chnuic mhòir an sin, ri taobh an loch. Bha e ag innse dhomh gu robh sia pìobairean a' coiseachd ron a' phrocession a' dol chun a' bhonfire a bhuineadh dhan bhaile fhèin. Fhios agad, 's e latha mòr a bha siud. Latha a bha comharrachadh deireadh a' Chogaidh Mhòir, a choisinn uiread de dhaoine a bhith air am bàs fhaighinn.

Bha an t-uabhas de bhalaich òga sa bhaile sa a bh' anns an Arm. Chan urrainn dhomh innse cuin a thòisich iad a' dol ann, ach bhiodh iad a' dol ann ro 1880 co-dhiù. Ghabh iad dhan Arm. Cha do chailleadh àireamh mhòr dhiubh idir a rèir na bha san Arm. 'S e seachdnar de mhuinntir a' bhaile fhèin a chaidh a mharbhadh de shaighdearan, agus chaidh aon fhear às an rathad san *Iolaire*. Chaidh aon fhear 's e òg 's e anns a' Mhailisidh dhan Fhraing, 's thug athair às e a chionn 's gu robh e under-age. Cha robh e ochd deug. 'S nuair a thàinig àm a thogail, chaidh e dhan RNR. Chaidh e às an rathad anns an *Iolaire*.

Ma sheallas tu anns an Roll of Honour airson an Dàrna Cogaidh, chì thu gu robh trì fichead neach 's a sianar ann às a' bhaile sa. Bha na boireannaich anns na WRNS, ach tha trì fichead ainm agus a sia ann, ach an-diugh tha nas lugha na ceud neach anns a' bhaile gu lèir. Mura biodh na Goill ann, cha bhiodh sin fhèin ann. Chaidh còignear a chall. Bha aon fhear dhiubh air a' bhattleship *Hood*. Chuir am *Bismark* fodha i. Mach às na ceudan mòra a bh' oirre, cha tàinig ach ceathrar beò far a' *Hood*.

Dh'fhalbh m' athair a sheòladh nuair a thòisich an Cogadh. Bhàsaich e. Dh'fhàs e tinn a' dol tron a' Phanama Canal. Thug e greiseag ann am Barbados. Nuair a dh'fhàs e na b' fheàrr, chuir iad air ais gu muir e. Bhàsaich e a-mach à Halifax, an Alba Nuadh. 'S ann aig muir a tha e air a thiodhlacadh.

Cha robh mise ach ceithir bliadhna deug nuair a thòisich an Cogadh. Air sgàth 's gu robh mo fhradharc cho bochd, cha deach mo thogail airson a dhol dhan Chogadh. Bha mi dìreach ag obair air a' chroit. Bha mi a' fighe bho bha mi sia-deug.

'S e a' chiad obair air na thòisich mise, as t-samhradh 1939, ghabh mi obair ris an canadh iad 'An Cuairtear'. B' e siud a chanadh iad ri buachaille-baile. Bha agam ris na caoraich a chumail a-mach às a' bhaile, oir bha a h-uile sgòid fearainn fo arbhar agus fo bhuntàta. Bha an tìde cho math 's gun tug mi bho meadhan May gu toiseach November a' falbh na mòintich 's mi casruisgte. Cha robh e ceadaichte na caoraich a leigeil tron bhaile gus an robh an t-arbhar gu lèir a-staigh. Cha chreid mi nach e trì latha san àm sin a chuir mi brògan orm. Fhuair mi deich nota fichead airson na h-obrach a rinn mi ann am faisg air sia mìosan. B' e sin mo thuarastal, agus leis an fhìrinn innse, cha robh an cosnadh sin agam an-asgaidh! Bhithinn a' cur a-mach nam beathaichean uaireannan trì uairean san latha. Cho luath 's a ruiginn a-mach leotha chon na mòintich 's a chuirinn cùl riutha, thòis-icheadh iad ag èaladh air ais a-steach. Fhios agad, bha am feur air taobh a-staigh gàrradh a' bhaile na bu mhilse na feur na mòintich. Bu mhi an duine mu dheireadh anns a' bhaile againne a rinn an obair ud. Nuair a sguir an Dàrna Cogadh, chaidh feansaichean mòra a chur an-àird agus cha robh feum air Cuairtear an deidh sin. Chuir na feansaichean às dha.

Tha mi fhìn fhathast a' dèanamh beagan de dh'obair an fhearainn. Seadh, beagan. Och, cha mhòr sin an-diugh an taca ris na bh' ann o chionn beagan bhliadhnaichean. Tha còrr is trì fichead beathach caorach agam. A' chiad bhliadhna a thàinig iad an seo airson 'sheep quota' – cunntadh nan caorach – bha dà cheud agam. Their cuid gun do rinn mi fortan air subsadaidh nan caorach. Uill, cha d' rinn mi fortan, ach bha e na chuideachadh mòr. Cha robh mise riamh ris an iasgach. Cha robh e anns an fhuil agam idir. Bha e ann am fuil mo bhràthar. B' e sin a b' fheàrr a dhèanadh mo bhràthair. Cha dèanadh e càil le caoraich. Dheigheadh e a-mach le slat no ann an eathar. Nuair a bha mise òg, nan deigheadh tu a-mach mun tìde sa le lìon, gheibheadh tu làn clèibh de dh'adagan no leòbagan agus corra chnòdan. Ach bho chionn bhliadhnaichean, chan eil leithid de rud ri fhaicinn. An t-aon iasg a tha mise a' faicinn, 's ann anns a' gheamhradh, 's chan eil sin fhèin ann pailt mar a chleachd. Cudaigean. Ach nuair a bha mise òg leis na balaich, bhithinn a' dol bho thigeadh deireadh August gu deireadh November – nan deigheadh tu le slat a-mach chon nan creagan, gheibheadh tu làn peile.

Nise, seall thusa air an loch a tha am meadhan a' bhaile sa. Uill, tha an loch sin iongantach. Dh'fhaodadh tu breac fhaighinn air no dh'fhaodadh tu iasg-mara fhaighinn air. Tha am muir a' tighinn a-steach thuige aig a h-uile làn agus tha an sàl a' tighinn a-steach ann. Tha a-nis loch eile shìos an siud agus tha an sàl a' tighinn ann aig a h-uile làn, ach chan fhaigheadh tu gin a bhreac air an fhear sin. Chan eil allt a' tighinn ann. O, corra uair, gheibheadh tu bradan ann. Tha iasg gu math annasach air an fhear tha shìos an siud. Tha e mì-choltach duilich a ghlacadh. 'S e *mullet* [geadais] a' Bheurla a th' air. Ach dè a' Ghàidhlig a th' air? Cha chuimhnich mi. 'S bhiodh iad ann an seo a' feuchainn ri ghlacadh. Cho luath 's a tha e a' faicinn gluasad air tìr, tha e a' dèanamh a-mach air druim an loch.

Bha seann daoine ann an seo uaireigin air an robh na Doilich. 'S iad an aon fheadhainn a dh'fhuirich air a' cheann sa dhan a' bhaile nuair a dh'fhalbh càch a dh'Ameireaga. 'S e MacLeòid a bh' orra. Agus bha tòb ghiomach aca air an loch. 'S mathaid nach cuala tu riamh iomradh air dè a th' ann an tòb ghiomach. Uill, seo mar a bha an tòb air a dhèanamh. Bha ballachan aca air an togail air dhòigh 's gu robh rudeigin de dh'amar ann gus nach fhaigheadh na giomaich a dheigheadh ann às. 'S e daoine a bh' annta a bha rudeigin iomraiteach gu muir. 'S ann dhiubh a bha Clann 'IcLeòid aig an robh am *Mùirneag* anns an Rubha. Fear a chaidh a-null à seo a bh' ann. Chan eil duine de Chlann 'IcLeòid sin a bha ri giomaich beò anns a' bhaile sa an-diugh. Bhiodh iad ag ràdh riumsa gur e freumh nan Leòdach sin anns a' bhaile sa an fheadhainn bu shine de Chlann 'IcLeòid.

Tha dòigh-beatha nan daoine an-diugh cho eadar-dhealaichte ris an dòigh a bh' againne 's a ghabhas a bhith. 'S e an telebhisean an rud a th' air an fhìor òigridh a mhilleadh an-diugh. Chan eil iad ag iarraidh ach a bhith a' coimhead siud. Rud eile: nuair a bha mise òg, bha e na chleachdadh aig a h-uile duine clainne a bhith a' cuideachadh am pàrantan leis an obair. Cho fada 's a chì mise, chan eil na pàrantan ag iarraidh càil air an cuid chlainne an-diugh. Tha iad a' falbh mar a thogras iad fhèin. Cha tèid iad a dhèanamh càil dham pàrantan. Chan eileas ag iarraidh orra. 'S e na pàrantan fhèin a tha rin coireachadh anns an rathad sin. Nuair a bha sinne òg cha robh e gu diofar dè an obair a bha ri dèanamh, dh'fheumadh a h-uile duine a bhith 'g obair a rèir an comais. Feadhainn dhiubh a bha gu math, math òg cuideachd, dhèanadh iad a h-uile càil a b' urrainn dhaibh. Dh'fheumadh an t-athair a bhith dian ag obair uaireannan air feadh an t-saoghail a' cosnadh. 'S e am màthair a bhiodh a' dèanamh na dachaigh.

Nise, bu chòir dhomh innse dhuibh gur e latha sònraichte a tha an seo. 'S e St Swithin's Day a th' aca air ann am Beurla. Ach dhuinne, mar Ghàidheil, 's e Latha Fir Bhuilg a their sinn ris. Sin a' Ghàidhlig a bhithinn-sa a' cluinntinn air bho riamh. Ach cò aige a tha fios dè tha sin a' ciallachadh. 'S e an seanchas a chuala mise man an latha gu robh e a' beantainn ri fear a bhathas a' dol ga chrochadh. Bha e a' feuchainn ri toirt

air an fheadhainn a bha dol ga chur gu bàs creidsinn gu robh e neoichiontach. A rèir na h-aithris, cha robh iad a' gabhail ri fhacal. Mu dheireadh, 's
ann a thàinig an t-àm aig an robh iad a' dol ga chrochadh. "Uill," thuirt
an duine riutha, "mar chomharradh gu bheil mise neoichiontach, chì sibh
gu bheil m' fhacal-sa fìor. Chì sibh gum bi an seòrsa aimsir a bhios ann
an-diugh, air latha mo bhàis – gur e sin an aimsir a bhios ann airson sia
seachdainean às dèidh seo. Agus chì sibh gum bi sin mar sin gu deireadh an
t-saoghail."

Bhiodh iad ag ràdh, nam biodh e fliuch air Latha Fir Bhuilg, gu
fuiricheadh e fliuch airson sia seachdainean. Co-dhiù, chan eil tòrr a'
creidsinn anns an rud sin an-diugh. Ach bha bodaich ann an seo nuair a bha
mise òg, agus eadhon nuair a bha mi greis mhath aois, a bha a' làn-
chreidsinn anns an t-seanfhacal ud. Anns an latha sin, bha geasagan dhan
t-seòrsa sin ann. O, tud, bha. Chiall, bha. Tòrr gheasagan aig na seann
fheadhainn.

Bha feadhainn a bhiodh a' tighinn timcheall an seo a h-uile bliadhna – na
ceàrdan. Agus bhiodh iad an-còmhnaidh ann as t-earrach nuair a bhiodh
sinn a' treabhadh: glè thric mun àm sin, thigeadh banacheard timcheall, no
ceàrd fireann le basgaid. Mura tugadh tu càil bhuapa – seadh, ri a
cheannachd – dhèanadh iad achanach dhut. Dhèanadh: achanach. Bha
sin a' ciallachadh gun dèanadh iad droch ghuidhe dhut. Nan tugadh tu
bhuapa rud, cha dèanadh iad càil ort. Agus bhiodh feagal am beatha aig tòrr
an seo ro na ceàrdan anns an t-seagh sin. Bha feagal orra, mura toireadh iad
bhuapa rud, gun tachradh rud uabhasach dhaibh. Bheireadh iad uighean
dha na ceàrdan, is bheireadh feadhainn pìos feòil. Bha na geasagan an
seo aig na seann daoine gus na dh'fhalbh iad. Bha tòrr gheasagan aig na
h-iasgairean. O, bha, aig na h-iasgairean. Nan deigheadh duine air an rathad
le lìon-beag aige ann an sgùil fo achlais, bhiodh feagal air gun coinnicheadh
boireannach ris. 'S nan coinnicheadh boireannach ris mus ruigeadh e an
eathar, bha gruaimean air. Cha robh càil gu bhith aige airson a thurais. Fìor
dhroch chomharradh a bh' ann.

Bha fear thall an siud a bha creidsinn gu robh feadhainn ann aig an robh
cumhachd am bainne a thoirt bhon a' chrodh 's gum biodh iad a' dol ann an
cruth rabaid. Bha tòrr de rudan eagalach ac'. B' ann do dh'Ùig a thàinig a'
chiad mhinistear a thàinig dhan eilean leis an t-Soisgeul mar a tha e againn
an-diugh. An t-Urramach Alasdair MacLeòid. Bha am ministear sin a'
feuchainn ri toirt air na daoine gun a bhith a' toirt gèill dha na geasagan
agus dha na buidsichean. Latha bha siud, nach tàinig searbhant a' mhinisteir a-steach 's thuirt i nach robh i a' faighinn deur bainne aig dà bhò a'
mhinisteir. Sheas dìth a' bhainne airson dà latha. Dà bhò a' mhinisteir, 's

cha robh deur bainne aca. B' ann mar seo a bha an seanchas a bh' aig a' bhodach a bha thall an seo.

Ars an t-searbhant, "Tha a cheart cho math dhuibh cur a dh'iarraidh a leithid seo a bhean ach an cur i stad air an droch rud a bha a' cosnadh dhan bhoin a bhi anns an t-suidheachadh seo."

A rèir na h-aithris, thàinig air a' mhinistear 'give in' a dhèanamh, 's gun deach fios a chur air seann duine glic a bh' ann an sin airson gu faigheadh an crodh faothachadh 's gu faigheadh iad am bainne. Thàinig an duine glic gun dàil, agus dh'iarr e air an t-searbhant mùn na bà a ghoil. Rinn an t-searbhant mar a chaidh iarraidh oirre. Agus mus robh mùn na bà ach air tòiseachadh a' goil, gun tàinig boireannach a-steach 's i ag eigheachd, "Murt! Murt! Dèanaibh cobhair orm 's mi gu bàsachadh!"

Agus gur e sin an tè a bha ag adhbharachdainn dhan dà bhò a bhith a' cleith a' bhainne. Cho luath 's a thug iad a' phrais far an teine, thuirt an duine glic ris an t-searbhant, "Theirig thusa a-nise a-mach a bhleoghan a' chruidh, agus gheibh thu pailteas dhan bhainne." Agus b' ann mar sin dìreach a thachair. O, bha tòrr de sgeulachdan buisneachd aca. Bha dotairean aca airson Tinneas an Rìgh a leigheas. Nam biodh càil de nàdar niosgaid air d' amhaich, dh'fheumadh iad fios a chur air dotair Tinneas an Rìgh. Uill, 's mathaid nach tigeadh e. Cha leigeadh e a leas a thighinn. Bha sin an urra ris fhèin. Teaghlach sam bith anns an robh seachdnar mhac air sàilibh a chèile, bha am fear a b' òige na dhotair. 'S ma bha seachdnar nighean ann, bha an t-seachdamh nighean na dotair. Sin ma bha an t-seachdnar nighean air sàilibh a chèile. Bha teaghlaichean mòra ann, agus le sin, bha dotairean pailt gu leòr. 'S e dotair a bha nam sheanair a thàinig an seo. 'S iongantach gu robh mòran de phàigheadh aca dhaibh. 'S mathaid gu faigheadh an dotair tiodhlac bheag air choreigin.

Bhiodh iad a' faighinn botal man screwtop 's a' cur bùrn ann. Dh'fheumadh an dotair a làmhan a bhith anns a' bhùrn. Bha e a' cur a làmhan fliuch air far an robh an èiginn. 'S bha bonn sia sgillinn ga chur air sreang timcheall ceann a' bhotail. Bonn sia sgillinn airgid. Sia sgillinn airgid an ceann a' bhotail. Bhiodh am bonn airgid sin crochaichte mu amhaich an fhir a bha a' gearain. Bhiodh e cuideachd a' rubaigeadh a' bhùirn far an robh an lot. Bha gu leòr mòr a' creidsinn ann. Tha cuimhne agamsa piuthar dhomh – tha i beò fhathast – agus bha i bochd. Tha cuimhne agam i a bhith na nighean bheag, 's bha niosgaid air a h-amhaich 's chaidh m' athair sìos gu fear ann an Càrlabhagh – fear a bha na dhotair, dotair Tinneas an Rìgh. Fhuair e botal le bùrn dìreach man a dh'innis mi dhut, agus cha robh teagamh nach b' e siud a thug mo phiuthar air ais gu slàinte. B' e siud aon dha na h-ìocshlaintean a bha air bith aca anns an t-seann aimsir. Ach cha robh na dotairean a bha air a dhol tron fhoghlam a' creidsinn anns na h-ìocshlaintean ud idir, idir.

Nuair a bha mise nam bhalach òg, bha e na chleachdadh aig dhà na thrì de bhailtean anns an sgìre bhith a' dol a h-uile samhradh leis a' chrodh chun na h-àirigh. Bhithinn a' dol a-mach a chuideachadh mo mhàthar gu àirigh mo sheanar ann an Ciribhig. 'S ann thall faisg air mòinteach an Rubha a bha àireachan Chiribhig. Nise, Ciribhig, 's e th' ann baile shìos seachad air Dùn Chàrlabhaigh. 'S ann às a bha mo mhàthair.

Bhiodh bò agus gamhainn leinne a' dol a-mach còmhla ris a' chrodh acasan, agus chan fhaca sibh càil a-riamh coltach ris a' phiseach a thigeadh air na beathaichean fhad 's a bha iad air an àirigh airson còig seachdainean no, air a' char a b' fhaide, sia. Bhiodh iad air an àirigh beò air feurach agus fraoch na mòintich, agus nuair a thigeadh na beathaichean sin dhachaigh, bhiodh gleans asta. Bhitheadh, às dèidh feurach na mòintich. Agus bhiodh am bainne aca a cheart cho làidir ri sin. Nuair a bha mi òg, bhiodh sinn a' dol chon na h-àirigh. Bha an seòrsa àirigh anns an robh sinn a' fuireachd as t-samhradh glè chumanta anns an latha sin. Bha na ballachan aice air an deanamh de chip. Bha i mòr gu leòr airson dithis cadal innte – triùir aig a' char bu mhotha.

Bha dà dharas air an àirigh agus bha staran beag de làr bhon an dàrna daras tarsainn chun an darais eile. Dhùineadh tu aon dharas le cip, a rèir 's de an àirde bhon robh a' ghaoth a' sèideadh. Bha àirigh shìos bìdeag bhuainne ceart gu leòr agus bha daras fiodha oirre, ach cha robh dorsan fiodha idir anns an fhasan. 'S e tuill a bh' air a' chòrr, gun chòmhla idir. B' e sin an seann nòs. Agus 's e cip a bh' anns a' chuid mhòr dha na ballachan. Ann am ballachan na h-àirigh bha preasan anns am biodh iad a' cur nam miasan bainne. Bha sin anns a h-uile h-àirigh. Bha an t-àite-teine ris a' bhalla eadar an dà dharas agus bha ceò na mònach a' dol a-mach tro toll bhos a chionn. Mu choinneamh an teine bha seòrsa de bheing, 's cha chreid mi nach e cip a bh' inntese cuideachd, air a dèanamh bho thaobh gu taobh. Na bha suas bhon a sin, bha e na àite-cadail. Cha robh leapannan anns an àirigh idir. Cha robh aca ach seide air an làr, agus chaidleadh iad air an t-seid gu math sona.

Bhiodh muinntir an Rubha a' toirt nan cearcan a-mach chon na h-àirigh, agus chluinninn-sa an coileach aca a' gairm ged a bha na h-àireachan aca pìos bhuainn. Nam bhalach, bhithinn a' gabhail iongnadh gu robh mi a' cluinntinn coileach a' gairm, 's mi air a' mhòintich mìltean air falbh bho taighean nam bailtean. Ach air madainn bhrèagha samhraidh, chluinneadh tu an coileach cho brèagha ri càil. Cha bhiodh muinntir an taobh sa a' toirt chearcan a-mach idir – càil ach an crodh.

Tha cuimhne agam là eile (bha mi air fàs na bu mhotha an uair sin) a bhith còmhla rim uncail agus dithis eile à Ciribhig. Bha iadsan shìos aig an abhainn – Abhainn Ghrìoda. Tha bruthaichean mòra shìos ris an abhainn, agus fhuair na fir a bha còmhla rium caora ann an sin agus twins mhòr uabhasach aice. Bha naodh aitheamh de ròp às a dèidh air a dhol timcheall nam bruthaichean. Man a bha an ròp ceangailte, cha b' urrainn dhi faighinn às. O, chan fhaigheadh a-chaoidh. Thug na fir dhith an ròp agus leig iad às a' chaora. Dh'fheumadh iad an ròp a thoirt dhith no thachradh an aon rud a-rithist. Tha mi a' creidse gur e feadhainn air choreigin a thug a' chaora a-mach chon na mòintich 's gun d' fhuair i às.

Bha mòinteach an Rubha, air taobh thall an eilein, air a roinn eadar bailtean na sgìre sin. B' ann aig muinntir Shiadair a bhiodh stoc air Abhainn Ghrìoda. Bhiodh muinntir Gharraboist a' cur an cuid-san gu cùl na Beinne a' Mhuine. Bhiodh feadhainn à Pabail ag ràdh rium gu robh iadsan a' cur an cuid stoc a-nall taobh nam Beannaibh – iad sin agus muinntir Mhealboist. Nise, bha muinntir na h-Àirde timcheall air Loch a' Chòcaire agus Àirigh na Bèist. O, tha mi eòlach air a h-uile cnoc a tha sin.

Tha iad ag ràdh gu bheil còig mìle eadar Crois Àirigh na Bèist agus Cidhe Steòrnabhaigh. Chì thu fhathast tobhtaichean na tuatha a bha aig Àirigh na Bèist. Chì thu iad a-muigh anns a' mhonadh, tuath air Rathad a' Phentland mus ruig thu an Crois. Tha na h-imrichean anns an robh an t-arbhar aca farasta gu leòr am faicinn. Chan eil fhios agam dè a choisinn dhan an tuath sin a dhol à bith. Bha an taigh ann agus, ri thaobh, tòrr bhothagan. O, saoilidh mi gu robh daoine a' fuireach ann an siud fad na bliadhna. 'S cinnteach gu robh, fhad 's a bha an tuath ga cumail le beathaichean agus arbhar. Ach 's fhada bho chaidh an tuath bàn.

Bliadhnaichean às dèidh dhomh sgur a dhol chon na h-àirigh, chaidh mi chon an làraich, 's cha robh aon sgath dhith an-àird. Cha robh càil ach dhà na thrì chlachan a bha uair air cùl an teine. Ach bha mi uair aig àireachan air an Taobh Siar, 's tha cuimhne agam a bhith aig àirigh aon duine nuair a bha e beò 's a' fuireachd innte, agus bha na h-àireachan sin tòrr na b' fheàrr air an togail. Cha mhòr nach b' e clach a bh' annta gu lèir. Tha feadhainn dha na h-àireachan cloiche sin an-àirde fhathast. Dh'fhaodadh tu fhathast mullach a chur orra. Tha iad sin a-steach mòinteach Bhradhagair is Shiaboist. Bha ballachan nan àireachan air an dèanamh a rèir an àite far an robh iad air an togail. Bha àitichean ann far nach robh clachan faisg orra idir, agus le sin, b' fheudar na ballachan a bhith air an togail le cip. Cha robh gin a chlach faisg air àirigh mo sheanar-sa. Chan fhaiceadh tu ball cloich air àireachan ach feadhainn a bha faisg air bòrd locha, far am faigheadh iad pailteas chlachan. Agus tha cuid mhòr dhiubh an-àirde fhathast. Rud eile mu bhallachan àireachan Bhradhagair: bha ballachan àrd orra. Cha mhòr nach coisicheadh tu a-steach air an daras gun dad a chrùbadh a dhèanamh. Leis a' mhòr-chuid de dh'àireachan eile, cha robh na dorsan ach mu cheithir troighean a dh'àirde.

Chleachd muinntir nan àireachan a bhith buain mòine nuair a bha iad a-muigh air a' mhòintich agus bha iad ga cur ann an cruach tughaidh nuair a dh'fhalbhadh iad dhachaigh. Bhiodh i aca nuair a thigeadh iad a-mach air an ath bhliadhna. Fhad 's a bhiodh iad a-muigh bha an tè a bha iad a' buain a' dèanamh cruach-tughaidh dhaibh. Bha a' chruach-tughaidh air a dèanamh biorach agus air a tughadh le sgrathan oirre. Bha na sgrathan a' cumail na mònach seasgair anns a' gheamhradh. O, bhiodh i cho tioram 's a ghabhadh.

Tha cuimhne agamsa cruachan-tughaidh fhaicinn aig na bailtean, agus iad le còmhdach sgrathan air am mullaich. Nuair a bha na daoine gu lèir a' losgadh mòine, bha cuid ann nach biodh a' toirt dhachaigh ach cliabh an siud 's an seo mar a dh'fheumadh iad. Bha muinntir air an Dùn shìos ri taobh a' hotel nach biodh a' toirt dhachaigh ach man a bhiodh iad ga losgadh. 'S ann aig na boireannaich a bhiodh a' mhòr-chuid dhan obair sin ri dhèanamh, a h-uile fàd ga ghiùlain air an dromannan. Bho àm gu àm, bhiodh na boireannaich a' falbh dhachaigh bho na h-àireachan le eallaich de bhainne agus de dh'ìm aca anns na clèibh. Nuair a thilleadh iad, bhiodh iad a' toirt iasg a-mach gu muinntir nan àireachan. Bhiodh iad cuideachd a' toirt a-mach cnàmhan èisg dhan a' chrodh. Bha an crodh dèidheil air a bhith 'g ithe cnàmhan an èisg shaillt.

Anns an àirigh air an robh mise nam òige, cha robh duine a' dol dhachaigh bho dheigheadh sinn a-mach. Ach nuair a bhiodh mo shean-mhair a' dèanamh ime, bha dòigh àraid aice air a dhèanamh. Bha crogaich-ean aice: man an àirde sin. Bhiodh iad a' tighinn dha na bùithtean le siùcar annta – crogaichean buidhe. Agus nuair a bha fear dha na crogaichean sin aice an ìre mhath làn bàrr ('s cha robh sin fada air an àirigh), bha i a' cur pìos craicinn timcheall a' bheul aige – rud ris an canadh iad 'iomaideal'. Nise, bha an t-iomaideal aice ga cheangal timcheall beul a' chroga le sreang. Agus bha i an uair sin ga ruideal a-null 's a-nall mar seo. O, cha bhiodh deich mionaidean ann gus am biodh an t-ìm aice deiseil. Ach bha e math ri ithe, an t-ìm ud! Gruth agus bàrr agus ìm gu leòr, is aran ùr. Sgadan cuideachd. Sin rud eile. Bhiodh bhanaichean a' tighinn le sgadan chon nan àireachan. Tha mi a' smaoineachadh gu faigheadh tu fichead sgadan air sia sgillinn. No an e deich? Chan urrainn dhomh bhith cinnteach. Ach bhithiste gam chur-sa le sia sgillinn gu àirigh a bha faisg air an rathad gus am faigheadh an fheadhainn a bh' ann sgadain dhuinn. Biadh math

fallain air an àirigh! Bha àirigh mo sheanar pìos mòr air falbh às a seo. O,
dhìol, bha! Timcheall air dà mhìle dheug. Cha bhitear a' coiseachd ann is às
gu tric idir. Bha sinn ann bho dheigheadh sinn ann gus an tigeadh sinn
dhachaigh. An dà rud a chitheadh tu an uair a bha sinne air an àirigh, 's e
geàrran agus cearcan-fraoich. Ge-tà, chan eil mi ag ràdh gu faiceadh tu a
bheag de gheàrran agus cearcan-fraoich an-diugh. Ach an uair a bha mise
nam bhalach, bha a' mhòinteach làn dhan an dà sheòrsa creutair sin.

Fhuair mi grèim air geàrr aona latha. Rug mi air anns a' gheamhradh, leis
a' chù. Cù luath a bh' agam. Fhios agad, tha na geàrran a' dol geal anns a'
gheamhradh. 'S chunnaic mi fear a-muigh anns a' mhòintich 's chuir mi an
cù às a dhèidh agus bha an cù ga chròthadh thugam. Bha e a' buannachadh
air a' chù nuair a bha e a' dìreadh ach cha robh nuair a bha e cromadh.
Nuair a bha an geàrr a' dol aon taobh bha e a' buannachadh air a' chù, ach a'
dol an taobh eile, bha an cù a' buannachadh airsan. Uill, chrò an cù
thugamsa e agus fhuair mise grèim air mu dheireadh. Bha e air a
shàrachadh. Ach cha mhòr nach do chuir e às dhomh mu dheireadh.
Mharbh mi e gus an tugainn e sìos gu m' antaidh an Ciribhig, an geàrr.
Dh'fhalbh mi à seo air baidhsagal le grèim agam air a' gheàrr air a chasan-
deiridh. Bha mi a' dol aig astar math, ach gun fhaireachdainn dhomh,
chaidh ceann a' gheàrr a-steach do spògan na cuibhle-toisich 's chaidh mise
a thilgeil tarsainn air na handlebars!

Nuair a bhithinn-sa a' dol chun na mòintich an uair ud anns a'
gheamhradh, bhiodh sealgairean le gunnaichean a' coinneachadh rium
gu math tric. Bhiodh iad le coin airson toirt air na beathaichean sin èirigh
a-mach às na leapannan a bh' aca anns an fhraoch. Cho luath 's a nochdadh
iad, loisgeadh na sealgairean orra. Tha iad air a h-uile càil a th' ann a
spùilleadh. Thòisich an obair ud ann an seo bho chionn fichead bliadhna.
Cha chreid mise nach eil shooting rights aig Loidse Gheàrraidh na
h-Aibhne air a' mhòintich agus bhiodh iad a' falbh anns a h-uile h-àite
bhon an treas latha deug de dh'August. Cha chreid mi gun dh'fhàg iad càil
idir.

Tha mi a' smaoineachadh gur e an t-àite bu chunnartaiche anns an robh
mise riamh, gur e latha a bha mi air a' mhòintich agus a chuir mi mi fhìn
ann an cunnart. Latha brèagha bh' ann. Thàinig mi gu breunloch mhòr,
mhòr, agus bha rud man eilean anns a' mheadhan aige. Thug mi leum
thuige, agus 's ann às dèidh dhomh sin a dhèanamh a chunnaic mi cho fada
's a thug mi mo leum. Cha b' urrainn dhomh leum air adhart, oir bha e na
bu leathainne buileach. O, bhoill, bha làn-dùil agam gu robh mi a' dol
fodha. Bha prosbaig agam air mo ghualainn 's thilg mi am prosbaig 's am
bata a-null air ais an taobh bhon tàinig mi. Thuirt mi beag leam fhìn, nan

deighinn sìos, gum biodh cothrom an dà làimh agam airson greimeachadh air rudeigin.

Dh'fheuch mi a h-uile càil a bha nam chorp agus rinn mi cruinn-leum. Gu fortanach, chaidh agam air leum air ais chon na bruaich on tàinig mi. O, chaidh mi am bogadh air a' mhòintich fichead uair, ach cha do dh'èirich càil dhomh. Ach tha àitichean cunnartach a-muigh an siud gun teagamh. Bha beathaichean uaireannan gan call. Crodh is caoraich. Thàinig mise aon uair air toll agus chan eil fhios cia mheud closach caorach a bha shìos san toll.

Bha uair a bha saighdearan ainmeil anns a' bhad sa. Bha aon fhear ann a bhàsaich ann an 1932 anns na h-Innseachan. Bha e na lieutenant an uair sin. Bha e anns an Arm bhon a' Chiad Chogadh agus chaidh e tron a' chogadh sin gun beud èirigh dha. Bha e na shàirdseant an toiseach, 's an uair sin na regimental sergeant-major. Bha am Military Cross agus an Distinguished Conduct Medal aige. B' esan Calum MacAoidh – Malcolm MacKay. A-nis, bha tòrr de shaighdearan mar sin ann a fhuair beag no mòr de dh'àrdachadh anns an Arm, ach cha robh duine aca a chaidh tron fhoghlam. Ach ged nach deacha, bha an comas fhèin aca. Bha feadhainn às a' bhaile seo a chaidh tron fhoghlam 's a ràinig ìre a bhith nan ceannardan-sgoile. Mar eiseamplair, bha Coinneach MacLeòid – Kenneth MacLeod – na cheannard-sgoile – na Rector – ann am Fortrose Academy. 'S e fìor dhuin'-uasal a bh' annsan. Chleachd e bhith a' tighinn dhachaigh an seo a h-uile bliadhna airson holidays an t-samhraidh. Chan fhaigheadh e àite eile na b' fheàrr leis na Tolastadh a' Chaolais. 'S leis an fhìrinn innse, chan eil mòran àitichean ann dha shamhail. Tha e eireachdail air leth, agus tha a' bhuil: chan eil conadal a thig air an astar nach iarr fuireachd ann.

Duncan MacKenzie

1924–2007

My name is Duncan MacKenzie and, at the moment, we are sitting in my home at Tolastadh a' Chaolais on the west side of Lewis. I'm best known by my Gaelic name, which is 'Donnchadh Toggan'. Toggan is a byname given long ago to my father and all his offspring are identified by it – as if it were our surname. It is said that it was the local schoolmaster who first called my father by that name, when my dad was just a wee boy. No one has been able to figure out what the name means. Suffice to say that even my nephew who has come here from England is known by the byname Toggan.

I've spent my entire life, more or less, in this village. My earliest recollection relates to the old lady who lived in the house over there that is just a ruin now. You can see the ruin from this window. There were two bachelors living in the house – the woman's sons. I can see the woman just now in my mind's eye, just as if I am seeing a dream. I don't believe that I was more than three years of age.

I'm six-foot-two and my sister Annie is also pretty tall. Very tall, my father's lot – the MacKenzies. On the other hand, my father himself wasn't all that tall – just about five-foot-eight, the smallest among his brothers. But my grandfather's brother in the Gearrannan and there were eight brothers in the family all reputed to have been more than six feet tall. One of my grandfather's brothers was on the police somewhere near Glasgow. In my paternal grandfather's family three of the sons took off for America. Yes, three of them went over there. In my father's generation, the houses were full of family. But those people melted away and the houses are now standing empty. Their offspring chose not to live in them. It makes you think!

I'm sometimes asked what the placename 'Tolastadh' means. Well, I've always heard it means 'in-by the narrows'. There was a time when this place was quite remote but it is no longer like that. Plenty of incomers from the

south of England have discovered us. There's as many incomers now as
there are of the original islanders. They are here of every kind but they
bother no one. On the other hand, they have none of our traditional ways.
They don't mingle with us or participate in the croft work such as
communal work with tractors or lorries or at the sheep-fanks. The incomers
stay aloof from all that. Of course, some must have come to our community
comparatively well off. A lot of them work for the Western Isles Hospital or
Council. On the other hand, the majority of the indigenous people from the
village are employed away from the island. Very few young people here
now: they are earning a living elsewhere.

The Harris Tweed looms kept a fair number employed here after the
Second World War. Very few are weaving now – six at the most. For years,
the tweed industry was in the doldrums. Weavers were months without
getting a tweed to weave. Three weavers purchased the wide looms for
making the kind of cloth required by the fashion industry. My nephew was
one of those but even he has given it up. He was offered employment by the
local authority and he finds that that suits him better. It's an easier life in
the sense that he is assured of a wage at the end of every week.

In 1851, the inhabitants deserted this village. Ten families took off for
Canada. They went to Bruce County in Ontario. It was into the vacuum left
by those families that others came and occupied their crofts. Those
included my forebears. A fellow called John Young took the croft that
is now ours. I believe that his father had come to Lewis from elsewhere – an
incomer. Before migrating here, John Young had been in a place over by
Loch Roag [on the west side of Lewis]. I don't think he was a Lowlander.
In any case, he married the daughter of Donald MacLeod of Uig and they
were given the croft here.

The crofts here are big – each about twenty acres– but they include a lot
of hills. They extend along the seashore. In addition to that, we had ground
outside the village on what you might call the village common. It's a big
area. In the old days, a great deal of the actual crofts was arable; it was tilled
and grew crops. At one time, there were three families on our croft. I used
to be astonished by the crofts at the inner end of the village where, I believe,
the most fertile ground was. They extended from the loch and on either side
of the road right down to the sea. Every square yard was cultivated. The
crofters there were cutting their peats out near where the cemetery is and
they were, even there, cultivating lazy-beds in the wake of where their peats
had been cut – that in addition to all the ground they had under crops in the
village. You should have seen their crops in those days! At that time, the

people were poor compared to the conditions of people today. But, in spite of it all, folks were happy in those days with what little they had. Many of them had nothing but what they were able to earn from their crofts – and that was not a lot. Of course, they not only had their harvest of cereals, potatoes and vegetables, they also owned a few cattle and some sheep.

When I was young, one or two men would go off to the mainland to work, especially when the tunnels were being dug through the mountains to make roads for railways and motorcars. I think that that was probably before the big hydro electricity schemes started up. It would be a while before the Second World War. A number of lads went to the sailing. My father was a sailor. Others followed the herring industry. That was particularly true of the young women. Those were the older girls. I was a young lad at the time. Oh, yes, hundreds of girls and women left Lewis every year – hundreds, if not thousands. They followed the herring shoals from Stronsay in Orkney to Lowestoft and Yarmouth, Leverburgh in Harris, and Fraserburgh – everywhere curers were looking for herring-gutters.

The 'season' started at the beginning of the summer. For the winter season, they had to travel down to England. I well remember my aunt, my mother's sister, going off to Yarmouth 'to the herring'. One year, she brought back two dogs – ornaments they were, of the kind you often saw in houses. One of them was accidentally broken and I don't know what became of the other.

When I was a lad, there weren't any boys of my own age living near me. There were plenty in towards the middle of the village. But, in spite of our being a little out of the way, our house was the ceilidh house. The men would come in of an evening and tell stories of ghosts and witchcraft and everything weird. I'd be shivering with fright whenever I'd open the door to go out. When my mother would tell me to go out to the stack for peats for the fire, I'd be afraid that there was a ghost waiting for me outside the door! I'd look round the wall to see if there was any lurking there. On reaching the age of twelve, the fear deserted me and I became quite accustomed to roaming the district at night without any fear. I used to go to the dances in Carloway. The dances were held in the Territorials' drill hall. That's where I used to dance when I was young.

In my young days there were excellent weddings. I believe that weddings throughout the island were of a standard form. But round about 1950 things changed and young couples used to hold their weddings in Stornoway. I much preferred the weddings when they were held locally in our own village. Arranging a village wedding entailed a great deal of preparation.

Women did most of the work. Most of the people related to the bride and groom attended the wedding. The women in every house boiled a hen. At some of the weddings there were probably as many as eighty hens prepared – enough to feed everybody who came to the wedding feast. It took three days to prepare: dispatching the fowls, cleaning them and cooking them. In addition to the hens, a wedder [castrated male sheep] belonging to someone who had a flock of sheep would also be slaughtered.

Oaten bread had to be baked and butter, crowdie and cream prepared. The women used to spend time making the butter into small balls and setting them in a pile on plates. Once a little boy went to a wedding and saw the plates of butterballs and imagined them to be sweeties. What disappointment when he stuffed some into his mouth!

For a traditional village wedding, you had to have the barns prepared. They used to cover the interior walls with sheets where the food was stored. These were hung with decorations of the sort you get at Christmas. A separate barn was prepared for the dancing. Often, two barns were used for a wedding dance and, again, would be nicely prepared for the occasion. Their interior walls were hung with white bedsheets which were sewn together to make the place look bright and attractive.

I used to marvel at how narrow the interior of the dwelling houses and the barns were in those days. When you stand at the ruins and peer down on the living quarters they are very narrow and I wonder how the families could have lived in such a cramped space. While the wedding was in full swing, there was a plank of wood laid along one side of the barn when guests wanted to sit while the rest were dancing. There was very little space between the seated onlookers and the opposite wall – the space left as a dance floor. I marvel that couples could dance there.

At one time two old bachelors were my neighbours, one living on either side of me. I looked upon them as *bodaich* [old men] but they weren't that old really. In those days the most popular dances were the Highland Schottische and the two-step reels and the eightsome reel. Every young person wanted to learn to dance. There was a bridge at the south end of the village and the generations before mine used to go to the bridge to dance to melodeon music. That's where all the young folks danced in those days. The melodeon was their musical instrument. But at a wedding there was also the bagpipes and there was always some individual who was a good enough piper.

I once met an old man at the south end of the village who was resident in Ireland. He told me that he was raised for a time at the south end over there. He could remember when they were building the bonfire for the armistice that brought the First World War to an end. They had the bonfire on top of the big hill by the loch. Six pipers led the procession that went up from the village to the bonfire. It was all in remembrance of the Great War that had resulted in the deaths of so many people.

Lots of young men from this village were in the army. I'm not sure how many had gone to the army but I know that they started going from about 1880. Yes, they took off to the army. Seven men from the village were killed in the war and one was lost on the *Iolaire*. One young fellow who was in the militia went to fight in France, but his father was able to have him released owing to the fact that he was under-age. He was under eighteen years old. However, when it was time for him to go he joined the Royal Naval Reserve. He lost his life on the *Iolaire*. If you look in the Roll of Honour for the Second World War, you will find sixty-six service personnel from this village. Five lost their lives in that war. One of them was lost when the German battleship sank HMS *Hood*, the most powerful battleship in the British Navy. Only six men survived the *Hood* out of a crew of more than 2,000. Some of those called up were women who served in the Women's Royal Naval Service. All told, less than one hundred people live in the village today. If it weren't from the incomers, that number would be far less.

My father was sailing when the Second World War started. He died abroad. He became ill while the ship he was on was sailing through the Panama Canal. He recuperated for a while in Barbados, but when he became a wee bit better they put him back to sea again. He died off Halifax, Nova Scotia, and was buried at sea.

I was only fourteen when the war broke out. Owing to my sight being so poor, I was not deemed fit to be in the armed services. I was left to work the croft. I was weaving Harris Tweed from the age of sixteen. That was my first real paid employment.

In the summer of 1939, I took the job as *Cuairtear* [village shepherd]. My job was to ensure that all the sheep were to be herded out of the village so that they wouldn't get inside the fields where the crofters' precious crops were growing. At that time all the arable ground in the village was under oats, barley and potatoes. The weather was so good that I was able to walk the moor barefoot from mid May to the beginning of November. I believe that I wore shoes only on three days. It was a demanding job, for I had to be vigilant all the time. It was absolutely vital that the sheep weren't allowed to invade the crops. Sometimes I had to round up the animals thrice each day. As soon as I drove them out to the moor and began my homeward journey, they would start to wander back again. The grass was greener and sweeter in the village, you see! After the harvest was done, of course, and all the potatoes and grain was safely taken off the fields, the animals were allowed in. When it was all over I was paid £30 for the work I had done during my six months' stint and, to tell you the truth, I had earned every penny of it! I was the last *Cuairtear* the village appointed. The reason for that was that after the Second World War, great fences were erected and the sheep were prevented from entering the village during the growing season. The job of village shepherd was eliminated. The fences killed him off!

I'm still continuing to do some croft work. Just a little. Och, it doesn't compare with the amount of work on the croft only a few years ago. I have more than sixty sheep. In the first year that they came here regarding the 'sheep quotas', I was registered as having 200. I didn't exactly make a fortune through the subsidy but it was a great help to me. Fishing didn't ever interest me. It wasn't in my blood but it was in my brother's. That was his forte. He was useless when it came to sheep. He was ever ready to go out with the rod or on a boat. When I was young, you could go out about this time of year with a net and you'd catch a creelful of haddock or flounders and the occasional gurnet. But for the past number of years fish like that are not to be found. The only time of the year in which fish is obtainable hereabouts is in winter but, even then, it is not as plentiful as it once was. Cuddies – that's young saithe about six inches long. But when I was young and going about with the rest of the village boys, you could go out to the rocks with a rod and come back with a pailful.

Now, have a look at the loch that's in the middle of the village there. Well, that's a most unusual stretch of water. You can get a trout there or you can catch a fish that normally lives in the sea. The reason for that is that the sea flows into it at the high tide. Now, there's another loch over there and the seawater comes into it with every high tide but you cannot find any trout in it. There is not a freshwater stream emptying into it. Very occasionally, you'd find a salmon in it. There's a very unusual fish in the loch that's down there but it's very difficult to catch. It's called a mullet. The locals used to catch one but whenever it detects any movement on the bank it rushes off into deep water.

There was a family here at one time called the 'Doilich'. They lived at this end of the village and they decided to stay put when the others took off for America. They were MacLeods and had a *tòb ghiomach* [lobster enclosure] on the loch. Maybe you have never before heard of a *tòb ghiomach*? Well, I'll tell you how it was made. They built a stone wall to form a basin so that any lobster that occupied it couldn't escape. The

Doilich were rather famous as seafarers. The MacLeods of Point who owned the Zulu herring-boat called the *Mùirneag* were of that ilk. It was said that the MacLeods who lived in this village were descended from the original chiefs of the clan.

Our lifestyle today is totally different from the lifestyle that I was accustomed to when I was young. Television is the thing that has spoiled today's youth. When I was young, it was expected of every young person that they help the parents with whatever work had to be done. So far as I can see, parents don't ask their children to do anything. The children are free to do as they choose. They don't volunteer to help. Nobody asks them. In that, nobody is to blame but the parents. When we were growing up, everyone had to contribute according to his or her ability. Some who were very, very young did whatever they could. Of course, the father had to be out earning – sometimes in far corners of the world. Homemaking was left to the mother.

I should mention that today is a significant date in the calendar [15 July]. It is St Swithin's Day, which was known to the Gaels as 'Latha Fir Bhuilg'. That was the name that I heard given it since I was very young. Goodness only knows where the [Gaelic] name comes from. According to folklore, a man was being tried and was in prospect of being hanged. His accusers would not accept his innocence. In the end, they decided that he should hang. The condemned man said, 'As a sign that I am innocent, you will find that, henceforth, the kind of weather we have today will continue for the next six weeks. If it be dry it will remain dry for six weeks and if wet it will continue wet. That will be consistently so until the world's end.'

It used to be said that if the weather was wet on Latha Fir Bhuilg, you could be sure that it would continue to be wet for six weeks thereafter. Anyway, belief in the old saying is far less nowadays. But when I was a lad, and even when I was up in years, the old men here fully believed in that old saying. But, och, at that time folk believed in superstitions of that kind. Goodness, they certainly did! Lots of superstitions.

Tinkers used to visit the village every year. Their visit used to coincide with our ploughing the fields. Very often, either one woman or one man would arrive with a basket. If you refused to buy of their wares, they would put a spell on you. Yes, a spell! In effect, they would wish you to be cursed. If you bought something from them you'd escape their displeasure. The people here were afraid of the tinkers because of that. They were afraid that if they failed to please the tinkers something terrible would happen to them. Some would give them a present of eggs or a joint of meat. The old folks here were under those superstitions until their generation passed away. The fishermen were particularly superstitious. If a fellow walked along the road with a baited small-line, he'd be worried that a woman would meet him. If he should meet her before he reached the boat, he'd be in the dumps! It was regarded as a bad omen.

There was one man over yonder who believed that some had power to deprive a cow of her milk. He claimed that they travelled in the guise of a rabbit. A lot of terrible things of that nature. The first church minister who came to the island to preach the Gospel as we know it today was resident in Uig. He was the Rev. Alasdair MacLeod and he tried hard to dissuade his congregation from believing in superstition and witchcraft. One day, the minister's servant came in to announce that she was unable to get any milk from either of the two cows that the minister owned. The deprivation continued for two days. Neither of the cows yielded a drop! This is the manner in which the man over yonder related the story. Said the servant, 'You might just as well send for such-and-such a woman to put a stop to the cause for the cows' condition.'

According to folklore, the minister was forced to give in. A wise old man was sent for and his advice sought as to how best to relieve the cows of their discomfort and yield their milk. The wise old man came at once. He told the servant to boil the cows' urine. The servant did as she was bid. But as the cows' urine was about to reach boiling, a woman came rushing in shouting, 'Murder! Murder! Help me or I shall die!'

By that means, the woman who was responsible for preventing the two cows from yielding their milk was identified. As soon as the pan of urine was taken off the fire, the wise old man addressed the servant thus: 'Go now out to the two cows and you will be given plenty of milk.'

And that is exactly what happened. Oh, there were lots of stories about witchcraft. They had doctors who specialised in curing King's Evil.* If you happened to have a boil on your neck, you had to send for the 'king's evil doctor'. Well, perhaps he would choose not to come. He was not obliged to come, you see. That was up to him. Any family which had seven sons one after the other was identified as having the seventh son as the doctor. Similarly, if there were seven sisters born, one after the other without a break, the last born had the gift. In those days, families were big and 'King's Evil doctors' were not uncommon. My own grandfather – the one who came here – was one. I don't think that much was paid to them for their services – maybe some little gift.

---

* A malady also known as scrofula.

What did the doctor have to do? Well, they came with a bottle about the size of an old 'screw-top' [beer bottle] and filled it with water. The doctor had to wash his hand in that water and, with his hands still wet, place his hands on the area of the neck that was affected. A silver sixpenny bit which was hung round the neck of the bottle was taken off the bottle and hung round the neck of the invalid as an amulet. They also used to rub the water from the bottle on to the invalid's neck. Many people believed that that procedure was effective. I remember a sister of mine, who's still living, being very ill. I remember that she had a boil on her neck, so my father went down to Carloway to a fellow who was a 'King's Evil doctor'. The man took a bottle of water and applied the water in the way that I described. My sister recovered and nobody had any doubt that she had been cured by the 'king's evil doctor'. Mind you, that was only one of the remedies they had in the old days. However, qualified doctors who had had formal education dismissed those beliefs.

When I was a boy, two or three villages in the district used to go to the shieling [hut on the moor] in the summer. I used to go out to help my mother who occupied my grandfather's shieling on Ciribhig's land. My mother came from Ciribhig, which is a village south of Dùn Chàrlabhaigh. My grandfather's shieling was a great distance from here. Gosh, yes. It was. I'd say it was about twelve miles out on the moor, near those belonging to the people of the Rubha, which is on the far side of the island.

Our cattle used to follow the cattle from that village and you wouldn't believe how quickly the condition of the cattle improved during their five or six weeks on the summer grazing. On the moor, their diet was deer grass and heather, and when we came home with them their coats had a sheen. Yes, excellent feed on the moor. Their milk also was very strong. As I said, going to the shieling in summer was part of the routine when I was young. The design of our shieling was the standard one. Its walls were of turf and it was big enough to allow two, or perhaps at the most three, persons to sleep in it.

The shieling had two doors, one in opposite walls with a short path between the two. Depending on the direction of the wind, you would close one door with turfs. A little distance from ours, there was a certain shieling which had two wooden doors. That was most unusual and was not typical. The other shielings, as I have indicated, had only rectangular gaps in the wall, one of which had to be turfed up depending on the weather. The fireplace was against the wall, between the two doors, and the smoke escaped through a hole immediately above the fire. Now, facing the fire and placed athwart the shieling was a kind of bench again made, I believe, of turf. Behind that bench was the space which was the sleeping quarters. There were no beds as such. What you had was only a bolster stuffed with rushes. On top of the bolster there was placed a large sack stuffed with fodder. Then, on top of that was laid a white sheet, which may have been made from a couple of flour sacks which had been sewn together. Though those 'shake-downs' were rough and ready, folk slept soundly in them.

Those who came to the moor from the Rubha brought their poultry, and I was able to hear their cockerels crowing when I was many miles away in the moor. As a lad, I used to wonder that the sound carried so far. It was good to listen to such a bright sound on a lovely summer's morning. The people from this part of the island took only their cattle to the shieling – never the poultry.

I mind of one day – I had grown up somewhat by then – when I was out with my uncle and another couple of fellows from Ciribhig. My companions had gone down to the river – the River Creed, which had tall, steep banks on either side. The men found a ewe which had lovely big twins with her. Attached to the ewe was a rope nine fathoms long. The rope had become entangled in rough ground so that the animal was trapped. It was impossible for her to escape. The men had no alternative but to remove the rope or the same thing would have happened to her again. I believe that somebody had taken the animal out to the moor and tethered her to keep an eye on her but she had managed to escape.

That part of the moor belonging to the Rubha was divided between all the villages in that parish. The Shader crofters had their sheep in the catchment area of the Creed River. The Garrabost people had theirs over by Beinn a' Mhuine. Bayble had theirs over by Na Beannaibh and so had the Melbost folk. The Aird folk had theirs by Loch a' Chòcair and Àirigh na Bèist. Oh, I'm very familiar with all of those places.

You can still see the ruins of the shielings at Àirigh na Bèist beside the old farmhouse. They are visible out in the moor to the north of the Pentland Road before you reach the Cross. The fields where their crops were grown are easily visible. I don't know what caused that farm to become defunct. The house is there and, beside it, a number of bothies. I believe that people were living on the farm throughout the year, and that farming there was not just a seasonal activity. Surely there were animals on the farm to make use of all the crops that were grown there. However, I believe that the place was abandoned a long time ago.

Years after I stopped going to the summer shieling during the summer, I visited the site on which my grandfather's stood. There wasn't any trace of it – nothing except the half dozen stones which indicated where the hearth had been. Of course, the reason for the disappearance of that shieling is that its walls were made of turf. Now, by contrast, there were some shielings of the Taobh Siar [West Side] made almost entirely of stone. I remember visiting one man's in particular – and he was living in it at the time – and it was very substantial in its construction. The ruins of some of those stone shielings are still standing. Indeed, you could make use of them even now. All you would have to do is roof them. They can be seen if you go in by the stretch of moor belonging to Bragar and Shawbost. Of course, the material used for the building of the shieling walls depended on where, on the moor, the shieling was built. In some places, stones were not to be found in the vicinity, so that they had no alternative but to use the building material to hand – namely, turf. Of course, there wasn't a stone anywhere near where my grandfather's shieling was built. So it had to be turf. Stone walls were to be seen only in the case of those shielings close to the banks of lochs, where there was a plentiful supply of stones. There was another feature which made the Bragar shielings different from ours: their walls were that much higher. You could enter them without having to bend down. In the case of most shielings, the doors were only about four feet high.

It was customary for the shieling people to cut peats while they were out on the moor in summer. When the peats were dry, they used to stack them before returning to their villages. You'd always find somebody who was skilled at making a *cruach-tughaidh* [thatched stack] which was particularly weatherproof. For that design of stack they needed *sgrath* cladding [a mat cut out of a sward of short, tough grasses]. It was somewhat conical in shape. When expertly built, the *sgrath* kept the peat in the *cruach-tughaidh* nice and dry.

Och, I've occasionally seen a *cruach-tughaidh* built at houses in the villages – stacks built with *sgrath* cladding up to their tops. In those days, everybody burned peat for heating and cooking. There were some folk living on the Dùn [Carloway] who took home only the amount of peat that they burned on a daily basis. The women did most of the work of carrying home their peats in creels on their backs. They transported the peat-stack which had been built on the moor bit by bit. It was also women's work to transport the milk and butter from the shielings back to their homes in the villages. On the return journey back from the village, they often brought back lots of bones from the fish which had been salted. The salt fishbones were to feed the cattle. The cows loved to chew them and that made them drink lots of water. I suppose it was to improve their milk yield.

It was traditional for the older women to stay put on the shieling for the duration. When my granny made butter, she had her own way of making it. She had yellowish pottery jars about a foot tall – jars which had originally contained sweeties in the shops. When a jar was, say, three-quarters full of cream, she attached an *iomaideal* as a lid on the top of it. An *iomaideal* was a special, perfectly clean sheepskin which was tightly bound to the jar with a piece of string. Having done that, she would agitate the contents of the jar by shaking it up and down. It took only ten minutes for the butter to form. What beautiful butter it was – very tasty! Plenty of crowdie and cream and butter on the shieling. Also, plenty of herring. That was the other thing! Fishmongers' vans used to come out as far as they could on the moor. You could buy twenty herrings for sixpence. Twenty, or was it ten herrings? I'm not sure. But I used to be sent with the money to the shieling nearest where the vans stopped so that we could get our supply of herrings. Oh, yes, all told, we had wonderful healthy food on the moor. The two creatures that you would commonly see out on the moor were hares and grouse. Very few of those are to be seen on the moor today.

I actually caught a hare on the moor one winter's day. I had a very fast dog with me. You know, the hares change their colour to white in winter. I saw this hare quite clearly some distance from me and sent the dog in pursuit. The dog began to round up the animal as if it were rounding up sheep, all the while bringing the hare in my direction. It outpaced the dog when ascending the hillocks but lost that advantage when descending. Well, it took some time, but, in the end, I leapt on it and caught it. I dispatched it at once and brought it home, intending to take it to my aunt in Ciribhig. I leapt on my bicycle, holding the hare by its hind legs. I was travelling at some speed and wasn't aware that the animal was swinging so much. Its head went into the spindles and I was thrown headlong over the handlebars.

When I was out on the moor, I often saw hunters with guns and dogs trained to make game leap out from where they were sheltering in the heather. As soon as a bird or hare sprang into the open, the hunters shot it. They have denuded the moor of its wildlife. This carry-on began twenty years ago. I believe that the Geàrraidh na h-Aibhne Lodge have the shooting rights to the moor and the open season begins on the twelfth day of August. I'm afraid that the destruction has gone to its limit.

The most dangerous situation I was ever in was out on the moor when I was out there on my own. It was a nice day. As I walked, I came upon one of those lochans in the middle of an area of soft peat. It was directly in the middle of the line I was travelling. As it so happened, there was a small island in the middle of the lochan and I decided that I could easily leap to the island. My intention was to leap from the island to the opposite side of the lochan.

Well, I took a running jump and managed to make it to the island. However, when I arrived there, I discovered that the distance between it and the opposite bank was too great for me to jump – much too great. There was no way forward, so I had to go back. To be honest, I expected to find myself in the water when trying to get back. The island was too small to allow me to make a running jump. I threw the binoculars I had on my shoulders and the walking stick to the bank. At least if I were to land in the water, my hands would be free! I took a standing jump and by good fortune I managed to scramble out of harm's way. It was not a pleasant experience, for some of those lochans on the moor are very, very deep and muddy.

Oh, I went into moorland bogs time after time and got wet but nothing untoward ever happened to me even though there are some pretty dangerous places on the moor. Animals were sometimes lost in some of the traps created by Nature. Both cattle and sheep. On one occasion, I came on a moorland hole and goodness only knows how many carcasses were down there.

There was a time when some famous soldiers came from here. Calum MacKay continued in the army from the time of the First World War. He was promoted from sergeant to regimental sergeant major. When he died in India in 1932 he was a lieutenant. He was very fortunate, for he got through the fighting without suffering any injury. He won the Military Cross and the Distinguished Conduct Medal. In fact, there was a number of soldiers who made progress in the army though none of them had had higher education. In spite of that, they seem to have had plenty of ability.

There were some born in this village who chose to follow careers in education. Kenneth MacLeod, for example, became rector of Fortrose Academy. A really nice chap he was. He used to come back here for his summer holidays every year. Well, he could not find a better place in which he could relax. To tell you the truth, I don't think that you could find many other places that are so peaceful and relaxing. The scenery here in Tolastadh a' Chaolais is exceptional, with the result that every stranger who visits here wishes to settle here.

Allan Campbell

1922–

I was born at Dingwall on 17 October 1922. This world-shattering event happened at the Ross and Cromarty Police HQ in Ferry Road in the house which now houses the Registrar of Births, Deaths and Marriages.

My first few minutes in this world were not happy ones; when I made my exit I was seen to be very blue, silent and not breathing. My mother was very distressed and the doctor gave me up, more or less, as a lost cause, turning all his attention on a very ill mother. However, the nurse persisted against the odds and eventually got me breathing and I am sure rejoiced when a muted whimper announced success. I owe my life to her and a photo of me as a teenager with her is a treasured possession of mine. I feel fairly certain that my mother experienced what psychical researchers call a near-death experience, of which many cases have been recorded. She told me that she distinctly saw her much-loved father, who died of influenza in 1918, waving his hands to indicate that she was not to 'pass over'.

At the time of my birth, my father was a police sergeant. His Campbell family came from Redcastle in the Black Isle. My mother was born in Glasgow in 1897 and for most of her life before marriage lived in Garnethill. I stayed there with my grandmother while at university in the 1940s.

My father was promoted to the post of police inspector in Stornoway in May 1924, and my earliest memory of being with my father and my mother's cousin Sergeant John Campbell is my walking with both of them on the railway track at Invergordon station. My parents were staying at Invergordon for the weekend after the long train journey from Dingwall by train to Kyle of Lochalsh. They were preparing to embark on David MacBrayne's famous ship the ss *Sheila*, a small, single-screw, coal-burning ship with the renowned Captain Cameron in command. Of the journey across the Minch and subsequent instalment in the police station at 41 Kenneth Street, I have no memories.

My father knew Stornoway quite well, having spent some time there as a constable in 1907 some three years after he joined the police force. While there he stayed on Point Street with Mr and Mrs 'Jocky' Henderson. Old Stornowegians will remember that they stayed in the 1920s and '30s over at the sawmill at the Shoe Burn which, when we were young, we regarded as 'a spooky place'. The sawmill is now replaced by a pleasant café, small museum and toilets, open six days in the week only. Old Donald Henderson, well known in Stornoway, was born in Beauly, and at least two of my father's relatives around that area were married to Hendersons. During his period in Stornoway, the Hendersons were friends of my parents and I can clearly recall old Donald, with a magnificent white beard, in the house in Kenneth Street with his third wife and three girls. One of those girls, named Nancy, became a life-long friend of mine.

My liberation into the wider world outside the police station was for me the 'Beginning of Life'! Kenneth Street was a place with a large population of children and, as I grew stronger and taller, the attraction of this young life became irresistible Although it is now a tarmac road completely cluttered with parked cars, in those far-off days the road was rough-made of clay and stones and with numerous potholes which resulted in a high incidence of cut knees. Cars were few and the main traffic was horse-driven carts and lorries. Indeed, in those days it was often possible to have a good game of relatively uninterrupted football on the street in front of the Free Church. Of course, because of the traffic, that would not be possible now.

There were many families living in Kenneth Street, especially in that area from the Free Church to Church Street, and down that street to Cromwell Street. What a great contrast between childhood in Stornoway then and that of so many children at the present time. Today's children lack the kind of freedom we enjoyed – the degree of freedom that is so important during the formative, character-building period of the children's lives when play is so necessary. Here in Stornoway, we had almost unlimited opportunity to exercise our imagination with games. The space in which we were allowed to roam was relatively uninhibited. The castle grounds were an obvious attraction, with vast acres freely available for walking and expeditions, subject only to the supervision of the 'Watchers'. One was never quite sure when Mr Bayfield or Mr MacIver – 'Goosey' – would appear from the undergrowth to check any excesses. Apart from one episode where we decided to build a tree house and felled a small tree in the Willow Glen, I can say that we were, on the whole, devoid of a tendency to vandalism. The tree episode, which was reported by a passer-by, left a deep impression on my old friend Donald Stewart who, many years later, said that, during his time in local government, he tried to absolve his sin by encouraging the planting of as many trees as possible.

The police station was at 41 Kenneth Street, a rather forbidding place with tall iron railings in front; however, it became a focus for much activity, especially on wet and cold winter days. At the back was a small building known as 'the shed', which was slowly disintegrating. The process of disintegration was encouraged by our activities! Also, during really cold weather, my father, who was a most benign and kindly person, allowed us to congregate in the 'charge room' at the back of the house, where boxing matches were supervised by one of the constables. There were three old cells at the back and these were, of course, an attraction to young boys. On one occasion, we were playing cops and robbers and three of the latter, including Donald Stewart [later a Member of Parliament] were locked in. When the time for liberation arrived, I recall trying to turn the key, which to my horror broke. This was a major catastrophe. My parents were out. There weren't any constables present to help and the prisoners were becoming increasingly agitated. In desperation, Donald's father was summoned and, after some effort, managed to turn the lock using pliers. I remember Donald telling me that his journey along the street was accelerated by the implant of his father's foot on his posterior!

Summertime saw us frequently fishing at the piers, especially at Cromwell Street – 'Billingsgate'. Cuddies were the most frequent fish caught but an occasional dogfish or mackerel – known as 'mog' – added excitement. As we got older, some of us became interested in trout fishing on the Willow Glen Burn. That is where I caught my first trout. On one occasion, armed with 'cane-forest rods', we proceeded to fish on the protected and hallowed waters of the Creed. That one episode ended abruptly when Mr Mitchell, the gamekeeper, 'planted' behind a bush, challenged us as we gazed with wonder and envy at a half-pound trout caught by Donald, the future MP for the Western Isles. Rods and the fish were confiscated. We parted with Mr Mitchell, who warned that further trespass would be notified to our parents. No more poaching! My favourite place was – and still is – the Angus River at Coll. When I was big enough to cycle, I was able to spend very many hours fishing there.

The laws of the country require a certain number of attendance days at school and I made my entrance into the Scottish educational system in August 1927. While excited about the prospect of going to school, I think that many of my generation had some initial reservations. The Infant mistress was Miss Reid, who had a reputation as a strict disciplinarian. Months before entering the school at the top of Francis Street on Matheson

Road any misdemeanour at home led to the ultimate maternal threat: 'Wait till Miss Reid gets you!'

It was a remark that usually had the desired calming effect. But, in fact, the reality was that the Infant mistress was much less forbidding than I was led to believe and, after a weeping catharsis at the morning interval on the first day, I soon settled down to the successive encounters with Miss Belle Morrison of 61 Kenneth Street; Miss Steven, an attractive young lady with one arm; Miss Alina MacLeod, who lived at the Bayhead end of Kenneth Street; and the greatly respected, rather stern Miss Pope, who lived on Shell Street. It soon became apparent to my teachers and others that, as a young student, I was not 'a natural', my mind being taken up more with non-educational activities. However, in those early days, I managed to sit quietly in the grey, amorphous body of each successive class. But an awakening was soon to take place when I left the so-called 'Tin School' and entered 'Pryde's School'. The only remnant of that building is the Clock Tower, which sits incongruously in isolation. In my opinion, it is a tragedy that the old building was torn down.

Miss Alina's class had some interesting extramural associations which I clearly remember. The first of these was the destruction by fire of the boarding house known in SY as the 'Beehive'. It was situated at the corner of Kenneth Street and Church Street where the police station now sits. In the 1920s and '30s, it was a regular happening that large naval vessels visited and lay outside the Arnish lighthouse. Local people were allowed to visit well-known battleships such as the *Hood* and the *Nelson*. The crews of those vessels had the opportunity to have an overnight stay in the town. One night in the summer of 1930, the Beehive caught fire as a result of an intoxicated sailor pushing over a lamp. No electricity at that time. Sadly, the sailor lost his life. The handcart fire-fighting equipment proved useless. Things improved later when John Bain of Chicago gifted a modern Merryweather fire engine to the town.

The second notable affair that I recall occurred at school one early summer afternoon. The semi-hypnotic state of the class I was in was suddenly interrupted by a loud engine noise above the school. The class, including the teacher, rushed to the windows just in time to see a flying boat passing overhead. We were released early and most of the pupils, particularly the boys, rushed down to the harbour to see our first flying machine. Although the very first to arrive in Stornoway was on Sunday 9 September 1932, this was the first that most had seen. It stayed for a day or two. It is interesting to recall that the first land-plane was a Fox Moth, which landed on the second fairway at the Steinish golf course on Saturday, 9 June 1933.

It was followed by a seven-seater of Midland and Scottish Air Ferries. This arrival heralded the frequent visits of the aviation pioneer Captain Fresson.

My entry into Pryde's School in 1932 marked a turning point in my schooling. In the school, there were four teachers: two in the pre-qualifying class, named Chrissie MacArthur, known as 'Chrissie Carthur' and Miss MacDonald, known as Sarah – pronounced 'Saa-rah' – who was my teacher; and the two 'Qualifying' class teachers, Mr Pryde and Mr Kenneth MacDonald, who was known as 'Veegan'. I was in the latter's class and, to me, Veegan was a superb teacher. I prospered in his class, enabling me to improve my educational progress considerably. I still keep in touch with Veegan's daughter Margaret, who lives in Toronto. The transition from the primary to the secondary school on Francis Street was accomplished satisfactorily. In my new environment, I soon learned that I had to adopt a more positive learning mode. I was now under the gaze of the Nicolson Institute's well-known teachers of that time: Miss Black; Miss Cheyne; Mr Chalmers the art-master – who, out of pity, usually gave me 50 per cent in the class exam; Mr Smart the music-master – whose Class 2 boys with breaking voices was the star turn in the 1936 prize-giving; Miss ('Meg') Stewart; Mr MacPherson – 'Cloggy'; Mr MacKenzie – Cainey; and the Urquharts – Alex and Gordon.

My class teacher in 1B was Miss ('Pollack') MacKenzie, who trailed unwilling scholars through Scott's *Marmion*, to be followed by that racy Victorian travelogue, Lord Dufferin's journey in Iceland [*Letters from High Latitudes*]. She was also the guardian of the girls in the Carnegie hostel, now no longer there, at the corner of Kenneth Street and South Beach. As we boys got older, her charges were a distinct attraction as they strolled along Cromwell Street on a summer evening. It is important not to forget that Classics teaching duo of Messers Bill ('Soft') MacLeod and Trail. Suffice to say that, for reasons quite unknown to me, my position in the prize list went from the Perfect Attendance slot to the Educational Attainment one. The year 1936 ended my contact with the Nicolson, as we moved down south to the town of Alloa in Clackmannanshire, but before I leave this very important period I should mention one situation which arose and which, I believe, played an important part in my future life.

In 1934, we noticed that one of the young people in the street called Elma Thomson – who lived with her parents in the lower flat of 45 Kenneth Street – was not only having to rush into her home for frequent drinks of water but was also becoming very thin. The upshot was her emergency admission to the hospital in diabetic [ketotic] coma. Sterling work by Mr

Jamieson, the surgeon, and Dr Alex Matheson rescued her — a difficult task, as I discovered later in life. This illness, of course, caused much community interest and it made a deep impression on me and, I am sure, was responsible for my long interest and involvement in diabetic care later in life.

The transition from the familiar surroundings, friends and culture of the previous eleven years was certainly difficult. Most summers my mother and I went to stay for part of the holiday with my grandmother in Glasgow. Thus, I was not a stranger to travelling. In those days air transport was not an option, so an overnight journey on the ss *Lochness* (Captain MacArthur) to Kyle of Lochalsh was inevitable. After that, we had the choice of two routes to Glasgow. Sometimes we got the early morning LMS [London, Midland & Scottish Railway] train to Inverness and thence on a different one to Buchanan Street Station, arriving in the early afternoon. The more favoured was to continue by boat to Mallaig. Initially this was on an old paddle boat named the *Plover* but later by the continued sail of the *Lochness* and then by LNER [London and North Eastern Railway] via Fort William to Queen Street Station. A special interest on this journey was to see the large number of ships which were the World War One surplus moored in the Gareloch near Helensburgh. Fortunately the break-up theory which seems to be popular at present did not prevail and these ships, maintained in good condition, were a welcome and important source of much-needed shipping in the not-too-distant Second World War. I greatly enjoyed the second part of the holiday, which I spent at my father's farm home above Beauly.

It was initially planned that I should attend Dollar Academy but since I had no modern language, the headmaster insisted that I repeat my second year. The headteacher in Alloa Academy admitted me into third year, on condition that I caught up with his third-year French pupils. This I managed, though how I did so is an unanswered question, as I didn't inherit any linguistic ability. I soon made friends and my new companions soon got used to my Stornoway accent. As I journeyed through the school I was able to 'ditch' both Latin and French.

Having got my Highers, I got provisional acceptance into medicine at Glasgow University. I was strongly advised to do a sixth year, thus ensuring a place in the 1940 intake into the medical course at Glasgow University.

As 1939 approached while our attention was primarily on the examinations, my friends and I became very conscious of the possibility of the outbreak of war with Germany. In the school there was a tradition involving class five and six which saw a group of seniors doing a midnight climb to the summit of Ben Cleuch, the highest point in the Ochil Hills, to see the sunrise. A late May evening in 1939 saw the group winding its way up the Tillicoultry Glen and then into the hill country. I recall vividly climbing with my great friend John ('Jock') Laing. We stopped for a rest on a hillside facing south and sat watching the searchlights located in the Grangemouth area practising. It was an eerie experience, although spectacular. It was then that I came to the point of facing up to probable war. I clearly recall Jock and myself discussing what war might mean to us and what might happen to us. For me it meant studying at Glasgow University, for Jock, a call–up from Jordanhill College, where he was training to be teacher of physical education. He entered the RAF, trained as a pilot and perished in his Lancaster Bomber in that disastrous 1,000–bomber raid on Berlin on 24 March 1944.

In 1939, I returned to Stornoway for a long holiday, staying with the Hepburn family, who lived at that time in a flat above what was the Baltic Shoe Shop on North Beach Street and for part of the time with the family of my great friend Calum Angus MacInnes in the house on Kenneth Street above what is at present Alex Dan's Cycle Shop. The Minch crossing was superb, sitting up on the top deck with that most attractive young lady who had been in my class in the Nicolson called Marjorie MacIvor of Barvas Lodge. During my stay I met many of my old friends but, all too soon, the holiday was over, but I clearly remember three things. The first was my timed arrival to coincide with the marriage of Nancy Henderson, whom I have already mentioned. I had a present to deliver from my parents. She lived on the ground floor of the houses in the close opposite No. 39 Kenneth Street, which is occupied by Andrew Cabrelli. The second was a fishing trip. Calum and I did the Angus River at Coll, which was in full spate. With the worm as bait, we caught about seventy-five trout of varying sizes. The third memory was the heading on the front page of the *Daily Express* which Calum's father was reading in the evening. In those days, papers arrived with the 'mail-boat'. In large letters were the words 'War Clouds are over Europe'. Sadly, I did not again visit Stornoway for many years.

When I was demobbed in May 1948, I was faced with the problem of deciding my future in civilian medicine. I returned to the Western Infirmary, Glasgow and I got a very pleasant welcome back from my old chief in the unit where I had been a resident physician in 1945. When asked what my future plans were I was rather vague, so I was dispatched to the department of physiology to see one of the senior members of the medical unit and given a postgraduate grant and an 'order' to appear at the unit in the Western as soon as possible. This was the determining factor in guiding me to a future career in hospital medicine.

The next seventeen years were spent in obtaining extra qualifications and slowly climbing the ladder to consultant grade working in the Glasgow Western Infirmary, Paisley Infirmary and eventually Hairmyres Hospital East Kilbride. In addition I acquired a wife and a family of four.

Although I did not return to Lewis until 1965, I was in frequent touch and in continuing friendship with two of my Kenneth Street childhood friends, Calum Angus MacInnes, a brilliant chemist in ICI, and Allan Murray, a PR specialist in the Glasgow area.

At last I had the time to return to Lewis in the company of Allan Murray and his wife in the summer of 1965. It is difficult to explain just exactly how I felt starting out on this journey back to a place I had not visited since 1939. It was a mixture of excitement and quite unexplained apprehension. Thoughts of what Stornoway would be like, what changes would I see, would my memories of yesteryear be compatible with the expected changes?

As the *Loch Seaforth* entered the harbour, the sight of the Castle and the war memorial were most reassuring, but the change in the harbour was immediately apparent. Goat Island, so often sailed round in childhood, was no longer an island. The harbour which in the summer of the Twenties and Thirties was packed with fishing-boats was strangely rather empty and this struck me most forcefully. Once we were ashore, the absence of the herring-gutting activities with the very skilled ladies bent over the large quantities of herring and the stacks of barrels on the various piers was very apparent. Once installed in the County Hotel, I recall taking my first steps up Kenneth Street.

Immediately, I was struck by the smooth tarmac surface of the street, so different from when I lived there. In those early days the surface was rough with a fair distribution of potholes and very few cars. Football on that street was usually a rarely disturbed activity. However, the rough surface did yield a regular crop of skinned knees. Attendance at the domestic A&E department in the kitchen was usually greeted by the maternal minor-injury specialist with 'Not Again!' Treatment expertly applied consisted of a good, and vigorous, wash with carbolic soap followed by the much dreaded but highly effective tincture of iodine, perhaps a bandage and then, back to the battlefield.

Yes, Calum 'Soda' MacLeod's garage doors were still there, but time and other scribes had obliterated the initials which I sought cut in the wood many years ago. The Free Church was reassuringly still there, but the house beside it was demolished and was now a much-needed car park for the church. The houses opposite Andrew Cabrelli's were, I think, not occupied and MacIver and Dart had taken over the house where Allan Murray lived as a store. Murray's court where many fine families lived in poor circumstances with very primitive sanitary services had been abandoned. Such places as the Cowie sisters' house was of course still occupied by them, the Masonic lodge still looked in good shape and the Smiths' business, the Shoe Shop was, as I was latter to discover, a hive of great activity, its products sealing off the weather from the feet of Stornowegians. The throw-away culture had not yet reduced to a trickle the need for the shoe repairer's skills. However, the most striking change was the vast expansion of the town. On ground once occupied by the Manor Park Farm now had a new crop – that of council houses rather than of grass. I well remember Goathill Road when it was not developed as a residential area. Down towards Matheson Road was the original sloping football pitch so important to the town's young footballers. On the west side of the road were fields which harboured the corncrake whose call was so typical of rural Lewis on a summer's evening. By the mid Sixties the fields and the call of the corncrake had become a distant memory. In their stead, on boths sides of Goathill Road, was a continuous street of expensive houses. The buildings of the Nicolson Institute had been extended. Although the old gym building was still there, the addition to the school along Springfield Road was very obvious. As my friend was staying with his mother, now housed in a new house, I had quite some time on my own and could not resist re-visiting my old haunts in the castle grounds. I was interested to see within the precincts of the grounds the town's new golf course which replaced the superb old course at Steinish. Of course, the old course at Steinish with which I was once so familiar was used to house the RAF's aerodrome during the Second World War. Since then, it has become Stornoway Airport. A walk along the Creed River at the southern extremity of the castle grounds was a 'must'.

When the weekend visit finished, my two companions and I felt wonderfully refreshed and ready to tackle the challenges of city life. We embarked for Kyle of Lochalsh and, by the time I had collected my car by the pier there, I had made up my mind to return to the Isle of Lewis the following summer with my family for a more prolonged visit.

In the summer of 1966 we did return to Stornoway – my wife and our four children. The journey on the _Loch Seaforth_ was a turbulent one due to a strong north-east wind gathering strength on its journey down from

Spitzbergen. In spite of the buffeting we received, we much enjoyed the stay. In the course of our exploration of the town, I had the opportunity to make more observations of the changed face of 'SY'. Very quickly it became apparent that, outside houses on Kenneth Street, there was an absence of the traditional stacks of peat used for household fuel. I remembered that in my early youth our family used to await the arrival of our yearly load of peats. I remembered how the peat enhanced the winter fire with a distinctive glow and comforting smell. This yearly occurrence always presented my father with a problem: the deposited load outside No. 41 caused quite large obstruction on the street and had quickly to be transported into the disused cell at the back of the house – our fuel depot. A solution to the challenge was not too hard to find, for the ever-present Kenneth Street boys were readily at hand. After meaningful negotiations with my father, the peat mountain was rapidly removed from the street. After the payout, a quick walk to Finlay Morrison's sweet shop on Church Street ended the day on a high note. It was remarkable what could be bought for tuppence in those days!

One of the advances in the Isle of Lewis since the days of my childhood was that of the widespread use of electricity in the home. The old DC electric power supply which had started in the early Thirties with a power station up Coulegre, had been replaced by a modern Standard AC supply from the power station in the Newton area. By the 1960s, most houses were well supplied with electrical power. The lowly peat for heating and cooking and the paraffin lamp had 'received their P45' in most parts of the island!

One day during this holiday I happened to be walking along Cromwell Street when suddenly, and indeed pleasantly, I came face to face with Matron Anna MacLeod. She had been senior nurse and then sister in the unit in the Western Infirmary, Glasgow when I was a resident physician in the mid Forties. She had been new to that senior post at a time when I was just finding my feet after graduation. This was a happy coincidence for both of us as we had the Lewis/Stornoway close binding connection. Subsequently in my post-graduate period in the unit after military service, I occasionally had the pleasure of her company. Our chance meeting on Cromwell Street was pleasant for both. She was matron in what had been, in my youth, the Sanitorium, which was now used for elderly care. This brought forcibly to me the changing pattern of disease in the island. The 'Sani', as it was known, was a busy unit in the Twenties, Thirties and Forties not only for pulmonary tuberculosis but also for bone and joint disease, this latter being most usually caused by the drinking of unpasteurised milk from cows with bovine tuberculosis, which I suspect was not too uncommon in Lewis in those days. The precipitous fall in clinical tuberculosis was due to the introduction of streptomycin and other anti-tubercule medication – that, coupled with the great improvement in the living conditions of many families in post-war years and the elimination of infected cows.

Having recently passed the relevant examination diet and obtained my amateur radio licence, I took a small radio transmitter and receiver to use during my holiday. After we had left the island in 1936 to stay in the south of Scotland, I received my usual Christmas book present from Nancy Henderson, the youngest child of the large family of Donald Henderson, who was in part instrumental in introducing regular bus services in Lewis and Harris. Nancy was a lifelong friend until her death in extreme old age some years ago. In this book was the description of how to build a radio crystal set. I became captivated by the whole theory of radio and, in the end, it led me to building more advanced receivers with the use of valve rather than of crystal. Gradually, I became a very earnest shortwave listener. But then the Second World War intervened. The rigours of my higher education, my involvement in the war and, then, my having to develop my career, rather blunted my interest in radio. My interest in the medium was rekindled in the early Sixties when I obtained my licence. I approached the younger of the MacIver brothers of MacIver & Dart, who gave me permission to use the old radar mast at Peighinn na Dròbh. Already rigged with a power supply, I was able to set up my station.

In 1987, shortly after I retired from full-time NHS hospital work, I acted as locum physician at the Lewis Hospital while the eminently popular physician, Dr John Goodall, was on holiday. That was to provide cover during the New Year period. Casting my mind much further back, I recall that, in 1927, I arrived one morning accompanied by my father at the original two-warded Lewis Hospital in Goathill to have my tonsils removed. The operation was not particularly challenging for the surgeons of that time. The speed of events was evidence of great professionalism. I remember it all so clearly. Once inside the door and saying goodbye to father, my outdoor clothes were speedily removed and replaced by a gown. Then I was quickly conducted to the operating theatre where a mask was gently placed over my face. Next, I was aware of unpleasant drops of anaesthetic ether being applied to the mask, a sensation quickly followed by oblivion. Awakening in the male ward with a rather sore throat was not an enjoyable sensation. Night-time was a strange experience as I lay half-awake listening to the snores and sleep-talk of the adults in the beds around me. Many years later, similar night-time sounds would become very familiar to me. Almost exactly sixty years later, I found myself temporarily acting as consultant physician in charge, in the old Lewis Hospital. By then, the precinct was much increased in size, but one of the first things I did was to walk into the original ward to have a look at the position of the bed which I had occupied as a youngster. I'm a hopeless nostalgic at heart!

Fortunately, the hospital was very quiet over the festive season and my dread that one of my peer group might be admitted as a patient proved unfounded.

Most elderly inhabitants of the island would agree that sixty years ago Hogmanay and the arrival of another year had a 'spiritual' dimension and certainly seemed to eclipse Christmas as the occasion to celebrate. Of course, it seems that, all over the country, the old Scottish way of celebrating Ne'er Day has largely been abandoned. Although some revellers overdid the occasion by consuming too much alcohol, I think that the old-style Hogmanay had much to commend it. At a very young age, I was always wakened just before midnight to hear the ships' hooters welcoming the New Year. It was a special privilege to be allowed to listen to the cacophony while sitting with the adults in front of the 'room' fire. The presence of the Baltic Klondykers in the harbour always added volume to the local boats' noisy celebration. I remember my parents' affectionate welcome to each other as we entered the New Year and how, for the following two hours or so, there was a constant arrival of first-footers, including all the police personnel employed in the town.

Sitting in the hospital, away from home and family, I felt a little remote as the New Year of 1988 swept in on the island, as it happened on a windless and dry night. However, for me the most disappointing fact was the almost total absence of the midnight cacophony of ship hooters in the harbour and, as I walked down Goathill Road to the Tower Boarding House, I saw only two first-footers and one car on Matheson Road. Time continuously brings changes. And, to a visitor like myself, that was certainly a big change from the old days. It is probably that, by 1988, all the inhabitants of the town were sitting in front of television sets watching the Rev. I.M. Jolly, who, alas, himself has passed into Hogmanay lore.

That renewal of my contacts with Stornoway and in different parts of the island set in motion the annual or twice-annual visit which has been my wont over many years. In my professional career, I have had the pleasure of seeing many of my books and learned papers published. Since retiring, the urge to write has been a feature of my leisure time. Our holiday visits to

Lewis always resulted in my recording little stories which the *Stornoway Gazette* kindly published. Over the years, I spent many happy hours looking over archive material in the *Gazette* office, renewing old friendships and making new ones.

Understandably, the reader might ask why I have found the Isle of Lewis such a lasting attraction. The answer is not a simple one.

I have been very fortunate in my work and on holidays to have visited many countries. A few of those have left an indelible impression on my memory. Foremost among those is New Zealand, which, in many ways, is very similar to Scotland. But the haven to which my mind often flits is the Isle of Lewis and which has a unique attraction for me. Entering Stornoway either by car from Harris or via the harbour gives me a great feeling of tranquillity. Approaching the harbour from the south, with the Castle and the war memorial in the background, is a special treat. Walking the old streets and recalling the very happy days of my youth, fishing on the Angus River at Coll and my daily walk round the River Creed give me untold pleasure. Not least, my visit to the 'parliament' in Smiths' shoe shop is a most satisfying experience, for there, conversation and debate bring back memories of personalities and incidents which belong to an almost-forgotten era when the island was famous for its herring industry and Harris Tweed. It was an era in which almost every able-bodied man spent time as a seaman on British merchantmen or working on the farms or factories of North America, cattle ranches in South America, sheep-farms in Australia, gold-mines in South Africa – in fact, in places in the most remote corners of the world. How satisfying to renew friendships which we forged together so long ago. The sense of belonging, the hospitality, the warmth of the welcome is indeed very precious. In 'SY', I have a sense of relaxation and peace that cannot be evaluated in material terms.

Lang syne, Joyce, my dear wife of more than half a century, and I made our home in the Lowlands, but it gives me untold pleasure to hope that I still have time left to enjoy further visits to the island I have always regarded as my original base and spiritual home.